Application of Artificial Intelligence in the New Era of Communication Networks

Application of Artificial Intelligence in the New Era of Communication Networks

Guest Editors

Teodor B Iliev
Lorant Andras Szolga
Gani Sergazin

Basel • Beijing • Wuhan • Barcelona • Belgrade • Novi Sad • Cluj • Manchester

Guest Editors

Teodor B Iliev
Department of
Telecommunication
University of Ruse
Ruse
Bulgaria

Lorant Andras Szolga
Basis of Electronics
Technical University of
Cluj-Napoca
Cluj-Napoca
Romania

Gani Sergazin
Global Education & Training
University of Illinois
Urbana-Champaign
Champaign
United States

Editorial Office
MDPI AG
Grosspeteranlage 5
4052 Basel, Switzerland

This is a reprint of the Special Issue, published open access by the journal *Electronics* (ISSN 2079-9292), freely accessible at: www.mdpi.com/journal/electronics/special_issues/F67Z2SR1ES.

For citation purposes, cite each article independently as indicated on the article page online and using the guide below:

Lastname, A.A.; Lastname, B.B. Article Title. *Journal Name* **Year**, *Volume Number*, Page Range.

ISBN 978-3-7258-3776-2 (Hbk)
ISBN 978-3-7258-3775-5 (PDF)
https://doi.org/10.3390/books978-3-7258-3775-5

© 2025 by the authors. Articles in this book are Open Access and distributed under the Creative Commons Attribution (CC BY) license. The book as a whole is distributed by MDPI under the terms and conditions of the Creative Commons Attribution-NonCommercial-NoDerivs (CC BY-NC-ND) license (https://creativecommons.org/licenses/by-nc-nd/4.0/).

Contents

About the Editors vii

Teodor Iliev, Lorant Andras Szolga and Gani Sergazin
Editorial for the Special Issue on "Application of Artificial Intelligence in the New Era of Communication Networks"
Reprinted from: *Electronics* 2025, 14, 1315, https://doi.org/10.3390/electronics14071315 1

Abdulagha Dadashev and Árpád Török
SmartDENM—A System for Enhancing Pedestrian Safety Through Machine Vision and V2X Communication
Reprinted from: *Electronics* 2025, 14, 1026, https://doi.org/10.3390/electronics14051026 4

Minseok Choi, Myeongjin Lee, Hyungchul Im, Joosock Lee and Seongsoo Lee
Shallow Learning-Based Intrusion Detection System for In-Vehicle Network: ASIC Implementation
Reprinted from: *Electronics* 2025, 14, 683, https://doi.org/10.3390/electronics14040683 20

Arjon Turnip, Muhamad Arsyad Faridhan, Bambang Mukti Wibawa and Nursanti Anggriani
Autonomous Medical Robot Trajectory Planning with Local Planner Time Elastic Band Algorithm
Reprinted from: *Electronics* 2025, 14, 183, https://doi.org/10.3390/electronics14010183 38

Shilpa Manandhar, Sneha Saravanan, Yu Song Meng and Yung Chuen Tan
A Linear Regression-Based Methodology to Improve the Stability of a Low-Cost GPS Receiver Using the Precision Timing Signals from an Atomic Clock
Reprinted from: *Electronics* 2024, 13, 3321, https://doi.org/10.3390/electronics13163321 56

Abrar Alkhamisi, Iyad Katib and Seyed M. Buhari
Blockchain-Based Control Plane Attack Detection Mechanisms for Multi-Controller Software-Defined Networks
Reprinted from: *Electronics* 2024, 13, 2279, https://doi.org/10.3390/electronics13122279 69

Yanhan Zhu, Yong Li and Zhu Duan
Adaptive Whitening and Feature Gradient Smoothing-Based Anti-Sample Attack Method for Modulated Signals in Frequency-Hopping Communication
Reprinted from: *Electronics* 2024, 13, 1784, https://doi.org/10.3390/electronics13091784 89

Rehab H. Serag, Mohamed S. Abdalzaher, Hussein Abd El Atty Elsayed, M. Sobh, Moez Krichen and Mahmoud M. Salim
Machine-Learning-Based Traffic Classification in Software-Defined Networks
Reprinted from: *Electronics* 2024, 13, 1108, https://doi.org/10.3390/electronics13061108 109

Miroslav Markov, Yasen Kalinin, Valentina Markova and Todor Ganchev
Towards Implementation of Emotional Intelligence in Human–Machine Collaborative Systems
Reprinted from: *Electronics* 2023, 12, 3852, https://doi.org/10.3390/electronics12183852 139

Mustafa Tasci, Ayhan Istanbullu, Selahattin Kosunalp, Teodor Iliev, Ivaylo Stoyanov and Ivan Beloev
An Efficient Classification of Rice Variety with Quantized Neural Networks
Reprinted from: *Electronics* 2023, 12, 2285, https://doi.org/10.3390/electronics12102285 153

Omayma Belkadi, Alexandru Vulpe, Yassin Laaziz and Simona Halunga
ML-Based Traffic Classification in an SDN-Enabled Cloud Environment
Reprinted from: *Electronics* 2023, 12, 269, https://doi.org/10.3390/electronics12020269 169

About the Editors

Teodor B Iliev

Teodor Iliev received his M.Sc. and Ph.D. degrees in telecommunication engineering from the University of Ruse "Angel Kanchev," Ruse, Bulgaria, in 1999 and 2007, respectively.

He is currently a Full Professor with the Department of Telecommunication, University of Ruse "Angel Kanchev". He has a background with qualifications and experience in electronics and telecommunications engineering from institutions, including the University of Ruse "Angel Kanchev" and the University of Telecommunications and Post. He has authored or co-authored over 120 papers in refereed academic journals and international conferences in the areas of telecommunications, electronics, and energy. His research interests include mobile communications networks, signal processing, wireless technologies, and satellite navigation.

Prof. Iliev is serving as the Conference Chair for the International Scientific Conference on Communications, Information, Electronic and Energy Systems—CIEES—and the International Conference on Electronics, Engineering Physics and Earth Science—EEPES. He is also the Editor-in-Chief for *The Journal of CIEES*.

Lorant Andras Szolga

Lorant Andras Szolga received his PhD degree in Electronics from the Technical University of Cluj-Napoca (TUCN), Cluj-Napoca, Romania, in 2013. After completing his PhD, he joined the Department of Basis of Electronics, Faculty of Electronics, Telecommunications and Information Technology of the TUCN as an assistant professor. Since 2022, he has been an Associate Professor in the same structure of the TUCN. In the last ten years, he has participated in and been responsible for national and international research projects. His main research fields are optical fiber sensors, biomedical sensors, organic photovoltaics, and the IoT. He is a member of the technical committee in more than ten IEEE/Scopus index conferences and is a member of IEEE.

Gani Sergazin

Dr. Gani Sergazin is a dedicated researcher specializing in robotics, mechatronics, rehabilitation robotics, and AI-integrated systems. He began his academic career at Almaty University of Power Engineering and Telecommunications (AUPET), where he served as an assistant, senior lecturer, and later as an associate professor.

In 2012, he was awarded the prestigious Bolashak scholarship to pursue doctoral studies at the University of Cassino and Southern Lazio (Italy), where he successfully defended his PhD dissertation in 2015. Additionally, in 2011, he received an ITEC scholarship from the Indian Ministry of External Affairs to study at APTECH University in Delhi, India.

Dr. Sergazin has actively contributed to the international research community, frequently presenting at conferences and symposiums in cities such as Bilbao (Spain), Brașov (Romania), Rome (Italy), and Tokyo (Japan). In recognition of his academic excellence, he was named The Best University Teacher in 2018.

Through the ERASMUS+ program, he has participated in several European projects, including APPLE (Applied Training Program on the Development of Outer Space Affairs and Intellectual Robotic Systems) and InnoCENS (Enhancing Innovation Competencies and Entrepreneurial Skills in Engineering Education). His expertise has led him to research visits and internships at renowned institutions such as the Turku University of Applied Sciences (Finland), Thomas More University (Belgium), Tohoku University and Sendai University (Japan), Belarusian State University (Belarus), Sorbonne University (France), and Palermo University (Italy).

Since 2016, Dr. Sergazin has taken on various administrative roles while continuing his research endeavors. He has served as the principal investigator for multiple funded projects in his field. In 2024, he joined the University of Illinois Urbana-Champaign, USA, as a research fellow.

Editorial

Editorial for the Special Issue on "Application of Artificial Intelligence in the New Era of Communication Networks"

Teodor Iliev [1,*], Lorant Andras Szolga [2] and Gani Sergazin [3]

1. Department of Telecommunication, University of Ruse, 7017 Ruse, Bulgaria
2. Basis of Electronics, Technical University of Cluj-Napoca, 400114 Cluj-Napoca, Romania; lorant.szolga@utcluj.ro
3. Global Education & Training, University of Illinois Urbana-Champaign, Champaign, IL 61820, USA; sergazin@illinois.edu
* Correspondence: tiliev@uni-ruse.bg

1. Introduction

The applications of machine learning in wireless and mobile communication net-works have been receiving increasing attention, especially in the new era of big data and the Internet of Things (IoT), where data mining and data analysis technologies are effective approaches to solving wireless system issues. Artificial intelligence is one of the leading technologies in 5G, beyond 5G, and future 6G networks. Intelligence is playing a crucial role in unlocking the full potential of the 5G networks and the future 6G mobile wireless networks by leveraging universal infrastructure, open network architectures, software-defined networking, network function virtualization, multi-access edge computing, vehicular networks, etc. The implementation of blockchain and mobile edge computing have become a significant part of the new wireless and mobile communication networks, helping to perform computations as close to IoT devices as possible.

2. Insights on the Application of Artificial Intelligence in the New Era of Communication Networks

This Special Issue offers valuable contributions to wireless and mobile communication technologies, mobile edge computing, and blockchain, using modern artificial intelligence and machine learning techniques. We received over 24 submissions. After rigorous manuscript screening and a peer-review process, ten articles were accepted for this Special Issue. In the following paragraphs, we provide summaries of these contributions.

Contribution 1 carries out traffic classification in a software-defined network (SDN)/cloud environment using supervised learning with four different algorithms—Naive Bayes, Support Vector Machines (SVMs), Random Forest and J48 tree (C4.5). The authors discuss the methodology used based on the Weka tool and explain how the testbed was deployed using two sets of features.

The goal of Contribution 2 is to create Quantized Neural Network (QNN) models to efficiently classify rice varieties while reducing resource usage on edge devices. The authors state that QNN is an effective method for alleviating high computational costs and power requirements in response to many deep learning (DL) algorithms. They also create/develop eight different QNNs using MLP and LeNet-5-based deep learning models with varying quantization levels to be trained by the dataset.

In Contribution 3, task-related adaptation on the machine side is proposed to account for a person's momentous cognitive and emotional state. The authors validate the practical significance of the proposed approach in both person-specific and person-independent

Received: 20 March 2025
Accepted: 25 March 2025
Published: 26 March 2025

Citation: Iliev, T.; Szolga, L.A.; Sergazin, G. Editorial for the Special Issue on "Application of Artificial Intelligence in the New Era of Communication Networks". *Electronics* **2025**, *14*, 1315. https://doi.org/10.3390/electronics14071315

Copyright: © 2025 by the authors. Licensee MDPI, Basel, Switzerland. This article is an open access article distributed under the terms and conditions of the Creative Commons Attribution (CC BY) license (https://creativecommons.org/licenses/by/4.0/).

setups. The analysis of results in the person-specific setup shows that the individual optimal performance curves for that person, according to the Yerkes–Dodson law, are dis-placed.

In Contribution 4, the authors presents a comprehensive research study on integrating software-defined networking (SDN) with machine learning (ML) to improve network performance and Quality of Service (QoS). The study primarily investigates ML classification methods, highlighting their significance in the context of traffic classification (TC). Traditional methods are discussed to clarify the observed outperformance of ML throughout the investigation, underscoring the superiority of ML algorithms in SDN TC.

Contribution 5 proposes a method to generate adversarial samples of frequency-hopping communication signals using adaptive whitening and feature gradient smoothing. The proposed method targets the DNN cognitive link of the jammer, aiming to reduce modulation recognition accuracy and counteract smart interference.

In Contribution 6, the authors state that the detection of MC-SDN security attacks is crucial for improving network performance. For this reason, they designed blockchain-based controller security (BCS), which exploits the advantages of immutable and distributed ledger technology among multiple controllers and securely manages controller communications against various attacks. The experimental results of the proposed BCS approach demonstrate its performance under various scenarios, such as attack detection, number of attackers, number of controllers, and number of compromised controllers, by applying different performance metrics.

The objective of Contribution 7 is to develop a model to improve the stability of a low-cost receiver. To achieve this, the authors propose a machine learning-based linear regression algorithm to predict the differences in the low-cost GPS receiver compared to the precision timing source.

Contribution 8 aims to create an autonomous indoor navigation system for medical robots using sensors such as Marvelmind, LiDAR, IMU, and an odometer, along with the Time Elastic Band (TEB) local planning algorithm to detect dynamic obstacles. The algorithm's performance is evaluated using metrics such as path length, duration, speed smoothness, path smoothness, Mean Squared Error (MSE), and positional error. In the test arena, TEB demonstrates superior efficiency with a path length of 155.55 m, 9.83 m shorter than the Dynamic Window Approach (DWA), which covered 165.38 m, and a lower yaw error of 0.012 radians.

Contribution 9 presents an Application-Specific Integrated Circuit (ASIC) implementation and Field-Programmable Gate Array (FPGA) verification of a Convolutional Neural Network (CNN)-based Intrusion Detection System (IDS) designed to enhance the security of an in-vehicle Controller Area Network (CAN) bus and detect malicious messages. In this article, the authors also conduct functional verification by configuring a simplified CAN bus environment using the Xilinx Nexys Video FPGA and PEAK-System PCAN-USB, which is validated in real time against DoS, spoofing, and fuzzy attack scenarios.

The YOLO-based object detection model is used in Contribution 10 to identify pedestrians and extract key data such as bounding box coordinates and confidence levels. These data are encoded afterward into decentralized environmental notification messages (DENMs) using ASN.1 schemas to ensure compliance with V2X standards, allowing for real-time communication between vehicles and infrastructure. The authors identify that the integration of pedestrian detection with V2X communication resulted in a reliable system wherein the roadside unit (RSU) broadcasts DENM alerts to vehicles. Upon receiving the messages, the vehicles initiate appropriate responses, such as slowing down or lane changing, with the testing demonstrating reliable message transmission and high pedestrian detection accuracy in simulated–controlled environments.

The guest editors wish to thank the authors for their contributions and their commitment to improving their work, the reviewers for their valuable comments, and the administrative staff of MDPI for their support in completing this Special Issue. We hope that the selected publications will have a lasting impact on the scientific community and serve as a motivating factor for other researchers to pursue their scientific goals.

Author Contributions: Writing—original draft preparation, T.I., L.A.S. and G.S.; writing—review and editing, T.I., L.A.S. and G.S. All authors have read and agreed to the published version of the manuscript.

Funding: This research received no external funding.

Conflicts of Interest: The authors declare no conflicts of interest.

List of Contributions:

1. Belkadi, O.; Vulpe, A.; Laaziz, Y.; Halunga, S. ML-Based Traffic Classification in an SDN-Enabled Cloud Environment. *Electronics* **2023**, *12*, 269.
2. Tasci, M.; Istanbullu, A.; Kosunalp, S.; Iliev, T.; Stoyanov, I.; Beloev, I. An Efficient Classification of Rice Variety with Quantized Neural Networks. *Electronics* **2023**, *12*, 2285.
3. Markov, M.; Kalinin, Y.; Markova, V.; Ganchev, T. Towards Implementation of Emotional Intelligence in Human–Machine Collaborative Systems. *Electronics* **2023**, *12*, 3852.
4. Serag, R.H.; Abdalzaher, M.S.; Elsayed, H.A.E.A.; Sobh, M.; Krichen, M.; Salim, M.M. Machine-Learning-Based Traffic Classification in Software-Defined Networks. *Electronics* **2024**, *13*, 1108.
5. Zhu, Y.; Li, Y.; Duan, Z. Adaptive Whitening and Feature Gradient Smoothing-Based Anti-Sample Attack Method for Modulated Signals in Frequency-Hopping Communication. *Electronics* **2024**, *13*, 1784.
6. Alkhamisi, A.; Katib, I.; Buhari, S.M. Blockchain-Based Control Plane Attack Detection Mechanisms for Mul-ti-Controller Software-Defined Networks. *Electronics* **2024**, *13*, 2279.
7. Manandhar, S.; Saravanan, S.; Meng, Y.S.; Tan, Y.C. A Linear Regression-Based Methodology to Improve the Stability of a Low-Cost GPS Receiver Using the Precision Timing Signals from an Atomic Clock. *Electronics* **2024**, *13*, 3321.
8. Turnip, A.; Faridhan, M.A.; Wibawa, B.M.; Anggriani, N. Autonomous Medical Robot Trajectory Planning with Local Planner Time Elastic Band Algorithm. *Electronics* **2025**, *14*, 183.
9. Choi, M.; Lee, M.; Im, H.; Lee, J.; Lee, S. Shallow Learning-Based Intrusion Detection System for In-Vehicle Network: ASIC Implementation. *Electronics* **2025**, *14*, 683.
10. Dadashev, A.; Török, Á. SmartDENM—A System for Enhancing Pedestrian Safety Through Machine Vision and V2X Communication. *Electronics* **2025**, *14*, 1026.

Disclaimer/Publisher's Note: The statements, opinions and data contained in all publications are solely those of the individual author(s) and contributor(s) and not of MDPI and/or the editor(s). MDPI and/or the editor(s) disclaim responsibility for any injury to people or property resulting from any ideas, methods, instructions or products referred to in the content.

Article

SmartDENM—A System for Enhancing Pedestrian Safety Through Machine Vision and V2X Communication

Abdulagha Dadashev [1,†] and Árpád Török [2,*,†]

1 Department of Automotive Technologies, Budapest University of Technology and Economics, 1521 Budapest, Hungary; abdulaghadadashev@edu.bme.hu
2 Safety and Security Team, BME Automated Drive, 1111 Budapest, Hungary
* Correspondence: torok.arpad@kjk.bme.hu
† These authors contributed equally to this work.

Abstract: A pivotal moment in the leap toward autonomous vehicles in recent years has revealed the need to enhance vehicle-to-everything (V2X) communication systems so as to improve road safety. A key challenge is to integrate real-time pedestrian detection to permit the use of timely alerts in situations where vulnerable road users, especially pedestrians, might pose a risk. Seeing that, in this article, a YOLO-based object detection model was used to identify pedestrians and extract key data such as bounding box coordinates and confidence levels. These data were encoded afterward into decentralized environmental notification messages (DENM) using ASN.1 schemas to ensure compliance with V2X standards, allowing for real-time communication between vehicles and infrastructure. This research identified that the integration of pedestrian detection with V2X communication brought about a reliable system wherein the roadside unit (RSU) broadcasts DENM alerts to vehicles. These vehicles, upon receiving the messages, initiate appropriate responses such as slowing down or lane changing, with the testing demonstrating reliable message transmission and high pedestrian detection accuracy in simulated–controlled environments. To conclude, this work demonstrates a scalable framework for improving road safety by combining machine vision with V2X communication.

Keywords: V2X communication; pedestrian detection; autonomous vehicles; machine vision

Academic Editors: Paul Mitchell and Stefano Scanzio

Received: 31 December 2024
Revised: 10 February 2025
Accepted: 28 February 2025
Published: 4 March 2025

Citation: Dadashev, A.; Török, Á. SmartDENM—A System for Enhancing Pedestrian Safety Through Machine Vision and V2X Communication. *Electronics* **2025**, *14*, 1026. https://doi.org/10.3390/electronics14051026

Copyright: © 2025 by the authors. Licensee MDPI, Basel, Switzerland. This article is an open access article distributed under the terms and conditions of the Creative Commons Attribution (CC BY) license (https://creativecommons.org/licenses/by/4.0/).

1. Introduction

The complexity of urban mobility and the rise in the number of vulnerable road users have made road safety a top priority in contemporary transportation systems [1]. To remedy the issue of having many traffic accidents, V2X technology is among those most often proposed, acting as one of the core parts of automated transport. In detail, the way mobility issues are handled has changed dramatically as a result of the growing integration of intelligent transportation systems (ITS) in highway and urban settings. Since pedestrian-related traffic accidents are responsible for a sizable percentage of traffic deaths globally [2,3], pedestrian safety is still considered one of the issues that requires immediate attention and creative solutions to minimize dangers for vulnerable road users. Conventional safety measures, such as advanced driver-assistance systems (ADAS) and sensors mounted on vehicles, are frequently constrained by their dependence on localized processing and line-of-sight detection [4]. V2X communication systems [5,6], on the other hand, provide a more comprehensive strategy by granting access to real-time situational data sharing between infrastructure, vehicles, and other organizations [7]. As the need for dependable V2X communication to enable intelligent transportation systems grows, creative architectures are crucial to overcoming scalability, resilience, and robustness issues. Recent developments, such the combination of blockchain technology and mobile edge computing, have shown promise in resolving these issues by facilitating secure data transfer and hierarchical computing. For example, Muhammad Awais Khan (2021) suggested a strong V2X architecture that uses blockchain for safe, low-overhead communication and integrates cloud, edge, and fog computing nodes for dynamic resource allocation [8]. The study demonstrated notable improvements in network scalability and reliability by predicting automobile connectivity with near-perfect accuracy. While V2X communication has significantly improved connectivity and autonomy in modern transport systems, it also introduces critical security challenges. Recent studies have surveyed V2X security vulnerabilities, providing comprehensive classifications of attacks and countermeasures. Roshan Sedar (2023) [9] performed a systematic review of V2X attacks, categorizing them by security and privacy requirements, and highlighted the potential of AI-driven solutions to enhance V2X security. These insights emphasize the need for robust security mechanisms to ensure safe and reliable operation of V2X-enabled systems. Another problem occurs when various detection technologies, such as cameras, radar, and lidar, are employed for pedestrian detection. Each has its own data formats and communication protocols, complicating the integration into a unified V2X system [10]. Target detection networks, such as those in the YOLO series, are widely used in transportation applications due to their high detection accuracy and real-time performance. It is true that limitations such as handling large-scale variations and computational resource demands remain challenges; nevertheless, recent advancements, such as those proposed by Bo Wang (2024) [11] as well as by Bakirci (2024) [12], have introduced improvements to the YOLOv8n model to address these limitations. In the former case, these enhancements include embedding attention mechanisms, adding small-scale detection heads, and optimizing loss functions, leading to significant increases in detection accuracy (such as mAP50 reaching 95.9/100), and the latter achieved an accuracy exceeding 80 percent. Due in part to these advantages, the YOLO model, albeit YOLOv5, lighter version, will be used in this implementation, which will be discussed further in the next section.

This study is also immensely significant as it addresses the gap in current intelligent transportation systems by integrating real-time pedestrian detection with V2X communication protocols. The findings contribute to ongoing global initiatives such as Vision Zero and cooperative intelligent transport systems (C-ITS), supporting safer and more intelligent transportation systems.

Some of the research conducted in this area, while having a role in advancing this field, is still lacking in some aspects when being deployed as a real-time system. In a study carried out by Fabio and Giovanni (2019) [10], they researched the possibility of the integration of V2X into the pedestrian and vehicle alert system. While this system is promising, some specific issues can be mentioned, including the possibility of pedestrians not carrying their smartphones with them as well as the concept of pedestrian detection systems (cameras, radar) being integrated with V2X communication networks. Another research study performed by Faisal, Robinet, and Frank (2024) showed better results in detection, though they also need to be tested in dynamic environments, and the impacts of mobility on network latency, considering factors such as signal strength, handovers, obstacles, interference, and network congestion, should be analyzed [13]. As for the use of mobile applications in sending information, the study by Capallera (2019) highlighted the importance of providing instructions on automation limitations and context-related information through mobile applications in order to improve drivers' situational awareness and takeover performance in conditionally automated vehicles. Their findings suggest that while instructions are essential for understanding takeover requests, the use of a mobile application to convey context-related information may not always be beneficial, particularly in critical situations like avoiding moving obstacles. However, the study's limitations, such as the small, non-representative sample and the use of a driving simulator, call for further research to validate these results in real-world scenarios [14], and are, therefore, not in a position to be overlooked. The paper by Veena et al. (2019) introduced a smart car automated system aimed at assisting drivers, particularly new drivers, in detecting and resolving minor vehicle issues through a mobile application. This system provides a user-friendly interface through which drivers can identify problems using alert signals and search for solutions, ensuring that they can address issues quickly and continue driving without interruption. However, the system's focus on minor problems and its reliance on an Android-based application may limit its applicability to more complex vehicle issues or non-Android users. Nonetheless, the system's low-cost and secure design offers a practical tool for enhancing vehicle maintenance and driver confidence [15]. Uchida et al. (2020) proposed a mobile traffic accident prevention system that uses wireless signals and sensors on mobile devices. The system monitors data to detect dangerous smartphone usage and approaching vehicles or bicycles, employing a Markov Chain algorithm for analysis. Field experiments with WiFi detection show the system's effectiveness, but further research is needed to enhance decision-making and include additional sensors for better detection [16]. When it comes to the data transmission properties, the paper by Han et al. (2019) addresses the challenges of data fusion in V2X networks, particularly the necessity for a trust system to handle multi-source and multi-format data exchange. They, therefore, proposed a four-level trust model for data transmission in V2X networks and introduced a location-based public key infrastructure system to improve key distribution efficiency while ensuring high trust. The performance evaluation shows that their system meets the strict latency requirements of V2X networks. Yet, the proposed approach depends heavily on accurate vehicle route predictions, which could require improvement by integrating deep learning techniques [17]. LiDAR sensors provide high-resolution 3D environmental data beneficial for autonomous vehicle perception systems; nevertheless, their integration was not prioritized in this study. This decision stems from the significant computational complexity associated with processing LiDAR data, aside from them being costly, which requires advanced algorithms and substantial processing power [18]. In contrast, camera-based systems offer a more cost-effective and computationally efficient solution, aligning with the objectives of developing accessible and efficient road safety enhancements, leading them being deemed beyond the scope of this initial system implementation.

The primary objective of this study is to design a framework for pedestrian detection and alert transmission via I2V (infrastructure-to-vehicle) communication [19], one of the major types of V2X communication used to collect traffic data generated by vehicles and wirelessly deliver information, such as relevant messages and instructions from the infrastructure, to the vehicle and notify the driver about safety, mobility, or environmental conditions. The most instrumental part is the decoding and encoding of the information being transferred via DENM message type with ASN.1 (abstract syntax notation one) coding, which will be thoroughly investigated in the Materials and Methods section.

This study builds upon previous works by addressing critical gaps in existing pedestrian safety systems. For instance, Fabio and Giovanni (2019) [10] explored the integration of V2X in pedestrian and vehicle alert systems but highlighted limitations such as reliance on pedestrians carrying smartphones and the lack of integration between detection systems and V2X communication. In contrast, the proposed framework leverages RSUs equipped with cameras and radar to eliminate the dependency on smartphones, ensuring broader applicability. Similarly, the system improves on Faisal et al.'s [13] approach (2024) by incorporating real-time hazard notifications in dynamic environments, addressing concerns related to network latency and signal reliability, albeit with are some limitations regarding latency as well since this project is still in its experimental phase, meaning that before being deployed to the real-world, a larger dataset should be used in training for pedestrian detection. Hence, the challenge of network latency remains an important factor, as the proposed system is still in its initial phases and has yet to be validated for real-world deployment. While prior research like Capallera (2019) [14] emphasized mobile applications for improving driver awareness, this study adopts a decentralized DENM-based approach to enhance situational awareness without relying on centralized infrastructure. This decentralized model ensures faster communication and reduces potential bottlenecks, making it more suitable for real-time safety-critical scenarios. By focusing on ASN.1-based DENM encoding, this study also offers a more standardized and efficient communication protocol compared to alternative methods like IEEE 802.11p or Wi-Fi-based V2V solutions [20–22]. Consequently, this work provides a more reliable and scalable solution for pedestrian safety in autonomous driving applications.

The key objectives are as follows:

1. Implementing an object detection algorithm to identify pedestrians,
2. Encoding detection data into standardized DENM formats,
3. Designing a V2X communication pipeline for seamless data exchange,
4. Validating the system's performance through simulation.

By employing DENM in the context of V2X communication, this study presents a novel strategy that makes use of the said protocol created especially to improve safety in autonomous driving situations. DENM provides a more focused solution for real-time safety hazard notifications than conventional communication methods, like using the IEEE 802.11p protocol [20] or Wi-Fi-based communication [21,22], which concentrate on vehicle-to-vehicle (V2V) communication for general data exchange [23,24]. By establishing decentralized communication between automobiles, pedestrians, and RSUs, DENM enhances situational awareness in dynamic contexts and allows for instantaneous hazard notifications [25,26]. Instead of depending on centralized infrastructure, which may cause delays or single points of failure, this system enables cars and pedestrians to get fast-paced information about possible crashes or safety hazards. That being said, in comparison to centralized systems, where a single point of failure could lead to delays in data transmission and system operation, this proposed approach leverages a decentralized structure using DENM for I2V communication. This decentralized model ensures more robust and real-time decision-making without relying on a central server, reducing the risk of communication bottlenecks and enhancing the overall safety and responsiveness of the system. The DENM-based system improves safety by enabling faster communication between vehicles and infrastructure, making it a more reliable solution for autonomous driving applications.

This project explores the integration of DENM with V2X communication, particularly using the ASN.1 encoding for standardized protocols, which is an area with limited prior research. The goal is to demonstrate the feasibility of this integration through simulation results. Although latency is a critical factor for real-world V2X applications, especially pedestrian safety, the current testing environment has limitations. The object detection algorithm, implemented using YOLO and converted to ONNX format, was integrated with ROS2 Humble running on a VMware virtual machine. This setup, while functional, introduces overheads that do not fully reflect real-world latency performance. Factors such as network congestion, hardware acceleration, and real-world V2X conditions were not fully accounted for in the simulations.

Despite these limitations, the system demonstrated reliable communication and high-accuracy pedestrian detection in controlled environments, serving as a proof-of-concept. The project highlights the potential of combining DENM-based hazard notifications with

V2X for pedestrian safety, although real-world validation and latency optimization (targeting 100–500 ms) remain future goals. This work is conceptual, focusing on prototyping and early-stage testing, and lays the foundation for future research. Key contributions include its innovative approach (DENM, ASN.1, YOLO integration), focus on pedestrian safety, scalability, decentralization, and establishing a reliable communication pipeline. While the dataset and latency testing are limited, the project provides a stepping stone for further exploration, optimization, and real-world deployment in autonomous vehicle safety systems.

A key novelty of this research lies in the integration of real-time pedestrian detection with DENM in a standardized V2X communication framework, which has not been extensively explored in prior studies, as could be seen in previous study comparisons. The study introduces new relationships between machine vision-based detection systems and V2X communication protocols, demonstrating how pedestrian detection outputs can be efficiently encoded into DENM messages using ASN.1 schemas.

On top of that, this research identifies a new system concept by presenting an end-to-end framework that enables I2V hazard warnings through RSUs. Unlike existing pedestrian safety mechanisms that rely on onboard vehicle sensors or mobile applications, this approach eliminates the dependency on pedestrian-owned devices and ensures broader safety coverage, particularly in urban environments with occlusions and blind spots. Additionally, the study describes a new phenomenon in message propagation efficiency, analyzing how ASN.1-based DENM encoding works in which experimental validation in controlled simulations demonstrates reliable real-time hazard communication and a clear path for scalability in real-world implementations, albeit with the need for more emphasis on latency requirement in the future. Unlike previous V2X-based pedestrian alert systems, which rely on onboard sensors or pedestrian devices, this new approach ensures hazard detection and alert dissemination without requiring any action from pedestrians themselves. This, in turn, significantly improves safety in environments where pedestrian smartphone usage is inconsistent or unreliable, such as in school zones or crowded city centers. Last but not least, this study contributes a novel practical impact by laying the groundwork for real-world deployment in smart city infrastructure. The findings show that DENM-based pedestrian alerts can be seamlessly integrated into existing V2X architectures, improving situational awareness for autonomous and human-driven vehicles alike, obviously with a bit more testing in the real-world. This work, hence, provides a scalable, decentralized, and real-time pedestrian safety enhancement strategy that can be extended to other traffic scenarios, such as cyclist detection and intersection safety management.

By explicitly defining these contributions, the research underscores its scientific significance in the broader context of intelligent transportation systems and autonomous vehicle safety.

2. Materials and Methods

To provide an overview of the system and address potential ambiguities prior to detailing specific components, the SmartDENM system is a framework designed to improve road safety by combining pedestrian detection with V2X communication protocols. The said architecture comprises subsystems, each with specific functionalities that work in tandem to achieve reliable and efficient operation. The system workflow begins with cameras capturing real-time scenes. These images are processed by the detection subsystem, which extracts critical pedestrian data. This data is then converted into a DENM and transmitted via the RSU to surrounding vehicles. Upon receiving the message, vehicles assess the information and take timely actions to mitigate potential hazards.

This study follows a systematic approach, dividing the development process into four distinct components to ensure clarity and scalability, as well as for simplicity when it comes to understanding the concept. The methodology is structured as follows:

1. Pedestrian detection system: Implementation of a deep learning-based object detection model to identify pedestrians in real time, generating bounding box coordinates, confidence scores, and class IDs.
2. DENM message encoding: Conversion of detection data into standardized DENM formats using ASN.1 schemas to ensure compliance with V2X communication standards.
3. V2X communication pipeline: Design and deployment of a communication framework where an RSU publishes DENM alerts, and a subscribing vehicle node processes these alerts for real-time safety actions.
4. System integration and testing: Integration of all components within an ROS2 environment, utilizing JSON serialization for efficient message transmission, and conducting rigorous simulations to evaluate system performance.

To put it mildly, indisputably, each component was independently developed and tested to make sure of reliability before being integrated into the final system, as this modular structure facilitates scalability and adaptability for future enhancements. The flowchart, Figure 1, has been handcrafted for a better understanding of the process going on when the system is activated:

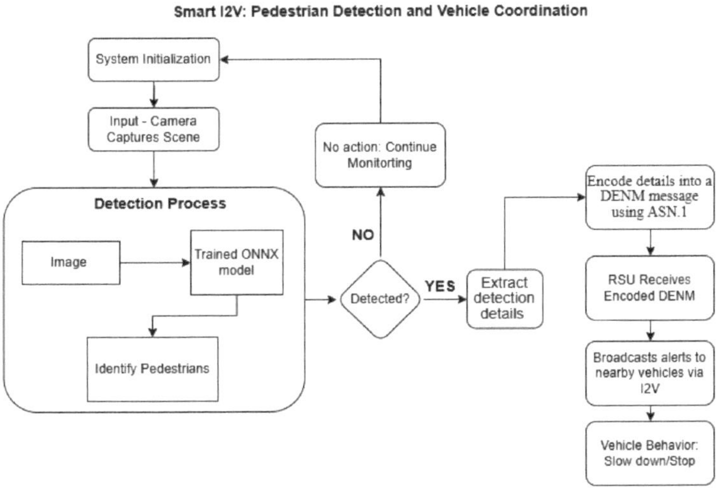

Figure 1. Smart I2V system process flowchart for pedestrian detection and vehicle coordination. The system integrates V2X communication protocols, AI-based detection, and vehicle behavior coordination to enhance real-time traffic safety.

The flowchart in Figure 1 illustrates the Smart I2V system for pedestrian detection and vehicle coordination. To offer further insight, the process begins with system initialization, where the input camera captures the surrounding scene in real-time. The captured image is then fed into a detection pipeline, encompassing a trained ONNX model specifically designed to identify pedestrians. Provided that pedestrians are detected, their details, including position, bounding box, and confidence rates, are extracted for further processing. In case no pedestrians are detected, the system continues monitoring the environment without additional action, having the vehicles pass through the crosswalks. When pedestrian detection occurs, the extracted details are encoded into a DENM using ASN.1 encoding standards. Subsequently, the RSU receives this encoded message and uses the I2V communication channel to propagate notifications to surrounding vehicles, respectively. To preserve the safety of pedestrians, the car responds to the signals by changing its behavior, such as slowing down or stopping. This system displays a durable integration of V2X communication protocols, AI-based detection, and vehicle behavior coordination to augment real-time decision-making and traffic safety.

2.1. Pedestrian Detection System

The YOLOv5 architecture, a deep learning model intended for real-time object recognition, albeit a lighter version, was used to create the pedestrian detection system. In a specific order, the implementation consists of preparing the dataset, training the model, and deploying the model in accordance with the particular needs of this investigation.

The dataset used for training the YOLOv5 model was acquired from Kaggle's "Pedestrian Detection" dataset [27]. The reason for choosing this specific dataset was its richness with person and nonperson-like pictures in a variety of environments, contributing to even detecting cyclists, aside from pedestrians. Although the primary objective of this study is to detect pedestrians as vulnerable road users, the system's capabilities extend beyond this scope. Due to the diversity of the dataset and the robustness of the YOLO-based detection model, cyclists can also be detected effectively.

The raw data were thereafter preprocessed and structured to fit YOLOv5's requirements:

- Data organization: The dataset was divided into training and validation subsets (with the test dataset subset analyzed in the next phases), having a balanced representation of pedestrian images in diverse scenarios, such as urban areas, varying lighting, and weather conditions.
- Annotation conversion: Since the provided annotations were in XML format, they were converted into YOLO-compatible ".txt files" using a custom script. The conversion included normalizing bounding box coordinates and mapping the "person" class to a unique class ID, in this case "0".
- Verification of annotations: A sample of converted annotations was inspected to ensure proper formatting and accuracy during the conversion process.

The YOLOv5 model was trained using transfer learning with pre-trained weights (yolov5s.pt), with the training process having to resize and normalize images to 640 × 640 pixels as part of the input configuration. Following that, the model was trained over 50 epochs with a batch size of 16, using a "dataset.yaml" file to define the dataset structure, comprising the paths to training and validation images, and specifying the "person" class. During training, evaluation metrics such as precision, recall, and mean average precision (mAP) were tracked to assess performance, and hyperparameter tuning was performed to optimize these metrics for better results.

The trained model was in due course deployed for real-time inference with the use of the YOLOv5 framework. The deployment process involved several key steps. First, a detection script was executed to process images from a test dataset, generating bounding boxes, class IDs, and confidence scores for identified pedestrians. Afterward, the detection results were saved as annotated images, with bounding boxes displayed around pedestrians, and were visualized using tools like Matplotlib 3.3.4 for verification. Lastly, the model was integrated into an ROS2 node, where it published the detection results, including bounding box coordinates, confidence scores, and class IDs, to the "detectiontopic" for downstream processing, which will be explained in more detail in the following section.

After training the YOLOv5 model, the trained weights were exported in a format suitable for deployment in diverse environments, with this process guaranteeing the model's portability and compatibility with real-world applications. To that end, the trained weights (best.pt) were to be exported to the ONNX (open neural network exchange) format using the YOLOv5 export utility. To elucidate, the ONNX format is widely supported across platforms and frameworks, authorizing the use of seamless integration with systems optimized for GPU or CPU inference. The exported ONNX file was then downloaded locally for deployment. The exported ONNX model was tested on sample images to verify that it retained the performance metrics achieved during training. The exported "best.onnx" file was downloaded for further deployment and testing.

2.2. DENM Message Encoding

The DENM is a standardized V2X message format used to share event-based safety information. In this study, the YOLOv5 pedestrian detection results were encoded into DENM messages using ASN.1 schemas, verifying compliance with ETSI ITS standards. The procedure involved the following steps. The DENM message structure is defined by ETSI ITS standards and includes multiple components that describe the event's nature, location, and timing. Key elements include

- ActionID: A unique identifier for the DENM message.
- Management container: Details the origin and type of the event.
- Situation container: Describes the specific scenario triggering the message, such as a pedestrian being detected.
- Location container: Encodes geographic coordinates (latitude, longitude, and altitude) of the event.

For that to work out, what is needed are the relevant ".asn" files, encompassing all the details mentioned. They were acquired from "ETSI TS 102 894-2 V1.3.1 (2018-08)", which are "DENM-PDU-Descriptions.asn, ETSI-ITS-CDD.asn, and ITS-Container.asn" [28], that were used to define these components and their relationships. The ASN.1 schemas were compiled into Python-compatible encoders and decoders using an ASN.1 compiler, "asn1c". This step enabled automated encoding of detection data into the DENM structure.

The process of mapping detection data to DENM fields was carried out as follows: First, the geographic coordinates of the detected pedestrian were extracted and mapped to the location container. Next, the detection timestamp was encoded into the management container to indicate when the event occurred. As a final step, the detection event was categorized as "pedestrian detected" and mapped to the appropriate field in the situation container.

Lastly, message encoding should be conducted as well in the way that the mapped data was encoded into binary format using the generated encoder functions. This ensures that the DENM messages comply with ETSI ITS communication standards. In this regard, each encoded message was validated for compliance with the DENM specification to ensure compatibility with V2X communication systems. The encoded DENM messages were intended to be published by the RSU node in the ROS2 framework. The messages were then sent as a dedicated topic for the subscribing vehicle nodes to process and react to.

2.3. V2X Communication Pipeline

The V2X communication pipeline integrates the pedestrian detection system with the DENM message encoding and broadcasting framework. This pipeline involves a series of interconnected ROS2 nodes, each responsible for specific tasks, securing efficient and reliable communication between infrastructure and vehicles. Regarding the nodes, the "detectionnode" and "denmnode" are designed to operate sequentially. The "detectionnode" detects pedestrians and publishes results. The "denmnode" encodes the detection results into DENM messages and broadcasts them for consumption by subscribing vehicles.

The YOLO-based object detection system is a critical component of the SmartDENM framework, serving as the primary source of input for the I2V communication pipeline.

Upon detecting a pedestrian, the system extracts key attributes, such as bounding box coordinates and confidence scores, which are encoded into DENM messages using ASN.1 schemas. These messages are then transmitted via I2V protocols from the RSU to nearby vehicles, enabling them to take timely safety actions. As is explained, this communication enables real-time data exchange from infrastructure components, such as RSUs, to vehicles. This allows vehicles to receive critical information about road conditions, hazards, or detected objects, speeding timely and informed decision-making. This seamless integration ensures that the detection results are effectively utilized to enhance real-time decision-making and road safety.

To facilitate effective inference, the "detectionnode" loads the YOLOv5 model in ONNX format using the ONNX Runtime library. Pre-processing involves scaling input photos to 640 × 640 pixels, standardizing pixel values, and transforming them into a model-appropriate tensor format. The node performs inference to generate bounding boxes, confidence scores, and class IDs, filtering results with confidences greater than 0.5 (anything below this value was tested to produce mostly inaccurate results, leading to this value after numerous iterations for threshold selection). These filtered detection results are serialized into JSON format and published on the "detectiontopic", enabling downstream processing by other nodes in the pipeline, just as pictured in the diagram below (Figure 2). The JSON format is utilized owing to its capability as an intermediary format to structure detection results and encode them into a simple, human-readable, and interoperable format.

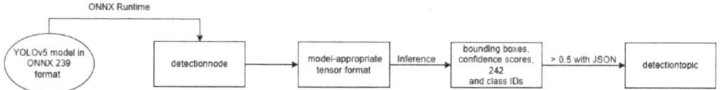

Figure 2. Detection workflow with YOLOv5: Model loading, inference, and JSON-based result publishing for downstream processing.

The "denmnode" then subscribes to the "detectiontopic" to receive detection results in JSON format, parsing the data to extract critical details like bounding box coordinates, confidence scores, and class IDs. Using this information, the node constructs a DENM message compliant with ETSI ITS standards, incorporating additional contextual details such as event location (latitude and longitude), timestamp, and event type and encodes these results into a DENM with the help of ASN.1 encoding. The next process is about publishing the encoded DENM message on another topic called "denmalerts" for further process.

The vehicle behavior nodes are designed to process DENM messages received on the "denmalerts" topic and execute appropriate actions based on the alert's type and quality. These nodes makes sure that the vehicle responds in real time to potential hazards detected by the system. Both nodes contribute to the V2X ecosystem by translating DENM messages into actionable insights, enabling real-time responses. Node 1 focuses on direct action, while Node 2 extends communication by broadcasting the vehicle's status, supporting monitoring and further decision making in the system. Vehicle Behavior Node 1 is designed to subscribe to the "denmalerts" topic and process incoming DENM messages. Its key functionalities include message parsing, where relevant fields such as informationQuality and causeCode are extracted to assess the reliability and type of the alert. Based on these fields, the node applies decision logic to determine appropriate vehicle actions. For instance, high-quality alerts prompt the vehicle to slow down for significant hazards, medium-quality alerts result in cautious actions, and low-quality alerts lead to no immediate action. Additionally, the node maintains simplified logs of alerts and corresponding actions for debugging and monitoring purposes. Vehicle Behavior Node 2 builds upon the first node's behavior by incorporating a status publishing capability. Like the first node, it processes DENM messages and determines vehicle actions such as slowing down or taking no action. However, it further publishes the vehicle's status on the "vehicle2status" topic after an action is determined. This status includes details such as the vehicle ID and the chosen action, serialized in JSON format for downstream applications. To ensure traceability, the node also generates logs for each received alert and the published status.

3. Results and Discussion

The pedestrian detection and V2X communication system was rigorously tested to evaluate its performance across different components. The testing process focused on the accuracy of pedestrian detection and the efficiency of encoding and broadcasting DENM messages, coupled with the vehicle's real-time responses to alerts. Key performance metrics such as precision, recall, mAP, and latency were analyzed to ensure the system's reliability and readiness for deployment. Below, it is planned to delve into the results for each component, starting with the pedestrian detection system.

3.1. Pedestrian Detection Results

The training configuration for the model involved 50 epochs, as shown in Figure 2, promoting the model's efficient convergence. The best-performing model weights were saved as "best.pt" for validation and deployment purposes. This configuration upheld a stable and efficient training process.

The model demonstrated strong performance metrics. It achieved a precision (P) of 0.855, indicating a high ability to minimize false positives, and a recall (R) of 0.837, showcasing good sensitivity in detecting pedestrians. Furthermore, the model achieved an mAP50 (mean average precision at IoU = 0.5) score of 0.883, reflecting high accuracy in detecting objects with acceptable bounding box overlap. It also recorded an mAP50-95 score of 0.591, highlighting its robust detection performance across stricter intersection over union (IoU) thresholds. In terms of efficiency, the model consists of 157 layers with 7,012,822 parameters, striking a balance between computational complexity and inference speed. The training process was completed in just 0.291 h, demonstrating the computational efficiency of the YOLOv5 framework. Validation was performed on a dataset of 160 images containing 203 pedestrian instances. The results, saved in runs/train/exp, provide a visual representation of the model's detection capabilities and support further evaluation of its performance, as mentioned in Table 1.

Table 1. The results of the performance metrics provide a comprehensive evaluation of the model's ability to accurately detect pedestrians while minimizing errors.

Metric	Value
Precision (P)	0.855
Recall (R)	0.837
mAP50	0.883
mAP50-95	0.591
Number of epochs	50

To further evaluate the model, a separate analysis was conducted on 116 common files from the test dataset. At an IoU threshold, the model achieved a precision of 0.88, recall of 0.75, and an F1 score of 0.81. These results highlight the model's ability to detect pedestrians effectively, even under lenient overlap criteria, which aligns with real-world scenarios where bounding boxes may not perfectly align. It provided insights into the model's robustness and practical applicability, showcasing its ability to balance detection accuracy with real-world considerations. To say the least, the results could be improved with more epochs and more datasets along the way since the size of the dataset used in this could be limited to fully determine its capability to be deployed to the real-world.

These results given in Tables 1 and 2 indicate that the trained YOLOv5 model is well suited for real-time pedestrian detection, laying a strong foundation for integration into the V2X communication pipeline. The pedestrian detection system was evaluated on a set of test images to verify its ability to accurately identify humans while ignoring non-human objects. Four images were selected for being included in this report out of 235 images used for testing, as given in Figure 3: two containing people and two containing non-human entities (statues and androids).

Table 2. Comprehensive evaluation of YOLOv5 detection performance on test dataset.

Metric	Value
True Positives (TP)	181
False Positives (FP)	24
False Negatives (FN)	61
Precision	0.88
Recall	0.75
F1 Score	0.81
Files Analyzed	116

Figure 3. Four selected tested images: The first two images depict scenes with two individuals present, while the latter two images represent scenarios without any individuals.

There are various actions that could be taken to enhance the model's performance. First, the model's capacity for generalization might be improved by training it on a bigger and more varied dataset that includes situations like dim lighting, occlusions, and complicated backdrops. Second, real-world variability could be addressed by adding changes to the dataset, such as cropping, scaling, and brightness adjustments. Lastly, performance could be further improved by implementing sophisticated strategies like attention mechanisms or optimizing the YOLOv5 architecture to increase small-object recognition or by employing the latest versions of YOLO as well. By taking care of these issues, false negatives will be decreased and the system's resilience in various operating conditions will be increased.

The model exhibited high confidence in detecting humans, achieving confidence scores of 0.90 and 0.94 in the first two test images. Additionally, it successfully disregarded non-human entities, such as statues and androids, in the subsequent two images. This demonstrates the model's robustness in minimizing false positives, as illustrated in Figure 3.

3.2. Integration and Simulation Results

The pedestrian detection and V2X communication system was tested under real-time conditions using a sequence of nodes: "detectionnode", "denmnode", "vehiclebehaviornode", and "vehiclebehaviornode2". The tests included two key scenarios: (1) an environment with a pedestrian present and (2) an environment without a pedestrian. The results are summarized as follows:

3.2.1. Scenario 1: No Pedestrian Present

When the "detectionnode" processed the input image using the YOLOv5 model in ONNX format, no detections were identified. The node logged that no valid objects were detected, and no messages were published on the detection topic. Consequently, no DENM was generated or published, and the vehicle nodes detected the absence of alerts. The system monitored the "vehiclestatus" topic, but no actions were initiated as no updates were received.

3.2.2. Scenario 2: Pedestrian Present

During testing, the "detectionnode" accurately identified pedestrians with high confidence scores exceeding the threshold. The detection results, including bounding box coordinates, confidence scores, and class IDs, were serialized into JSON format and published on the "detectiontopic". Upon confirming a valid detection, the node halted further processing to optimize resource utilization. The "denmnode" seamlessly integrated into the pipeline by receiving detection messages from the "detectiontopic". It encoded the detection data into a structured DENM message compliant with ETSI ITS standards. This message included details such as geographic coordinates, event time, and event type (causeCode: 1). The DENM was then published on the "/denmalerts" topic, with a single alert for each detection, with the use of ASN.1, as explained before. Upon receiving the DENM, the "vehiclebehaviornode" parsed the message and made real-time decisions. Based on an informationQuality score of 67 and a causeCode of 1, the node decided to "be cautious" and logged this action. This demonstrated the node's ability to translate V2X alerts into practical vehicle responses. The enhanced "vehiclebehaviornode2" replicated this cautious behavior while adding status publishing functionality. In addition to processing DENM messages, it broadcasted its response ("be cautious") on the "vehicle2status" topic, extending inter-vehicle communication capabilities, paving the way for a future project implementation with other message types.

3.3. System Validation

The integrated pedestrian detection and V2X communication system has been validated through real-time simulations. The system successfully detected pedestrians with high confidence, encoded alerts into DENM messages, and facilitated vehicle responses via RSU-based and inter-vehicle communication mechanisms. The flow of data across the pipeline is illustrated in Figure 1, demonstrating seamless interaction among the nodes:

- Detection node: Identifies pedestrians and publishes detection results.
- DENM node: Encodes these results into ETSI ITS-compliant messages and broadcasts them on the "denmalerts" topic.
- Vehicle behavior nodes: Process these alerts to determine appropriate actions, with the second node extending functionality for inter-vehicle communication when RSU coverage is unavailable.

The workflow begins with a camera detecting a pedestrian in a crosswalk. Using advanced detection algorithms, the system sends these data to a RSU, which broadcasts an alert to nearby vehicles via I2V communication. Upon receiving the alert, the approaching vehicle adjusts its behavior, such as slowing down, to ensure pedestrian safety. This process highlights how I2V systems amplify traffic safety through real-time detection and communication, as depicted in Figure 4. By way of conclusion, the proposed system performed as intended, providing both security of passengers and smooth operation of traffic flow. The detected pedestrians were fed into the system mounted in the vehicle approaching, enabling the vehicle to use the help of said system to perform the necessary course of action of either slowing down or stopping entirely if the threshold determined is passed through.

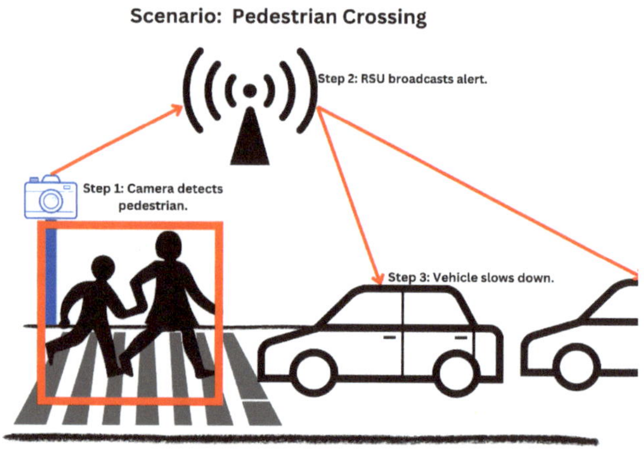

Figure 4. Scenario: Pedestrian Crossing: Demonstrates the integration of real-time pedestrian detection and V2X communication, showcasing how alerts enable vehicles to adapt their behavior for enhanced safety.

Another addressable matter is that the primary focus of this system is to ensure pedestrian safety at crosswalks by enabling vehicles to detect and respond to pedestrians in real time. While recognizing traffic lights and road signs can provide additional contextual awareness, these elements were not incorporated into this study, as they are not directly relevant to the system's core functionality. For instance, the presence of a pedestrian in a crosswalk necessitates an immediate response regardless of traffic signal states, as the priority is to prevent collisions. Future iterations of the system, however, might explore integrating traffic lights and signs to augment situational awareness and improve traffic flow management (such as alerting drivers about jaywalking or detecting a "school zone" sign, making the vehicle adjust its behavior).

4. Conclusions

This study effectively illustrated how real-time pedestrian identification and V2X communication can be integrated, highlighting how it can improve road safety in situations with fluctuating traffic, with the utilization of DENM. What the proposed system did was to identify pedestrians effectively, convert the data into structured DENM messages, and equip cars to make rapid and intelligent decisions by merging machine vision techniques with standardized ETSI ITS-compliant communication protocols. High detection accuracy, dependable message encoding and broadcasting, and efficient vehicle decision-making in simulated situations were all demonstrated throughout testing step by step. By tackling important issues in real-time detection and V2X communication with DENM, the research advances the continuous development of ITS. Nonetheless, it is of utmost importance to recognize some of this study's limitations. A controlled simulation environment was used for the evaluation, which does not adequately represent the intricacies and unpredictability of real-world situations. Real-world testing is the paramount step when deciding to deploy the system to be utilized in dynamic environments. Not overlooking the fact that simulation could give insight into how the proposed approach would work, the real-world has complexities which sometimes cannot be imitated in the experimental setup. Some crucial ones include network latency and connectivity issues as well as packet loss and variations in signal strength, causing DENM messages to have delays or even the worst case of resulting in incomplete messages being delivered, especially in rural areas or urban areas with high population density. The detection model's ubiquitousness across a variety of pedestrian appearances and environmental conditions may be impacted by its reliance on a small training dataset—occlusions caused by other vehicles, objects, and environmental features could be taken as examples, producing the need for a large amount of data to be used in the detection process.

Future work will focus on addressing these limitations to enhance the system's robustness and applicability. The detection model's accuracy will increase across a larger variety of scenarios on the off chance that the dataset used to train it is expanded. Real-time GPS inputs and other dynamic geographic data would grant approval for the system to adjust to quickly changing settings. Validating the system's performance in real-world scenarios involving dynamic vehicle interactions and live infrastructure connectivity is of significance. Extended research will also explore enlarging the system's functionality to support cooperative driving and advanced safety applications. What is meant is the incorporation of additional V2X message types, such as CAM (cooperative awareness message) and MCM (maneuver coordination message), which could enable broader use cases, including cooperative lane changes, intersection management, and coordinated responses in complex traffic situations, as well as highway merging and crowded pedestrian crossings. Not forgetting about the impact of the varying weather conditions, the emphasis being put on enhancing the system's environmental adaptability to ensure robust performance under diverse weather and lighting conditions, such as heavy rain, fog, snow, or nighttime scenarios, might also correspondingly be deemed necessary. Additionally, recognizing traffic signals and road signs could provide contextual awareness, thereby enhancing decision making and allowing the system adapt better to varied traffic flow dynamics. Last but not least, for the safety issues, though, incorporating cutting-edge cybersecurity features like intrusion detection, authentication, and encryption will protect the V2X communication pipeline from possible cyber-attacks and improve system dependability in practical applications.

Author Contributions: The authors contributed equally to this work. All authors (Á.T. and A.D.) have read and agreed to the published version of the manuscript. All authors have read and agreed to the published version of the manuscript.

Funding: This research received no external funding.

Data Availability Statement: The original data presented in the study are openly available in FigShare at [DOI: https://doi.org/10.1007/978-981-15-7031-5_103].

Conflicts of Interest: The authors declare no conflicts of interest.

Abbreviations

The following abbreviations are used in this manuscript:

V2X	Vehicle-to-everything
DENM	Decentralized environmental notification message
ONNX	Open neural network exchange
ADAS	Advanced driver assistance system

I2V	Infrastructure-to-vehicle
V2V	Vehicle-to-vehicle
JSON	JavaScript object notation
CAM	Cooperative awareness message
MCM	Maneuver coordination message
ID	Identification number
GPS	Global positioning system
ITS	Intelligent transport systems
C-ITS	Cooperative intelligent transport systems
ETSI	European telecommunications standards institute
ROS	Robot operating system
ASN.1	Abstract syntax notation one
RSU	Roadside unit

References

1. Sosik-Filipiak, K.; Osypchuk, O. Identification of solutions for vulnerable road users safety in urban transport systems: Grounded theory research. *Sustainability* **2023**, *15*, 10568. [CrossRef]
2. Deb, S.; Rahman, M.M.; Strawderman, L.J.; Garrison, T.M. Pedestrians' receptivity toward fully automated vehicles: Research review and roadmap for future research. *IEEE Trans. Hum.-Mach. Syst.* **2018**, *48*, 279–290. [CrossRef]
3. Preisen, L.; Helgeson, C.; Roelofs, T. *Pedestrian Detection Systems for Improved Safety*; Report No. ENTERPRISE Pooled Fund Study TPF-5(359), Michigan DOT; Athey Creek Consultants: Maplewood, MN, USA, 2022.
4. Silva, C.M.; Silva, L.D.; Santos, L.A.L.; Sarubbi, J.F.M.; Pitsillides, A. Broadening understanding on managing the communication infrastructure in vehicular networks: Customizing the coverage using the delta network. *Future Internet* **2018**, *11*, 1. [CrossRef]
5. Schulte-Tigges, J.; Rondinone, M.; Reke, M.; Wachenfeld, J.; Kaszner, D. Using V2X Communications for Smart ODD Management of Highly Automated Vehicles. In Proceedings of the 2023 IEEE 26th International Conference on Intelligent Transportation Systems (ITSC), Bilbao, Spain, 24–28 September 2023; pp. 3317–3322. [CrossRef]
6. Arena, F.; Pau, G.; Severino, A. V2X communications applied to safety of pedestrians and vehicles. *J. Sens. Actuator Netw.* **2019**, *9*, 3. [CrossRef]
7. Li, L.; Zhang, W.; Wang, X.; Cui, T.; Sun, C. NLOS Dies Twice: Challenges and Solutions of V2X for Cooperative Perception. *IEEE Open J. Intell. Transp. Syst.* **2024**, *5*, 774–782. [CrossRef]
8. Khan, M.A.; Ghosh, S.; Busari, S.A.; Huq, K.M.S.; Dagiuklas, T.; Mumtaz, S.; Rodriguez, J. Robust, resilient and reliable architecture for V2X communications. *IEEE Trans. Intell. Transp. Syst.* **2021**, *22*, 4414–4430. [CrossRef]
9. Sedar, R.; Kalalas, C.; Vázquez-Gallego, F.; Alonso, L.; Alonso-Zarate, J. A comprehensive survey of V2X cybersecurity mechanisms and future research paths. *IEEE Open J. Commun. Soc.* **2023**, *4*, 325–391. [CrossRef]
10. Arena, F.; Pau, G. An overview of vehicular communications. *Future Internet* **2019**, *11*, 27. [CrossRef]
11. Wang, B.; Li, Y.Y.; Xu, W.; Wang, H.; Hu, L. Vehicle–pedestrian detection method based on improved YOLOv8. *Electronics* **2024**, *13*, 2149. [CrossRef]
12. Bakirci, M. Real-time vehicle detection using YOLOv8-nano for intelligent transportation systems. *Trait. Signal* **2024**, *41*, 1727. [CrossRef]
13. Hawlader, F.; Robinet, F.; Frank, R. Leveraging the edge and cloud for V2X-based real-time object detection in autonomous driving. *Comput. Commun.* **2024**, *213*, 372–381. [CrossRef]
14. Capallera, M.; de Salis, E.; Meteier, Q.; Angelini, L.; Carrino, S.; Khaled, O.A.; Mugellini, E. Secondary task and situation awareness, a mobile application for conditionally automated vehicles. In Proceedings of the 11th International Conference on Automotive User Interfaces and Interactive Vehicular Applications: Adjunct Proceedings, Utrecht, The Netherlands, 21 September 2019; pp. 86–92.
15. Veena, S.; Ramyadevi, K.; Elavarasi, K.; Preetha, M. Smart car automated system to assist the driver in detecting the problem and providing the solution. *Int. J. Innov. Technol. Explor. Eng.* **2019**, *8*, 727–731.
16. Uchida, N.; Takeuchi, S.; Ishida, T.; Shibata, Y. Mobile Traffic Accident Prevention System based on Chronological Changes of Wireless Signals and Sensors. *J. Wirel. Mob. Netw. Ubiquitous Comput. Dependable Appl.* **2017**, *8*, 57–66.
17. Han, Q.; Qiu, M.; Lu, Z.; Memmi, G. An efficient key distribution system for data fusion in V2X heterogeneous networks. *Inf. Fusion* **2019**, *50*, 212–220.
18. Li, Y.; Ibanez-Guzman, J. Lidar for autonomous driving: The principles, challenges, and trends for automotive lidar and perception systems. *IEEE Signal Process. Mag.* **2020**, *37*, 50–61. [CrossRef]

19. Sluis, J.v.d.; Op den Camp, O.; Broos, J.; Yalcinkaya, I.; De Gelder, E. Describing I2V communication in scenarios for simulation-based safety assessment of truck platooning. *Electronics* **2021**, *10*, 2362. [CrossRef]
20. Arshad, S.; Feng, C.; Elujide, I.; Zhou, S.; Liu, Y. SafeDrive-Fi: A Multimodal and Device Free Dangerous Driving Recognition System Using WiFi. In Proceedings of the 2018 IEEE International Conference on Communications (ICC), Kansas City, MO, USA, 20–24 May 2018; pp. 1–6. [CrossRef]
21. Malladi, A.; Chandrashekhar, A. WIFI for Vehicular Communication Systems. *J. Emerg. Technol. Innov. Res.* **2015**, *2*, 1939–1943.
22. Abidi, B.; Moreno, F.M.; El Haziti, M.; Hussein, A.; Al Kaff, A.; Gomez, D.M. Hybrid V2X Communication Approach Using WiFi and 4G Connections. In Proceedings of the 2018 IEEE International Conference on Vehicular Electronics and Safety (ICVES), Madrid, Spain, 12–14 September 2018; pp. 1–5.
23. Campolo, C.; Molinaro, A.; Vinel, A.; Zhang, Y. Modeling Event-Driven Safety Messages Delivery in IEEE 802.11p/WAVE Vehicular Networks. *IEEE Commun. Lett.* **2013**, *17*, 2392–2395. [CrossRef]
24. Klapež, M.; Grazia, C.A.; Casoni, M. Experimental Evaluation of IEEE 802.11p in High-Speed Trials for Safety-Related Applications. *IEEE Trans. Veh. Technol.* **2021**, *70*, 11538–11553. [CrossRef]
25. Santa, J.; Pereñíguez, F.; Moragón, A.; Skarmeta, A.F. Experimental evaluation of CAM and DENM messaging services in vehicular communications. *Transp. Res. Part C Emerg. Technol.* **2014**, *46*, 98–120. [CrossRef]
26. Monteuuis, J.-P.; Petit, J.; Chen, C.; Das, S.; Nekoui, M.; Yang, S. V2X Misbehavior in Decentralized Notification Basic Service: Considerations for Standardization. In Proceedings of the 2024 Cyber Security in CarS Workshop, Salt Lake City, UT, USA, 20 November 2024; pp. 76–84.
27. Karthika, N.J.; Saravanan, C. Addressing the False Positives in Pedestrian Detection. In Proceedings of the 2020 Electronic Systems and Intelligent Computing, Singapore, 23 September 2020; Lecture Notes in Electrical Engineering; Springer: Berlin/Heidelberg, Germany, 2020; Volume 686. [CrossRef]
28. *Technical Specification ETSI TS 103 831 V2.1.1*; Vehicular Communications; Basic Set of Applications; Decentralized Environmental Notification Service, Release 2. ETSI: Valbonne, France, 2022.

Disclaimer/Publisher's Note: The statements, opinions and data contained in all publications are solely those of the individual author(s) and contributor(s) and not of MDPI and/or the editor(s). MDPI and/or the editor(s) disclaim responsibility for any injury to people or property resulting from any ideas, methods, instructions or products referred to in the content.

Article

Shallow Learning-Based Intrusion Detection System for In-Vehicle Network: ASIC Implementation

Minseok Choi [1], Myeongjin Lee [1], Hyungchul Im [1], Joosock Lee [2] and Seongsoo Lee [1,*]

[1] Department of Intelligent Semiconductors, Soongsil University, Seoul 06978, Republic of Korea; 1102342004@soongsil.ac.kr (M.C.); mjlee7466@soongsil.ac.kr (M.L.); tory@soongsil.ac.kr (H.I.)
[2] School of Electronic Engineering, Soongsil University, Seoul 06978, Republic of Korea; jslee@ssu.ac.kr
* Correspondence: sslee@ssu.ac.kr

Abstract: This paper presents an Application-Specific Integrated Circuit (ASIC) implementation and Field-Programmable Gate Array (FPGA) verification of a Convolutional Neural Network (CNN)-based Intrusion Detection System (IDS) designed to enhance the security of an in-vehicle Controller Area Network (CAN) BUS and detect malicious messages. The CNN model employs a lightweight architecture with a single convolution layer using a 2×2 kernel and integrates a filter algorithm optimized for Fuzzy and Spoofing attacks to improve the performance. The IDS is implemented on an Electronic Control Unit platform powered by an ARM Cortex-M3 core and uses SRAM to store the parameters utilized by the CNN model and filter algorithm, targeting ASIC implementation with TSMC 180 nm technology. Functional verification was conducted by configuring a simplified CAN bus environment using the Xilinx Nexys Video FPGA and PEAK-System PCAN-USB, which was validated in real-time against DoS, Spoofing, and Fuzzy attack scenarios. The proposed lightweight CNN-based IDS achieved a fast detection speed of 0.0233 ms and an average accuracy of 99.6879%, thereby demonstrating its potential to enhance the security of in-vehicle CAN BUS.

Keywords: controller area network; intrusion detection system; convolution neural network; lightweight; in-vehicle network; automotive security

Academic Editor: Taeshik Shon

Received: 30 December 2024
Revised: 27 January 2025
Accepted: 8 February 2025
Published: 10 February 2025

Citation: Choi, M.; Lee, M.; Im, H.; Lee, J.; Lee, S. Shallow Learning-Based Intrusion Detection System for In-Vehicle Network: ASIC Implementation. *Electronics* 2025, 14, 683. https://doi.org/10.3390/electronics14040683

Copyright: © 2025 by the authors. Licensee MDPI, Basel, Switzerland. This article is an open access article distributed under the terms and conditions of the Creative Commons Attribution (CC BY) license (https://creativecommons.org/licenses/by/4.0/).

1. Introduction

The automotive industry has recently required significant computational performance due to the advances in Advanced Driving Assistance Systems (ADASs) and autonomous driving technologies [1,2]. Furthermore, the growing network connectivity with electric devices to accommodate various vehicle features has significantly elevated the importance of Controller Area Network (CAN) BUS, the primary communication protocol for vehicles [2,3].

The CAN bus enables efficient data exchange among various Electronic Control Units (ECUs) within the vehicle, thereby supporting a wide range of functionalities. However, owing to a lack of security features, they are vulnerable to malicious attacks. An attacker can gain access to a network and manipulate it, posing a serious threat to the safety of drivers and passengers [3].

To address the threats posed by the lack of security features, various models have been implemented to Intrusion Detection Systems (IDS) [4], such as Convolutional Neural Network (CNN)-based IDS using Inception-ResNet [5] and Generative Adversarial Networks (GAN)-based IDS using an Auxiliary Classifier [6]. However, Deep Learning approach is often unsuitable for vehicles due to its high computational complexity and the limited resources available in vehicle environments.

This paper proposes a lightweight CNN-based IDS using shallow learning to address the security vulnerabilities of the CAN BUS and establish an IDS for vehicle networks. The proposed approach includes Application Specific Integrated Circuit (ASIC) implementation and Field Programmable Gate Array (FPGA) verification of an IDS. The proposed IDS can be summarized as follows.

1. The error-handling mechanism of the CAN protocol is utilized to impose communication penalties on the hacked ECU or isolate them from the bus.
2. Data preprocessing methods, such as Sliding Window and Data Insertion, are utilized to facilitate the real-time analysis of ongoing communication data.
3. The CNN model performs multiclass classification to identify attack types, and the corresponding filter algorithm is applied to mitigate performance degradation caused by the lightweight design.

2. Background

2.1. CAN

CAN is a network protocol designed to communicate among various ECUs within a vehicle. In the CAN protocol, each data packet is assigned a unique message ID to form a message-based communication structure [7,8]. This allows all ECUs within the network to control communication independently without a central control unit. Additionally, it provides error detection and recovery features capable of identifying and managing various types of errors.

Additionally, as shown in Figure 1, the ECU within a vehicle adopts a multi-master architecture, where collisions can occur if multiple ECUs attempt to communicate simultaneously. To prevent this, an arbitration process is performed to determine the communication priority. The arbitration process operates on a bit-level comparison. When a Dominant Bit (Logic 0) and a Recessive Bit (Logic 1) are transmitted simultaneously, the Dominant Bit takes precedence. Through this method, the message IDs are compared, and ultimately, the message with the lowest ID is assigned the highest priority.

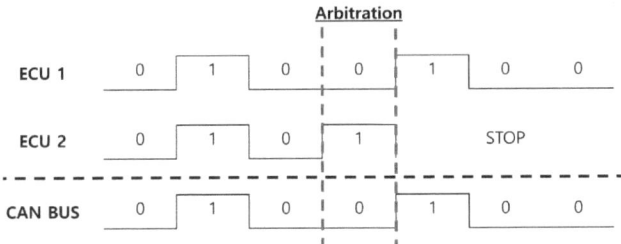

Figure 1. Controller Area Network (CAN) arbitration procedure.

2.1.1. Frame

A CAN Frame is the basic unit of data transmission, containing the transmitted data, along with its associated control information. CAN Frames are categorized into four types: Data Frame, Remote Frame, Overload Frame, and Error Frame, each serving the following roles, respectively:

1. Remote Frame: A frame used to request data associated with a specific message ID. It does not transmit any data but only includes the ID for the request.

2. Overload Frame: A frame transmitted when the network is in an overloaded state, temporarily halting communication and requesting additional time for data processing.
3. Error Frame: A frame transmitted when an error is detected, notifying the network of its occurrence.
4. Data Frame: A frame used for actual data transmission, sending information from the transmitting ECU to receiving ECU.

In this study, only Error and Data Frames were considered. The CAN Data Frame is shown in Figure 2, and the role of each field is as follows.

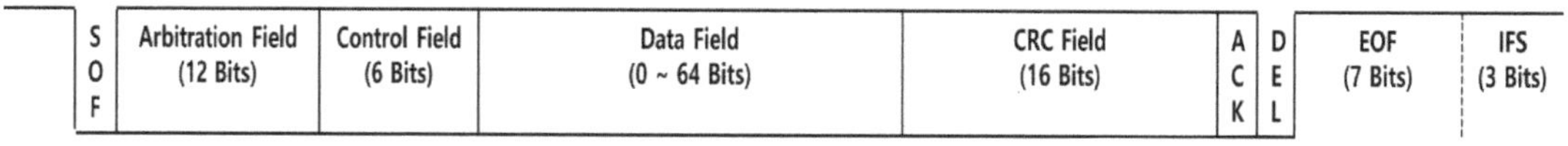

SOF	Arbitration Field (12 Bits)	Control Field (6 Bits)	Data Field (0 ~ 64 Bits)	CRC Field (16 Bits)	ACK	DEL	EOF (7 Bits)	IFS (3 Bits)

Figure 2. Data Frame structure.

The Start of Frame (SOF) is a single bit that signals the start of a frame, enabling the ECU connected to the network to recognize and synchronize the beginning of the frame accordingly.

The Arbitration Field contains the unique ID of the message and is responsible for determining its priority. It is composed of the Identifier (ID) and Remote Transmission Request (RTR). The ID is 11 bits long in the CAN Standard and 29 bits long in the Extended format. In this study, the Standard format is used, with the ID set to 11 bits. The RTR is a single bit used to differentiate between Data Frames and Remote Frames. A Dominant Bit is used to indicate a Data Frame.

The control Field contains information regarding the size and type of the Data Field of the current frame. It is composed of 6 bits, including Reserved Bits and the Data Length Code (DLC). The Reserved Bits are the two bits allocated to the future functionality. In this study, DLC was limited to values between 0 and 8.

The data Field contains the actual transmitted data. The size of the data is determined by the DLC, and the data are transmitted in the order of Most Significant Bit.

The CRC Field performs error detection in the frames. It is composed of a Cyclic Redundancy Check (CRC) Sequence and a Delimiter Bit. The CRC Sequence contained a 15-bit CRC value calculated using the SOF, Arbitration Field, Control Field, Data Field, and the CRC-15 Polynomial. The Delimiter Bit is a single Recessive Bit used to mark the end of a CRC Field. The transmitted CRC value in the CRC Sequence is compared with the CRC value calculated using the receiving ECU. If the values do not match, the receiving ECU can request the transmitting ECU to resend the frame.

The ACK Field indicates to the transmitting ECU whether data were successfully received by the receiving ECU. It comprises an ACK Slot and the Delimiter Bit. If the data were successfully received, a Dominant Bit was transmitted in the ACK Slot.

The End of Frame (EOF) is the field that signals the End of Frame. It comprises seven consecutive Recessive Bits.

The Interframe Space (IFS) represents the gap between frames. It consists of three consecutive Recessive Bits indicating the minimum interval between frames. This prevents collisions between consecutive frames and enhances communication reliability.

2.1.2. Error Handling

CAN communication detects and manages errors in stages such as error detection, error counter management, and error state transitions. It can identify five types of errors: Bit, Stuff, CRC, Form, and ACK Error.

A Bit Error occurs when the bit transmitted by the sending ECU is different from the actual bit received by the CAN BUS. However, exceptions include cases where a Stuff Bit or the ACK Slot is transmitted as a Dominant Bit, in which no Bit Error is triggered [7,8]. In addition, Bit Errors do not occur when a transmitting ECU in the Passive Error Flag state detects a Dominant Bit.

A Stuff Error occurs when the sixth consecutive identical bit appears in an encoded Frame Field, violating the bit-stuffing rule. As shown in Figure 3, bit-stuffing is used to maintain synchronization and assist in error detection during data transmission. This method inserts the opposite bit when five identical consecutive bits are detected.

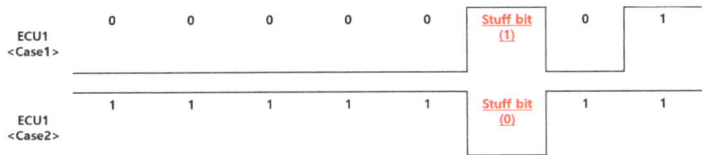

Figure 3. Bit Stuffing.

A CRC Error occurs when the CRC value calculated by the receiving ECU is different from the CRC value transmitted by the sending ECU.

Form Error occurs when a fixed-format Bit Field, such as a Delimiter Bit or EOF contains a bit that does not conform to the required format. However, a Form Error does not occur if the receiving ECU detects a Dominant Bit in the last bit of the EOF or monitors a Dominant Bit in the last bit of the Error Delimiter.

An ACK Error occurs when, after sending a message, the transmitting ECU detects a Recessive Bit in the ACK Slot instead of a Dominant Bit from the receiving ECU connected to a CAN BUS.

The ECUs connected to the CAN BUS exist in one of three error states, as shown in Figure 4. These states are managed through a Transmission Error Counter (TEC), which counts errors occurring during transmission, and the Receive Error Counter (REC), which counts errors occurring during reception. When an error is detected, the TEC typically increases by eight and the REC increases by one [5,6]. Conversely, when communication occurs without errors, both the TEC and REC decrease by 1.

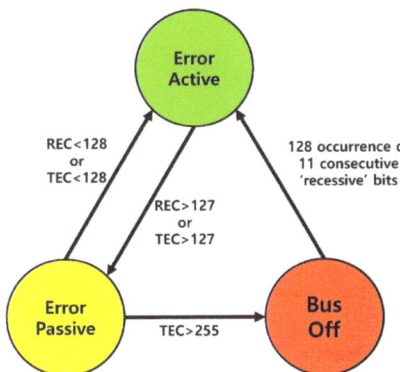

Figure 4. Error state.

Error Active is the default state of an ECU that allows normal participation in CAN BUS communication. When either the TEC or REC reaches 128, the state transitions to Error Passive. If the counters fall below 128, the state reverts to Error Active. Additionally, when an error occurs, the ECU transmits an Active Error Frame, as shown in Figure 5.

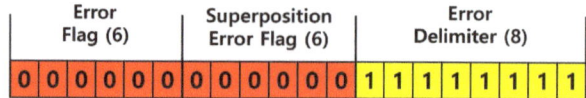

Figure 5. Active error frame.

Passive error is a state in which the ECU transmits a Passive Error Frame when an error occurs, as shown in Figure 6. After transmitting the Passive Error Frame, any subsequent transmission requires the ECU to wait before retrying. If TEC exceeds 255, the ECU transitions to a bus-off state.

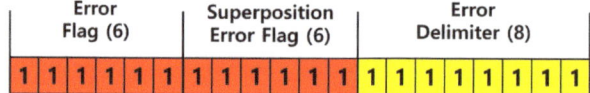

Figure 6. Passive error frame.

A bus-off is a state in which the ECU can no longer participate in communication and cannot influence the bus. This occurs when an ECU is isolated from the network. If 11 consecutive Recessive Bits are detected 128 times on the bus, the TEC and REC are reset to zero, and the ECU transitions back to the error-active state.

2.1.3. Attack Type

Network attacks within vehicles involve hacking an ECU to inject malicious messages into the CAN BUS, thereby disrupting the normal functionality of the vehicle [9]. This study addresses Denial of Service (DoS), Fuzzy, and Spoofing attacks.

DoS Attack is, as shown in Figure 7, where a hacked ECU leverages the CAN communication arbitration process to send a large number of low-priority messages, disrupting normal communication. By transmitting these messages repeatedly at short intervals, an attack can saturate the CAN BUS, thereby preventing the transmission of legitimate messages.

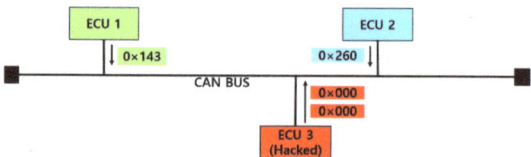

Figure 7. DoS attack.

A Fuzzy Attack, as depicted in Figure 8, involves transmitting messages with randomly generated IDs and data to the CAN BUS. This disrupts the transmission of legitimate messages and causes devices to malfunction. From the perspective of the hacker, the attack is relatively simple to execute, as it only requires sending messages with random IDs and data. However, these messages are uncommon in normal communication scenarios, which makes them easier to detect from the perspective of an IDS.

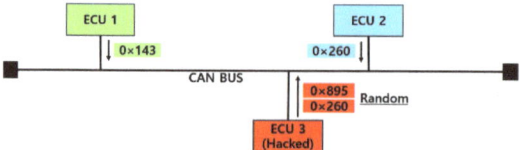

Figure 8. Fuzzy attack.

A Spoofing Attack, as shown in Figure 9, occurs when a compromised ECU monitors messages transmitted on the CAN BUS for a period of time and then impersonates a legitimate ECU to send false data to the bus. By mimicking a specific ECU, the attack causes other ECUs to operate based on incorrect information. In some cases, the attack replicates the exact data of legitimate messages, making a distinction between normal and malicious messages difficult for the receiving ECU. This makes the attack particularly dangerous from the perspective of the driver.

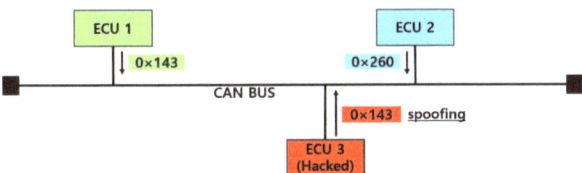

Figure 9. Spoofing attack.

3. CNN-Based Intrusion Detection System Model

3.1. CNN Model

This study proposes a lightweight CNN model with a simplified Multi-Layer Perceptron (MLP) structure and a single convolution layer, based on shallow learning designed for a vehicle IDS, as shown in Figure 10.

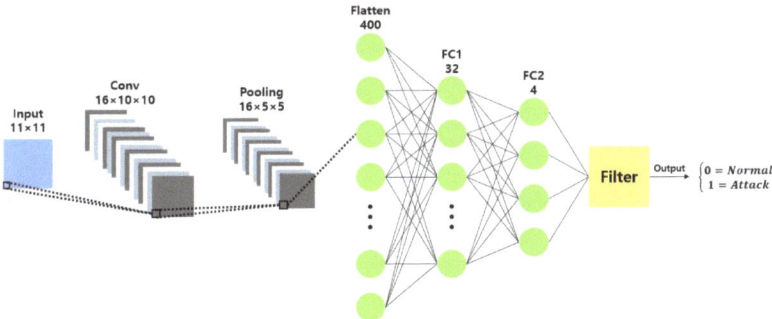

Figure 10. Proposed CNN model.

The proposed model uses 11 CAN IDs, each consisting of 11 bits, as the input. It uses a $16 \times 2 \times 2$ kernel to form a $16 \times 10 \times 10$ convolution layer, followed by a 2×2 filter to construct a $16 \times 5 \times 5$ max-pooling layer. The processed data are then passed through two fully connected layers. The first fully connected layer reduces the input of 400 nodes to 32 nodes, and the second fully connected layer further reduces the input to four nodes. These four nodes represent the classification results, indicating whether the current CAN BUS message is normal, or belongs to one of the following attack types: DoS, Fuzzy, or Spoofing. Based on the detected attack type, the message was processed using the corresponding filter algorithm [10] to determine whether it was an actual attack.

3.2. Data Preprocessing

The lightweight CNN model used in this study is designed to process the status of data frame shown in CAN BUS in real time, as shown in Figure 11, 11-bit CAN IDs were preprocessed using Sliding Window and Data Insertion method to generate a convolution layer input in the form of 11×11.

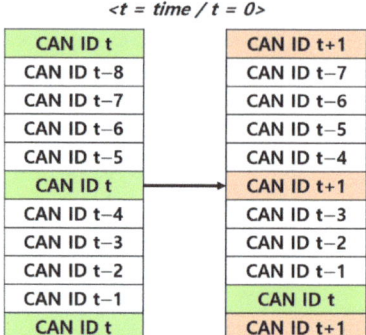

Figure 11. Proposed data preprocessing.

A Sliding Window is a technique that processes specific segments of continuous data by selecting and shifting them over a defined range. In this study, as shown in Figure 12a, the current CAN ID on the CAN BUS is placed at the bottom of the matrix, whereas the earliest received CAN ID is positioned at the top. When a new CAN ID arrives, the earliest CAN ID is removed, and the previous data shift upward, creating space for the current CAN ID at the bottom. This approach has the advantage of allowing individual evaluation of each CAN ID. However, this poses challenges in assessing the state of current CAN ID because of the emphasis on historical data.

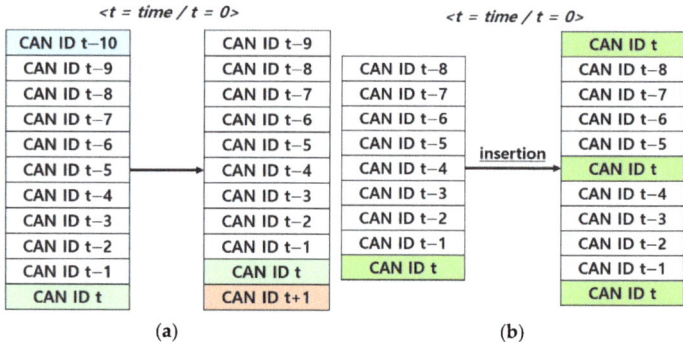

Figure 12. (a) refers to the sliding window and (b) refers to the data insertion.

Data Insertion is a preprocessing technique used to address the difficulty of assessing the state of the current CAN ID in the Sliding Window method. As shown in Figure 12b, this technique appends the three most recent CAN IDs to the previous eight CAN IDs to create an 11×11 structure. By placing more emphasis on the current CAN IDs, this method provides the advantage of evaluating the state of the current CAN ID more accurately.

3.3. Filter

The lightweight CNN model proposed in this study, which uses only a single convolutional layer, shows a lower performance compared to standard CNNs. To address this limitation, a Cross-Check Rule-Based Filter algorithm is introduced to enhance the detection capabilities of the model [10]. Of the three available filter algorithms, this study focuses on those targeting Spoofing and Fuzzy attacks because these demonstrate significant performance degradation.

For DoS Attacks, rely solely on the IDS determination results without using the filter algorithm. For Spoofing Attacks, the filter algorithm was refined by revising Rule 2 and introducing Rule 3. For Fuzzy Attacks, modifications included removing Rule 1 and adjusting Rule 2. These improvements were made to enhance detection accuracy while maintaining compatibility with the lightweight CNN-based IDS.

The Spoofing Filter Algorithm detects Spoofing attacks that exploit normal IDs by assigning predefined FP_{Max} values to each normal ID. To determine if an attack is taking place, the algorithm compares this value with the number of times the IDS has identified the attacked ID as malicious (Rule 1). Additionally, because Spoofing attacks often use the same ID with repeated Data Fields, the algorithm calculates and compares the Hamming Distance between Data Fields of the same ID to determine if an ongoing attack (Rule 2). Because normal communication can also involve the use of the same ID with repeated Data Fields, the algorithm mitigates performance degradation caused by Rule 2 by reviewing previous IDS results for the same ID to make a final determination (Rule 3). (Algorithm 1).

Algorithm 1: Spoofing Attack

Input: IDS Decision (0: Normal, 1: Spoofing, 2: DoS, 3: Fuzzy)
Output: Final Decision (0: Normal, 1: Attack)
1 **While** Monitoring results of the IDS **do**
2   **if** Result of the IDS is Spoofing Attack **then**
3   **if** $AC[ID_{cur}] > FP_{max}$ **then**   ▷ (Rule 1)
4   **if** Present or Previous Hamming Distance is Zero **then**   ▷ (Rule 2)
5 | Attack ← True;
6   **else**
7 | Attack ← False;
8   **else**
9 | Attack ← True;
10   **else**
11   **if** $AC[ID_{cur}] > FP_{max}$ **then**
12   **if** Present or Previous Hamming Distance is Zero **then**
13   **if** Previous Result of the IDS is Normal **then**   ▷ (Rule 3)
14 | Attack ← False;
15   **else**
16 | Attack ← True;
17   **else**
18 | Attack ← False;
19   **else**
20 | Attack ← False;
21 **end**

The Fuzzy Filter Algorithm detects Fuzzy attacks that involve the transmission of randomly generated IDs and Data Fields by analyzing the Hamming Distance between Data Fields with the same ID in normal data. The algorithm determines the maximum Hamming Distance, H_{Max} from the normal data and compares it with the Hamming Distance between Data Fields with the same ID during communication to identify an attack (Rule 1). Because randomly transmitted IDs and Data Fields typically exhibit higher Hamming Distances than normal IDs and Data Fields, the algorithm can effectively detect such attacks. (Algorithm 2).

Algorithm 2: Fuzzy Attack

Input: IDS Decision (0: Normal, 1: Spoofing, 2: DoS, 3: Fuzzy)
Output: Final Decision (0: Normal, 1: Attack)

```
1  While Monitoring results of the IDS do
2    if Result of the IDS is Fuzzy Attack then
3      | Attack ← True;
4    else
5      if H_cur > H_max[ID_cur] then                    ▷ (Rule 1)
6        | Attack ← True;
7      else
8        | Attack ← False;
9  end
```

4. Hardware Implementation

The hardware architecture of an in-vehicle IDS using a lightweight CNN model is shown in Figure 13. The IDs transmitted on the CAN BUS were processed using Data Preprocessing to form an 11 × 11 input structure, which was converted to match the kernel size for feature extraction. The converted values are used for Convolution and Max Pooling, followed by operations in Dense Layer 1 and 2. Finally, the data communicated on the CAN BUS and the output from Dense Layer 2 were provided as inputs to the filter, which produced the final attack determination.

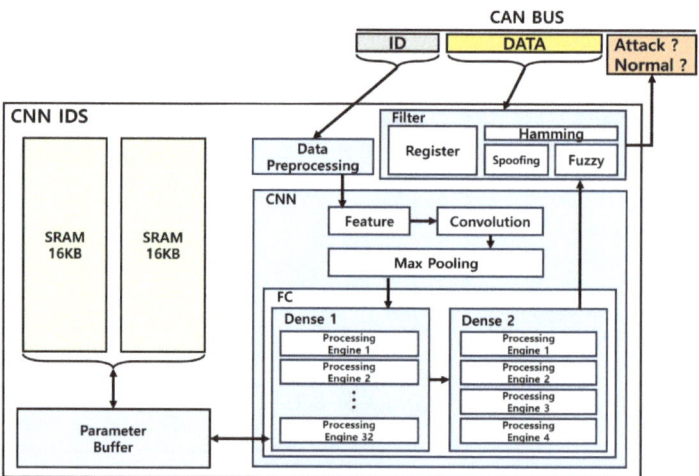

Figure 13. Hardware structure of vehicle IDS.

4.1. Parameter

This study presented a lightweight CNN model tailored for in-vehicle networks, trained using 32-bit floating-point data. However, this format leads to high resource consumption and slower detection speeds when implemented in hardware [11].

To overcome these challenges, as shown in Figure 14, a fixed-point representation was adopted, eliminating the need for normalization. Additionally, all parameters were quantized to 16 bits. This optimization effectively reduced resource usage and enhanced detection speed.

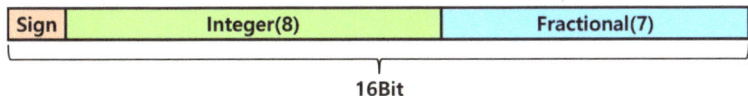

Figure 14. Fixed point.

Additionally, two 16 KB SRAM modules were utilized to store the parameters required for the CNN and filter. To enable real-time attack detection on messages transmitted over the CAN BUS, as shown in Figure 15, the parameters required for the next operation are preloaded from the SRAM into the buffer while the Dense Layer 1 computation is underway [12,13]. This approach ensures seamless execution of subsequent operations, enabling uninterrupted real-time processing.

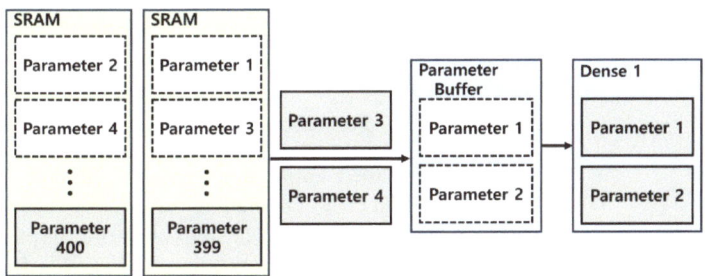

Figure 15. Parameter buffer operation.

4.2. Convolution, Max Pooling, Fully Connected Layer

The main operations in a CNN are performed by the convolution layer and the pooling layer, which require optimization for hardware implementation [14–16].

This study utilizes the hardware architecture of the convolution layer, as shown in Figure 16, where 11×11 input is processed through feature extraction and transformed into a 2×2 output. Feature input value consists of binary values (1 and 0), allowing the multiplication operations in the convolution process to be replaced by AND operations. This approach significantly reduces resource usage and optimizes the hardware for real-time processing.

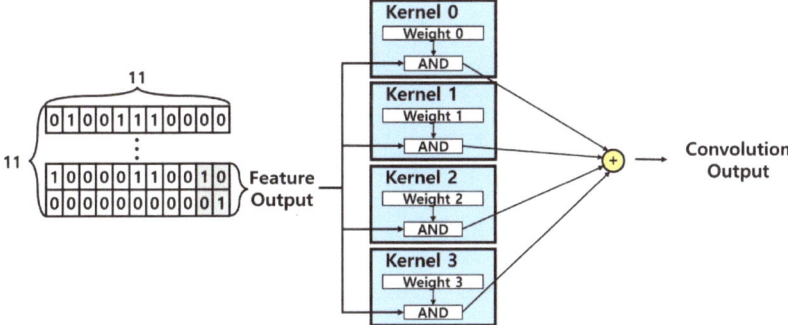

Figure 16. Convolution layer hardware architecture.

Additionally, we propose modifying the computational sequence shown in Figure 17a to the sequence shown in Figure 17b, for only four values required for Max Pooling were processed through convolution operations and stored in the registers for comparison. By performing computations only on necessary values, this method reduces resource usage and, regardless of the input format, the Max Pooling result can be output in only four cycles, minimizing the latency.

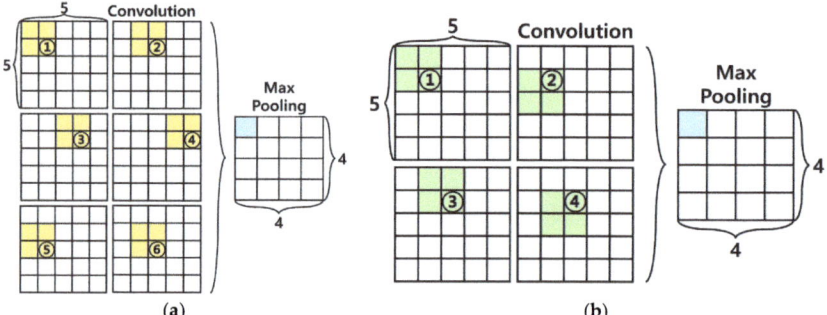

Figure 17. (a) refers to the standard sequence of operations in a convolution process, and (b) represents the modified convolution process proposed in this study for hardware implementation.

By modifying the computation sequence, the Feature, Convolution, Max Pooling, and Fully Connected Layer 1 operations can be structured into a pipelined architecture, as shown in Figure 18. According to Table 1, comparing the parallel processing of Convolution and Max Pooling operations with their reuse in a pipelined structure shows a 65% reduction in LUT usage. However, this increased detection time, which is a drawback. This is addressed by comparing the detection time with the criteria for determining whether the current message in the CAN communication is valid. The results show that even with a longer detection time, the determination of attack for the current frame is possible. Regarding ECU transmission, a message can be considered valid if no errors occur up to the last bit of the EOF. Similarly, for receiving ECU, a message is considered valid if no errors occur up to the bit immediately preceding the last bit of the EOF. Considering the worst-case scenario with a CAN communication speed of 500 Kbps, DLC of 0, and no Stuff bits, the minimum time required to invalidate a message is calculated as follows:

$$Minimum\ Time = \frac{Frame\ bit\ at\ Worst\ Case}{Baud\ Rate} \quad (1)$$

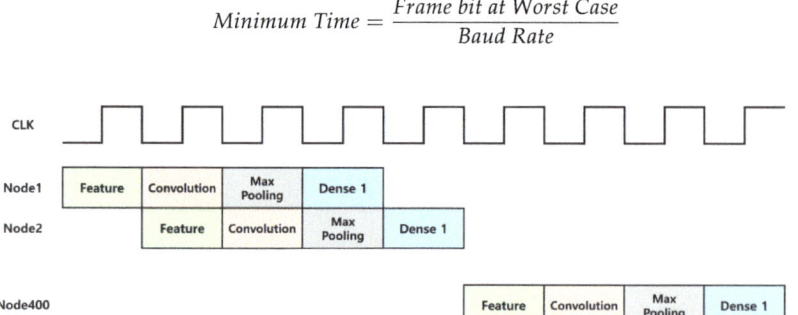

Figure 18. Timing diagram of the lightweight CNN model.

Table 1. Performance comparison based on pipelining and execution order.

Method	Detected Time (ms)	Resource (LUT)
Pipeline + Propose Step	0.023	11,062
Not Pipeline + General Step	0.012	32,291

To invalidate a message, the transmitting ECU must detect an error within 0.088 ms, whereas the receiving ECU must detect an error within 0.086 ms. Thus, the proposed IDS in this study is sufficient to detect attacks and invalidate the message because it has a detection time of 0.0234 ms. Additionally, by implementing a pipelined structure, the Dense 1 operation can proceed without the need for a flattening process, which means that no additional registers are required.

This study utilized the structure of the Processing Engine as shown in Figure 19, within the Fully Connected Layer. The Processing Engine receives a 16-bit input and executes the Multiply-Accumulate (MAC) operation, but during computation, overflow may occur due to the limitations of the 16-bit fixed-point representation. To address this issue, as depicted in Figure 20, the 16-bits input is extended to 32-bits during the MAC operation [17,18]. Once the computation is complete, the result is converted back to 16-bits for output. This approach effectively resolves the overflow problem while enhancing the accuracy of the computation process.

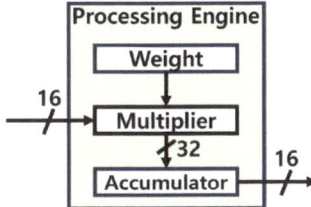

Figure 19. Processing engine structure.

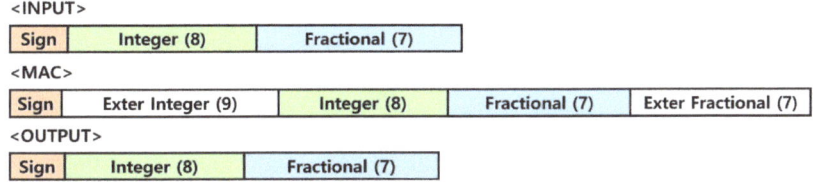

Figure 20. Bit extensions in MAC operations.

4.3. Filter

The hardware design of the filter structure is shown in Figure 21. The filter register is a crucial component in the process. At the start of CAN communication, it reads and stores the values of FP_{Max} and H_{Max} values from the SRAM, which are essential for the Spoofing and Fuzzy attack detection algorithms. During communication, the register also holds the current CAN ID, DATA, Hamming Distance, and attack counter. The output from Dense 2 is routed to all detection algorithms. If no attack is identified, the output is marked as Normal (Logic 0). Conversely, if a Fuzzy, DoS, or Spoofing attack is detected, the output is marked as Attack (Logic 1), triggering an Error Frame on the CAN BUS.

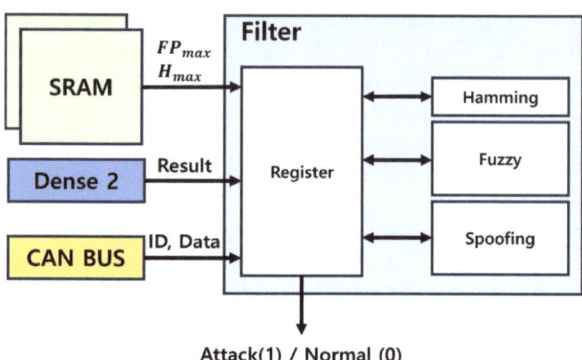

Figure 21. Filter hardware structure.

5. Validation and Performance Evaluation

5.1. Verification Environment

In this study, the dataset configuration used for training the lightweight CNN model in the IDS is shown in Table 2. This dataset was constructed by recording CAN traffic from a real vehicle through the OBD-II port. The DoS attack uses CAN ID "0×000", the Fuzzy attack utilizes random values for both CAN ID and DATA, and the Spoofing attack uses information related to RPM and Gear, along with the corresponding CAN ID [5,9,19,20]. Additionally, the dataset configuration used for verification, with 100,000 instances of each attack type used for testing is shown in Table 3.

Table 2. Configuring the dataset used to train the lightweight CNN model.

Attack Type	# of Messages	# of Normal Messages	# of Injection Messages
DoS	3,665,771	3,078,250	587,521
Fuzzy	6,838,860	3,347,013	491,847
Gear (Spoofing)	4,443,142	3,845,890	597,252
RPM (Spoofing)	4,621,702	3,966,805	654,897
Normal	988,987	988,872	

Table 3. Configuring the data set used for FPGA validation.

Attack Type	# of Normal Messages	# of Injection Messages
DoS	76,327	23,673
Fuzzy	87,979	12,021
Gear (Spoofing)	81,183	18,817
RPM (Spoofing)	81,048	18,952

The FPGA verification environment used to validate the real-time response of the lightweight CNN-based IDS proposed in this study is shown in Figure 22. The verification environment utilizes Universal Asynchronous Receiver Transmitter (UART) communication was used to transmit the IDS results to a PC, and the PEAK system's PCAN-USB was employed to implement the transmitting ECU on the CAN BUS. An API was developed in Python to control PCAN-USB. The TLE 9250 V transceiver was used to convert the CAN-H and CAN-L signals, as well as for RX and TX signal conversion. In addition, a Nexys Video FPGA board was selected for debugging to provide the necessary resources for the verification process. The verification sequence is as follows.

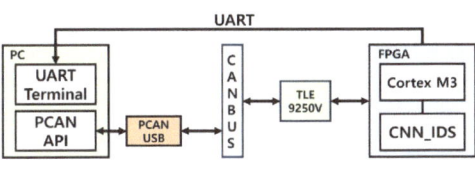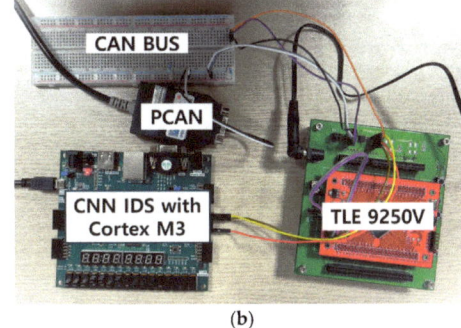

(a)   (b)

Figure 22. (a) the block diagram of the FPGA environment for IDS verification; (b) the actual FPGA environment configured for IDS verification.

1. Transmit the test data to the CAN BUS through the PCAN USB using the PCAN API.
2. Transmit data from the CAN BUS to the FPGA, where the verification system is implemented via a transceiver.
3. The FPGA board transmits signals, such as ACK and error flags, to the CAN BUS while sending the IDS results to the PC via UART.

To check for errors during the transmission and reception processes, PCAN View and an oscilloscope were used to monitor the transmission/reception waveforms and data.

5.2. Performance Evaluation

We compared the performance of different data preprocessing methods applied to the same lightweight CNN model, utilizing dataset used for model training, to verify that the proposed Data Insertion method can assist in determining attacks in real time. Specifically, we evaluated the performance of using the Sliding Window method alone and the combined approach of Sliding Window and Data Insertion. As shown in Table 4, the combined approach of Sliding Window and Data Insertion achieved a 10% performance improvement compared to using the Sliding Window method alone.

Table 4. Comparison of accuracy based on data preprocessing methods.

Attack	Sliding Window (%)	Sliding Window + Data Insertion (%)
DoS	90.4153	99.9255
Fuzzy	87.2578	98.4888
Gear (Spoofing)	86.1185	97.9245
RPM (Spoofing)	86.9854	97.8995

For IDS performance evaluation on the FPGA, 100,000 test datasets were used, and the evaluation was based on the metrics of accuracy, precision, recall, and F1-Score. The accuracy represents the ratio of correct predictions made by the IDS. Precision refers to the proportion of actual attacks among instances that the IDS identified as attacks. Recall measures the proportion of actual attacks correctly identified by an IDS. The F1-Score is the harmonic mean of precision and recall, offering a balanced evaluation, particularly for imbalanced datasets.

For this evaluation, the following terms were defined: True Positive (TP) refers to instances in which the IDS correctly identified an attack, and True Negative (TN) refers to instances in which the IDS correctly identified a normal message. A false Positive (FP) refers to instances in which the IDS incorrectly identifies a normal message as an attack, and a False Negative (FN) refers to instances in which the IDS incorrectly identifies an attack as normal.

$$Accuracy = \frac{TP + TN}{TP + FP + TN + FN} \quad (2)$$

$$Precision = \frac{TP}{TP + FP} \quad (3)$$

$$Recall = \frac{TP}{TP + FN} \quad (4)$$

$$F1 - Score = \frac{2 * Precision * Recall}{Precision * Recall} \quad (5)$$

The software and hardware performance metrics for the lightweight CNN model with filters applied are shown in Tables 5 and 6. An evaluation was conducted for four types of attacks: DoS, Fuzzy, Gear (Spoofing), and RPM (Spoofing). The data format used in the software implementation was a 32-bit floating point, whereas the hardware implementation utilized a 16-bit fixed-point representation.

Table 5. Lightweight CNN model software performance indicators.

Attack Type	Accuracy (%)	Precision (%)	Recall (%)	F1 Score (%)
DoS	99.9255	99.6212	99.9983	99.8094
Fuzzy	98.4888	96.6246	94.1021	95.3467
Gear (Spoofing)	97.9245	91.8077	96.4587	94.0758
RPM (Spoofing)	97.8995	91.1108	97.5583	94.2244

Table 6. Filter application performance indicators of lightweight CNN-based IDS implemented in hardware.

Attack Type	Accuracy (%)	Precision (%)	Recall (%)	F1 Score (%)
DoS	99.9540 → 99.9110	99.8061 → 99.6255	100 → 100	99.9029 → 99.8124
Fuzzy	98.7479 → 99.3039	95.8294 → 94.6605	93.6611 → 99.8419	94.7329 → 97.1822
Gear (Spoofing)	97.7508 → 99.6790	90.7757 → 98.6583	98.0071 → 99.6493	94.2529 → 99.1513
RPM (Spoofing)	97.9738 → 99.8580	91.4244 → 99.5365	98.5542 → 99.7151	94.8555 → 99.6257

A comparison of the results shows that the hardware implementation outperformed the software in some aspects. This improvement is attributed to the difference in the Bit Resolution that occurs when converting from a 32-bit floating point to a 16-bit fixed point during hardware implementation. The CNN model did not achieve the highest possible results because of its lightweight design. A filter algorithm was applied to address this reduced performance. As listed in Table 6, the performance of the model improved significantly, with notable increases in the Recall for the Fuzzy attack and Precision for the Spoofing attack.

The time required by different IDS models to determine an attack is shown in Table 7. The proposed IDS is shown to be 0.22 ms faster on average than the fast detection models, QMLP and BNN. As shown in Table 8, the proposed IDS was implemented with 70% fewer LUTs and 85% fewer FFs than the QMLP, with a memory requirement of 0.288 MB. Additionally, similar to the BNN, the proposed model can perform multiclass classification to determine the type of attack and can also use the filter algorithm for binary classification to detect attacks.

Table 7. Comparison of inference time with other IDS models.

Model	Latency (ms)	Detection Unit	Platform
ACGAN [6]	0.203	Per CAN frame	Raspberry Pi 4
MA-QCNN [21]	0.43	4 CAN frame	Zynq Ultrascale +
DCNN [5]	5	29 CAN frame	Tesla K80
MTH [22]	0.574	Per CAN frame	Raspberry Pi 3
QMLP [23]	0.24	Per CAN frame	Zynq Ultrascale +
BNN [24]	0.259	30 CAN frame	Zedboard
Proposed IDS	0.023	Per CAN frame	Artix 7

Table 8. Metric comparison of proposed IDS and other FPGA implementation cases.

Metric	QMLP	BNN	MA-QCNN	Proposed IDS
FPGA Device	Zynq Ultrascale + XCZU7EV	Zedboard XC7Z020	Zynq Ultrascale + XCZU3EG	Nexys Video XC7A200T
LUTs	56,733	33,224	30,726	17,059
FFs	72,146	54,175	48,400	11,062
BRAM (Mb)	3.06	4.85	2.5605	0.288
URAM (Mb)	6.75	0	0	0

The results of the ASIC implementation of the CNN-based IDS proposed in this study are shown in Table 9. The implementation was based on the TSMC 180 nm process and Synopsys Design Compiler, with a die size of 5000 μm × 5000 μm. The clock used in the ASIC for the IDS was set to 50 MHz, and the Gate Count was calculated based on a 2-input NAND gate. The IDS, including the SRAM used for storing parameters, occupies 39.1762% of the total chip area, while the remaining portion consists of the Cortex-M3 and Debug Logic, and SRAM used by the Core. The utilized area of the total chip is shown in Figure 23, while the blue section represents the unused area.

Table 9. ASIC implementation of proposed IDS.

Metric	Proposed IDS
Using System Clock	50 MHz
Total area of Chip	1,146,194 gate
Total area of SRAM in IDS	203,876 gate
Single area of IDS(CNN)	135,866 gate
Single area of IDS(Filter)	55,510 gate

Figure 23. Physical layout.

6. Conclusions

This study aims to detect attacks on in-vehicle networks using a Shallow Learning-based lightweight CNN IDS. The lightweight CNN employs a single Convolution Layer and applies data preprocessing methods such as Sliding Window and Data Insertion for real-time detection. In hardware implementation, the use of a fixed-point representation that does not require normalization, and a pipelined structure resulting from changes in the Convolution operation order, lead to reductions in both resource usage and delay. Additionally, performance degradation caused by the lightweight design is mitigated by up to 8.1121% through the application of filter algorithms to handle Fuzzy and Spoofing attacks.

A total of 400,000 attack injection dataset were used to verify the real-time detection and response actions for DoS, Fuzzy and Spoofing attacks. Despite being implemented utilizing 17,059 LUTs and 191,376 gates, the Shallow Learning-based CNN IDS achieved an accuracy of 99.6879% and a recall of 99.8014% across these three types of attacks. However, the proposed model uses supervised learning, which has the limitation of being unable to detect attack types not present in the training data. This is a known limitation of supervised learning-based IDS. In future research, we plan to implement an IDS with lower resource usage and reduced delay by utilizing an unsupervised

Author Contributions: Conceptualization, M.C.; methodology, M.C. and M.L.; software, H.I. and J.L.; validation, M.C. and M.L.; formal analysis, M.C. and M.L.; investigation, M.C.; resources, M.C.; data curation, M.C. and H.I.; writing—original draft preparation, M.C.; writing—review and editing, J.L. and S.L.; visualization, M.C.; supervision, J.L. and S.L.; project administration, S.L.; funding acquisition, S.L. All authors have read and agreed to the published version of the manuscript.

Funding: This research was supported in part by the National R&D Program through the National Research Foundation of Korea (NRF) funded by the Ministry of Science and ICT (2021M3H2A1038042) and in part by the R&D Program of the Ministry of Trade, Industry, and Energy (MOTIE) and the Korea Evaluation Institute of Industrial Technology (KEIT) (RS-2022-00154973, RS-2023-00232192, and RS-2024-00403397) and in part by the Technology Innovation Program funded by the Ministry of Trade, Industry, and Energy (MOTIE) (RS-2024-00433615).

Data Availability Statement: Available online: https://ocslab.hksecurity.net/Datasets/car-hacking-dataset (accessed on 13 December 2024).

Acknowledgments: The EDA tool was supported by the IC Design Education Center (IDEC) in the Republic of Korea.

Conflicts of Interest: The authors declare no conflicts of interest.

References

1. Okuda, R.; Kajiwara, Y.; Terashima, K. A Survey of Technical Trend of ADAS and Autonomous Driving. In Proceedings of the Technical Papers of 2014 International Symposium on VLSI Design, Automation and Test, Hsinchu, Taiwan, 28–30 April 2014; pp. 1–4.
2. Cheng, T.; Wu, Z.; Wang, C.; Shi, Q.; Zhang, X.; Xu, P. Research on Vehicle-to-Cloud Communication Based on Lightweight Authentication and Extended Quantum Key Distribution. *IEEE Trans. Veh. Technol.* **2024**, *73*, 12082–12095. [CrossRef]
3. Zeng, W.; Khalid, M.A.S.; Chowdhury, S. In-Vehicle Networks Outlook: Achievements and Challenges. *IEEE Commun. Surv. Tutor.* **2016**, *18*, 1552–1571. [CrossRef]
4. Quadar, N.; Chehri, A.; Debaque, B.; Ahmed, I.; Jeon, G. Intrusion Detection Systems in Automotive Ethernet Networks: Challenges, Opportunities and Future Research Trends. *IEEE Internet Things Mag.* **2024**, *7*, 62–68. [CrossRef]
5. Song, H.M.; Woo, J.; Kim, H.K. In-Vehicle Network Intrusion Detection Using Deep Convolutional Neural Network. *Veh. Commun.* **2020**, *21*, 100198. [CrossRef]
6. Zhao, Q.; Chen, M.; Gu, Z.; Luan, S.; Zeng, H.; Chakrabory, S. CAN Bus Intrusion Detection Based on Auxiliary Classifier GAN and Out-of-Distribution Detection. *ACM Trans. Embed. Comput. Syst.* **2022**, *21*, 45. [CrossRef]
7. Bosch. *CAN Specification Version 2.0*; Rober Bosch Gmbh: Stuttgart, Germany, 1991; p. 72.

8. *ISO 15031-1:2010*; Road Vehicles—Communication Between Vehicle and External Equipment for Emissions-Related Diagnostics—Part 1: General Information and Use Case Definition. ISO: Geneva, Switzerland, 2010. Available online: https://www.iso.org/standard/51828.html (accessed on 13 December 2024).
9. Lee, H.; Jeong, S.H.; Kim, H.K. OTIDS: A Novel Intrusion Detection System for In-Vehicle Network by Using Remote Frame. In Proceedings of the 2017 15th Annual Conference on Privacy, Security and Trust (PST), Calgary, AB, Canada, 28–30 August 2017; pp. 57–5709.
10. Im, H.; Lee, D.; Lee, S. A Novel Architecture for an Intrusion Detection System Utilizing Cross-Check Filters for In-Vehicle Networks. *Sensors* **2024**, *24*, 2807. [CrossRef]
11. Moolchandani, D.; Kumar, A.; Sarangi, S.R. Accelerating CNN Inference on ASICs: A Survey. *J. Syst. Archit.* **2021**, *113*, 101887. [CrossRef]
12. Chen, Y.-H.; Krishna, T.; Emer, J.S.; Sze, V. Eyeriss: An Energy-Efficient Reconfigurable Accelerator for Deep Convolutional Neural Networks. *IEEE J. Solid-State Circuits* **2017**, *52*, 127–138. [CrossRef]
13. Chen, Y.-H.; Yang, T.-J.; Emer, J.; Sze, V. Eyeriss v2: A Flexible Accelerator for Emerging Deep Neural Networks on Mobile Devices. *IEEE J. Emerg. Sel. Top. Circuits Syst.* **2019**, *9*, 292–308. [CrossRef]
14. Ma, Y.; Cao, Y.; Vrudhula, S.; Seo, J. Optimizing Loop Operation and Dataflow in FPGA Acceleration of Deep Convolutional Neural Networks. In Proceedings of the 2017 ACM/SIGDA International Symposium on Field-Programmable Gate Arrays, Monterey, CA, USA, 22–24 February 2017; Association for Computing Machinery: New York, NY, USA, 2017; pp. 45–54.
15. Zhao, B.; Chong, Y.S.; Tuan Do, A. Area and Energy Efficient 2D Max-Pooling For Convolutional Neural Network Hardware Accelerator. In Proceedings of the IECON 2020 The 46th Annual Conference of the IEEE Industrial Electronics Society, Singapore, 18–21 October 2020; pp. 423–427.
16. Bailer, C.; Habtegebrial, T.; varanasi, K.; Stricker, D. Fast Feature Extraction with CNNs with Pooling Layers. *arXiv* **2018**, arXiv:1805.03096.
17. Simić, S.; Bemporad, A.; Inverso, O.; Tribastone, M. Tight Error Analysis in Fixed-Point Arithmetic. *Form. Asp. Comput.* **2022**, *34*, 3. [CrossRef]
18. Bečvář, M.; Štukjunger, P. Fixed-Point Arithmetic in FPGA. *Acta Polytech.* **2005**, *45*, 2. [CrossRef] [PubMed]
19. Seo, E.; Song, H.M.; Kim, H.K. GIDS: GAN Based Intrusion Detection System for In-Vehicle Network. In Proceedings of the 2018 16th Annual Conference on Privacy, Security and Trust (PST), Belfast, Ireland, 28–30 August 2018; pp. 1–6.
20. HCRL—Car-Hacking Dataset. Available online: https://ocslab.hksecurity.net/Datasets/car-hacking-dataset (accessed on 13 December 2024).
21. Khandelwal, S.; Shreejith, S. A Lightweight Multi-Attack CAN Intrusion Detection System on Hybrid FPGAs. In Proceedings of the 2022 32nd International Conference on Field-Programmable Logic and Applications (FPL), Belfast, UK, 29 August–2 September 2022; pp. 425–429.
22. Yang, L.; Moubayed, A.; Shami, A. MTH-IDS: A Multitiered Hybrid Intrusion Detection System for Internet of Vehicles. *IEEE Internet Things J.* **2022**, *9*, 616–632. [CrossRef]
23. Khandelwal, S.; Shreejith, S. A Lightweight FPGA-Based IDS-ECU Architecture for Automotive CAN. In Proceedings of the 2022 International Conference on Field-Programmable Technology (ICFPT), Hong Kong, 5–9 February 2022; pp. 1–9.
24. Rangsikunpum, A.; Amiri, S.; Ost, L. An FPGA-Based Intrusion Detection System Using Binarised Neural Network for CAN Bus Systems. In Proceedings of the 2024 IEEE International Conference on Industrial Technology (ICIT), Bristol, UK, 25–27 March 2024; pp. 1–6.

Disclaimer/Publisher's Note: The statements, opinions and data contained in all publications are solely those of the individual author(s) and contributor(s) and not of MDPI and/or the editor(s). MDPI and/or the editor(s) disclaim responsibility for any injury to people or property resulting from any ideas, methods, instructions or products referred to in the content.

Article

Autonomous Medical Robot Trajectory Planning with Local Planner Time Elastic Band Algorithm

Arjon Turnip [1,*], Muhamad Arsyad Faridhan [1], Bambang Mukti Wibawa [1] and Nursanti Anggriani [2]

[1] Department of Electrical Engineering, Faculty of Mathematics and Natural Sciences, Universitas Padjadjaran, Kabupaten Sumedang 45363, Indonesia; muhamad20059@mail.unpad.ac.id (M.A.F.); b.mukti.wibawa@unpad.ac.id (B.M.W.)

[2] Department of Mathematics, Faculty of Mathematics and Natural Sciences, Universitas Padjadjaran, Kabupaten Sumedang 45363, Indonesia; nursanti.anggriani@unpad.ac.id

* Correspondence: turnip@unpad.ac.id

Abstract: Robots have made significant contributions across various industries due to their efficiency and effectiveness. However, indoor navigation remains challenging due to complex environments and sensor signal interference. Changes in indoor conditions and the limited range of GPS signals necessitate the development of an accurate and efficient indoor robot navigation system. This study aims to create an autonomous indoor navigation system for medical robots using sensors such as Marvelmind, LiDAR, IMU, and an odometer, along with the Time Elastic Band (TEB) local planning algorithm to detect dynamic obstacles. The algorithm's performance is evaluated using metrics like path length, duration, speed smoothness, path smoothness, Mean Squared Error (MSE), and positional error. In the test arena, TEB demonstrated superior efficiency with a path length of 155.55 m, 9.83 m shorter than the Dynamic Window Approach (DWA), which covered 165.38 m, and had a lower yaw error of 0.012 radians. TEB outperformed DWA in terms of speed smoothness, path smoothness, and MSE. In the Sterile Room Arena, TEB had an average path length of 14.84 m, slightly longer than DWA's 14.32 m, but TEB navigated 2.82 s faster. Additionally, TEB showed better speed and path smoothness. In the Obstacle Room Arena, TEB recorded an average path length of 21.96 m in 57.3 s, outperforming DWA, which covered 23.44 m in 61 s, with better results in MSE, speed smoothness, and path smoothness, highlighting superior path consistency. These findings indicate that the TEB algorithm is an effective choice as a local planner in dynamic hospital environments.

Keywords: autonomous navigation; ROS; global planer; time elastic bane

Academic Editor: Andrea Bonci

Received: 15 November 2024
Revised: 19 December 2024
Accepted: 26 December 2024
Published: 4 January 2025

Citation: Turnip, A.; Faridhan, M.A.; Wibawa, B.M.; Anggriani, N. Autonomous Medical Robot Trajectory Planning with Local Planner Time Elastic Band Algorithm. *Electronics* 2025, *14*, 183. https://doi.org/10.3390/electronics14010183

Copyright: © 2025 by the authors. Licensee MDPI, Basel, Switzerland. This article is an open access article distributed under the terms and conditions of the Creative Commons Attribution (CC BY) license (https://creativecommons.org/licenses/by/4.0/).

1. Introduction

The development of autonomous robot technology has become a key focus in industry and research, particularly in the context of addressing complex, monotonous, repetitive, and physically demanding tasks. This technology offers effective solutions for handling work that requires consistency, precision, and long-term durability without physical or mental fatigue. Several important reasons for the development of this technology include efficiency, safety, and increased productivity, which directly contribute to the quality of output across various sectors, including manufacturing, agriculture, logistics, and healthcare. Repetitive and monotonous tasks, such as assembling goods on production lines, monitoring crops in agriculture, or transporting items in warehouses, require consistency that is difficult for human workers to maintain over extended periods. Research has shown that autonomous robots can perform these tasks faster and more consistently, significantly improving operational efficiency [1]. Additionally, automation can reduce human error, which often occurs in repetitive tasks due to fatigue or boredom. Autonomous robots have the potential to boost productivity by working non-stop for 24 h, a feat that is impossible for human workers. This enables industries to increase production volumes without significantly increasing the workforce. A study by Jones et al. (2021) found that autonomous robots in production lines could reduce operational costs by up to 30% due to increased productivity and reduced downtime [2].

In agriculture, the use of autonomous drones for crop monitoring and pesticide spraying has led to a 20% increase in crop yields due to optimized water and pesticide use [3]. Autonomous robots also help reduce the risk of workplace accidents, particularly in hazardous environments such as mining, construction, or areas at risk of disease transmission [4]. Robots designed for specific tasks can be equipped with sensor systems to avoid accidents and detect potential hazards, providing additional protection for people in their vicinity. As the elderly population grows in many developed countries, labor shortages have become a serious issue, especially in sectors dependent on physical labor. Autonomous robots can serve as a solution to this labor shortage by replacing or assisting human workers in tasks that require significant physical effort and long durations [5]. Autonomous robots also support sustainability initiatives, particularly in resource management. For instance, plant watering robots in agriculture equipped with moisture sensors can ensure that water is only supplied to areas that need it, thereby reducing water consumption and optimizing irrigation. A literature review by Zhang and Wang (2022) showed that sensor- and AI-based automation can reduce resource usage by up to 40%, directly contributing to environmental sustainability [6].

Robots have made significant contributions to humans in various fields, such as warehouse delivery, floor cleaning, and as household assistants. Indoor navigation technology is becoming increasingly important due to its widespread use in various applications. However, indoor navigation remains a challenge due to the complex indoor environments and signal interference from sensors [7]. Indoor robot navigation requires the development of more accurate and effective technologies because of frequent environmental changes and the limited range of GPS signals indoors [8]. The development of indoor navigation technology for robots is advancing to improve accuracy. Challenges in developing these navigation systems include measurement accuracy, data processing with various filtering techniques, the robot's limited range of movement, and many other factors. To address the challenges of autonomous indoor navigation, artificial intelligence can be used to develop algorithms and systems capable of tasks such as decision-making, pattern recognition, and machine learning [9,10]. To tackle these issues, previous research has presented various approaches to indoor robot navigation. Zulfan J. and Rafly developed an autonomous robot using Marvelmind sensors, LiDAR, IMU, and rotary encoders with the Adaptive Monte Carlo Localization method and Extended Kalman Filter [11,12]. The results showed that the robot could avoid obstacles with low error rates. LiDAR was used for real-time environmental mapping but had limitations in measuring large distances and interference from surrounding objects.

Currently, much research is focused on the development of autonomous navigation robots. Arjon Turnip et al. [13] developed a medical assistant robot to replace nurses in patient isolation at hospitals, creating a robot that moves autonomously, interacts, and detects faces. Research by Rivai et al. [14] introduced a 2D mapping technique using an omnidirectional moving robot equipped with LiDAR, while a study by Hai Wang et al. [15] proposed a real-time vehicle detection algorithm based on the combination of vision and LiDAR point cloud. The implementation of interactive medical robots was explored by Turnip et al. [16], who examined the use of deep learning-based voice chatbots. This research highlighted the potential integration of chatbot technology to enhance interaction and functionality in medical robots. Furthermore, Suryawan et al. [17] demonstrated significant progress in this field. However, the research by Suryawan et al. used teleoperated manual control, which is considered ineffective due to the need for an operator and vulnerability to environmental disturbances in hospital settings. Alternatively, the medical assistant robot by Nurhayati [18–20] uses a line-following system, though it is difficult to implement in hospitals due to the need for obstacle-free paths. Zhao et al. [20] utilized the Robot Operating System (ROS) with the Karto SLAM algorithm for mapping, A* for global planning, and DWA for local planning. LiDAR, IMU, and odometers were used for accurate navigation, but the system was slow in building maps and tracking the robot's position.

Recent studies on mobile robot navigation emphasize advanced technologies and applications, including the use of LIDAR, indoor GPS, emerging trends, and developments in autonomous navigation systems [21–23]. Path planning is essential for enabling autonomous navigation and optimizing efficiency in robotic systems. Various approaches have been developed to address challenges such as navigating cluttered environments, achieving energy efficiency, and ensuring precision in diverse terrains. Advanced techniques, including reinforcement learning, hybrid algorithms, and motion capture technologies, demonstrate significant progress in both theoretical and practical applications. These advancements highlight the growing potential for enhancing navigation capabilities in robotics for both ground and aerial applications [24–29].

This study on an autonomous indoor navigation system for medical robots presents several novel contributions, particularly its focus on dynamic hospital environments. By integrating sensors such as Marvelmind, LiDAR, IMU, and odometers with the Timed Elastic Band (TEB) algorithm, this study addresses challenges like signal interference and environmental changes. Unlike many previous studies, this research evaluates TEB in real-world medical scenarios, demonstrating superior performance over the Dynamic Window Approach (DWA) in metrics such as path smoothness, speed smoothness, Mean Squared Error (MSE), and positional error. When compared to related work, this study stands out for its specialized application. For instance, "Comparison and Improvement of Local Planners on ROS for Narrow Passages" focuses on optimizing DWA and TEB for narrow environments but lacks the focus on dynamic human-centric conditions found in hospitals [30]. Similarly, while "Comparison of ROS Local Planners with Differential Drive Heavy Robotic System" analyzes planners in heavy robotics, it doesn't address the intricacies of hospital environments with frequent human interaction [31]. Papers such as "Enhancing Social Robot Navigation with Integrated Motion Prediction" explore social navigation, but the current study emphasizes hospital-specific metrics and real-time adaptability [32].

This research also differs from works like "Resilient Timed Elastic Band Planner for Collision-Free Navigation", which enhances TEB for high-obstacle-density environments using Voronoi maps, and "Improved Timed Elastic Band Algorithm for AGVs", which optimizes energy efficiency during turns [33,34]. In contrast, this medical robot study prioritizes navigation efficiency and obstacle avoidance in dynamic settings. Studies such as "A Study on the Effect of Parameters for ROS Motion Planners" and "Navigation for Mobile Robots to Inspect Aircraft" are broader in scope, focusing on parameter effects and aircraft inspection scenarios, respectively, rather than medical environments [35]. Finally, while "A Comparison Study Between Traditional and DRL Algorithms" highlights reinforcement learning, this medical robot study confines itself to traditional algorithms, with an emphasis on practical, dynamic, and human-interactive scenarios [36].

This study significantly advances medical robotics by addressing key challenges in indoor navigation and presenting an efficient, validated solution for real-world healthcare settings. It introduces a novel framework integrating multi-sensor fusion—Marvelmind, LiDAR, IMU, and odometer sensors—with the Time Elastic Band (TEB) algorithm, tailored for medical robots to overcome GPS limitations and adapt to dynamic indoor environments. By systematically evaluating TEB's performance across metrics such as path length, duration, speed smoothness, path smoothness, Mean Squared Error (MSE), and positional error, this study demonstrates its superiority over the Dynamic Window Approach (DWA) in navigation efficiency, accuracy, and reliability. The research further proposes a hybrid navigation strategy, leveraging TEB for narrow spaces and DWA for open areas, optimizing adaptability to varying hospital conditions. Validated across multiple controlled environments, such as the Test Arena, Sterile Class Arena, and Obstacle Class Arena, the system proves its practical applicability. By effectively combining sensor data and showcasing robust performance in dynamic scenarios, this work provides a practical and efficient solution for advancing autonomous medical robotics, setting a benchmark for local navigation systems in healthcare environments.

The remainder of this paper is organized as follows: Section 2 presents the proposed methodology and the experimental setup, detailing the integration of multi-sensor fusion and the TEB algorithm including the controlled environments used for validation. Section 3 discusses the results, benchmarking the TEB algorithm against DWA across various performance metrics. Finally, Section 4 concludes the paper by summarizing the findings, emphasizing the practical implications for medical robotics, and suggesting potential directions for future research.

2. Methods

This research was conducted at PPBS Laboratory C, 3rd Floor, Padjadjaran University, West Java, Indonesia. The testing arena was designed to represent a nurse's and a patient's room, as shown in Figure 1. The robot trajectory path is marked with seven waypoints, namely waypoints 1 to 7, where waypoints 1–6 are patient rooms. In the test scenario, the robot is designed to be able to deliver medicine or food to three patient rooms in sequence as well as take biosignal measurements, such as blood pressure, body temperature, and oxygen saturation, in a single trip. The robot's ability to perform these various tasks simultaneously aims to mimic the daily activities of a nurse in a hospital in Indonesia.

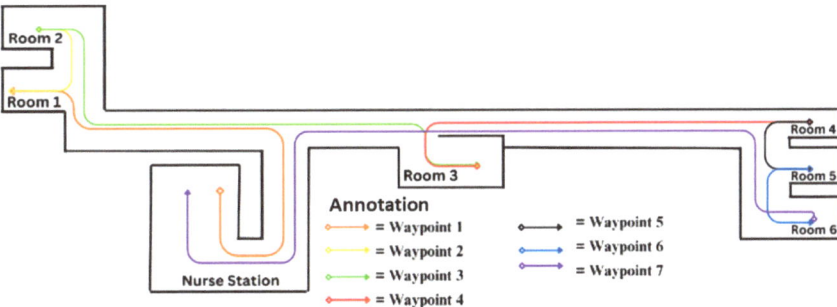

Figure 1. Waypoint for Arena PPBS C.

The testing process was conducted in 5 scenarios, with a total of 7 waypoints to each patient room. The robot moved sequentially from room to room, navigating automatically using the Trajectory Elastic Band (TEB) algorithm. An additional class-shaped test arena was used to test the effectiveness of the TEB algorithm in handling dynamic environments.

This arena includes conditions that represent environmental changes and moving obstacles, as shown in Figure 2. Figure 2a shows a narrow room condition, while Figure 2b depicts a narrow room with additional dynamic obstacles. This test aims to evaluate the ability of the TEB algorithm to plan safe and efficient paths under various scenarios with different navigation challenges. With the addition of the testing room, the robot's local planner system can be tested in more depth to assess its effectiveness in planning a path through narrow passageways, selecting the most efficient path to navigate, and observing the robot's movement characteristics in a confined area. In the initial stage, tests were conducted in an arena without obstacles (sterile conditions) using 8 setpoints to observe the basic characteristics of robot movement. Next, tests were conducted in a more complex arena with additional obstacles (Figure 2b) using 6 setpoints to evaluate the robot's ability to avoid obstacles and make navigation adjustments according to environmental conditions.

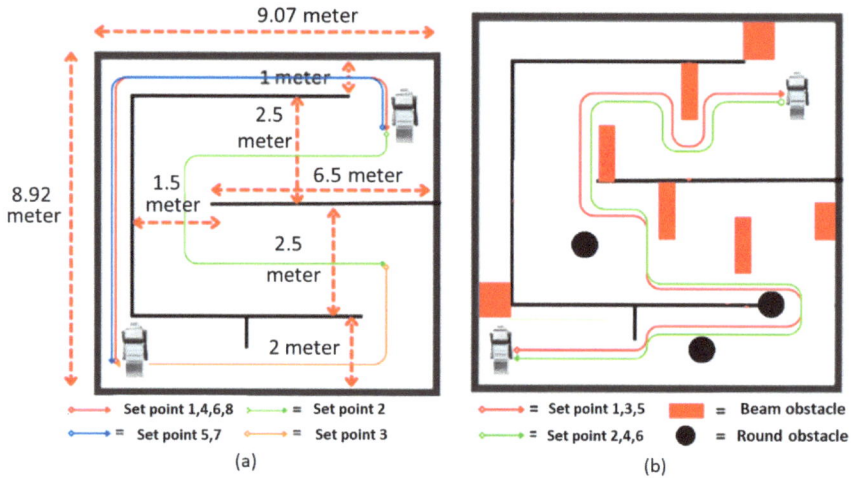

Figure 2. Waypoint for dynamic narrow room simulation: (**a**) with, (**b**) without Obstacle.

Figure 3 illustrates the circuit schematic of the medical robot, highlighting the integrated relationship between its components. The robot is powered by a 24-volt LiFePO4 battery, which is recharged using a battery charger and protected by a fuse to prevent power surges. The battery's power is distributed through step-down converters: one regulates the voltage to 19 Volts to power the Intel NUC mini PC, while another converts it to 5 Volts for the control PCB. A terminal block ensures efficient power distribution across the subsystems.

Control and processing are managed by the Intel NUC, a compact computer responsible for high-level processing and decision-making, and the ESP32 microcontroller, which handles communication and low-level control. A custom PCB control board centralizes connections and manages components such as motor drivers and sensors. The robot's sensor system consists of LiDAR, Marvelmind, IMU, and odometer sensors, working together to provide accurate navigation, orientation, and position data. The LiDAR sensor connects directly to the Intel NUC and integrates with the Robot Operating System (ROS). It uses a laser to measure object distances through light reflection with high accuracy, enabling obstacle detection and avoidance. The Marvelmind system connects to the mini PC via an HW receiver modem, receiving ultrasonic wave data from super beacons. This system calculates distances and delivers highly accurate x and y coordinate data, ensuring the robot stays on its intended path.

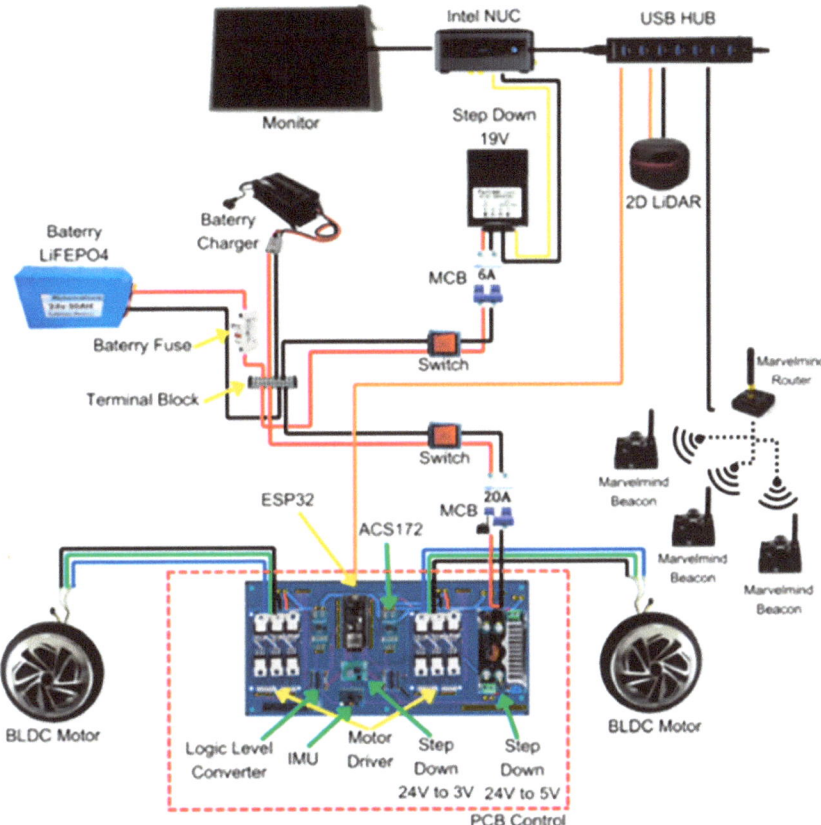

Figure 3. Robot Schematics.

Actuation is powered by two BLDC motors controlled by a motor driver that regulates their speed and direction. The system incorporates switches and miniature circuit breakers (MCBs) to ensure safe operation by protecting circuits from overload. Additionally, a USB hub connects peripherals to the Intel NUC, and a monitor displays system information for user monitoring. This integrated design supports the efficient, reliable, and safe operation of the medical robot in dynamic indoor environments.

The Inertial Measurement Unit (IMU) is connected to the ESP32 microcontroller to read the linear and angular acceleration values, which allows measuring and tracking the robot's orientation in three-dimensional space. The IMU sensors consist of accelerometers, gyroscopes, and magnetometers that provide motion and orientation data, used to correct and stabilize the robot's movements for greater precision. A rotary encoder is mounted on the BLDC motor to measure and calculate the rotation of the wheel or motor shaft. This magnetic incremental encoder produces output pulses that provide information about the wheel rotation and direction of rotation. This data, generated in real-time, supports more accurate control of the robot's position and speed, improving efficiency and precision in navigation and movement control. This interconnected set of components gives the robot the ability to perform better navigation and orientation, supporting its application in medical tasks that require high precision in movement and positioning in operational environments.

In Figure 4, the autonomous navigation system is composed of several integrated stages designed to determine the robot's position, create a map, and plan its route effectively.

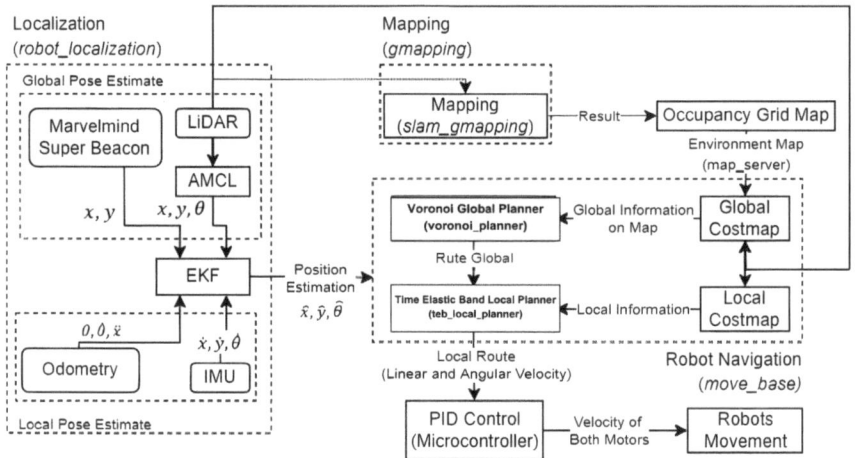

Figure 4. Autonomous Navigation System.

1. Localization Stage: This stage leverages the robot_localization package and various sensors to estimate the robot's position accurately. The Marvelmind Super Beacon provides global position estimates in x and y coordinates, while the LiDAR sensor generates distance data. This distance data is combined with the Adaptive Monte Carlo Localization (AMCL) method to estimate the robot's position in three dimensions (x, y, θ). Additionally, odometry tracks local position changes (Δx, Δy, Δθ), and the IMU supplies acceleration and rotation data. These data inputs are fused using an Extended Kalman Filter (EKF), which minimizes errors arising from the limitations of individual sensors, resulting in a more precise position estimate.
2. Mapping Stage: Data from the LiDAR sensor and the position estimates generated during localization are processed by the SLAM_GMapping algorithm to create an Occupancy Grid Map. This map identifies obstructed and navigable areas, serving as the foundation for autonomous navigation and obstacle avoidance.
3. Path Planning Stage: With the Occupancy Grid Map in place, the Voronoi Global Planner calculates a global route from the robot's starting point to its target destination. This global path is further refined by the TEB Local Planner, which incorporates dynamic factors such as the robot's speed, direction changes, and shifting environmental conditions, to create an optimal local route.
4. Speed Control: In the final stage, the PID Controller embedded in the robot's microcontroller uses the data from the local route to set the linear and angular velocities of the robot's motors. These velocity instructions are sent in the form of cmd_vel or command velocity commands, which enable the robot to move responsively along the planned route.

Overall, this autonomous navigation system seamlessly integrates advanced technologies across localization, mapping, path planning, and control. This ensures precise, efficient navigation while adapting to dynamic environmental changes, making the system highly effective in complex indoor scenarios.

2.1. Local Planner Time Elastic Band

Time-Elastic Band Algorithm is a path planning algorithm used to control the motion of autonomous robots with differential drive kinematics models. This algorithm optimizes the path based on several objectives, such as speed, safety, and energy efficiency, and is suitable for use in complex, dynamic environments and spaces with limited space. In robots with a -*-differential drive kinematics model, the speed of the left wheel and right wheel are used to determine the linear velocity (V) and angular velocity (ω) of the robot. The equation of velocity and acceleration is shown in Equation 1.

$$u(t) = \begin{bmatrix} V(t) \\ \omega(t) \end{bmatrix} = \begin{bmatrix} \frac{1}{2} & \frac{1}{2} \\ -\frac{1}{D} & \frac{1}{D} \end{bmatrix} \begin{bmatrix} V_L \\ V_R \end{bmatrix} \quad (1)$$

where V_L dan V_R are the left and right wheel speeds of the differential drive robot, and D is the distance between the two wheels. TEB increases the time interval between robot movements from one pose to the next based on the Elastic Band algorithm. These poses and time intervals are optimized using the G2o package Equations (2) and (3), resulting in smoother and more efficient trajectories.

$$\begin{cases} Q = \{S_i\}, i = 1, 2, \ldots, nn \in \mathbb{N} \\ \tau = \{\Delta T_i\}\, i = 1, 2, \ldots, nn - 1 \end{cases} \quad (2)$$

$$B := (Q, \tau) = [S_1, \Delta T_i, S_2, \Delta T_2, \ldots, \Delta T_{n-1}, S_n] \quad (3)$$

The objective constraint function in the TEB algorithm focuses on criteria such as speed and acceleration limits, obstacle avoidance, and time efficiency. These criteria ensure that the planned path is not only optimal but also safe and efficient under various operational conditions, both for static and dynamic obstacles. The penalty function in Equation (4) in the TEB algorithm is used to penalize violations of the constraints that robot path planning must adhere to. This function measures the extent to which a value violates certain constraints.

$$e_\tau(x, x_r, \varepsilon, S, n) \approx \begin{cases} \left(\frac{x-(x_r-\varepsilon)}{S}\right)^n &, x > x_r - \varepsilon \\ 0 &, x \leq x_r - \varepsilon \end{cases} \quad (4)$$

Punishment function e, plays a role in measuring the degree of violation of a value x against predetermined limits. Thus, this function provides a penalty value that is proportional to the amount of violation that occurs, so that it can direct the optimization process so that the resulting solution meets the existing constraints. In the Time- Elastic Band (TEB) algorithm, the multi-objective optimization function in Equation (5) is used to combine several criteria that need to be met in robot path planning. These criteria include speed, acceleration, obstacle avoidance, and travel time constraints. By considering all these criteria, the TEB algorithm aims to produce a path that is optimal and safe, while being efficient in achieving the desired goal.

$$f(B) = \sum_k \gamma_k f_k(B) \quad (5)$$

Optimization in the Time-Elastic Band algorithm aims to achieve a balance between various desired objectives or constraints. Each criterion $f_k(B)$ in path planning is given a weight of γ_k. The magnitude of the value γ_k determines how much influence the criteria have on the optimization results. In determining the value of γ_k, and the handling of each $f_k(B)$ system ensures that the final result not only meets the mathematical requirements but also represents the desired parameters of each weight with the aim that the robot navigation system runs as safely and efficiently as possible.

2.2. Local Planner Assessment Parameters

To test the performance of the TEB algorithm, it is necessary to process data from the ROS topic so that it can be analyzed regarding the characteristics of robot movement in implementing the algorithm used. Some of the performance assessments of the TEB and DWA local planners that will be tested include: (i) Mean Square Error (MSE) value to get a quantitative measure of how accurate the robot is in achieving position and orientation on the optimal path. The MSE value is calculated based on the error of x, y position, and yaw orientation on the robot against the optimal path. The calculation of the error value is shown in Equation (6).

$$\begin{aligned} \text{Error}_x &= X_{goal} - X_{odom}\, ; \\ \text{Error}_y &= Y_{goal} - Y_{odom}\, ; \\ \text{Error}_{yaw} &= \theta_{goal} - \theta_{odom} \end{aligned} \quad (6)$$

The MSE value is calculated as the mean square of the error through Equation (7).

$$\begin{aligned} \text{MSE}_x &= \tfrac{1}{n}\sum_{i=1}^{n}(\text{Error}_{xi})^2 \\ \text{MSE}_y &= \tfrac{1}{n}\sum_{i=1}^{n}(\text{Error}_{yi})^2 \\ \text{MSE}_{yaw} &= \tfrac{1}{n}\sum_{i=1}^{n}(\text{Error}_{yawi})^2 \end{aligned} \quad (7)$$

By calculating the MSE value for each of the x, y, and yaw variables the robot's performance in achieving the optimal position and orientation can be analyzed and compared; (ii) Navigation Duration is used to evaluate the robot's navigation efficiency in achieving the predefined target. This duration shows how fast the robot can reach the destination from the initial position after receiving the command as shown in Equation (8).

$$T = t_N - t_1 \quad (8)$$

where T is the navigation duration, t_N, is the time when the robot reaches the goal, and t_1 is the time when the robot receives the command to move; (iii) Path Length is needed to evaluate the efficiency of the path taken by the robot in achieving the predetermined goal. The path length shows the total distance traveled by the robot from the starting position until it reaches the goal.

$$Path\ Length = \frac{1}{n}\sum_{i=1}^{n}\sqrt{(x_{i+1} - x_i)^2 + (y_{i+1} - y_i)^2} \quad (9)$$

where x_i and y_i are the coordinates of the robot's position at the i-th point, and n is the total number of coordinate points recorded from the start to the destination. By calculating the path length, it can be evaluated whether the robot takes the optimal path or there is a significant deviation from the shortest path it should take; (iv) Path Smoothness is used to assess the quality of robot movement. The local planner algorithm is essential in navigating the robot from one point to another considering the surrounding conditions. Path smoothness calculates the vector displacement difference between two consecutive points in two dimensions (x and y) as shown in Equation 10.

$$f_{ps} = \sum_{i=2}^{N-1}\|\Delta x_{i+1} - \Delta x_i\|^2 \quad (10)$$

Path smoothness ensures the robot moves in a controlled and predictable manner, reducing sharp turns and sudden movements, maintaining stability, reducing component wear, and improving navigation safety and efficiency, especially in environments with obstacles or in tasks that require precision; (v) Velocity Smoothness to measure the smooth and controlled acceleration and deceleration of the robot over time. Smoother acceleration means that the robot moves with more stable changes in speed, without sudden acceleration or deceleration. The calculation of the velocity smoothness parameter is shown in Equation 11.

$$f_{vs} = \frac{1}{N-1}\sum_{i=1}^{N-1}\left|\frac{v_{i+1}-v_i}{t_{i+1}-t_i}\right| \qquad (11)$$

where v is the robot speed at the i-th time, t is the time at the i-th point, and N is the total number of data points. These metrics assess the change in velocity between points, helping to ensure stable and controlled movement of the robot.

3. Results and Discussion

In autonomous robot navigation, the system generates a map from the map topic, which is then used to create both local and global costmaps. The mapping is achieved using the SLAM-Gmapping algorithm, which processes lidar data from the /scan topic and hall sensor data from the /odom topic. The resulting maps are saved in Portable Gray Map (PGM) format within the /map_server topic and are further processed by the Voronoi Planner algorithm to generate safe and efficient global paths. During mapping, the robot is manually controlled through the teleop_twist_keyboard ROS package, which sends motion commands to the /cmd_vel topic based on keyboard input. Using lidar sensors and encoders, the robot maps the PPBS Building area and each room, capturing detailed environmental data. The mapping results for the PPBS rooms are shown in Figure 5a, while those for a smaller room representing limited space with dynamic obstacles are displayed in Figure 5b. This study compares two local planner algorithms: the Dynamic Window Approach (DWA) from the move_base package and the Time Elastic Band (TEB), known for its time efficiency and path-planning capability. Testing was conducted across three scenarios. Scenario 1 involves navigating the environment in Figure 5a along the path in Figure 1. Scenarios 2 and 3 involve navigating the space shown in Figure 5b, with paths depicted in Figure 2a (without obstacles) and Figure 2b (with obstacles), respectively. In Scenario 1, the robot traverses seven set points, each corresponding to those listed in Figure 1. The algorithm performance is assessed by comparing DWA and TEB to identify the more effective algorithm for navigating the PPBS rooms.

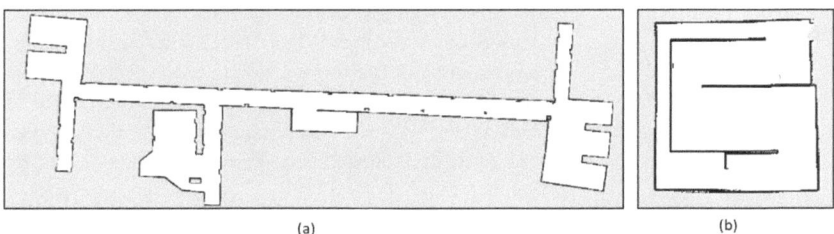

Figure 5. Map of Testing room: (**a**) Nurse's and a patient's room area (PPBS rooms), (**b**) Dynamic narrow room.

Robot navigation plots across five test scenarios as shown in Figure 6 compare the trajectories generated by the DWA and the TEB algorithms for autonomous navigation. Both graphs illustrate the robot's path along the X-Y plane in five different navigation scenarios. Figure 6a shows the trajectories produced by the DWA algorithm. In Section A, which highlights the robot's navigation in a complex, narrow region, DWA demonstrates the difficulty in maintaining consistent and smooth trajectories, exhibiting sharp turns and minor deviations. Section B depicts the robot's navigation of an initial curved segment.

While DWA successfully follows the route, there are observable variations in path accuracy and smoothness. Section C corresponds to a long, relatively straight path where the DWA trajectories exhibit oscillations, indicating inefficiencies in maintaining a steady course.

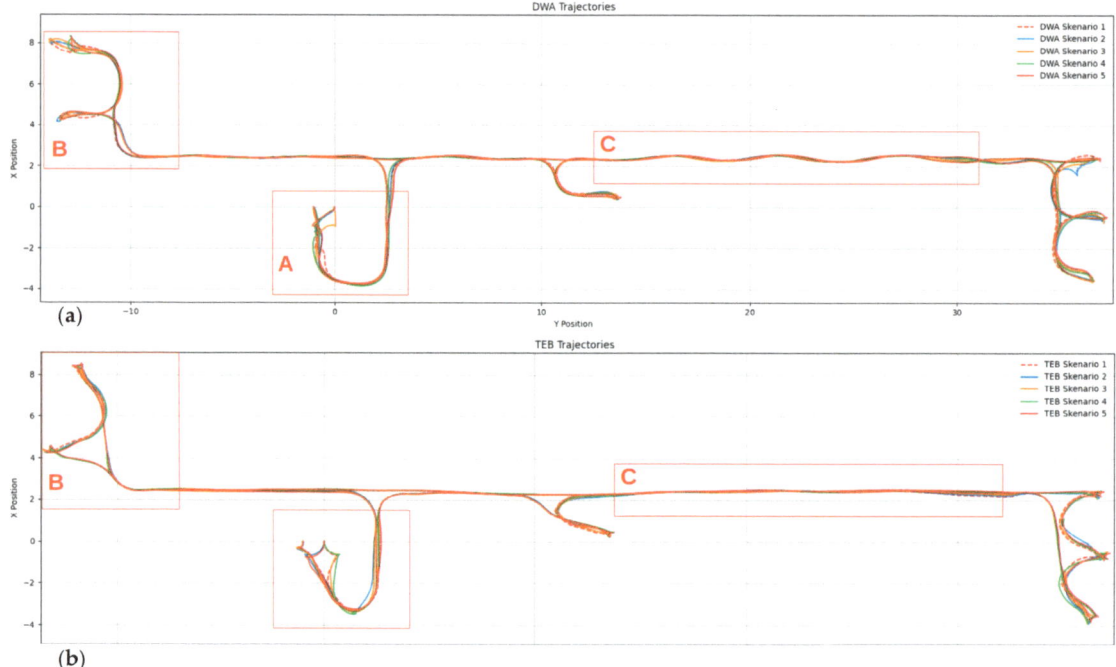

Figure 6. Plot Trajectory on Scenario 1.

Figure 6b presents the trajectories generated by the TEB algorithm. In Section A, TEB performs more consistently in the narrow region, with smoother and more uniform paths across scenarios compared to DWA. Section B shows the robot's effective handling of the initial curved segment, with improved path consistency and reduced variation. Section C highlights TEB's significant advantage in maintaining a steady trajectory along the straight path, with minimal oscillations or deviations. The comparison reveals that TEB consistently outperforms DWA in terms of path smoothness, accuracy, and uniformity across all scenarios. The smoother paths generated by TEB indicate better handling of dynamic obstacles and environmental complexities, making it a more reliable algorithm for navigation in dynamic environments. The results for the five PPBS scenarios are provided in Table 1.

Table 1 presents a comparative analysis of two navigation algorithms DWA and TEB across multiple path-planning scenarios. The metrics measured include path length, duration, velocity smoothness, path smoothness, and Mean Squared Error (MSE), each averaged across scenarios for both algorithms. Based on Path Length category, TEB consistently produces shorter paths (mean of 155.5 m) compared to DWA (mean of 165.38 m), suggesting that TEB can find more efficient paths for navigation. TEB takes slightly longer in three out of five scenarios and, on average, has a similar duration to DWA (429 s for TEB vs. 428.2 s for DWA). The velocity smoothness values highlight a notable advantage for TEB, with a mean of 0.0599 m/s^2 compared to 0.0871 m/s^2 for DWA. Lower values indicate smoother accelerations and decelerations along the path, which is beneficial in applications requiring steady movement, such as autonomous vehicles carrying sensitive cargo. This smoother velocity profile could improve passenger comfort or load stability in practical scenarios. Both algorithms exhibit similar path smoothness (0.0017 m^2 for TEB vs. 0.00183 m^2 for DWA on average). This metric suggests that the paths generated by both algorithms avoid abrupt turns, although TEB has a slight advantage. Higher path smoothness is often desired to reduce the wear on mechanical components by preventing sharp direction changes. The MSE values are comparable between the algorithms, with TEB at 0.60 and DWA at 0.613 on average. The MSE provides insight into the accuracy and reliability of the path in adhering to the desired trajectory. Here, TEB's slight improvement suggests better adherence to the planned path, which may result in a more predictable route.

Table 1. Performance Evaluation of Local Planners in Scenario 1.

Scenario/Rooms		Path Length (m)		Duration (s)		Velocity Smoothness (m/s^2)		Path Smoothness (m^2)		MSE (m^2)	
		DWA	TEB	DWA	TEB	DWA	TEB	DWA	TEB	DWA	TEB
1	1	166.07	156.5	423	446	0.0803	0.0740	0.00179	0.0018	0.620	0.61
	2	166.78	154.7	441	413	0.0976	0.0620	0.00196	0.0017	0.623	0.59
	3	165.41	154.4	415	421	0.0784	0.0299	0.00180	0.0016	0.636	0.60
	4	164.89	156.4	439	443	0.0886	0.0676	0.00184	0.0017	0.606	0.61
	5	163.75	155.5	423	426	0.0909	0.0662	0.00176	0.0017	0.578	0.58
Means		165.38	155.5	428.2	429.8	0.0871	0.0599	0.00183	0.0017	0.613	0.60

The comparison indicates that TEB generally performs better in terms of path length, velocity smoothness, and slightly improved path smoothness and MSE. These metrics suggest that TEB may be a preferable choice in applications where efficient path planning and smoother velocity profiles are critical. The trade-off, however, is a marginally increased travel time in some scenarios, which may or may not be significant depending on the use case. Overall, TEB appears to offer superior optimization in terms of navigation efficiency and smoothness, making it potentially more suitable for tasks requiring high precision and smooth navigation. DWA, while slightly less optimized in these areas, may still be preferable in situations where marginally faster response times are required and path efficiency is less critical.

In Scenario 2, it is made in the Room Arena which contains narrow and wide aisles according to the results of SLAM-Gmapping as many as eight set points according to Figure 2. Table 2 shows the performance assessment of the TEB and DWA algorithms for each goal as many as eight goals with six goals passing through a narrow hallway and two goals passing through a wide hallway.

In comparing the DWA and TEB methods across different metrics for a series of path goals in Scenario 2, several key insights emerge: The DWA method generally resulted in shorter path lengths, with an average of 14.32 m compared to TEB's 14.84 m. In most cases, DWA found a more direct route to the goal, which may suggest that it is more efficient in terms of distance traveled. However, TEB occasionally provided shorter paths, particularly noticeable in Goal 2 and Goal 3, which suggests TEB's flexibility in optimizing the path under certain conditions. While DWA and TEB performed similarly in terms of time, DWA showed a slightly longer average duration (46.12 s) than TEB (43.3 s). This difference could indicate that TEB was able to complete paths more quickly despite slightly longer distances, potentially due to a smoother trajectory or fewer adjustments during navigation. TEB generally achieved lower goal errors in the x and y directions. Across most goals, TEB demonstrated more consistent accuracy in reaching the target with lower error values. On average, TEB had a mean x-error of 0.071 m compared to DWA's 0.082 m and a mean y-error of 0.160 m versus DWA's 0.168 m, indicating its advantage in positional accuracy. A notable difference was observed in the yaw error. TEB consistently achieved a significantly lower yaw error, with an average of 0.066 radians, whereas DWA's average yaw error was much higher at 1.2485 radians. This suggests that TEB is more effective in aligning the orientation towards the target, which is essential for applications where precise final orientation is critical. TEB outperformed DWA in positional accuracy and orientation alignment while maintaining a competitive duration. This makes TEB more suitable for tasks requiring high precision in both position and orientation. Conversely, DWA may still be beneficial for applications prioritizing shorter paths, though with a trade-off in orientation precision. While DWA offers slight advantages in path length, TEB's accuracy in positioning and orientation makes it a more reliable option for precision navigation tasks. The selection of the approach should, therefore, depend on whether the priority is minimizing distance or achieving high positional and orientational accuracy.

Table 2. Performance evaluation of local planners in Scenario 2 for each goal.

Scenario/Goals		Path Length (m)		Duration (s)		Goal Error x (m)		Goal Error y (m)		Goal Error Yaw (rad)	
		DWA	TEB	DWA	TEB	DWA	TEB	DWA	TEB	DWA	TEB
2	1	15.97	16.95	56	56	0.039	0.086	0.193	0.222	1.552	0.097
	2	14.42	12.83	48	41	0.183	0.118	0.137	0.016	3.166	0.100
	3	9.48	8.15	29	26	0.178	0.171	0.062	0.022	0.074	0.058
	4	15.77	16.77	49	46	0.021	0.065	0.140	0.195	1.526	0.063
	5	14.86	15.91	44	44	0.066	0.022	0.198	0.193	0.045	0.021
	6	14.53	16.04	37	42	0.040	0.039	0.191	0.192	1.628	0.005
	7	15.23	16.04	48	46	0.052	0.019	0.111	0.219	0.003	0.081
	8	8.03	16.04	58	46	6.516	0.052	0.315	0.227	1.994	0.108
	Mean	14.32	14.84	46.12	43.3	0.082	0.071	0.168	0.160	1.2485	0.066

The TEB algorithm demonstrates superior performance over the DWA regarding velocity smoothness. TEB provides more controlled and gradual acceleration, particularly in confined spaces, significantly reducing sudden oscillations and improving maneuverability. In terms of path smoothness, TEB also surpasses DWA by enabling safer, more fluid movements, which are essential for complex or narrow environments. Furthermore, the lower Mean Square Error (MSE) value achieved by TEB indicates greater precision and reliability in adhering to the intended path, reflecting its robustness in path-following tasks. Figure 7 illustrates the trajectories toward each target for the Scenario 2 tests, visually highlighting TEB's smoother navigation and its advantage in dynamic path adjustments. These findings underscore TEB's suitability for applications requiring high levels of accuracy and smoothness in real-time navigation, such as autonomous robotic systems operating in cluttered or constrained environments. The TEB algorithm's ability to maintain stable, smooth motion trajectories minimizes abrupt directional changes, which can be critical in environments where safety, control, and efficiency are paramount.

Table 3 compares the performance of DWA and TEB path-planning algorithms across metrics like path length, duration, and goal errors (in x, y, and yaw) over six goals. On average, TEB produced slightly shorter path lengths (21.96 m) than DWA (23.44 m), with DWA requiring longer paths in early goals, though both converged to similar lengths (around 22 m) in later goals, suggesting TEB's efficiency in minimizing path length. TEB also showed faster completion times, with a mean of 57.3 s compared to DWA's 61 s, notably outperforming DWA in goal 1 (51 vs. 66 s), hinting at TEB's ability to generate smoother trajectories. In goal errors, TEB demonstrated greater accuracy, with a mean error of 0.147 m on the x-axis versus DWA's 0.26 m and outperforming DWA significantly in Goal 1 (0.155 vs. 0.728 m). TEB maintained a lower y-axis error (0.097 m) than DWA (0.842 m), especially in Goal 1, where DWA's error was over three times TEB's (3.831 vs. 0.214 m). In orientation (yaw), TEB had a superior mean error of 0.09 radians compared to DWA's 0.877 radians, with a striking performance in Goal 5 (0.003 vs. 0.074 radians). Overall, TEB achieved shorter paths, faster completion, and lower position and orientation errors, suggesting it is better suited for applications requiring high accuracy and efficiency, while DWA's higher errors, particularly in y-axis positioning and orientation, may limit its use in precision-dependent navigation.

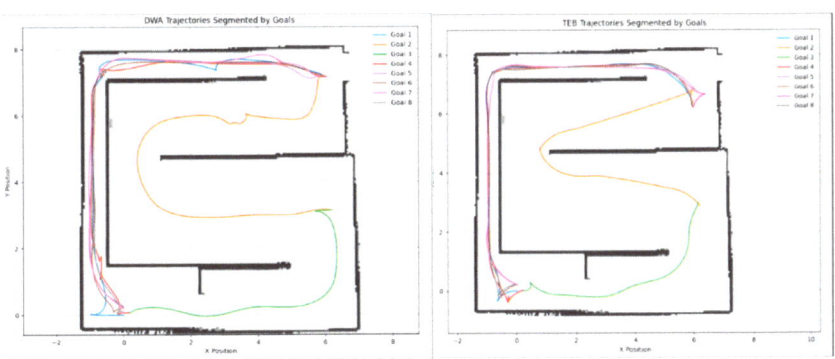

Figure 7. Scenario 2 with 8 Goal Waypoint.

Table 3. Performance evaluation of local planners in the narrow with obstacle scenario.

Scenario/Goals		Path Length (m)		Duration (s)		Goal Error x (m)		Goal Error y (m)		Goal Error Yaw (rad)	
		DWA	TEB	DWA	TEB	DWA	TEB	DWA	TEB	DWA	TEB
3	1	12.28	21.51	66	51	0.728	0.155	3.831	0.214	1.074	0.094
	2	15.52	22.94	50	73	0.151	0.146	0.140	0.025	1.596	0.248
	3	23.69	22.04	64	57	0.120	0.178	0.067	0.257	0.007	0.062
	4	23.68	22.04	64	54	0.112	0.067	0.168	0.023	1.638	0.085
	5	22.96	21.76	61	56	0.189	0.213	0.007	0.018	0.074	0.003
	6		21.49		53		0.124		0.046		0.053
Means		23.44	21.96	61	57.3	0.26	0.147	0.842	0.097	0.877	0.090

The performance comparison between the DWA and TEB local planners across scenarios with and without obstacles highlights key distinctions in path length, duration, velocity smoothness, path smoothness, and Mean Squared Error (MSE) as shown in Table 4. In terms of path length, DWA covered shorter distances in both scenarios—108.30 m vs. TEB's 118.79 m without obstacles and 98.86 m vs. TEB's 131.38 m with obstacles—suggesting that DWA generates more direct paths. TEB, however, completed the obstacle-free path faster (347 s vs. DWA's 369 s), although this advantage diminished in obstacle scenarios, with DWA taking 305 s compared to TEB's 344 s. Velocity smoothness favored TEB, which maintained lower acceleration values in both settings (e.g., 0.08828 m/s^2 vs. DWA's 0.11441 m/s^2 without obstacles), indicating smoother speed transitions, crucial in complex environments. For path smoothness, both planners were similar in obstacle-free conditions, but with obstacles, DWA's path smoothness dropped significantly (0.1421 m^2 vs. TEB's 0.00154 m^2), reflecting more abrupt movements around obstacles. TEB also consistently recorded a lower MSE, particularly in obstacle scenarios (0.0004 m^2 vs. DWA's 4.3462 m^2), underscoring its alignment with the desired path and adaptability. Overall, while DWA's shorter paths and durations are advantageous in open spaces, TEB's superior path smoothness, velocity consistency, and accuracy make it better suited for navigating obstacle-rich environments.

Table 4. Performance Evaluation of Local Planners in the narrow room without (scenario 2) and with (scenario 3) Obstacle.

Scenario	Path Length (m)		Duration (s)		Velocity Smoothness (m/s^2)		Path Smoothness (m^2)		MSE (m^2)	
	DWA	TEB	DWA	TEB	DWA	TEB	DWA	TEB	DWA	TEB
2	108.30	118.79	369	347	0.11441	0.08828	0.001531	0.00153	0.0220	0.0202
3	98.861	131.38	305	344	0.14014	0.08318	0.1421	0.00154	4.3462	0.0004

TEB algorithm successfully covered six goals with a total length of 131.38 m, while the DWA only reached three goals. TEB excelled in the velocity smoothness parameter due to its quick reaction to obstacles, keeping the velocity smooth and controlled. In path smoothness, TEB was more effective in plotting a path outside the global map than DWA, which was slower in adjusting the path. The MSE value of TEB is also much smaller, indicating consistency and efficiency in selecting the optimal path and adapting to the dynamic environment. The plot of each goal's journey for the Obstacle Class arena test is shown in Figure 8.

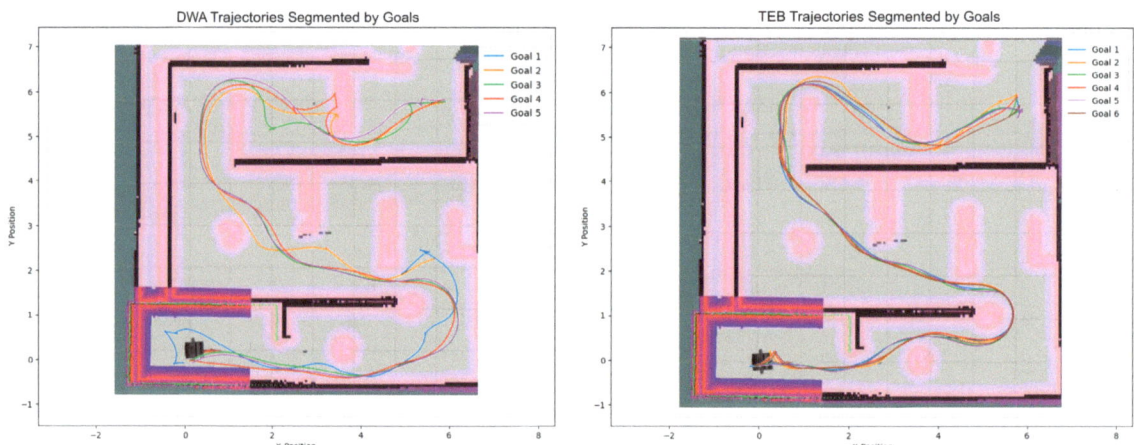

Figure 8. Scenario 3 with 6 Goal Waypoint.

TEB algorithm performed better than the DWA in the face of new obstacles. TEB instantly adapts by planning a new path, avoiding collisions, and improving navigation efficiency. In contrast, DWA often almost hit obstacles that were not recorded on the global map and took longer to perform recovery behaviors, such as backtracking and re-planning the path. The TEB successfully completed six goals, while the DWA had problems with the first two goals and delayed reactions to obstacles. This shows that TEB excels in environments with many obstacles and dynamic conditions, while DWA is more suitable for simple environments. Overall, the navigation results show that the TEB algorithm is superior in various aspects of navigation performance compared to the DWA algorithm. TEB is not only more effective in avoiding obstacles and maintaining smooth speed but also more efficient in path planning, especially in dynamic and complex environments. The

TEB algorithm shows better ability in achieving navigation goals with safer and optimized paths, making it a better choice for applications in diverse and challenging environments.

4. Conclusions

The performance evaluation of local planner algorithms demonstrates that the Time Elastic Band (TEB) algorithm outperforms the Dynamic Window Approach (DWA) across various test scenarios. TEB consistently exhibits better path efficiency, smoothness, and navigation consistency. In Scenario 1, TEB achieved a shorter path length, reduced position and yaw errors, and improved velocity and path smoothness compared to DWA. Similarly, in Scenario 2, TEB generated shorter paths with faster completion times and smoother trajectories. In Scenario 3, TEB continued to excel with shorter path lengths, reduced durations, and significantly smoother and more consistent navigation metrics. These results highlight TEB's superior performance, particularly in environments with obstacles and dynamic conditions, making it a more reliable choice for autonomous navigation tasks.

Author Contributions: Conceptualization, A.T.; Methodology, A.T.; Software, M.A.F.; Validation, M.A.F.; Formal analysis, B.M.W.; Investigation, B.M.W.; Data curation, A.T. and M.A.F.; Writing—original draft, A.T.; Writing—review & editing, B.M.W.; Supervision, A.T.; Project administration, N.A.; Funding acquisition, N.A. All authors have read and agreed to the published version of the manuscript.

Funding: This research was funded through the Academic Leadership Grant, No. 1518/UN6.3.1/PT.00/2024 awarded to Nursanti Anggriani and supported by the Department of Electrical Engineering, Faculty of Mathematics and Natural Sciences, Universitas Padjadjaran, Indonesia.

Data Availability Statement: The original contributions presented in this study are included in the article. Further inquiries can be directed to the corresponding author.

Conflicts of Interest: The authors declare that they have no known competing financial interests or personal relationships that could have appeared to influence the work reported in this paper.

References

1. Huang, Y.; Chen, X.; Liu, J. Automation in repetitive tasks in industrial settings. *J. Ind. Eng.* **2019**, *45*, 123–136.
2. Jones, T.; Smith, R.; Johnson, K. Cost reduction and productivity enhancement with autonomous robots. *Int. J. Autom.* **2021**, *52*, 232–245.
3. Smith, A.; Johnson, B. Autonomous drones in agriculture: Yield improvements and sustainability. *Precis. Agric.* **2020**, *10*, 298–315.
4. Lee, H.; Kim, S.; Park, M. Improving worker safety through autonomous robotics in hazardous environments. *Saf. Sci.* **2020**, *64*, 412–420.
5. Dufresne, T.; Dubois, L. Autonomous Robots in Hazardous Environments: Replacing Human Labor in Dangerous and Physically Demanding Tasks. *J. Robot. Mechatron.* **2019**, *31*, 220–232.
6. Zhang, L.; Wang, T. Environmental benefits of autonomous robots in sustainable agriculture. *J. Environ. Sci. Technol.* **2022**, *58*, 98–110.
7. Romanov, A.M. A navigation system for intelligent mobile robots. In Proceedings of the IEEE Conference of Russian Young Researchers in Electrical and Electronic Engineering (EIConRus), Saint Petersburg, Russia, 28–31 January 2019; pp. 652–656.
8. Yang, H. A multi-robot formation platform based on an indoor global positioning system. *Appl. Sci.* **2019**, *9*, 1165. [CrossRef]
9. Chempolil, S.S. Design of a medical prototype robot for nurse assistance. In Proceedings of the 2021 Seventh International Conference on Bio Signals, Images, and Instrumentation (ICBSII), Chennai, India, 25–27 March 2021; pp. 1–5.
10. Turnip, A.; Tampubolon, G.M.; Ramadhan, S.F.; Nugraha, A.V.; Trisanto, A.; Novita, D. Development of medical robot Covid-19 based 2D mapping LIDAR and IMU sensors. In Proceedings of the 2021 IEEE International Conference on Health, Instrumentation & Measurement, and Natural Sciences (InHeNce), Medan, Indonesia, 14–16 July 2021; pp. 1–4.
11. Manuky, Z.J. Lokalisasi Berbasis Marvelmind-Lidar-Imu Menggunakan Extended Kalman Filter Untuk Sistem Navigasi Otonom Robot Medis. Bachelor's Thesis, Universitas Padjadjaran, Bandung, Indonesia, 2023.
12. Rafly. Deteksi Rintangan Untuk Menghindari Tabrakan di Robot Medis Otonom Dengan Kamera LiDAR. Bachelor's Thesis, Universitas Padjadjaran, Bandung, Indonesia, 2023.

13. Turnip, A. Development of autonomous medical robot based artificial intelligence and Internet of Things. *Int. J. Artif. Intell.* **2024**, *22*, 20–37.
14. Rivai, M.; Hutabarat, D.; Nafis, Z.M. 2D mapping using omni-directional mobile robot equipped with LiDAR. *TELKOMNIKA Telecommun. Comput. Electron. Control.* **2020**, *18*, 1467–1474. [CrossRef]
15. Wang, H.; Lou, X.; Cai, Y.; Li, Y.; Chen, L. Real-time vehicle detection algorithm based on vision and LiDAR point cloud fusion. *J. Sens.* **2019**, *2019*, 8473980. [CrossRef]
16. Turnip, A.; Sudrajat, A.W.; Le Hoa, N.; Dharma, A.; Joelianto, E. Interactive development of medical robot using voice chatbot based on deep learning. In Proceedings of the 2023 29th International Conference on Telecommunications (ICT), Toba, Indonesia, 8–9 November 2023; pp. 1–6. [CrossRef]
17. Suryawan, D.; Adinandra, S.; Arifianto, J.; Nugroho, E.S.; Masykur, L.A.; Purnama, R.H. Rancang bangun robot pelayan medis untuk pasien karantina COVID-19 dengan kendali berbasis Android. *JTT J. Teknol. Terapan* **2021**, *7*, 68–76. [CrossRef]
18. Nurhayati, S. Sistem navigasi robot pembawa nampan obat pasien berbasis Internet of Things. In Proceedings of the Electro National Conference (ENACO) Politeknik Negeri Sriwijaya, Palembang, Indonesia, 1 June 2021; pp. 248–255.
19. Zhao, J.; Liu, S.; Li, J. Research and implementation of autonomous navigation for mobile robots based on SLAM algorithm under ROS. *Sensors* **2022**, *22*, 4172. [CrossRef] [PubMed]
20. Looi, C.Z.; Ng, D.W. A study on the effect of parameters for ROS motion planner and navigation system for indoor robot. *J. Electr. Comput. Eng. Res.* **2021**, *1*, 29–36.
21. Chikurtev, D.; Chivarov, N.; Chivarov, S.; Chikurteva, A. Mobile Robot Localization and Navigation Using LIDAR and Indoor GPS. *IFAC PapersOnLine* **2021**, *54*, 351–356. [CrossRef]
22. Sharma, N.; Pandey, J.K.; Mondal, S. A Review of Mobile Robots: Applications and Future Prospect. *Int. J. Precis. Eng. Manuf.* **2023**, *24*, 1695–1706. [CrossRef]
23. Loganathan, A.; Ahmad, N.S. A Systematic Review on Recent Advances in Autonomous Mobile Robot Navigation. *Eng. Sci. Technol. Int. J.* **2023**, *40*, 101343. [CrossRef]
24. Liu, L.; Wang, X.; Yang, X.; Liu, H.; Li, J.; Wang, P. Path Planning Techniques for Mobile Robots: Review and Prospect. *Expert. Syst. Appl.* **2023**, *227*, 120254. [CrossRef]
25. Hu, H.; Zhang, K.; Tan, A.H.; Ruan, M.; Agia, C.G.; Nejat, G. A Sim-to-Real Pipeline for Deep Reinforcement Learning for Autonomous Robot Navigation in Cluttered Rough Terrain. *IEEE Robot. Autom. Lett.* **2021**, *6*, 6569–6576. [CrossRef]
26. Al-Kamil, S.J.; Szabolcsi, R. Optimizing Path Planning in Mobile Robot Systems Using Motion Capture Technology. *J. Robot. Syst.* **2024**, *22*, 102043. [CrossRef]
27. Balasubramanian, E.; Elangovan, E.; Tamilarasan, P.; Kanagachidambaresan, G.R.; Chutia, D. Optimal Energy Efficient Path Planning of UAV Using Hybrid MACO-MEA* Algorithm: Theoretical and Experimental Approach. *J. Ambient. Intell. Hum. Comput.* **2022**, *25*, 1–21. [CrossRef]
28. Karur, K.; Sharma, N.; Dharmatti, C.; Siegel, J.E. A Survey of Path Planning Algorithms for Mobile Robots. *Vehicles* **2021**, *3*, 448–468. [CrossRef]
29. Liang, J.; Wang, S.; Wang, B. Online Motion Planning for Fixed-Wing Aircraft in Precise Automatic Landing on Mobile Platforms. *Drones* **2023**, *7*, 324. [CrossRef]
30. Yuan, H.; Li, H.; Zhang, Y.; Du, S.; Yu, L.; Wang, X. Comparison and Improvement of Local Planners on ROS for Narrow Passages. In Proceedings of the 2022 International Conference on High Performance Big Data and Intelligent Systems HPBD&IS, Tianjin, China, 10–11 December 2022. [CrossRef]
31. Naotunna, I.; Wongratanaphisan, T. Comparison of ROS Local Planners with Differential Drive Heavy Robotic System. In Proceedings of the 2020 International Conference on Advanced Mechatronic Systems ICAMechS, Hanoi, Vietnam, 10–13 December 2020. [CrossRef]
32. Canh, T.N.; HoangVan, X.; Chong, N.Y. Enhancing Social Robot Navigation with Integrated Motion Prediction and Trajectory Planning in Dynamic Human Environments. *arXiv* **2024**, arXiv:2411.01814. [CrossRef]
33. Kulathunga, G.; Yilmaz, A.; Huang, Z. Resilient Timed Elastic Band Planner for Collision-Free Navigation in Unknown Environments. *arXiv* **2024**, arXiv:2412.03174.
34. Wu, J.; Ma, X.; Peng, T.; Wang, H. An Improved Timed Elastic Band (TEB) Algorithm of Autonomous Ground Vehicle (AGV) in Complex Environment. *Sensors* **2021**, *21*, 8312. [CrossRef] [PubMed]

35. Mansakul, T.; Fan, I.-S.; Tang, G. Navigation for a mobile robot to inspect aircraft. In Proceedings of the 7th International Young Engineers Forum (YEF-ECE), Lisbon, Portugal, 7 July 2023. [CrossRef]
36. Arce, D.; Solano, J.; Beltrán, C. A Comparison Study between Traditional and Deep-Reinforcement-Learning-Based Algorithms for Indoor Autonomous Navigation in Dynamic Scenarios. *Sensors* **2023**, *23*, 9672. [CrossRef] [PubMed]

Disclaimer/Publisher's Note: The statements, opinions and data contained in all publications are solely those of the individual author(s) and contributor(s) and not of MDPI and/or the editor(s). MDPI and/or the editor(s) disclaim responsibility for any injury to people or property resulting from any ideas, methods, instructions or products referred to in the content.

Article

A Linear Regression-Based Methodology to Improve the Stability of a Low-Cost GPS Receiver Using the Precision Timing Signals from an Atomic Clock

Shilpa Manandhar [1,*], Sneha Saravanan [2], Yu Song Meng [1] and Yung Chuen Tan [1]

[1] National Metrology Centre (NMC), Agency for Science, Technology and Research (A*STAR), Singapore 637145, Singapore; meng_yusong@nmc.a-star.edu.sg (Y.S.M.); tan_yung_chuen@nmc.a-star.edu.sg (Y.C.T.)

[2] Department of Electronics and Instrumentation Engineering, Kumaraguru College of Technology, Coimbatore 641049, India; sneha.20ei@kct.ac.in

* Correspondence: shilpa_manandhar@nmc.a-star.edu.sg

Citation: Manandhar, S.; Saravanan, S.; Meng, Y.S.; Tan, Y.C. A Linear Regression-Based Methodology to Improve the Stability of a Low-Cost GPS Receiver Using the Precision Timing Signals from an Atomic Clock. *Electronics* **2024**, *13*, 3321. https://doi.org/10.3390/electronics13163321

Academic Editor: Ping-Feng Pai

Received: 30 July 2024
Revised: 20 August 2024
Accepted: 20 August 2024
Published: 21 August 2024

Copyright: © 2024 by the authors. Licensee MDPI, Basel, Switzerland. This article is an open access article distributed under the terms and conditions of the Creative Commons Attribution (CC BY) license (https:// creativecommons.org/licenses/by/ 4.0/).

Abstract: The global positioning system (GPS) is widely known for its applications in navigation, timing, and positioning. However, its accuracy can be greatly impacted by the performance of its receiver clocks, especially for a low-cost receiver equipped with lower-grade clocks like crystal oscillators. The objective of this study is to develop a model to improve the stability of a low-cost receiver. To achieve this, a machine-learning-based linear regression algorithm is proposed to predict the differences of the low-cost GPS receiver compared to the precision timing source. Experiments were conducted using low-cost receivers like Ublox and expensive receivers like Septentrio. The model was implemented and the clocks of low-cost receivers were steered. The outcomes demonstrate a notable enhancement in the stability of low-cost receivers after the corrections were applied. This improvement underscores the efficacy of the proposed model in enhancing the performance of low-cost GPS receivers. Consequently, these low-cost receivers can be cost-effectively utilized for various purposes, particularly in applications requiring the deployment of numerous GPS receivers to achieve extensive spatial coverage.

Keywords: GPS; time and frequency; stability of clocks; clock bias errors; precision timing applications; atomic clocks; time transfer

1. Introduction

The global positioning system (GPS) stands out as one of the most extensively utilized technologies, mainly known for its applications in navigation. With the advancement in science, GPS has been shown to achieve an accuracy of up to several meters in an open sky condition; however, the accuracy deteriorates for an urban canyon setting [1]. Various factors influence the accuracy of a GPS system, with the performance of the receiver clock being a key determinant. Receivers employ diverse clocks, ranging from high-end chip-scale atomic clocks to lower-grade options, such as crystal oscillators.

In Figure 1, we observe the performance of a specific low-cost GPS receiver (Ublox), which uses a lower-grade clock. The data are collected over a day at a fixed location. They show that the maximum 2D error can go up to 40 m. Vertical positioning for these receivers is even more challenging. The vertical accuracy of a GPS receiver is directly linked to the stability of the receiver clock. The higher the receiver clock bias error, the higher the error in vertical positioning [2,3]. An error as big as that shown by Figure 1 is totally unacceptable, especially for autonomous vehicles. Real-time kinematic (RTK) signals or differential GPS (DGPS) are widely used techniques to improve the positioning accuracy of a GPS receiver [4,5]. However, these methods only improve the positioning accuracy but do not improve the clock stability by correcting the receiver clock errors. Our proposed method here focuses on improving the stability of low-cost receiver clocks. Once the stability is improved, the positioning accuracy will be enhanced. RTK signals and DGPS could be applied further to enhance the precision of results.

The proposed methodology is to steer the GPS receiver periodically, hence improving its stability and accuracy. To achieve this, there are two main tasks: (a) generation of a precision timing source and (b) transfer of the steering information.

(a) Precision Timing Source: Atomic clocks have long been used as a source of precision time [6]. The accuracy of such timing is verified by comparing to the Universal Coordinated Time (UTC) generated and maintained by the Bureau of Weights and Measurement (BIPM) [7]. According to BIPM [8], cesium clocks are the current standards for time and frequency. Precision timing is generated from clocks that are traceable to the cesium standards. In our Time Lab at the National Metrology Centre (NMC) in Singapore, we maintain cesium clocks and hydrogen masers. The Singapore time scale is established by deriving frequency outputs from these clocks, which are meticulously preserved under optimal temperature and humidity conditions. The process of generation of precision timing based on a number of atomic clocks is almost similar for different laboratories [9–11]. However, they differ in the way they choose to combine the readings from these atomic clocks. It is important to analyze the precision time generation process. A detailed discussion on the time-scale generation process is presented in Section 2.

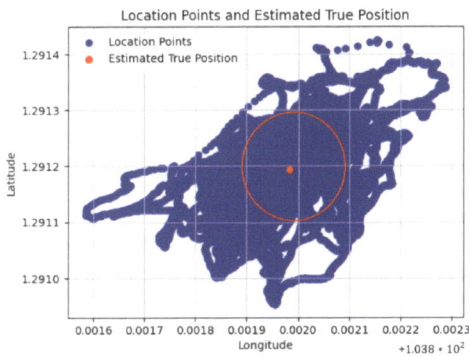

Figure 1. Scatter plot of the position recorded by Ublox for a randomly chosen day in a static condition for single point positioning (SPP). The latitude and longitude are in meters. The red circle represents a radius of 10 m error in 2D positioning.

(b) Time Transfer: Once the precision signals are generated from the lab, they can be used to correct the low-cost oscillators. The GPS time transfer technique can be applied for this purpose [12–14]. The GPS time transfer technique has previously been applied either in common view mode or all-in-view mode for the purpose of time comparison between any two laboratories [15,16]. This method has not been implemented yet for steering a low-cost GPS receiver. The paper will propose a machine-learning-based algorithm to explore the possibility of using this method to improve the stability of a low-cost GPS receiver. The details will be discussed in Section 3.2.

Contributions and Impacts

The major contribution of the paper is the model to steer the receiver clock of a low-cost receiver with the precision time information from labs. By doing so, it enhances the stability of the low-cost receiver and thus the positioning accuracy will be improved. As the proposed model is based on satellites and no physical connections are required, the advantage of the model is not only limited to improving the stability of a GPS receiver but any device that requires timing calibration can be benefited from the model. The proposed model has the capability of remotely transferring the time and frequency information.

In today's world of digitization and digitalization, such remote calibration capabilities are vital.

The proposed approach specifically targets low-cost receivers equipped with lower-grade clocks. By steering these clocks based on the devised model, the performance of such receivers can experience substantial improvement. This in turn will improve vertical positioning and the accuracy of overall positioning in general. The implications of this correction extends to applications such as autonomous vehicles, where precise positioning is imperative. Moreover, the correction of the receiver's clock performance can have a direct impact on the estimation of total GNSS signal delay. As the clock bias errors are improved, the signal delay estimation is expected to have less error. This is beneficial in climate-related studies like rainfall prediction, which relies on accurate estimation of atmospheric delay [17]. This enhancement is also particularly advantageous for studies requiring numerous GPS stations. For instance, GPS-based rainfall prediction, characterized by lower spatial resolution, necessitates the installation of multiple GPS receivers at diverse locations to enhance coverage. The current limitations posed by the high cost of receivers hinder this deployment strategy. However, the proposed methodology offers a solution by enhancing the performance of low-cost receivers, facilitating their cost-effective deployment across numerous locations.

2. Generation of Precision Timing Information

The correction of the low-cost oscillators like Ublox is based on the precision timing from the lab. This section will give an overview of the procedure involved in the generation of the precision timing in Singapore.

2.1. System Setup

There are two time and frequency laboratories under NMC in Singapore. They are located at 8 Clean Tech Loop (CT3) and Fusionopolis 2 (FP2). The lab at CT3 is the main lab traceable to UTC and the lab at FP2 is the backup lab traceable to $UTC(SG)$. The results discussed in this paper are with respect to the backup lab at FP2, where most of the R&D works are carried out. The hardware that we have at FP2 are shown in Figure 2. Here at the FP2 facility, we have three atomic clocks, which include two cesium clocks, and one hydrogen maser. We have one multi-channel measurement system (MMS), and one steering device (AOG-110, Microchip, Chandler, AZ, USA). We have higher-end GNSS equipment from Septentrio. This GNSS equipment has the option to be steered by an external clock as well.

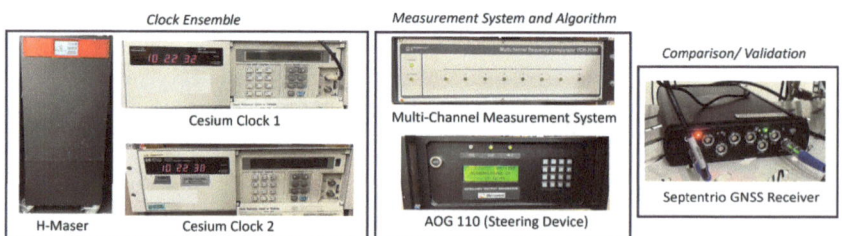

Figure 2. Hardware at Time and Frequency Lab of Singapore [located at Fusionopolis 2 (FP2)].

National Metrology Institutes (NMIs), like NMC, typically operate multiple atomic clocks, forming an ensemble [18] that contributes to the derivation of the $UTC(k)$ for a specific NMI, denoted as k. Ensemble timing capitalizes on the advantages offered by each clock within the ensemble. *AT1* is a very famous method to generate the ensemble timing that has been adopted by many NMIs [19]. ALGOS and Kalman filter-based methods are a few other techniques to generate the ensemble timings [20,21]. The next section will describe the time-scale algorithm that has been implemented for this paper.

2.2. Time-Scale Algorithm

Figure 3 shows the schematic of the system setup. It consists of all the hardware discussed in the previous section. As shown by the schematic, the MMS captures the time differences between a reference clock and the input clocks, with the H-maser serving as the reference in our case. Therefore MMS records two sets of differences, $x_r - x_1$ and $x_r - x_2$, differences between H-maser and cesium clock 1 and H-maser and cesium clock 2, respectively. These recorded differences are then used by a time-scale algorithm to calculate the ensemble time, x_{re}. For this paper, the *AT1* algorithm is implemented.

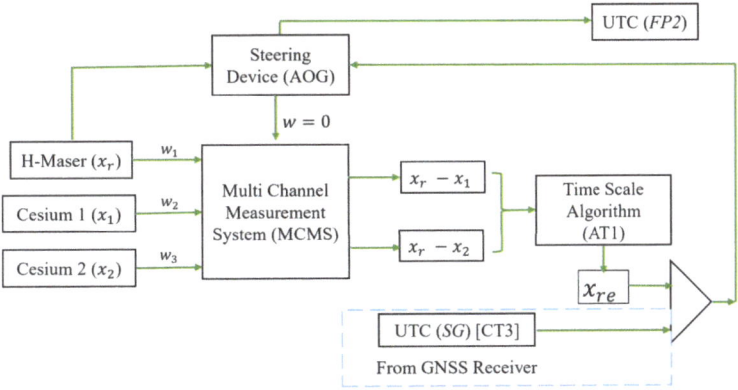

Figure 3. Flowchart of the system setup at the Time and Frequency Lab at FP2.

All time-scale algorithms share a common foundation, expressed by the general equation depicted in Equation (1).

$$\hat{x_{je}}(k) = x_{je}(k-1) + y_{je}(k-1)\tau + 0.5d_{je}(k-1)\tau^2 \qquad (1)$$

The equation shows the fundamental relationship used to estimate the behavior of a clock j with respect to an ensemble e, at time stamp k given the condition of clock at $k - 1$. Here, x_{je} is the phase difference, y_{je} is the frequency difference, and d_{je} is the frequency aging of clock j with respect to the ensemble e. The *AT1* algorithm is a recursive algorithm that can be used in the estimation of clock behavior. The procedural steps involved in the realization of the *AT1* algorithm have been described in our earlier paper [22].

Determination of Clock Weights

In the *AT1* algorithm, a crucial step involves determining the weights (w) assigned to each clock. These weights are generally inversely proportional to their errors i.e. clocks with higher errors receive lower weights. Different algorithms use different approaches for determining weights. Some rely on error variances [9]. Typically, an administrative weight limit is also put on the weights (like defining a maximum value of the weight that a clock in the ensemble can get) such that the ensemble is not biased to only one type of clock in the ensemble [20].

For this paper, the weights are determined based on the estimation error of each clock. Let A, B, and C represent the estimation errors and W_{HM}, W_{C1}, and W_{C2} represent the weights for the H-maser, cesium 1, and cesium 2, respectively. The weights and the errors are inversely proportional to each other: $W_{HM} \propto 1/A$, $W_{C1} \propto 1/B$, $W_{C2} \propto 1/C$. The sum of the weights equals 1, as shown by Equation (2). An administrative limit of 0.5 is imposed to ensure that the weight of any clock does not exceed 0.5. As an example, Equations (2) and (3) show how the weights for any given clock, e.g., hydrogen maser, are calculated.

$$W = K(W_{HM} + W_{C1} + W_{C2}) = 1 \tag{2}$$

$$K = ABC/(AB + BC + CA) \tag{3}$$

$$W_{HM} = K/A = BC/(AB + BC + CA) \tag{4}$$

The weights for the rest of the clocks can be estimated in a similar manner. The implementation of the algorithm results in the estimates of all clocks in the system with respect to the ensemble time i.e. x_{1e}, x_{2e}, and x_{re} for cesium clock 1, cesium clock 2, and H-maser, respectively.

2.3. Steering Algorithm

As illustrated by the system diagram in Figure 3, the steering process is facilitated by the AOG. This steering device takes in the signal from the H-maser and adjusts it based on the output provided by the time-scale algorithm (x_{re}). For this paper, frequency steering has been implemented, and the steering value s for a given timestamp k is calculated as shown in Equation (5). The process is automatic and is controlled by a script written in Python. The script generates the steering values every two-hours.

$$s(k) = (x_{re}(k) - x_{re}(k-t))/t \tag{5}$$

Enhancements to the steering process can be achieved by incorporating information on the difference between AOG and UTC(SG), as illustrated in the system diagram in Figure 3. This adjustment aims to refine the results obtained from our lab and FP2, and this optimization will be a focus of our upcoming work. In the meantime, the outcomes of AOG after the steering process, utilizing Equation (5), define the physical signal at FP2, denoted as the backup time for Singapore (UTC(FP2)). Subsequently, when this signal was compared to UTC(SG) for validation purposes, almost 82.5% of the differences were within ± 10 ns [23].

3. Data Processing & Methodology

This section describes the different data that have been used for devising the proposed model. Since the data come from two different sources, this section will introduce them separately. An overall methodology that has been implemented to achieve the objective will also be described.

3.1. Receiver Clock Offset w.r.t GPS Time

The time difference between a receiver clock and the satellites for a particular GPS receiver is documented in the Common GPS GLONASS Time Transfer Standard (CGGTTS) files. The Consultative Committee for Time and Frequency (CCTF) has published a set of guidelines based on which the CGGTTS files are created. These guidelines have been compiled with the aim of achieving a system that can transfer time with an accuracy of 1 ns or better. They can be applied to all available global navigation satellite system constellations, such as GPS, GLONASS, Beidou, QZSS, and Galileo. For this paper, we process these files to get information on the receiver clock performance w.r.t the satellite time.

The CGGTTS files record different important data types [24,25]. One of them is Refsys. This is the time difference between the receiver clock and the global navigation satellite system (GNSS) time. If the GPS constellation is considered then Refsys is the difference between the receiver clock and GPS time (GPST). The data available in CGGTTS files are generally 16 min apart and the values are reported in units of 0.1 ns.

We have used data from two different receivers with different grades of clocks; namely Ublox (Thalwil, Switzerland) and Septentrio (Leuven, Belgium) receivers. The Ublox that has been used for this paper is the Ublox from the M8T series [26]. It is a low-cost receiver steered by TCXO (temperature compensated crystal oscillator). However, it is very small in size and thus is portable and can be easily mounted in many locations. The Septentrio receiver, on the other hand, is expensive compared to Ublox. The Septentrio receiver model

PolaRx5TR has been used [27]. It is steered by Rubidium clocks and has the option to be steered by external clocks too.

The same Ublox was deployed at two different sites for data collection. The two sites were at Nanyang Technological University (NTU) and at Stirling Road. Figure 4 shows these two locations. The locations were chosen as per the convenience of the students to be able to record the data without intervention for as long as possible. The Septentrio receiver is located at the backup Time and Frequency Laboratory of the National Metrology Centre (NMC), Singapore (also shown in the Figure 4).

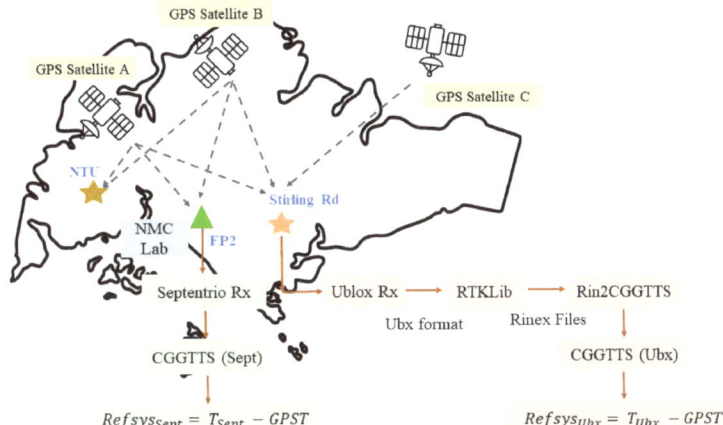

Figure 4. Map of Singapore showing the location of the receivers: Septentrio receiver at Time Lab in FP2 (in green triangle), Ublox receiver at NTU (in gold star), and Ublox receiver at Stirling (in orange star). The diagram also shows the flow of post-processing steps for a Ublox receiver.

Table 1 shows the common days that have been used for processing the results. The data from the NMC lab at Fusionopolis 2 for the corresponding date and time at both the Ublox locations (at NTU and Stirling Road) are used for the analysis.

Table 1. Data used for processing.

Location	Calendar Year	MJD
NTU	3 February 2024 to 5 April 2024	60343–60405
Stirling Rd	5 July 2023 to 1 September 2023	60130–60188

3.1.1. Ublox Data Processing

The Ublox records data in ubx format. It stores information that is useful in deriving the Refsys values. The flowchart in Figure 4 shows the general steps involved in getting the Refsys values from the raw ubx data. The ubx data are first converted into the receiver independent exchange (Rinex) observation and navigation files by using the rtklib software (version 2.4.3), which is freely available for use [28]. The Rinex observation files are then converted to the CGGTTS format by using the rin2cggtts program. The program is distributed by BIPM for non-commercial purposes [24].

3.1.2. Septentrio Data Processing

The Septentrio receiver records the data in standard CGGTTS format. The data are recorded for different constellations with an identifier. Since only GPS constellation is being considered for this paper, only the CGGTTS file with GPS identifier will be processed. For Septentrio receivers, the receiver can be steered to an external reference clock. For the experiments conducted for this paper, the Septentrio receiver will have an external reference, which is the precision timing generated at FP2.

An experiment was run to check on the data from the Septentrio receiver to study its performance in the presence of the external reference. For this experiment, a free-running cesium atomic clock was chosen as the external reference. Figure 5 shows the data with and without the external reference. The red dots are when the Septentrio receiver is running by its internal reference and the blue dots are when the external reference (from the FP2 Lab) is connected to the receiver. Almost the same number of days were considered for the comparison; however, there were some missing data for the case when the receiver is run by its internal clock. This is because there was a period when the instruments were shifted due to the relocation of the labs. The case was soon identified, and the devices were again working fine with no missing data after.

Figure 5 clearly shows that the distribution of the data with time is very much affected by the presence of an external reference. As expected, with the external reference, which is very precise, the data have a lesser range and less variation when compared to the case with the internal clock only. Also, there is a clear separation between the two when the amplitudes of the data are compared. The Refsys values in the presence of the external reference are more than 20 times smaller. For applications where the receiver clock bias errors are critical, like positioning, such differences can cause a huge impact.

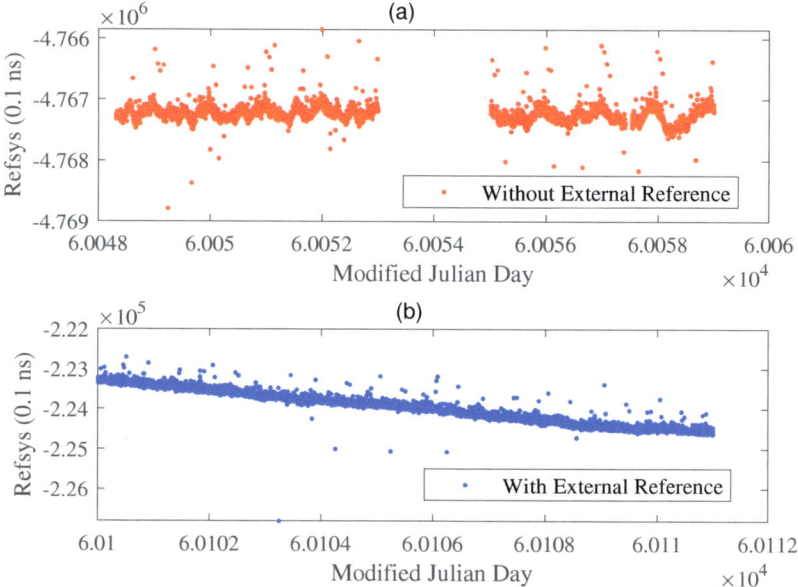

Figure 5. Results (**a**) before and (**b**) after synchronization to the external reference. The legend in each figure represents the condition. The graph with red dots is for "before" and the graph with blue dots is for "after" the synchronization.

3.2. Methodology

This section describes the procedure that is used in deriving the receiver clock differences between the two receivers Septentrio and Ublox. Both the receivers record the differences with respect to the GPST. $Refsys_{Sept}$ denotes the differences between the data from Septentrio and GPST, and similarly, $Refsys_{Ubx}$ denotes the differences between the data from Ublox and GPST. Here, we see that the GPST is the common time reference between the two receivers. If this common GPST is subtracted, we can compute the differences between the Septentrio and the Ublox receiver. This can be done by following either of the two approaches: *common view method* and *all-in-view method* [15,16].

Figure 4 shows that there are two satellites (GPS satellites A and B) that are viewed from both the receivers at that instant, whereas only GPS satellite C is viewed by the Ublox receiver. As the name suggests, if only common satellites (in this case A and B) are used, then it is termed as common view. If the data from all satellites are averaged first and then the difference is calculated, it is termed the all-in-view method. For this paper, the common view method will be implemented. However, there are not many differences between the two methods for the context of this paper as the distance between the two receiver locations is very short. The same satellites are visible almost all the time by both the stations.

4. Results and Analysis

This section will discuss the results processed for the Ublox receivers [located at two locations and the Time Lab at FP2]. A difference-correction algorithm will be introduced to correct the errors of a Ublox receiver. For all the experiments conducted for this section, the Septentrio receiver is connected to the external time reference provided by the FP2 lab (as described in Section 2).

4.1. Performance Comparison between Septentrio and Ublox Receivers

It is expected for the Septentrio receiver to perform better compared to the Ublox receiver. It is interesting to observe how the data for the Ublox fluctuates compared to the Septentrio. This gives us an opportunity to study and correct such fluctuations with reference to the stable output from Septentrio.

Figure 6 shows the respective Refsys values for the receivers at NTU, at Stirling Road, and at FP2. The x-axis of all three plots shows number of days. Each boxplot of one day shows the distribution of Refsys values. The Refsys values here are for all the satellites visible for that particular day. We can note two important variations here. Firstly, the daily variations: as Refsys represents the difference between the receiver clock and the GPST, it must be the same irrespective of the time of the day and the visible satellites. However, we observe that there are variations for each day for both receivers. This might be because of the satellite clock errors. Different satellites have their own clock errors. Thus, the Refsys calculated from Sat 1, for example, might have a difference compared to when calculated from Sat 10. The boxplot shows such discrepancies.

Secondly, a greater variation can be seen in the data when compared across the different days. It can be observed that the data vary quite distinctly with days for these two types of receivers. This is due to the fact that the receiver clock performance changes with time. The clocks have aging that affects their stability and performance. The Refsys data for Septentrio show a linear trend in the performance. Similar behavior is shown by the performance of the atomic clocks. Since the Septentrio receiver is disciplined by precision timing traceable to the cesium standards, it follows a similar pattern. No such linear trend is observed for the case of the Ublox receiver. The Refsys data for both the locations (NTU and Stirling Road) show that the performance is degrading with time but there is no fixed pattern. This was also observed for the case when Septentrio was freely running (without an external time source) in Figure 5. Moreover, the changing weather conditions for different days can add on to such variations.

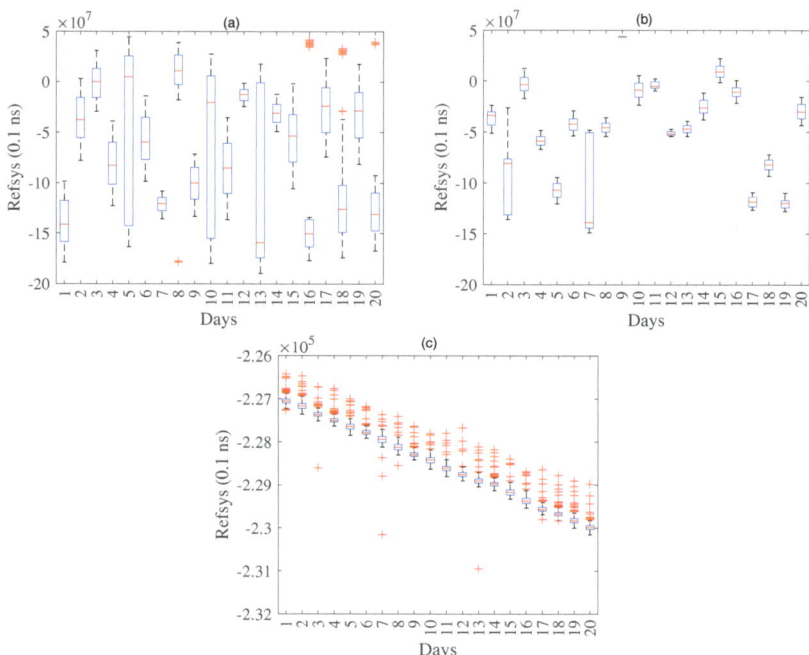

Figure 6. Boxplot to compare the data from Septentrio and Ublox receivers for (**a**) NTU, (**b**) Stirling Rd, and (**c**) Septentrio receiver. The x-axes for all plots are the number of days, as shown by Table 1 and the y-axes for all the plots are the respective Refsys values.

When the absolute amplitudes of these two types of receivers are compared, it shows that the performance of the Ublox receiver is very poor. The values for both the locations (NTU and Stirling Road) are poorer compared to the case when the Septentrio receiver was freely running. These higher errors can lead to greater uncertainty in the results produced by the Ublox receivers. This is one of the reasons that there is a greater variation in vertical height information when calculated using Ublox receivers [2]. This study shows that it is very important to build a method to correct such clock bias errors. The next section will propose the solution.

4.2. Data-Driven Correction Model

As established in the earlier section, the performance of a low-cost GPS receiver like Ublox is highly unstable and has higher clock-bias errors which can be translated into and not limited to longitudinal and latitudinal errors, vertical height errors, and errors in tropospheric delays. This section explores a way to correct the performance of such low-cost GPS receivers.

The GPS receivers have the advantage that they are connected to different receivers remotely via satellites. At a given instant, time differences between different GPS receivers can be compared based on the satellites in view. As explained in Section 3.2, this can be achieved by either the common view method or the all-in-view method. For this paper, the common view method is implemented.

At any given instant, all the Refsys values from two receivers, Septentrio ($Refsys_{Sept}$) and Ublox ($Refsys_{Ubx}$), are recorded. A machine-learning model is implemented that takes the differences between ($Refsys_{Sept}$) and ($Refsys_{Ubx}$) and predicts the correction factor for the Ublox receivers. The same procedure is repeated for the data from two Ublox locations (at NTU and at Stirling Road).

There are different machine-learning models that can be explored for difference prediction. We compared the few well-known ones. Support vector machine (SVM) is a powerful model that has been successfully applied in various real-life applications [29]. However, SVMs have some limitations that may make them less suitable for certain scenarios. One of the main issues with SVMs is their high time and memory training complexities, which depend on the size of the training set [29]. This can be problematic when dealing with large datasets, as it can lead to longer training times. While a k-nearest neighbors algorithm (KNN) is simple and can capture local patterns, it is sensitive to noise and requires careful tuning of the k parameter. In the case of aligning Refsys, where the relationship might not be strictly local, it may not perform optimally [30]. Random forest is also not suitable for this situation because it introduces unnecessary complexity. Random forest could lead to overfitting and is computationally more intensive compared to the task in hand [31]. Therefore, we explore a linear regression model, which can work best for our data.

Linear Regression Model

Linear regression is used in this context because it can provide a quick and relatively efficient solution to correct $Refsys_{ubx}$ with the $Refsys_{sept}$ values. The model works well when there is a linear relationship between the variables, and it converges quickly. Given that the data have a lot of outlier values, a more robust model like ridge regression or Huber regression could have been considered as well. However, in this case, linear regression seems to provide satisfactory results with a lower training time and is able to handle the linear relationship between the two datasets effectively.

Figure 7 shows the flowchart of the program that has been implemented for the paper. Python programming language has been used for this implementation. The data are pre-processed and any outliers are removed. The algorithm then calculates the differences between the $Refsys_{ubx}$ and $Refsys_{sept}$. These differences are the features for this machine-learning algorithm. In the next step, the model is trained with the difference values to predict the correction factor. A total of 80% of the data is split into the training set, and 20% is allocated for the validation (test) set. The linear regression model is then initialized and trained with the training dataset. The trained regressor will then be used to predict the differences for the test data. The predicted data will then be used to correct the test data. In this case, the Ublox receiver's timings will be corrected by adding these predicted differences.

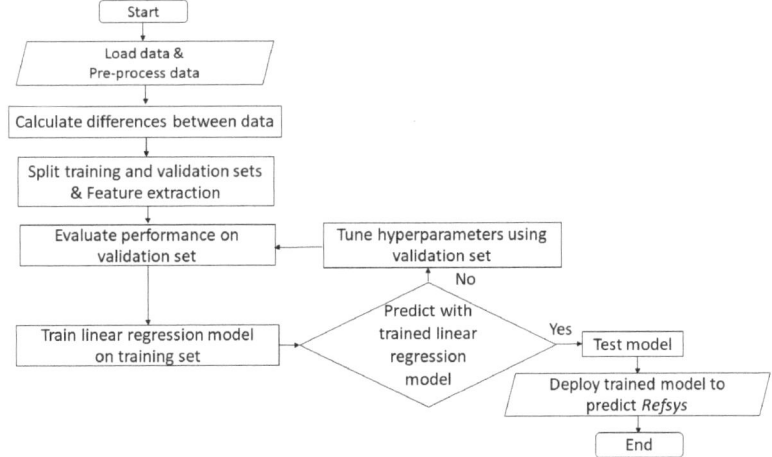

Figure 7. Flowchart of the proposed machine-learning-based correction model.

Here, the hyperparameters for the linear regression model are adjusted primarily through the selection of data splits and reproducibility settings. Specifically, the test size parameter defines the split between training and test data, while random state ensures consistent results across runs. Along with these, grid search and regularization are employed to optimize these parameters, enhancing the model's ability to correct $Refsys_{ubx}$ values and improve alignment with $Refsys_{sept}$ values.

4.3. Performance Comparison

Generally, the performance of a clock is reported in terms of its stability. Allan deviation is the most common form to express such stability. The lower the value of the Allan deviation, the higher the stability. Stable 32 is a well-known software that helps to generate such stability results [32]. This software is used to analyze the results for this paper too.

The stability graphs are plotted for the cases before the application of the correction factor and after the predicted correction factors are applied. In Figure 8, the dashed curves show the stability of the receiver before the application of the correction factor and the solid curves show the stability of the receiver after the application of the correction factor. The red and the blue colors are for the data from NTU and Stirling Road, respectively. It can be noted that the stability of the Ublox for the two locations look very similar for both the cases of before and after the application of the correction factor.

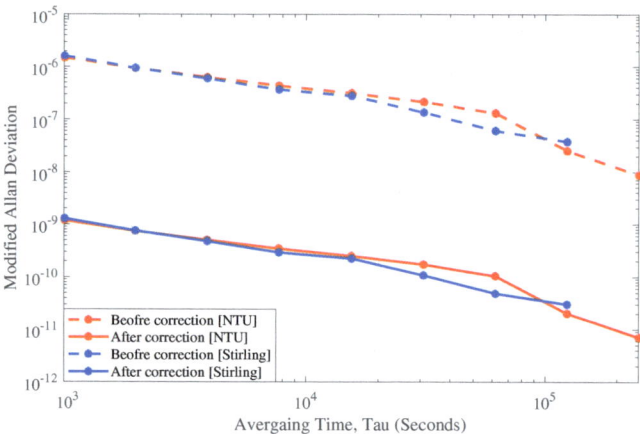

Figure 8. Modified Allan deviation for the $Refsys_{ubx}$ values. The red curve is for before the application of the correction and the blue curve is for after the correction has been applied.

There is a clear shift in the stability curves after the predicted correction factors were applied. The stability is improved for all the averaging times. This shows that the linear-regression-based model is able to improve the performance of a low-cost oscillator. For an averaging time of 1 day (x-axis reading of 86,400 s), the stability is improved by 10^3 times. This huge improvement in the stability validates that a simple data-driven algorithm-based steering is very much effective in correcting the performance of a low-cost oscillator.

5. Conclusions and Future Work

This paper identifies the significance of improving the stability of a low-cost GPS receiver. An improved low-cost receiver has a potential to provide location information as precisely and accurately as high-cost receivers. Thus, the spatial coverage could be increased by deploying a number of low-cost receivers. This leads to a better determination of location. The applications of a low-cost GPS receiver with improved stability are not only limited to positioning but the receiver could also be used for weather-related studies.

To achieve this, the paper proposed a machine-learning algorithm to predict the time differences between a low-cost GPS receiver and a higher-end receiver. The predicted differences were then used to correct the errors associated with the low-cost receiver. This then improved the stability of the receiver. Results show that for an averaging time of 1 day, the stability is improved by almost 10^3 times.

Moreover, the proposed methodology can extend its application in remote calibration of atomic clocks. Traditionally, the atomic clocks are transported to the calibration center, but with the proposed methodology, the clock can be calibrated remotely via GPS satellites. This saves both cost and time for the companies that need the calibration services.

In future work, the Ublox data, after being corrected, will be used in deriving location information and an improvement in the accuracy of the navigation will be shown. Also, the prediction of the differences will be done for different time steps in the future (say 6 h advance in time) and the effects of it will be studied.

Author Contributions: Conceptualization, S.M.; methodology, S.S. and S.M.; software, S.S.; validation, S.M., Y.S.M. and Y.C.T.; formal analysis, S.M. and Y.S.M.; investigation, S.M., S.S. and Y.C.T.; resources, Y.S.M.; writing—original draft preparation, S.M. and S.S.; writing—review and editing, S.M., Y.S.M. and Y.C.T.; visualization, S.M. and Y.S.M.; supervision, S.M. and Y.S.M.; project administration, S.M.; funding acquisition, S.M. and Y.S.M. All authors have read and agreed to the published version of the manuscript.

Funding: This research was funded by the Agency for Science, Technology and Research (A*STAR) under Project No. 222D800033 [Career Development Fund], and the National Research Foundation, Singapore and A*STAR under its Quantum Engineering Programme (NRF2021-QEP2-01-P03).

Data Availability Statement: The data collected for this research involve the time and frequency data from the cesium clocks of NMC, which are not allowed to be shared publicly.

Conflicts of Interest: The authors declare no conflicts of interest.

References

1. Jiménez-Martínez, M.J.; Farjas-Abadia, M.; Quesada-Olmo, N. An Approach to Improving GNSS Positioning Accuracy Using Several GNSS Devices. *Remote Sens.* **2021**, *13*, 1149. [CrossRef]
2. Misra, P.; Pratt, M.; Bruke, B.; Ferrantio, R. Adaptive modeling of receiver clock for meter-level DGPS vertical positioning. In Proceedings of the 8th International Technical Meeting of the Satellite Division of the Institute of Navigation (ION GPS 1995), Palm Springs, CA, USA, 12–15 September 1995; pp. 1127–1135.
3. Manandhar, S.; Meng, Y.S. Improvement in Vertical Positioning with GPS Receiver Clock Steered by Precise Time Reference. In Proceedings of the 2021 IEEE USNC-URSI Radio Science Meeting (Joint with AP-S Symposium), Singapore, 4–10 September 2021; pp. 82–83.
4. Niu, Z.; Zhao, X.; Sun, J.; Tao, L.; Zhu, B. A Continuous Positioning Algorithm Based on RTK and VI-SLAM with Smartphones. *IEEE Access* **2020**, *8*, 185638–185650. [CrossRef]
5. Ku, D.Y.; Patel, A. Kinematic State Estimation Using Multiple DGPS/MEMS-IMU Sensors. *IEEE Sens. Lett.* **2020**, *4*, 1–4. [CrossRef]
6. Jones, R.H.; Tryon, P.V. Estimating Time from Atomic Clocks. *J. Res. Natl. Bur. Stand.* **1983**, *88*, 17. [CrossRef] [PubMed]
7. Arias, F.; Jiang, Z.; Lewandowski, W.; Petit, G. BIPM comparison of time transfer techniques. In Proceedings of the 2005 IEEE International Frequency Control Symposium and Exposition, Vancouver, BC, Canada, 29–31 August 2005.
8. BIPM Technical Services: Time Metrology. Available online: https://www.bipm.org/en/time-metrology (accessed on 30 June 2024).
9. López-Romero, J.M.; Díaz-Muñoz, N. Progress in the generation of the UTC(CNM) in terms of a virtual clock. *Metrologia* **2008**, *45*, S59. [CrossRef]
10. Patrizia, T.; Claudine, T. Comparative Study of Time Scale Algorithms. *Metrologia* **2005**, *28*, 57.
11. Zhao, S.; Dong, S.; Qu, L.; Yuan, H.; Bai, S.; Wu, W.; Wang, X.; Yin, D. A new steering strategy for UTC(NTSC) based on hydrogen maser. In Proceedings of the IEEE International Frequency Control Symposium, IFCS, New Orleans, LA, USA, 9–12 May 2016.
12. Matsakis, D.; Defraigne, P.; Banerjee, P. Precise Time and Frequency Transfer. *Radio Sci. Bull.* **2014**, *351*, 29–44.
13. Lewandowski, W.; Azoubib, J.; Klepczynski, W.J. GPS: Primary tool for time transfer. *Proc. IEEE* **1999**, *87*, 163–172. [CrossRef]
14. Lee, S.W.; Lee, C.B.; Yang, S.H. A New Approach for Steering UTC(KRIS). *IEEE Trans. Instrum. Meas.* **2009**, *58*, 1247–1251.
15. Wang, J.L.; Huang, S.Y.; Liao, C.S. Time and frequency transfer system using GNSS receiver. *Radio Sci.* **2014**, *49*, 1171–1182. [CrossRef]
16. Weiss, M.A.; Petit, G.; Jiang, Z. A comparison of GPS common-view time transfer to all-in-view. In Proceedings of the 2005 IEEE International Frequency Control Symposium and Exposition, Vancouver, BC, Canada, 29–31 August 2005.

17. Manandhar, S.; Lee, Y.H.; Meng, Y.S.; Yuan, F.; Ong, J.T. GPS-Derived PWV for Rainfall Nowcasting in Tropical Region. *IEEE Trans. Geosci. Remote Sens.* **2018**, *8*, 4835–4844. [CrossRef]
18. Borregaard, J.; Sørensen, A.S. Efficient Atomic Clocks Operated with Several Atomic Ensembles. *Phys. Rev. Lett.* **2013**, *111*, 090802. [CrossRef] [PubMed]
19. Weis, M.; Weissert, T. A time-scale algorithm for post-processing: AT1 plus frequency variance. In Proceedings of the Conference on Precision Electromagnetic Measurements, Ottawa, ON, Canada, 11–14 June 1990.
20. Levine, J. Realizing UTC(NIST) at a remote location. *Metrologia* **2008**, *45*, S23–S33. [CrossRef]
21. Song, H.; Dong, S.; Qu, L.; Wang, X.; Guo, D. A robust Kalman filter time scale algorithm with data anomaly. *J. Instrum.* **2021**, *16*, P06032. [CrossRef]
22. Manandhar, S.; Meng, Y.S. Study on the Effect of using Different Weighting Techniques in a Time Scale Algorithm to Generate an Ensemble Time. In Proceedings of the 3rd URSI Atlantic and Asia Pacific Radio Science Meeting (AT-AP-RASC), Gran Canaria, Spain, 29 May–3 June 2022; pp. 1–4.
23. Manandhar, S.; Chai, J.Z.; Meng, Y.S.; Tan, Y.C. Performance Comparison of AT1 Algorithm for a Smaller Ensemble of Atomic Clocks. In Proceedings of the URSI Atlantic and Asia Pacific Radio Science Meeting (AT-AP-RASC), Gran Canaria, Spain, 19–24 May 2024.
24. Defraigne, P.; Petit, G. CGGTTS- Version 2E: An extended standard for GNSS Time Transfer. *Metrologia* **2015**, *52*, G1. [CrossRef]
25. CGGTTS Data Format. Available online: https://www.cnmoc.usff.navy.mil/Our-Commands/United-States-Naval-Observatory/Precise-Time-Department/Global-Positioning-System/GPS-Timing-Data-and-Information/ (accessed on 30 June 2024).
26. UBLOX:NEO/LEA-M8T Series. Available online: https://www.u-blox.com/en/product/neolea-m8t-series (accessed on 30 June 2024).
27. Septentrio PolaRx5TR. Available online: https://www.septentrio.com/en/products/gps/gnss-reference-receivers/polarx-5tr (accessed on 30 June 2024).
28. RTKLIB: An Open Source Program Package for GNSS Positioning- Version 2.4.3. Available online: https://www.rtklib.com/ (accessed on 30 June 2024).
29. Nalepa, J.; Kawulok, M. Selecting training sets for support vector machines: A review. *Artif. Intell. Rev.* **2019**, *52*, 857–900. [CrossRef]
30. Zeniarja, J.; Ukhifahdhina, A.; Salam, A. Diagnosis of heart disease using k-nearest neighbor method based on forward selection. *J. Appl. Intell. Syst.* **2020**, *4*, 39–47. [CrossRef]
31. Assuncao, J.; Fernandes, P.; Lopes, L.; Normey, S. Distributed stochastic aware random forests—Efficient data mining for big data. In Proceedings of the IEEE International Congress on Big Data, Santa Clara, CA, USA, 6–9 October 2013.
32. Stable32—Version 1.62. Available online: http://www.stable32.com/ (accessed on 30 June 2024).

Disclaimer/Publisher's Note: The statements, opinions and data contained in all publications are solely those of the individual author(s) and contributor(s) and not of MDPI and/or the editor(s). MDPI and/or the editor(s) disclaim responsibility for any injury to people or property resulting from any ideas, methods, instructions or products referred to in the content.

Blockchain-Based Control Plane Attack Detection Mechanisms for Multi-Controller Software-Defined Networks

Abrar Alkhamisi [1,*], Iyad Katib [1] and Seyed M. Buhari [2]

1 King Abdulaziz University, Jeddah 21589, Saudi Arabia; iakatib@kau.edu.sa
2 Universitiy Teknologi Brunei, Bandar Seri Begawan BE1410, Brunei; ismail.buhari@utb.edu.bn
* Correspondence: aalkhamisi0034@stu.kau.edu.sa

Abstract: A Multi-Controller Software-Defined Network (MC-SDN) is a revolutionary concept comprising multiple controllers and switches separated using programmable features, enhancing network availability, management, scalability, and performance. The MC-SDN is a potential choice for managing large, heterogeneous, complex industrial networks. Despite the rich operational flexibility of MC-SDN, it is imperative to protect the network deployment with proper protection against potential vulnerabilities that lead to misuse and malicious activities on the MC-SDN structure. The security holes in the MC-SDN structure significantly impact network survivability and performance efficiency. Hence, detecting MC-SDN security attacks is crucial to improving network performance. Accordingly, this work intended to design blockchain-based controller security (BCS) that exploits the advantages of immutable and distributed ledger technology among multiple controllers and securely manages the controller communications against various attacks. Thereby, it enables the controllers to maintain consistent network view and accurate flow tables among themselves and also neglects the controller failure issues. Finally, the experimental results of the proposed BCS approach demonstrated superior performance under various scenarios, such as attack detection, number of attackers, number of controllers, and number of compromised controllers, by applying different performance metrics.

Keywords: multi-controller; software defined networks; security attacks; blockchain technology; attack detection

1. Introduction

In the digital world, MC-SDN is emerging as a promising network paradigm that offers flexibility to manage the network infrastructure by clearly decoupling the data and control planes and managing the set of switches in a domain with multiple controllers [1]. The robust MC-SDN design provides a powerful architecture that offers scalability, flexibility, and failure resilience, making it a potential choice for large and complex network environments [2]. In the MC-SDN structure, each controller is responsible for managing a domain [3]. The capabilities of MC-SDN controllers are criticized for network availability, performance, and scalability. Thus, enabling multiple controllers is imperative for managing large-scale networks to improve the abovementioned issues, even though it increases network complexity and management [4]. Albeit, owing to the decoupling of planes with multi-controller structure, the MC-SDN applications are increasing day by day, and it is vulnerable to several types of attacks, such as Denial-of-Service (DoS), Man-in-the-middle, Flooding, and False Injection. Thus, paying attention to technological vulnerability challenges is paramount to applying proper solution strategies that effectively protect practical MC-SDN-based deployments [5,6]. In MC-SDN deployment, the distributed controller design spans several controllers to achieve scalability and attack resiliency. In this context, a compromised controller may greatly enhance the risk level of multiple controllers and switches. Hence, detecting such a vulnerable controller is crucial to protect the MC-SDN performance against various security attacks.

Blockchain is a powerful technology that detects the different MC-SDN attacks and prevents the controllers and switches from poor performance activities. In general, blockchain-based security models are highly influential solutions used to establish secure communication among controllers with immutable ledger data with different consensus, even in the presence of attackers [7–9]. However, an ingenious attacker can manipulate the immutable ledgers by getting hash knowledge series using sophisticated methods. Therefore, it is crucial to rate the blockchain controllers with a reward system to optimize the attack detection efficiency.

Therefore, the main research goal of the proposed BCS is to utilize the advantages of key enabling technologies such as blockchain to improve the security level of MC-SDN against various attacks in the control plane.

The main contributions of the proposed work are given as follows:

- The primary intention of the work is to maximize the MC-SDN security and efficiency against various attacks by utilizing the blockchain;
- The BCS improves the consistency and communication security among multiple controllers by incorporating reshaped Practical Byzantine Fault Tolerance (rPBFT) with a digit-coin assignment system. The BCS can also determine the malicious controllers affected by flow injection and man-in-the-middle attacks by providing equal priority to the genuine miners, resulting in high MC-SDN security;
- Finally, the experimental results demonstrate the superiority of the proposed BCS through MiniNet simulation. The simulation results are obtained in terms of diverse performance metrics.

The remaining part of the paper is organized as follows. Section 2 surveys the works related to controller security models of SDN and MC-SDNs. A detailed description of BCS design is provided in Section 3. Section 4 explains BCS experimental evaluation. Section 5 demonstrates the results of BCS. Finally, Section 6 concludes the paper.

2. Related Works

Recently, several works have been developed to provide SDN security using blockchain technology and have listed the advantages and limitations of the SDN strategies, especially from the security perspective, including DoS and illegal intrusion attacks on SDN control nodes. In [10], the flow-based traffic forwarding approach analyzes the security issues and lists possible loopholes in the SDN-blockchain environment, such as spoofing attacks, DoS attacks, hijacking attacks, latency issues, and privacy issues. This section reviews SDN security provisioning via blockchain-technology-based SDN security models.

A comprehensive review of security architecture platforms using SDN and blockchain technology is provided in [11]. Moreover, this study discusses the influence of blockchain technologies in protecting and securing the SDN architecture from the perspective of integrity, confidentiality, security, and availability. Blockchain-based lightweight security architecture (Bloc-Sec) [12] applies the Blake-256 hashing algorithm to authenticate all the IoT devices in the blockchain server. It applies the cuttlefish optimization algorithm to select the optimal Virtual Network Function (VNF). It securely stores the hashed flow rules in the VNF by invoking blockchain technology. Finally, the Bloc-Sec architecture employs the spiking dual fuzzy neural networks to leverage the packet classification through the packet header and content inspections. Some of the secure SDN architecture is designed only with specific DoS attacks in SDN, but still lacks data integrity-related attacks [13,14].

The SDN controller is responsible for dividing the data and control plane and controlling the SDN network activities without knowing the underlying structure. However, detecting malicious nodes or devices and securing SDN communication is prominent because it is vulnerable to insider threats. A hybrid network architecture [15] leverages the advantages of SDN and blockchain technology for the smart city. It comprises two parts, the core and edge networks, which inherit the power of the centralized and distributed network architectures. Moreover, it ensures security and privacy by modeling the Proof-of-Work (PoW) scheme without compromising the efficiency of the security mechanism. Blockchain applications in smart communities were briefly studied in [16], which discussed the various secure transaction process models, communication infrastructure, and applications. However, implementing blockchain technology across multiple controllers and enabling inter and intra-controller communication across controllers are still not effectively solved.

The framework proposed in [17] combines the advantages of trust management and blockchain technology. Trust management and blockchain technology estimate the trust value for each node and establish the communication without a trusted party, respectively. It helps in providing data integrity to the communication. However, it incurs communication delays and unnecessary energy consumption. In addition, the combined framework of trust and blockchain technology tends to a communication workload due to modeling the security mechanism on all the network nodes and enabling the storage of all the data flow entries. Most SDN approaches deploy a single controller to ensure security for SDN. If any problem occurs with a single controller, the overall functionality of the SDN is degraded.

Most of the attackers mainly target the functionalities of the controller. Therefore, the security of the controller plays an important role in the success of SDNs. To solve those issues, a security model using blockchain technology was suggested by [18], which attempts to maintain consistency among instances of the SDN controller. It also executes the Open DayLight controller operational flow. Many works have suggested utilizing the advantages of blockchain entirely for securing the SDN [17–19]. The work in [20] addresses the security and privacy constraints in the vehicular IoT environment and transportation system in SDN-enabled 5G-VANET. It presents the scheduling procedures in the blockchain-based security model. Designing the blockchain-based security framework ensures secure vehicular IoT services with the advantage of the immutable and decentralized characteristics of the blockchain. The main problem with blockchain-based SDN security schemes is the unnecessary delay in the overall functionality.

In a multi-controller SDN structure, it is crucial to maintain a consistent network view among all controllers for performance enhancement. To accomplish the aim, Smart Block-SDN [21] identifies and isolates the rouge switches to provide secure network communication, guaranteeing efficient cluster-head selection. Moreover, it maintains the consistent tracking of the flow rules in the switches within the controller cluster through its layered architecture. The blockchain-based security framework for NorthBound Interface (BC-NBI) in [22] utilizes blockchain security features and automatically verifies the credentials of the controller and application through token-based authentication. The work in [23] presents a novel secure blockchain-enabled multi-controller Rule Enforcement Verification (BlockREV) for SDNs. It exploits the blockchain architecture to verify rule enforcements over a multi-controller blockchain environment. It ensures correctness in cross-domain forwarding of multi-controllers in SDN. It uses the most significant cryptographic primitives and address-based signature aggregation model to perform rule enforcement verification. Consequently, the work in [24] presents an Intelligent blockchain-based SDN (IB-SDN) security architecture to attain a global trust model among multiple domain controllers. Hence, the controllers upload the topological abstractions to the blockchain and manage it through smart contracts.

The design of lightweight blockchain architecture secures the application controller interface and prevents malicious activities with reduced packet overhead and processing time. The work in [25] presents a blockchain-enabled SDN framework to secure transactions that uses SDN and Network Function Virtualization against man-in-the-middle attacks. Albeit, the lightweight blockchain security models are prone to ingenious attack activities in massive heterogeneous SDN-based networks. The Blockchain-Based Multi Controller architecture for secure SDN (BMC-SDN) in [26] ensures security against multi-controller SDN control-plane attacks. Each SDN domain is managed by one master controller that communicates through blockchain with the masters of the other domains. The work in [27] includes blockchain-based architecture and intent-driven mechanisms to implement Intent-driven security SDNs (IS2N). Specifically, it presents a novel four-layer architecture of the IS2N with security capabilities. Furthermore, the work in [28] introduces blockchain-based flow control consistency (B2-C2) for multi-controller SDNs. It incorporates blockchain and digital signatures into SDN infrastructure to assure consistency of flow control within MC-SDN. It can provide security against compromised controllers and switches, simultaneously maintaining a consistent network view among controllers. However, Ref. [28] failed to ensure entire network security.

Although the multi-controller-based SDN effectively overcomes the single point of failure issues, there are three major concerns, such as controller coordination, network view consistency, and security are still not addressed by the conventional multi-controller SDN strategies. Sudden changes in the controller state significantly impact the new configuration of flow tables at other controllers in the MC-SDN structure. Inconsistencies among multiple controllers can shrink the performance of the infrastructure layer routing process. Also, the decentralized nature of MC-SDNs is vulnerable to different types of security attacks, that are false injection, a man in the middle, and compromised controllers. Hence, efficient security is needed to improve the performance of multi-controller SDNs ultimately. The BMC-SDN [26] effectively addresses the issues mentioned above by employing blockchain technology among the redundant controllers in a domain. However, in a scenario where multiple controllers are compromised, relying only on the monitored data from redundant controllers within a domain is not sufficient for robust decision-making. Therefore, a novel security strategy is needed to solve the compromised controller effectively, and also inconsistent network view problems. The main objective of the BCS is to ensure high security against such attacks when multiple controllers are compromised through blockchain's advantage in both inter and intra controllers while maintaining the flow consistency at each controller. Table 1 compares various blockchain-enabled SDN security solutions with their limitations.

Table 1. Comparison of blockchain-based SDN security models.

Ref.	Work	Controller	Algorithms	Limitations
[18]	Security model using blockchain technology	Single	Secure hashing	High Delay and not suitable for controller-compromised attacks
[21]	Smartblock-SDN	single	Clustering and distributed flow verification	Not suitable for real-world large-sized networks
[22]	BCNBI	Single	Fine-grained access control with trust evaluation	Not adaptable to distributed controller environment
[23]	BlockREV	Multi	The address-based aggregate signature scheme	High computation cost and high overhead
[24]	IB-SDN	Multi	Local and Global Reputation, voting mechanism	High complexity and not suitable for a compromised controller environment
[25]	Blockchain-enabled SDN Framework	Single	Controller authentication strategy	Lacks to ensure entire network security
[26]	BMC-SDN	Multi	Reputation mechanism	Accomplish poor performance in more than one compromised controller
[27]	IS2N	Multi	Security store network-level snapshots	High complexity
[28]	B2-C2	Multi	Blockchain and digital signature	High computation cost and high overhead

3. The Proposed Work

Although the conventional works utilize the MC-SDN structure to handle the single point of failure issues effectively, they may suffer due to inconsistent network view and district security attacks. Notably, when multiple numbers of controllers are compromised, there is a chance that an attacker can control a specific domain, which is a more serious problem in the MC-SDN structure. The existing BMC-SDN utilizes a redundant controller structure with a blockchain advantage to solve such issues [26]. However, if an attacker compromises both the main and redundant controller of a domain to enhance its attack capabilities, the security of the entire network will be compromised. There is no effective existing solution, including BMC-SDN, to address multiple numbers of compromised controllers within a domain. Hence, it is crucial for a novel security solution to determine MC-SDN attacks even if the controllers of a domain have been compromised while maintaining a consistent network at each controller. Therefore, the proposed BCS aims to determine multiple MC-SDN security attacks with blockchain technologies under compromised controllers of a single domain. The features of blockchain technology make it a promising security strategy without sacrificing the performance level. The security design of BCS is shown in Figure 1. The BCS protects the controller communication against false injection, man-in-the-middle, and controller compromisation attacks by enabling blockchain-based digital reputation.

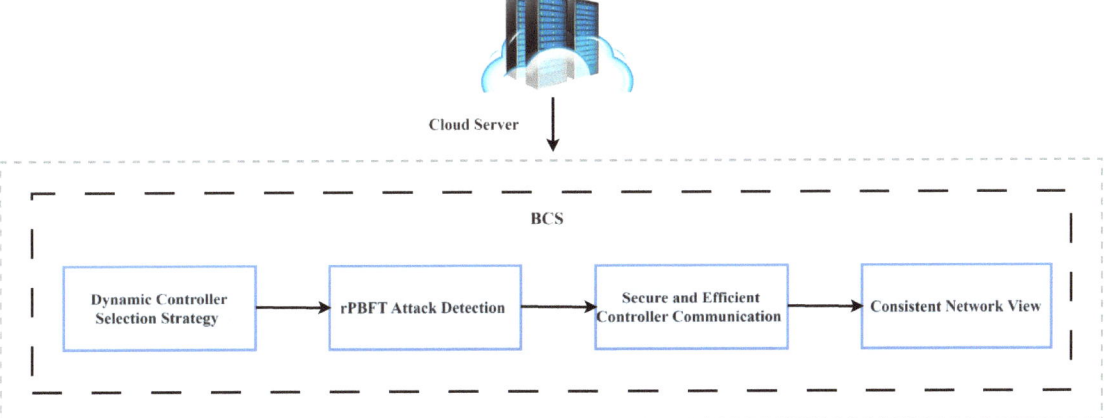

Figure 1. Overview of proposed BCS.

In this type, the BCS assigns the most suitable intra and inter-controllers to the main controller based on the digital reputation value estimated based on the sub-controller local reputation and blockchain history-based reputation. The tamper-resistance property of blockchain significantly improves the security and intra and inter-controller communication efficiency of MC-SDN against compromisation, false-injection, and man-in-the-middle attacks. The BCS estimates a reputation value for the available controllers in the intra and inter-controller domain and selects the most suitable sub-controllers to monitor the behaviors of the main controller. As described in work [26], the proposed BCS constructs the multi-controller architecture. The proposed BCS differs from BMC-SDN [26] by assigning inter and intra-redundant controllers to the main controller. Thus, it effectively handles the main controller failure issues without increasing the burden of redundant controllers and cost. In the proposed BCS, the same sub-domain has multiple controllers that are not always active. Hence, only one main controller is active at a time, and the others only monitor the main controller activity at the same time. The main controller role is rotated among the intra-sub controllers based on network traffic over a particular period to handle the massive network data efficiently.

3.1. Control Plane Attack Model

Different types of threats are possible in a multi-controller SDN environment. The false injection, man-in-the-middle, and DoS are prominent as they damage the entire controller performance. For instance, any change in the state controller significantly affects the performance of other controllers, resulting in in-consisting network view and SDN failures. The attack model for the MC-SDN control layer is shown in Figure 2.

- False Injection: An attacker spoofs the communication model of the controllers and injects false flow data, aiming to reduce the performance of the controller;
- Man-in-the-Middle: Attackers secretly intercept and relay the controller communications by exploiting any one of the methods. It leads to routing errors and creates routing loops, firewall leakages, and ineffective routing decisions;
- Compromised Controllers: An attacker compromises the controllers to obtain different topological views.

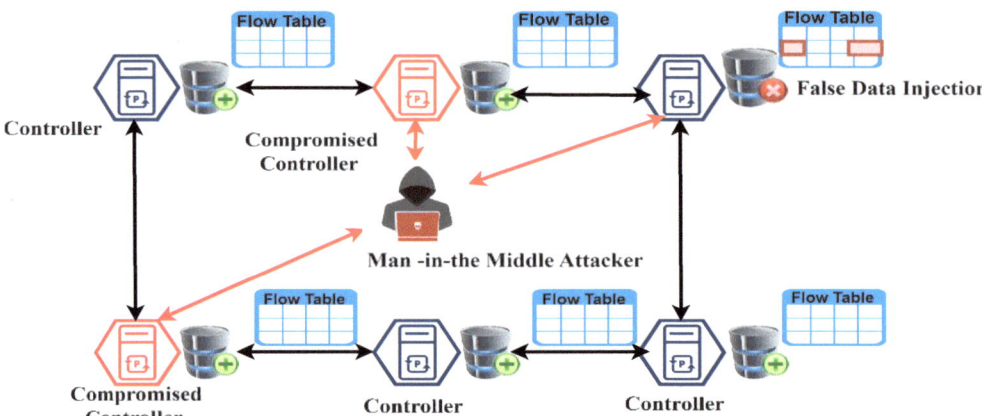

Figure 2. Attack model for the MC-SDN control layer.

3.2. Blockchain-Based Controller Security

The multi-controller SDN comprises several controllers that can work together to efficiently manage the traffic flow with a consistent network view over large-scale dynamic networks [26]. Sudden changes in the controller states should affect the performance of the new configuration flow of other controllers in the network, resulting in poor network performance. Also, the multi-controller SDNs are vulnerable to attacks such as false injection, a man in the middle, and compromised controllers. Thus, it ultimately impacts the entire performance of multi-controller SDN. Hence, efficient security is needed to protect the controllers against attacks and single-controller failure. Blockchain technology has proved as a promising security solution to mitigate MC-SDN security attacks, especially man-in-the-middle. Thus, it ultimately impacts the performance of multi-controller SDN. Detecting and mitigating the effects of attacks in an MC-SDN environment is crucial to maintaining the security and integrity of the multiple controllers. Also, efficient security is needed to protect the controllers against attacks and single-controller failure. To rectify the abovementioned issues and improve the security of multi-controller SDNs, this work intends to present a blockchain-enabled control plane security strategy named BCS. The main intention of the proposed BCS is to deliver distributed decentralized attack detection, providing strong security against multi-controller SDN systems by integrating the advantages of blockchain technology. The BCS design is explained in the following Figure 3, and it includes three mechanisms for the security of the multi-controller communication, the proposed model considers the work in [26] as a base model. Instead of assigning redundant controllers from the available controllers such as [26], the proposed BCS includes two redundant sub-controllers to the corresponding domain. Thus, it effectively handles the controller failure issues due to high load and optimizes the resource consumption among the controller without increasing the overhead.

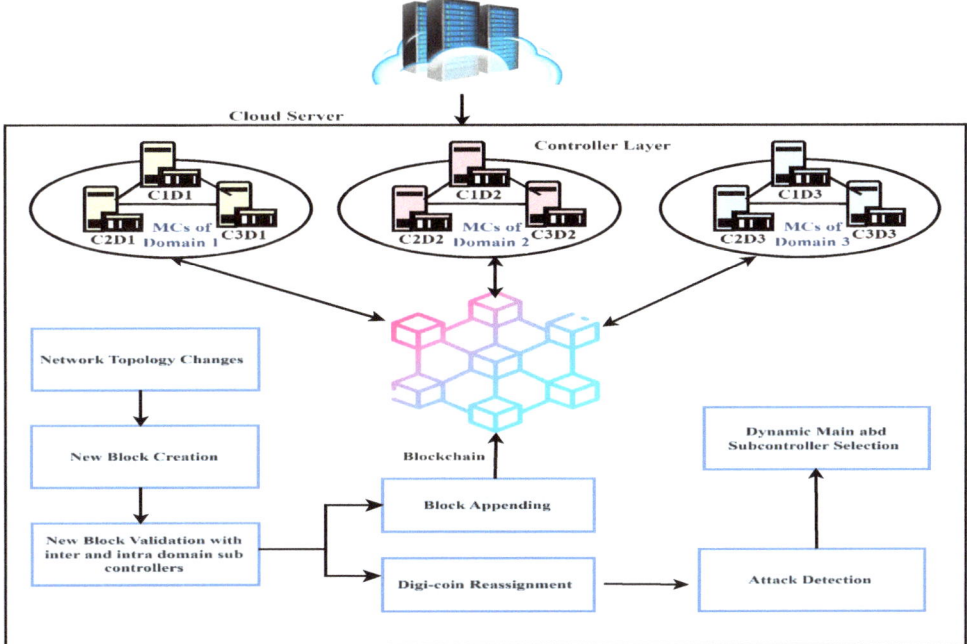

Figure 3. Design process of BCS for MC-SDN.

The blockchain system in BCS can yield security to intra and inter-controller communications and assist in maintaining a consistent network view at all controllers. More precisely, the multiple controllers in BCS architecture are becoming members of the blockchain network and establishing secure communication against attacks through the block creation and validation of immutable blockchain ledgers. The BCS includes three main mechanisms: digit-coin assignment, block validation with reputed rPBFT, and attack detection.

3.2.1. Digit-Coin Assignment in BCS

In a multi-controller SDN structure, the controllers establish communication whenever they observe changes in the network topology. In BCS, each controller receives digital coins based on the intra and inter-sub-controller monitoring data with blockchain after accomplishing topological changes. The BCS estimates the blockchain digit coins of main controllers, as demonstrated in Figure 4, with the assistance of the monitored data of both intra and inter-domain sub-controllers.

The BCS permits the nodes with high digit-coin to read and write the permissions of the proposed blockchain. During network initialization, each controller is considered a genuine node. After some rounds, the Genuity of the controllers is revised based on the digit-coin value. Thus, the proposed BCS can rectify the effects of compromised controllers in consensus participation. The main and sub-controllers of each domain are depicted in various colors. As shown in Figure 4, the controller C1D2 incurs flow changes and needs to update the corresponding changes to the main controllers C1D1 and C1D3 of other domains. Therefore, it inaugurates the digit-coin assignment system in which the monitored data of intra and inter-controllers are jointly considered with the blockchain historical data. The digit-coin system estimates the digit-coin of C1D2 (DC_{C1D2}) using Equation (1).

$$DC_{C1D2} = (\alpha \times (D_{C2D2} + D_{C2D2}))(\beta \times (D_{C1D1} + D_{C1D3}))(\gamma \times D_B) \qquad (1)$$

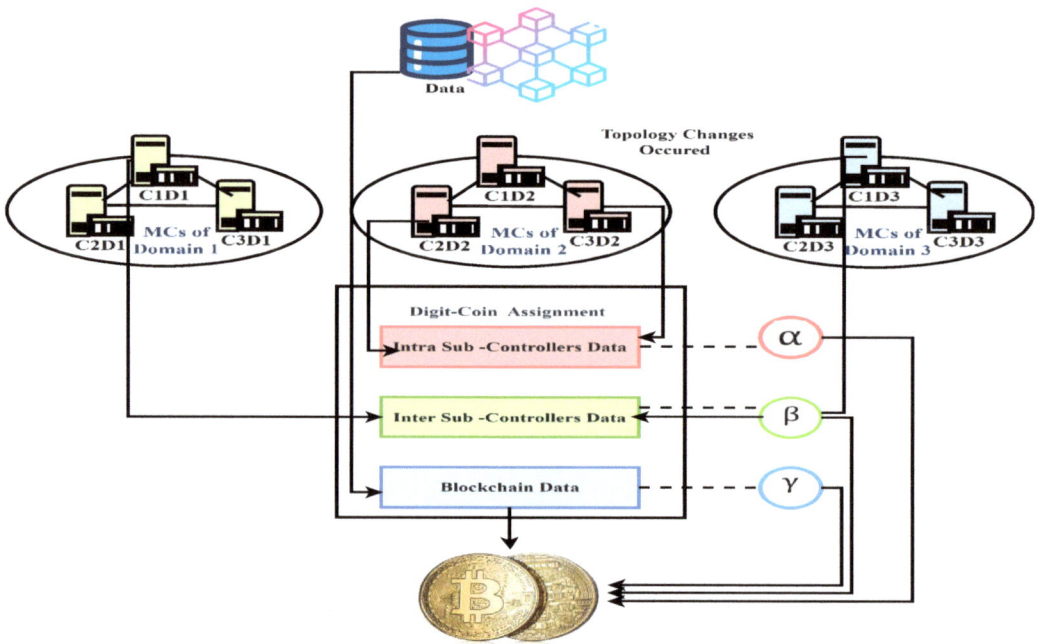

Figure 4. Digit-coin assignment of BCS.

In Equation (1), the factors α, β, and γ are weighting values of intra-sub-controller locally observed data. $(D_{C2D2} + D_{C2D2})$, inter sub-controller locally observed data $(D_{C1D1} + D_{C1D3})$, and blockchain historical data (D_B). The summation value of weighting factors α, β, and γ equals 1. The BCS assigns dynamic weighting values between 0 to 1 based on the behavior of the intra and inter-controllers in previous communications. Moreover, the BCS provides the DC_{C1D2} to rPBFT consensus to validate its newly created block. Consequently, the BCS initiates the block validation using the reputed rPBFT process. The digit-coin assignment process is explained in the following Algorithm 1.

Algorithm 1 Digit-Coin-Assignment Process.

1: **Input:** Contract balance in terms of digit-coin
2: **Output:** Assign digit coins to controllers
3: **BCS do**
4:         Initiate the digit-coin Assignment process
5:         Verifies the contract balance
6: **if** the Contract does not have sufficient balance **then**
7:         Insufficient balance
8: **else**
9:         Check the Controller Address
10:     **if** the Controller Address is not valid **then**
11:         Invalid Address
12:     **else**
13:         Valid Address
14:         Assign Digit-coins Successfully

3.2.2. Block Validation with Reputed rPBFT

In the proposed BCS, the intra and inter-domain sub-controllers perform the consensus. These controllers are called miners and are responsible for blocking validation before appending. The proposed BCS exploits the permissioned blockchain model with rPBFT to accomplish secure communication with minimum consensus delay among the controllers. Compared with other blockchain models such as public and permissionless, the customized consensus property and use case flexibility of permissioned blockchain make it highly adaptable to the MC-SDN environment. Initially, the controllers obtain a local topology view from their corresponding domain. By considering the opinions of optimally selected sub-controllers in block validation, the BCS neglects the contributions of attacks such as false injection, man-in-the-middle, and controller compromise in block creation, resulting in high accuracy of network consistent view. The proposed rPBFT is highly fit for a permissioned blockchain environment, compared to conventional PBFT, PoW, and PoS consensus mechanisms, as it assures fairness in consensus by providing equal chances to all benign miners during block generation.

The rPBFT utilizes a digit-coin assignment system to accomplish consensus fairness in the network. The three-stage process of rPBFT is pre-prepare, prepare, and respond. Most existing PBFT voting mechanisms only consider agreement and disagreement, which is insufficient for a practical MC-SDN environment. Therefore, the rPBFT utilizes fuzzy sets to optimize the digit-coin assignment process [29]. The fuzzy sets refer to the MC-SDN as U, then map the U to the fuzzy set interval [0, 1]. The fuzzy set is denoted as S. The digit-coin values of the controllers involved in block generation are evaluated based on the local monitoring information updated by the sub-controllers. Hence, all communication is performed via blockchain, which comprises immutable ledger technology. The fuzzy score of the main controller FS_{C1D2} is estimated using Equation (2).

$$FS_{C1D2} = [H_{SC}(u),\ 1 - M_{SC}(u)] \qquad (2)$$

In the above-shown equation, the terms $H_{SC}(u)$ and $M_{SC}(u)$ represents the honest score level and malicious score level of digit-coins of the controller FS_{C1D2} respectively. The consensus process of rPBFT is shown in Figure 5. By converting the monitor values of sub-controllers as digit-coin scores in controller block validation, the rPBFT maximizes the consensus efficiency and improves the security level of the control layer in the BCS model.

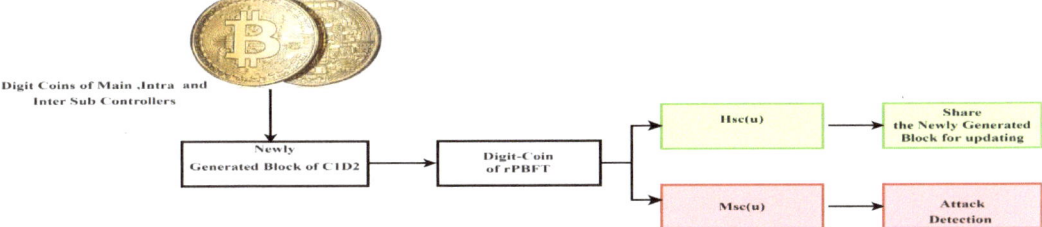

Figure 5. Digit-coin rPBFT consensus and block validation.

3.2.3. Attack Detection

The BCS determines the malicious controller based on the digit-coin and rPBFT consensus, referred to as additional security, as the blockchain offers fundamental security. The controller C1D2 can be in one of the following strategies, as shown in Equation (3).

$$C1D2 \sim \begin{cases} DC_{C1D2}\ \text{and}\ FS_{C1D2}\ \ 0.9 < 1, & C1D2 = \text{Honest} \\ DC_{C1D2}\ \text{and}\ FS_{C1D2}\ \ 0.5 \leq 0.9, & C1D2 = \text{Suspecious} \\ \text{Otherwise}, & C1D2 = \text{Malicious} \end{cases} \qquad (3)$$

In the proposed BCS, the attack detection threshold of DC_{C1D2} and FS_{C1D2} are fixed between 0 to 1. As explained in Equation (3), the controller is honest when it obtains the digit-coin and consensus values DC_{C1D2} and FS_{C1D2} lies between 0.9 to 1. The controller is considered suspicious when DC_{C1D2} and FS_{C1D2} lies between 0.5 to 0.9. Otherwise, the controller is compromised. Moreover, the BCS provides strong security against controller compromisation through blockchain-enabled security. Algorithm 2 explains the process of BCS. The miners performed the validation process with rPBFT by determining the similarity between the data of the invalid block and its local data. Upon validation, the new block is appending with the chain, and the BCS distributes the newly created block to all controllers. By determining and eliminating the interaction of compromised controllers from block updating, the BCS neglects the effect of false injection and man-in-the-middle attacks. Moreover, it maintains a consistent network view at all controllers in BCS through efficient reputation and rPBFT block validation. Thus, it greatly impacts improving the security and performance efficiency of the MC-SDN data layer. By rotating the main controller role among the available sub-controllers in the corresponding domain, the proposed BCS enhances the controller utilization efficiency without impacting the security and performance of the network. Also, selecting intra and inter-domain sub-controllers for mining can minimize the controller failure issues due to high burden and optimize resource utilization.

Algorithm 2 Digital Reputation Estimation and Block Validation of BCS.

1: **Input:** Monitored information from C2D2, C3D2, C1D1, C1D3, and BN
2: **Output:** Digit-coin and Block validation
3: **Main controller** ← true
4: **do while** Main controller
5:     Generating new block according to topological changes
6:     **BCS digit-coin system** ← true
7:     **do while** BCS digit-coin system
8:         Initiates the digit-coin assignment process for C1D2
9:         Collects the monitored information from C2D2, C3D2, C1D1, C1D3, and BN
10:         Estimates the DC_{C1D2} using Equation (2)
11:         Inputs the DC_{C1D2} to rPBFT mining
12:         **rPBFT** ← true
13:         **do while** rPBFT
14:         Maps the DC_{C1D2} as U sets
15:         Compute FS_{C1D2} to main controller C1D2
16:         Obtain the honest and malicious score level using Equation (3)
17:         **If** ($FS_{C1D2} > 0.9$ and $FS_{C1D2} < 1$)
18:             **then** C1D2 is trustworthy
19:         **else if** (FS_{C1D2} lies between 0.5 to 0.9)
20:             **then** C1D2 is suspicious
21:         **else if** ($FS_{C1D2} < 0.5$ and $FS_{C1D2} > 0$)
22:             **then** C1D2 is malicious
23:         end if
24:         **rPBFT** ← false
25:         end while
26:     **BCS digit-coin system** ← false
27:     end while
28: **Main controller** ← false

4. Experimental Evaluation

The experimental model virtually creates the SDN in a simulated environment with the help of the Mininet emulator. There are two communication environments created using Mininet. Firstly, inter-controller communication is created to evaluate the performance of BCS. Ryu [30] is a Python-based OpenFlow virtual controller that bypasses the incoming network traffic over the connection with the SDN controller. Each domain has multiple controllers, enabling developers to manage, program, and control the applications through its interface. The controllers effectively maintain a consistent network view by enabling blockchain-based communication environment creation. In the proposed model, a private blockchain assigns privileges to connect, send, and receive the flow information among the multi-controllers. In the simulated SDN, installed servers generate traffic flows across the multiple intermediate SDN switches. The configuration of the SDN devices or nodes relies on the applications executing on the Ryu controller through the OpenFlow. OpenFlow Ryu collects the statistical data from the SDN switches and devices. Hence, it is modeled as the firewall, switch, monitor, and router for the network traffic. The Ryu controller exploits the southbound Application Programming Interface (API) to establish the remote connection with Mininet, incorporating different hosts and switches. To design the processes involved in the proposed SDN research, the Ryu application development interface utilizes the Open vSwitch as the SDN switch for providing a switching stack for the virtualized environment. The proposed BCS approach is compared with existing IB-SDN [24] and BMC-SDN [26] to validate the effectiveness.

4.1. Implementation Parameters of BCS

The BCS security model is evaluated using Mininet, which creates virtual network support for implementation. The implementation parameters of BCS are shown in Table 2.

Table 2. Implementation parameters of BCS.

Parameters	Value
Simulator	MininetWiFi/PyEthereum
Type of SDN Controller	Ryu
Number of SDN Domain	5–20
Number of SDN main Controllers	5–20
Number of SDN Sub-Controllers	2 for each main controller
Blockchain Type	Permissioned Blockchain
Consensus Mechanism	Reshaped PBFT
Number of malicious Controllers	2 to 6
Type of SDN Nodes	OpenFlow Switches and Internet-enabled smart devices
Number of Switches	10 to 100
Number of SDN Nodes	10 to 500

The simulation environment creation is depicted in Figure 6.

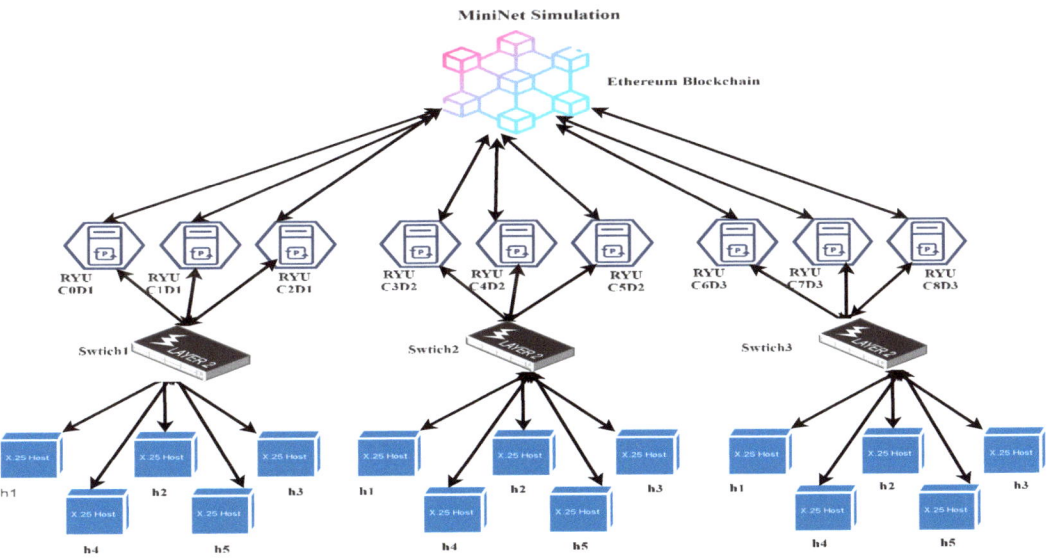

Figure 6. Simulation environment creation.

4.2. Performance Metrics

The performance of BCS is evaluated using the following metrics:

- Attack Detection Rate: The percentage of successfully detected attacks to the total number of injected attacks.
- Consensus Delay: The amount of time taken to reach a consensus.
- Detection Time: The amount of time required to detect malicious controllers.

5. Experimental Results of BCS

Figure 7a plots the relationship between the number of controllers and attack detection time for a compromised controller attack (CCA) attack scenario. The results are obtained for different controller scenarios, such as 10, 20, and 30. The attack detection rate is increased by adjusting the controller density from 10 to 30. The main reason is that the number of CCA escalated, varying the number of controllers from low to high. Albeit the BCS strategy provides a strong defense against the compromised controllers, most of the controllers are attackers under high controller scenarios. Hence, the digit-coin value estimation accuracy may diminish due to the high numbers of comprised controllers. For example, the BCS accomplishes 92.86% and 89.32% of the attack detection rate for 10 and 30 controllers.

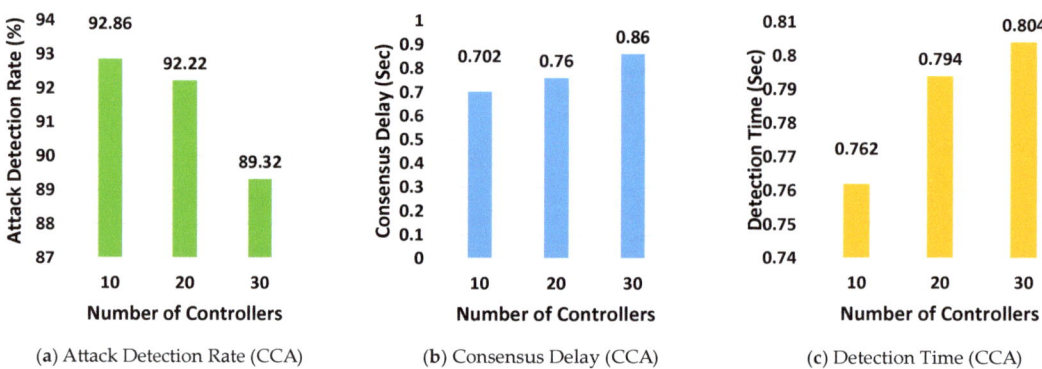

(a) Attack Detection Rate (CCA)   (b) Consensus Delay (CCA)   (c) Detection Time (CCA)

Figure 7. Compromised controller attack (CCA) performance metrics.

Figure 7b demonstrates the consensus delay results of the proposed BCS obtained for various controller scenarios with compromised controller attacks. The consensus delay escalates when the number of controllers varies from 10 to 30. The main reason is that many nodes compete to perform in the new block creation process, resulting in high consensus delay. Unlike fundamental PBFT, the proposed rPBFT provides an equal chance for miners to participate in consensus. For example, the consensus delay of the proposed BCS is 0.702 s for 10 controllers, and it varies by 0.86 for 30 controllers.

Figure 7c shows the relationship between the number of controllers and detection time for the CCA scenario. The BCS increases the detection time when varying the number of controllers from 10 to 30. This is caused because the percentage of CCA is high under 30 controller scenarios compared to 10 and 20 controller scenarios since the BCS needs adequate time to defend against the compromised controllers. For example, the BCS obtained 0.804 s of detection time for 30 controller scenarios.

Figure 8a illustrates the false injection attack (FIA) attack detection rate results of BCS obtained by varying the controller density from 10 to 30. The attack detection rate of BCS is decreased by varying the controller density from low to high. Under a low number of controller scenarios, the number of attackers is also minimal. Hence, the proposed model obtains accurate digit-coin values and quick rPBFT consensus. Thus, it improves the attack detection rate compared to many attacker scenarios with more controllers. The increase in controllers also has an impact on the number of controllers. For instance, the proposed BCS incurs an 89.74% attack detection rate for 10 controllers. However, the proposed model minimizes the attack detection rate at a very low percentage by 2.16 under 30 controllers, compared with 10 controllers.

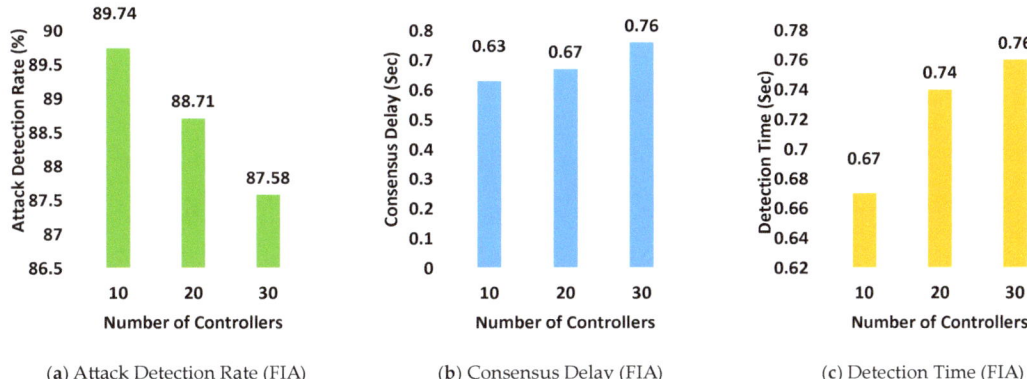

(a) Attack Detection Rate (FIA) (b) Consensus Delay (FIA) (c) Detection Time (FIA)

Figure 8. False injection attack (FIA) performance metrics.

Figure 8b compares the FIA consensus delay results of BCS obtained for the different number of controller scenarios. In the rPBFT, the consensus participation was decided according to the digit-coin value of nodes. The proposed model gives an equal chance to all the participants in the mining process. Thus, it accomplishes some delay in the consensus process, especially under many controllers. For example, the BCS obtained 0.63 s for 10 controllers. However, it varied by 20.63% when 30 controllers are present in the MC-SDN scenario.

Figure 8c depicts the detection time results of the FIA attack of BCS accomplished by varying the number of controllers from low to high. The detection time value was increased by adjusting the controller density from low to high. The proposed model considers 20% of controllers from the total controller density as attackers. Therefore, increasing the number of controllers also escalated the number of attackers in the network. Hence, the BCS needs significant time to detect such attackers in the MC-SDN scenario. For example, the BCS attained 0.67 and 0.76 s of detection time for 10 and 30 controller scenarios, respectively.

Figure 9a shows the attack detection rate results of BCS obtained for the Man-in-th-Middle Attack (MiMA) scenario. To analyze the attack detection efficiency of BCS, the number of controllers was varied from 10 to 30. The results demonstrate that the attack detection rate was reduced by varying the number of controllers from low to high. For example, the BCS incurred a 91.28% attack detection rate for 10 controllers, which is increased by 6.99% compared to the 30 controller scenarios. The main reason behind this is that the proposed model considers the digit-coin value and rPBFT consensus for attack detection in which the MiMA attacker contribution is high under many malicious scenarios.

The consensus delay results of the MiMA scenario are shown in Figure 9b. The BCS varies the number of controllers from 10 to 30 to obtain the consensus delay results. It increases the consensus delay by varying the number of controllers from low to high. For example, the BCS accomplishes 0.64 s of consensus delay for 10 controllers. Under the high number of controllers, the competing node density is also increased, resulting in maximum consensus delay. For example, the BCS decreases the consensus delay by 15.63% compared to the results obtained for 30 controllers.

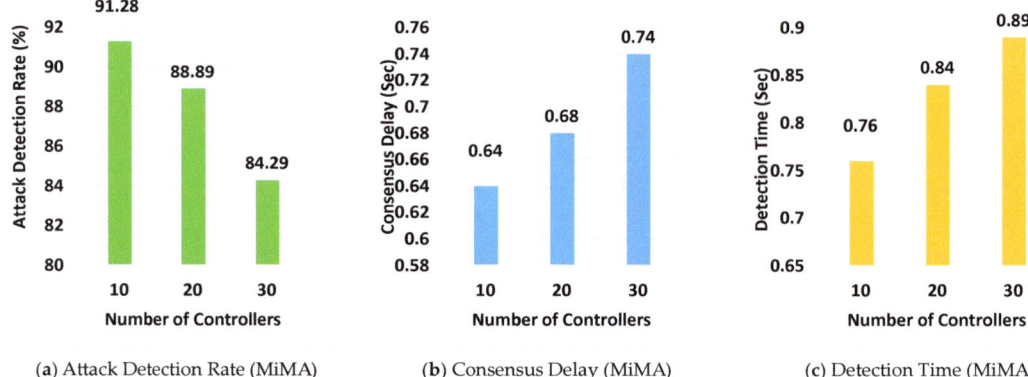

(a) Attack Detection Rate (MiMA)   (b) Consensus Delay (MiMA)   (c) Detection Time (MiMA)

Figure 9. Man-in-the-Middle Attack (MiMA) performance metrics.

Figure 9c plots the detection time results obtained for MiMA under various numbers of controllers. The BCS improves the detection time when varying the number of controllers from 10 to 30. The reason is that the BCS has to defend against the high number of MiMA under a high controller scenario. Thus, it increases the detection time under a high number of controllers present compared to a low number of controller scenarios. For instance, the BCS attained 0.76 and 0.89 s of detection time, respectively, for 10 and 30 controllers.

Figure 10 portrays the attack detection rate results of BCS obtained for the number of attackers (NoA) = 3, 6, and 9. To evaluate the performance efficiency of the BCS security model under different scenarios, the number of controllers was varied from 10 to 30. The attack detection rate slightly increased with varying the number of domains and controllers from low to high. The reason is that the increasing number of domains also increased the number of controllers, resulting in efficient intra and inter-sub-controller monitoring. Thus, it increases the efficiency of digit-coin computation accuracy and improves the attack detection performance. The proposed BCS detects malicious behaviors based on three pieces of information: intra-sub-controller data, inter-sub-controller data, and blockchain data. The maintenance of digit-coin values as blockchain ledgers increases the security level of the proposed system. For example, the BCS accomplished 99.35% and 99.56% attack detection rates under 10 and 30 controllers, respectively, where NoA = 9.

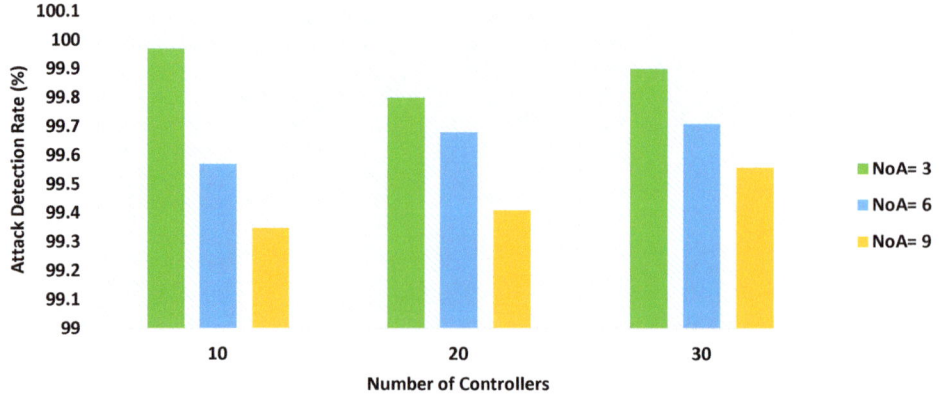

Figure 10. Number of controllers vs. attack detection rate.

The detection time of BCS is shown in Figure 11, and the numerical results are given. The results were obtained by varying the number of controllers from 10 to 30 under malicious controller scenarios 3, 6, and 9. The proposed system exploits the fuzzy-based rPBFT to detect malicious controllers, increasing the detection time when huge numbers of attackers and controllers are presented in the network. The proposed BCS includes different sub-controller monitoring and blockchain data to validate the newly generated blocks and attack detection. Hence, it provides strong security to the SDN even high number of attackers is presented in the network. The proposed model increases the detection time at an acceptable rate to provide strong security in the network. For example, the detection time of BCS is 0.56 and 1.3 s for the number of attackers, 3 and 9, respectively, when 30 SDN controllers are present in the network.

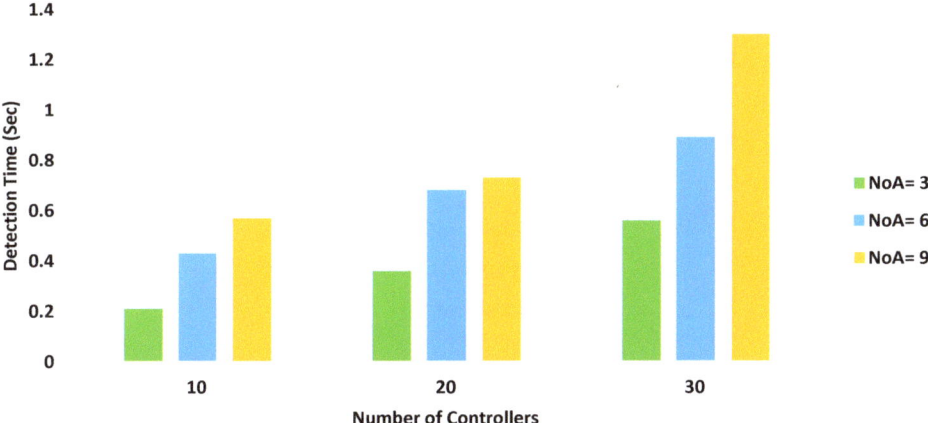

Figure 11. Number of controllers vs. detection time.

The consensus delay performance of rPBFT of BCS is demonstrated in Figure 12. Generally, the number of validators has some delay effect on the rPBFT consensus. The proposed model utilizes a digit-coin blockchain system where genuine miners are fairly involved in block creation and validation. Unlike fundamental PBFT, the rPBFT optimizes the miner selection process using digit-coin values. It selects an adequate number of genuine miners and performs equally to all the selected miner controllers during block validation. Thus, it minimizes the consensus delay and decreases overhead compared to existing PBFT. Also, it exploits various numbers of intra and inter-club-controllers in the consensus process, resulting in some consensus delays with secure mining. For example, the BCS accomplished 0.2 and 1.1 s of consensus delay for 1 and 5 validator scenarios, respectively.

Figure 13 portrays the attack detection rate of the proposed BCS, existing BMC-SDN, and IB-SDN. The proposed BCS model varies the number of attackers from 3 to 9 to show its superiority over existing BMC-SDN. Both models decrease the attack detection rate by adjusting the number of attackers from low to high. The reason is that both models consider the redundant controller monitoring information in attack detection, and most of the redundant controllers are malicious under the high malicious scenario. For instance, the proposed BCS accomplished a 99.54% and 99.14% attack detection rate for 3 and 9 attacker scenarios, respectively. However, the attack detection rate of the proposed BCS is better than the existing BMC-SDN and IB-SDN, as the proposed model includes the monitored data of both intra and inters controllers in attack detection. Unlike this, the existing BMC-SDN only includes the inter-controller reputation values for attack detection, resulting in a minimum attack detection rate. The IB-SDN exploits global trust maintenance among the distributed controllers, and it is unable to minimize the compromised controller effect in the network. For example, the BCS enhanced the attack detection rate by 0.3% and 0.9% compared with existing BMC-SDN and IB-SDN, respectively, when nine attacker nodes were presented in the network.

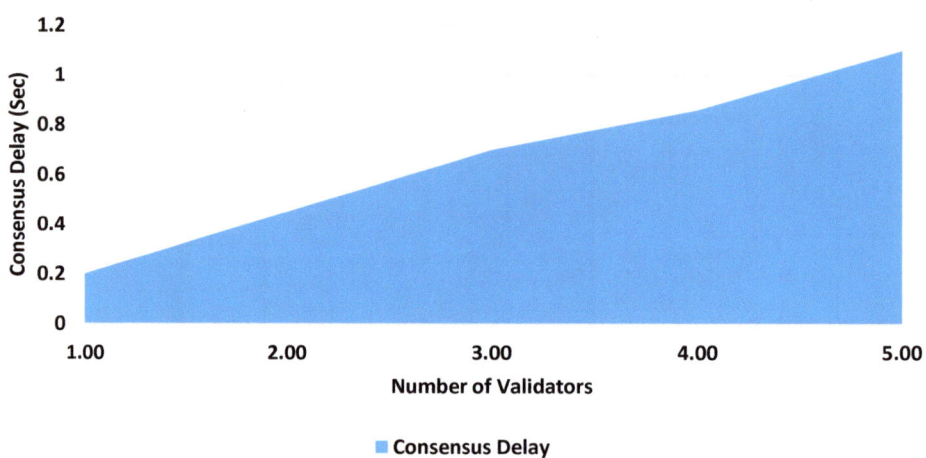

Figure 12. Number of validators vs. consensus delay.

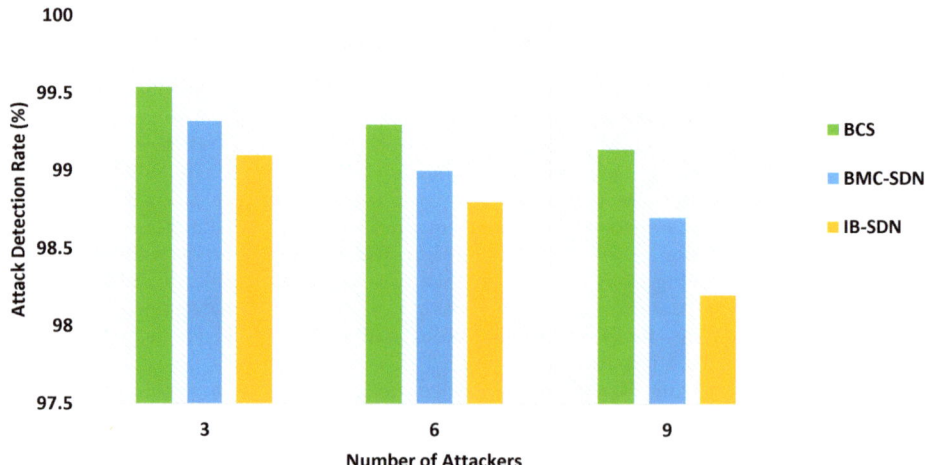

Figure 13. Number of attackers vs. attack detection rate.

Figure 14 illustrates the comparison of attack detection rate results of BCS, BMC-SDN, and IB-SDN. To show the superiority of BCS under multiple numbers of compromised controllers, the number of compromised controllers is varied from 1 to 3. The results demonstrate that all three works decreased the attack detection rate when adjusting the number of compromised controllers from low to high. For instance, the proposed BCS decreased the attack detection rate by only 0.4% by adjusting the compromised controller number from 1 to 3. However, it was minimal when compared with the attack detection rate results of BMC-SDN and IB-SDN. The reason is that the proposed model includes the advantage of inter and intra-controller monitoring strategy in the reputation estimation of the main controller. Although the BMC-SDN also includes the redundant controller structure to mitigate the compromised controller effect, it fails when multiple numbers of controllers within a domain are compromised. The IB-SDN fails to provide defense against compromised controller scenarios. For instance, the BCS minimized the compromised controller effects while improving the attack detection rate by 5.7% and 13.9% compared with BMC-SDN and IB-SDN, respectively, when three compromised controllers were present in the scenario.

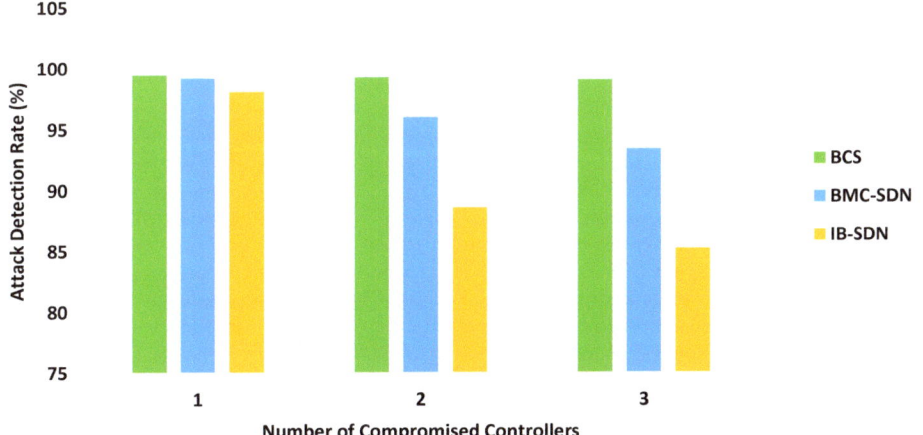

Figure 14. Number of compromised controllers vs. attack detection rate.

Figure 15 compares the attack detection time results of the proposed BCS, existing BMC-SDN, and IB-SDN obtained by varying the number of attackers from low to high. The attack detection time increased when adjusting the number of attackers from 3 to 9. The reason is that the attack detection models perform the computation for huge nodes. For example, the proposed BCS attained 0.12 and 0.23 s of attack detection time for 3 and 9 attackers, respectively. However, the reshaped PBFT provides fair consensus options to the genuine miners selected using blockchain and sub-controller data and neglects the participation of malicious nodes in the consensus process, resulting in quick validation. Thus, it also diminishes the attack detection time of BCS compared with the existing BMC-SDN and IB-SDN. For example, the proposed BCS minimized the attack detection time by 6% and 15% more than BMC-SDN and IB-SDN, respectively, when nine attackers were present in the scenario.

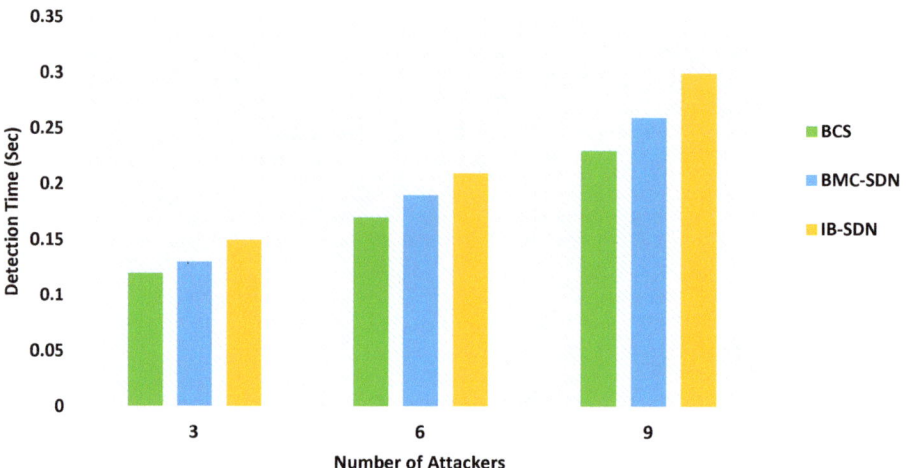

Figure 15. Number of attackers vs. detection time.

6. Conclusions

MC-SDN demonstrates potential advantages in data centers and enterprise network environments due to its scalability, fault tolerance, efficient network management, and performance. However, the compromised controllers in this environment have widespread implications and severe performance issues. The proposed BCS security model offers security against multiple compromised controllers and other security attacks at the controller level. The blockchain-based security model of BCS is implemented among the SDN controllers to detect attacks against controllers, especially in multiple numbers of compromised controller environments. By enabling the main controllers of every domain as sub-controllers to their preceding and succeeding domains, the BCS minimizes the impact of multiple compromised controllers and failure issues, thereby improving consistency among controllers. The rPBFT consensus with the digit-coin system mitigates compromised controllers' behaviors and improves flow table maintenance efficiency at all controllers. By eliminating the impact of multiple numbers of compromised controllers within a domain through inter and intra-controller structure, the BCS maintains a consistent network view among all controllers and improves the flow table update accuracy. Maintaining a consistent network view at the controller level also enhances efficiency at the infrastructure level. Finally, the evaluation results prove the superiority of BCS by improving the attack detection rate when varying the number of controllers and attackers under different network scenarios. For instance, the proposed BCS enhanced the attack detection rate by 5.7% and 13.9% compared with BMC-SDN and IB-SDN, respectively, even when an attacker could compromise three numbers of controllers within a domain. Thus, the BCS extremely minimizes the multiple compromised controller effects while maintaining a high attack detection rate. The notable enhancements demonstrated by the BCS have a significant advantage in the MC-SDN environment specifically large data centers and enterprise networks.

Some of the future directions of BCS are as follows:

- Future work plans to extend the BCS security model to cover the rest of security planes such as infrastructure, northbound, and southbound.
- Future work aims to improve the flexibility and integration capabilities and facilitate interoperability among distinct blockchain platforms exploited within MC-SDNs.

- BCS will be extended as an adaptive security framework that leverages immutable records of blockchain technology to dynamically respond against evolving real-time threat landscapes.
- BCS can exploit the advantage of blockchain to construct a secure, shared distributed repository of intelligence about threat information, where each controller can securely access threat information and improve their contribution to network consistency.
- Proposing a blockchain-enabled secure controller communication approach can enhance controller coordination and ensure that all controllers in the network can operate with similar trust levels.

Author Contributions: Methodology, A.A.; Software, A.A.; Validation, A.A.; Resources, A.A.; Writing—original draft, A.A.; Supervision, I.K. and S.M.B. All authors have read and agreed to the published version of the manuscript.

Funding: This research received no external funding.

Data Availability Statement: Data are contained within the article.

Conflicts of Interest: The authors declare no conflict of interest.

References

1. Hu, T.; Guo, Z.; Yi, P.; Baker, T.; Lan, J. Multi-controller Based Software-Defined Networking: A Survey. *IEEE Access* **2018**, *6*, 15980–15996. [CrossRef]
2. Blial, O.; Ben Mamoun, M.; Benaini, R. An Overview on SDN Architectures with Multiple Controllers. *J. Comput. Netw. Commun.* **2016**, *2016*, 9396525. [CrossRef]
3. Hu, T.; Yi, P.; Zhang, J.; Lan, J. Reliable and load balance-aware multi-controller deployment in SDN. *China Commun.* **2018**, *15*, 184–198. [CrossRef]
4. Yu, T.; Hong, Y.; Cui, H.; Jiang, H. A survey of Multi-controllers Consistency on SDN. In Proceedings of the 2018 4th International Conference on Universal Village (UV), Boston, MA, USA, 21–24 October 2018; pp. 1–6.
5. Maleh, Y.; Qasmaoui, Y.; El Gholami, K.; Sadqi, Y.; Mounir, S. A comprehensive survey on SDN security: Threats, mitigations, and future directions. *J. Reliab. Intell. Environ.* **2023**, *9*, 201–239. [CrossRef]
6. Bhuiyan, Z.A.; Islam, S.; Islam, M.; Ullah, A.B.M.A.; Naz, F.; Rahman, M.S. On the (in)Security of the Control Plane of SDN Architecture: A Survey. *IEEE Access* **2023**, *11*, 91550–91582. [CrossRef]
7. Indrason, N.; Saha, G. Exploring Blockchain-driven security in SDN-based IoT networks. *J. Netw. Comput. Appl.* **2024**, *224*, 103838. [CrossRef]
8. Fan, W.; Chang, S.Y.; Kumar, S.; Zhou, X.; Park, Y. Blockchain-based secure coordination for distributed sdn control plane. In Proceedings of the 2021 IEEE 7th International Conference on Network Softwarization (NetSoft), Tokyo, Japan, 28 June–2 July 2021; pp. 253–257.
9. Ahmad, S.; Mir, A.H. Securing centralized sdn control with distributed blockchain technology. *Comput. Sci.* **2023**, *24*, 5–30. [CrossRef]
10. Li, W.; Meng, W.; Liu, Z.; Au, M.H. Towards blockchain-based software-defined networking: Security challenges and solutions. *IEICE Trans. Inf. Syst.* **2020**, *103*, 196–203. [CrossRef]
11. Alharbi, T. Deployment of Blockchain Technology in Software Defined Networks: A Survey. *IEEE Access* **2020**, *8*, 9146–9156. [CrossRef]
12. Abdulqadder, I.H.; Zhou, S.; Zou, D.; Aziz, I.T.; Akber, S.M.A. Bloc-sec: Blockchain-based lightweight security architecture for 5G/B5G enabled SDN/NFV cloud of IoT. In Proceedings of the 2020 IEEE 20th International Conference on Communication Technology (ICCT), Nanning, China, 28–31 October 2020; pp. 499–507.
13. Goksel, N.; Demirci, M. Dos attack detection using packet statistics in sdn. In Proceedings of the 2019 International Symposium on Networks, Computers and Communications (ISNCC), Istanbul, Turkey, 18–20 June 2019; pp. 1–6.
14. Phan, T.V.; Park, M. Efficient Distributed Denial-of-Service Attack Defense in SDN-Based Cloud. *IEEE Access* **2019**, *7*, 18701–18714. [CrossRef]
15. Sharma, P.K.; Park, J.H. Blockchain based hybrid network architecture for the smart city. *Future Gener. Comput. Syst.* **2018**, *86*, 650–655. [CrossRef]
16. Aggarwal, S.; Chaudhary, R.; Aujla, G.S.; Kumar, N.; Choo, K.K.R.; Zomaya, A.Y. Blockchain for smart communities: Applications, challenges and opportunities. *J. Netw. Comput. Appl.* **2019**, *144*, 13–48. [CrossRef]
17. Li, W.; Tan, J.; Wang, Y. A framework of blockchain-based collaborative intrusion detection in software defined networking. In *Network and System Security*; Springer: Cham, Switzerland, 2020; pp. 261–276.
18. Lokesh, B.; Rajagopalan, N. A Blockchain-based security model for SDNs. In Proceedings of the 2020 IEEE International Conference on Electronics, Computing and Communication Technologies (CONECCT), Bangalore, India, 2–4 July 2020; pp. 1–6.

19. Barka, E.; Dahmane, S.; Kerrache, C.A.; Khayat, M.; Sallabi, F. STHM: A Secured and Trusted Healthcare Monitoring Architecture Using SDN and Blockchain. *Electronics* **2021**, *10*, 1787. [CrossRef]
20. Xie, L.; Ding, Y.; Yang, H.; Wang, X. Blockchain-Based Secure and Trustworthy Internet of Things in SDN-Enabled 5G-VANETs. *IEEE Access* **2019**, *7*, 56656–56666. [CrossRef]
21. Rahman, A.; Islam, M.J.; Montieri, A.; Nasir, M.K.; Reza, M.M.; Band, S.S.; Pescape, A.; Hasan, M.; Sookhak, M.; Mosavi, A. Smartblock-sdn: An optimized blockchain-sdn framework for resource management in IoT. *IEEE Access* **2021**, *9*, 28361–28376. [CrossRef]
22. Algarni, S.; Eassa, F.; Almarhabi, K.; Algarni, A.; Albeshri, A. BCNBI: A Blockchain-Based Security Framework for Northbound Interface in Software-Defined Networking. *Electronics* **2022**, *11*, 996. [CrossRef]
23. Li, P.; Guo, S.; Wu, J.; Zhao, Q. BlockREV: Blockchain-Enabled Multi-Controller Rule Enforcement Verification in SDN. *Secur. Commun. Netw.* **2022**, *2022*, 7294638. [CrossRef]
24. Zeng, Z.; Zhang, X.; Xia, Z. Intelligent Blockchain-Based Secure Routing for Multidomain SDN-Enabled IoT Networks. *Wirel. Commun. Mob. Comput.* **2022**, *2022*, 5693962. [CrossRef]
25. Das, D.; Banerjee, S.; Dasgupta, K.; Chatterjee, P.; Ghosh, U.; Biswas, U. Blockchain enabled sdn framework for security management in 5g applications. In Proceedings of the 24th International Conference on Distributed Computing and Networking, Kharagpur, India, 4–7 January 2023; pp. 414–419.
26. Derhab, A.; Guerroumi, M.; Belaoued, M.; Cheikhrouhou, O. BMC-SDN: Blockchain-based multicontroller architecture for secure software-defined networks. *Wirel. Commun. Mob. Comput.* **2021**, *2021*, 984666. [CrossRef]
27. Song, Y.; Feng, T.; Yang, C.; Mi, X.; Jiang, S.; Guizani, M. IS2N: Intent-Driven Security Software-Defined Network with Blockchain. *IEEE Netw.* **2023**, *38*, 118–127. [CrossRef]
28. Medury, L.; Kandah, F. B2-C2: Blockchain-based Flow Control Consistency for Multi-Controller SDN Architecture. In Proceedings of the 2024 IEEE International Conference on Consumer Electronics (ICCE), Las Vegas, NV, USA, 6–8 January 2024; pp. 1–6.
29. Ekel, P.; Queiroz, J.; Parreiras, R.; Palhares, R. Fuzzy set based models and methods of multicriteria group decision making. *Nonlinear Anal. Theory Methods Appl.* **2009**, *71*, e409–e419. [CrossRef]
30. The Ryu. Available online: https://ryu-sdn.org/ (accessed on 14 July 2023).

Disclaimer/Publisher's Note: The statements, opinions and data contained in all publications are solely those of the individual author(s) and contributor(s) and not of MDPI and/or the editor(s). MDPI and/or the editor(s) disclaim responsibility for any injury to people or property resulting from any ideas, methods, instructions or products referred to in the content.

Article

Adaptive Whitening and Feature Gradient Smoothing-Based Anti-Sample Attack Method for Modulated Signals in Frequency-Hopping Communication

Yanhan Zhu [1,2,*], Yong Li [2] and Zhu Duan [1]

1. School of Electronics and Information Engineering, Nanjing University of Information Science and Technology, Nanjing 210044, China; duanz@nuist.edu.cn
2. Sixty-Third Research Institute, National University of Defense Technology, Nanjing 210007, China; liyong17@nudt.edu.cn
* Correspondence: 202212490441@nuist.edu.cn; Tel.: +86-15189561788

Abstract: In modern warfare, frequency-hopping communication serves as the primary method for battlefield information transmission, with its significance continuously growing. Fighting for the control of electromagnetic power on the battlefield has become an important factor affecting the outcome of war. As communication electronic warfare evolves, jammers employing deep neural networks (DNNs) to decode frequency-hopping communication parameters for smart jamming pose a significant threat to communicators. This paper proposes a method to generate adversarial samples of frequency-hopping communication signals using adaptive whitening and feature gradient smoothing. This method targets the DNN cognitive link of the jammer, aiming to reduce modulation recognition accuracy and counteract smart interference. First, the frequency-hopping signal is adaptively whitened. Subsequently, rich spatiotemporal features are extracted from the hidden layer after inputting the signal into the deep neural network model for gradient calculation. The signal's average feature gradient replaces the single-point gradient for iteration, enhancing anti-disturbance capabilities. Simulation results show that, compared with the existing gradient symbol attack algorithm, the attack success rate and migration rate of the adversarial samples generated by this method are greatly improved in both white box and black box scenarios.

Keywords: frequency-hopping communication; modulation recognition; deep neural network; adaptive whitening; feature gradient; adversarial example

1. Introduction

In recent years, with the rapid development of electronic countermeasure technology, jamming means have become complex and diverse, which puts forward higher requirements for the reliability of communication. Owing to its excellent performance, frequency-hopping communication has become widely utilized and is regarded as a secure method in military applications for hostile environments [1]. However, the emergence of targeted interference has highlighted the limitations of traditional frequency-hopping techniques. To enhance the anti-interference ability of wireless communication systems [2], this paper studies the anti-interference strategy based on Game Theory in frequency-hopping communication to deal with the interference attack in frequency-hopping communication and puts forward new ideas to solve the interference countermeasure problem, which is of great significance to improve the anti-interference ability of frequency-hopping communication systems.

As an important research topic in the field of digital signal processing, modulation recognition of communication signals has shown great potential in military and civil fields. In the military field, modulation recognition provides an important technical means for obtaining enemy intelligence in electromagnetic countermeasures and selecting the best jamming and suppression method. Accurately identifying the modulation mode of frequency-hopping signals can provide strong support for military information warfare by, for example, judging the attributes of enemy and our own targets and jamming enemy signals [3]. Generally, after successfully intercepting enemy communication signals, it is undoubtedly a crucial task in communication countermeasure technology to determine the number levels and extract the feature level of the obtained mixed modulation signals and use the extracted features for further modulation recognition.

Traditional modulation recognition methods usually rely on manually designed features and complex signal processing algorithms, including maximum likelihood estimation based on hypothesis testing [4] and feature extraction based on pattern recognition [5]. These methods tend to perform poorly in the face of complex and variable frequency-hopping signals. In recent years, modulation recognition technology based on deep learning (DL) has attracted the close attention of researchers. Compared with traditional methods, modulation signal recognition based on DL does not need to rely on prior knowledge and can automatically extract features from data and classify them, so it not only has high classification accuracy but also stronger generalization ability in the face of large-scale data training. Mohamed A and others used a convolutional filter to use the basic convolutional neural network Alex Net and a residual neural network for compatibility with a constellation diagram, which significantly improved the accuracy of signal modulation classification [6]. Lihong Guang et al. removed noise from a two-dimensional time–frequency map of a frequency-hopping signal by adaptive Wiener filtering and accurately extracted the time–frequency map of each hop signal by using the algorithm in image processing, which achieved the accurate recognition of the modulation mode of the frequency-hopping signal and achieved good results at -4 db [7]. At present, DNNs are widely used in automatic modulation recognition (AMR) to complete signal detection and demodulation [8], which greatly improves the accuracy of modulation recognition. In communication countermeasures, a jammer can accurately identify the modulation mode being used in a target communication system and decode the frequency-hopping signal by training a DNN to more effectively interfere with and destroy the enemy's communication link.

Although deep learning modulation recognition technology has brought great convenience to people, its anti-interference performance has been questioned since 2013. In 2013, Szegedy et al. [9] found adversarial examples that can attack the neural network model—examples that can make the machine learning model misjudge or misclassify by perturbing the normal examples slightly and imperceptibly. The study indicates that deep neural network (DNN) models are typically characterized by their high complexity and sensitivity, which enable them to detect minute variations within the input space. Exploiting this characteristic, it is possible to enhance resistance to attacks by introducing precisely calibrated minor perturbations to the original samples. This method constructs adversarial examples that can provoke incorrect classifications by the model, thereby demonstrating a critical vulnerability in its predictive accuracy. Goodfellow et al. [10] proposed the fast gradient sign method (FGSM) in 2014. They added adversarial noise to the linear model and observed that when processing high-dimensional data input, the linear model was more vulnerable to the interference of adversarial examples, which overturned the theoretical explanation that the existence of adversarial examples was because the model was highly nonlinear. Kurakin et al. [11] introduced the iterative fast gradient sign method (I-FGSM), building on prior work. This approach incrementally introduces perturbations through multiple iterations and reprojects the currently generated adversarial samples back into a predefined constraint set. Classification outcomes indicate that most of these adversarial examples are misclassified, thereby demonstrating the efficacy of adversarial attacks on neural network classifiers in practical scenarios. Dong et al. [12] proposed a momentum iterative fast gradient sign method (MI-FGSM) to enhance resistance against sample attacks. This method integrates momentum into the gradient and gets rid of the bad local maximum in the iteration process to generate more mobile adversarial examples. Mardy et al. [13] proposed projected gradient descent (PGD), which is different from the clipping operation of I-FGSM. It limits the size of a disturbance by projecting the results of each iteration to the $\in -l_\infty$ field of pure input.

At present, research on adversarial examples is mainly focused on image and audio. In the field of communication signals, communicators can add adversarial examples with specific disturbances to modulated signals. These adversarial examples can attack the modem of a communication system so that the DNN model of the reconnaissance party cannot correctly demodulate the signal or cause wrong decoding results, which significantly improves the ability of the communicators to resist smart interference. Therefore, this paper proposes a frequency-hopping modulation signal adversarial example attack method based on adaptive whitening and feature gradient smoothing to reduce the recognition rate of the modulation signal in the DNN model. The main contributions of this paper can be summarized as follows:

1. Experiments show that the conventional method of generating countermeasure samples has shortcomings when attacking the frequency-hopping modulation recognition model, and, according to the particularity of the frequency-hopping signal and the rich space–time characteristics of the hidden layer of the model, a countermeasure sample generation method AWFGS-MIFGSM suitable for the field of frequency-hopping signal modulation recognition is proposed.
2. The method initially considers that frequency-hopping signals are non-stationary signals whose frequencies change non-linearly over time. This typical time-varying characteristic results in a relatively concentrated energy distribution within a short time frame. To address this, the acquired frequency-hopping signals undergo an adaptive whitening process. This treatment enables a more uniform distribution of energy across frequencies, eliminates correlations between signals, and simplifies the generation of adversarial samples.
3. This method uses the high-dimensional spatial features of the hidden layer of the target model to calculate the gradient to launch the attack, which ensures that the amount of characteristic information of the spectrum signal sample is rich enough. Considering that single-point gradient information might be unreliable due to loss function surface oscillations, the characteristic gradient is smoothed using surrounding sample data to identify the optimal direction for countering disturbances and improving adversarial sample transfer.

Section 2 of this paper introduces the basic principle of adversarial samples and adversarial attack based on DNN modulation recognition. In Section 3, the system model and the generation method of countermeasure samples based on adaptive whitening and feature gradient smoothing are described and analyzed. In Section 4, the experimental setup is explained, and a series of experiments are described from the perspective of white box attack and black box attack, and the experimental results are analyzed. Finally, we discuss and conclude this work in Section 5.

2. Related Literature Review
2.1. Adversarial Example Attack

Adversarial examples refer to the special samples formed by artificially adding subtle disturbances that are difficult to detect by the naked eye or that are visible to the naked eye after processing but that do not affect the overall system in the original data set. These disturbances are not random disturbances in the learning process but artificially constructed disturbances that can deceive the neural network model, as shown in Formula (1):

$$\min_{\delta}||\delta||_2 \text{ s.t. } C(x+\delta) = I; x + \delta \in [0,1]^m \qquad (1)$$

where δ represents the added disturbance, C represents the neural network classifier, x represents the original image, and I represents the specified class. Since the minimum value of $||\delta||_2$ is not easy to calculate, the loss function is introduced to change Formula (1) to Formula (2):

$$\min_{\delta} C|\delta| + J(X+\delta, I) \text{ s.t. } X+\delta \in [0,1]^m \tag{2}$$

where J is the loss function, which is realized by calculating the cross entropy.

Adversarial samples possess strong camouflage capability, exploiting model vulnerabilities to launch targeted attacks that mislead the model into categorizing these samples into incorrect categories with high confidence. The impact of an adversarial example on modulation recognition is illustrated in Figure 1. By introducing counter disturbance, the signal originally identified as a sine wave with 97.85% confidence is misclassified as a square wave with 99.92% confidence. This demonstrates that despite the incorrect classification results, the waveforms of the two signals are nearly identical.

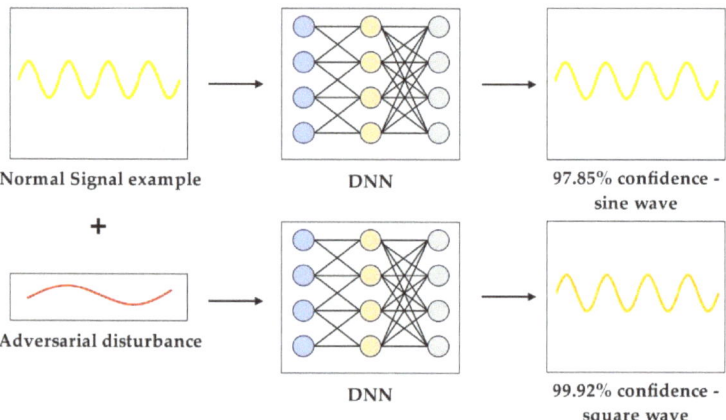

Figure 1. Example of modulated signal adversarial example.

Below are descriptions of the four most commonly used methods to generate adversarial examples.

2.1.1. FGSM

FGSM is an efficient and fast adversarial example generation method proposed by Goodfellow [10] that is committed to generating adversarial examples close to original images. The generation formula is shown in Formula (3):

$$x^{adv} = x - \varepsilon \cdot \text{sign}(\nabla_x L(\theta, x, t)) \tag{3}$$

where ∇_x is the gradient of loss function L to input x, ε is the parameter controlling the size of the disturbance, and t is the target category of the attack, that is, a single gradient iteration is performed in the direction of reducing the loss function corresponding to model category t. When the intention is to launch a no-target attack, the above formula is simply updated as follows:

$$x^{adv} = x + \varepsilon \cdot \text{sign}(\nabla_x L(\theta, x, y)) \tag{4}$$

where y is the correct category corresponding to the input sample x. The biggest feature of FGSM is its efficient running speed, so it is often widely used in scenarios that need to generate many adversarial examples, such as confrontation training. However, its disadvantage is that the overall performance of the generated adversarial samples is somewhat poor.

2.1.2. I-FGSM

I-FGSM [11] can be regarded as a multiple-iteration version of FGSM. The original FGSM only adds a single-step disturbance along the direction of gradient increase, while I-FGSM makes a multi-step small disturbance along the direction of gradient increase through iteration and cuts the iteration results after each iteration update to ensure that they are kept within the valid interval (for example, it is usually the [0, 1] or [0, 255] interval for image data). Compared with FGSM, I-FGSM can construct more accurate disturbances, but the amount of calculation is increased. This method can be expressed as follows:

$$x_{i+1}{}^{adv} = clip_{x,\alpha}(x_i{}^{adv} - \varepsilon \cdot \text{sign}(\nabla_x L(\theta, x, t))) \tag{5}$$

where the subscript i denotes the number of iteration rounds, $clip_{x,\alpha}(x^{adv}) = \min[1, x + \alpha, \max(0, x - \varepsilon, x^{adv})]$.

2.1.3. MI-FGSM

MI-FGSM [12] attack incorporates momentum into the I-FGSM attack by introducing a small number of gradients generated by the current step while retaining some gradients from the previous step to stabilize the update direction and avoid falling into the local extremum. The improvement of this method is the accumulation of the velocity vector in the gradient direction by using momentum. The formula is as follows:

$$g_{t+1} = \mu \cdot g_t + \frac{\nabla_x J(x_t{}^{adv}, y)}{||\nabla_x J(x_t{}^{adv}, y)||_1} \tag{6}$$

$$x_{i+1}{}^{adv} = x_i{}^{adv} + \alpha \cdot \text{sign}(g_{t+1}) \tag{7}$$

First, $x_t{}^{adv}$ is input to classifier f to obtain gradient $\nabla_x J(x_t{}^{adv}, y)$; then, the velocity vector is accumulated in the gradient direction through Formula (6) to update g_{t+1}, and $x_{i+1}{}^{adv}$ is updated by applying the symbol gradient in Formula (7), finally generating disturbance F. Compared with FGSM and I-FGSM, MI-FGSM gives higher mobility of adversarial examples.

2.1.4. PGD

Compared with the one-step confrontation of FGSM, PGD [13] adopts the strategy of small-step and multi-step. PGD initializes with uniform random noise to project the gradient and clips the disturbance to a specified range after each iteration. The attack process is shown in Formula (8):

$$x_{t+1}^{adv} = \text{proj}_{x,\varepsilon}(x_t^{adv} + \alpha \cdot sign(\nabla_x J(x_t^{adv}, y, \theta))) \tag{8}$$

where $\text{proj}_{x,\varepsilon}(\cdot)$ is the projection operation.

2.2. Modulation Recognition Adversarial Example Attack Based on a DNN

Modulation recognition can be regarded as a classification problem involving N modulation modes. The signal received by the communication receiver can be expressed as $y = \alpha e^{j(2\pi\omega + \varphi)} x + \sigma$, where x is the signal modulated by the transmitter according to a specific modulation scheme, α transmits the impulse response of the wireless channel, ω is the frequency offset, φ is the phase offset, and σ indicates additive white Gaussian noise (AWGN). The purpose of any modulation classifier is to identify the modulation type $P(x \in N|y)$ of the signal given the received signal y.

Modulation recognition can be categorized into classical and DL-based methods, depending on the use of deep learning algorithms. DL-based modulation recognition automates feature extraction and classification by feeding preprocessed signals directly into the network, significantly reducing the time needed to manually analyze communication signal characteristics. This advantage makes the method better adapted to future situations following the development of wireless communication where the amount of information may increase significantly, and it has higher recognition accuracy. The process is shown in Figure 2.

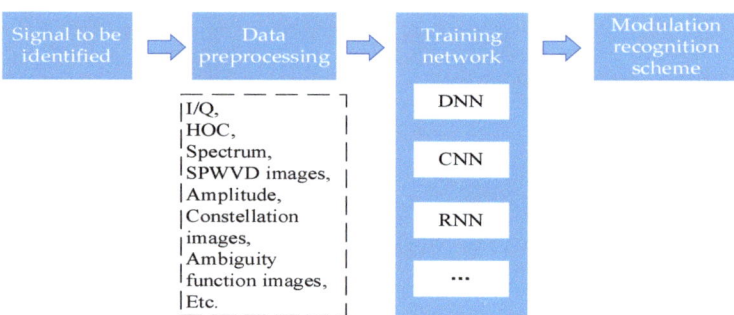

Figure 2. Modulation recognition process based on DL.

DNNs are central to DL-based modulation recognition technology. They process signal characterization results, analyzing preprocessed and extracted signal data to infer and output the modulation mode. O'Shea et al. [14] achieved the recognition and classification of three analog modulation signals and eight digital modulation signals based on a DNN model for the first time, and the accuracy rate reached 80%, proving the feasibility of applying DNNs to radio data recognition under the condition of a low signal-to-noise ratio. Ali et al. [15] employed IQ samples, constellations, and high-order cumulants to train sparse self-coding for modulation recognition, confirming the DNN's effectiveness in AWGN and flat fading channels via simulations. Xie et al. [16] used high-order cumulants to extract different features of each signal type to train a DNN for modulation recognition. When the signal-to-noise ratio was −5 dB and −2dB, the overall recognition accuracy of the algorithm exceeded 99%. At present, research on the modulation recognition of communication signals mainly focuses on fixed-frequency signals, and there is a big gap in research on the modulation recognition of frequency-hopping signals at home and abroad. For frequency-hopping modulation signal recognition, reference [17] introduced an algorithm that extracted instantaneous features and high-order cumulants from spread spectrum and conventional signals, enhancing recognition accuracy and reliability. Reference [18] developed a method using time–frequency energy spectrum texture features for modulation recognition, employing a support vector machine classifier for training and classification.

Although DNNs have many advantages in the field of signal modulation recognition, there are also some problems and challenges, such as the large amount of data demands and lack of model generalization ability; the deep learning model is also more sensitive to targeted adversary attacks. Small and intentional disturbances may lead to classification errors in the model, which seriously affect the reliability and security of signal recognition.

Research on countermeasure samples for modulation recognition started late. In recent years, the academic community has gradually turned its attention to research on countermeasure sample attack methods based on modulation classification. In 2018, Sadeghi [19] and others took the lead in research on countering sample attacks against the modulation recognition model of communication signals based on DL. The research results show that the modulation recognition model based on a DNN automatic encoder is vulnerable to interference. The paper further expounds on how attackers can effectively counterattacks. In 2020, Zhao [20] and others studied and tested counterattack in the process of signal recognition, successfully reduced the recognition accuracy of the model through experiments, and verified the generalization ability of the model. In 2021, Lin et al. [21] analyzed the effects of various gradient-based counterattack methods on modulation recognition; the experimental results showed that when the disturbance intensity was set to 0.001, the prediction accuracy could be reduced by 50%.

At present, the primary goal of counterattacks in modulation recognition is to improve attack performance, but research in the field of communication is still in its infancy, lacking the theoretical interpretation of counter samples. Most of the existing explanations are limited to a hypothetical interpretation and do not fully analyze the characteristics of the communication signal. Furthermore, current methods inadequately address the characteristics and gradient reliability of modulation signals, leading to issues like poor counterattack performance and limited black box adaptability. Improving the processing of the modulation signal's characteristic gradient can significantly enhance both the effectiveness of attacks and the model's security.

3. Anti Attack Method Based on Adaptive Whitening and Feature Gradient Smoothing
3.1. System Model

In the wireless communication environment, both the transmitter and receiver of frequency-hopping signals use the same communication protocol. During the communication process, the sender first modulates the frequency-hopping signal onto a carrier using a particular method to create a frequency-hopping modulation signal, which is then transmitted over the channel. The receiver needs to use the same modulation method as the sender to demodulate and reconstruct the received modulated signal and finally complete the communication process. Considering the existence of the reconnaissance party in the communication process, this party intercepts the communication signal and uses the intelligent DNN model to identify the modulation type of the signal, aiming to capture the content of the frequency-hopping signal. The system model is shown in Figure 3.

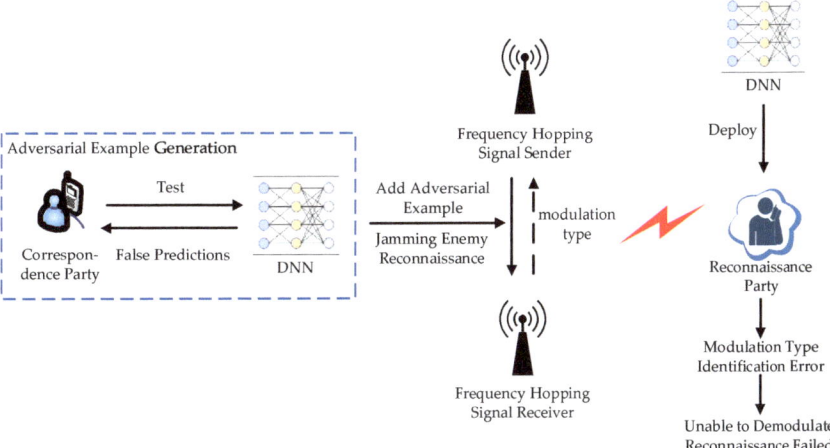

Figure 3. System model adversarial example attack in communication system.

To avoid this situation, the communication party needs to add adversarial examples to the communication signal on the premise of ensuring that its own communication is not affected as much as possible. This is done to flexibly attack the reconnaissance party deploying the DNN model and interfere with and mislead the identification results of the DNN model of the reconnaissance party so that the reconnaissance party cannot correctly identify the modulation type or demodulate and recover the intercepted signal, achieving the purpose of anti-reconnaissance. In this paper, an anti-attack method based on adaptive whitening and feature gradient smoothing (AWFGS) is proposed. Initially, the obtained frequency-hopping signal is adaptively whitened to enhance the useful features of the signal and facilitate subsequent feature extraction. Subsequently, the hidden layer feature extracted by the DNN model is used as the attack object, which significantly improves the attack accuracy and produces more refined adversarial examples, and the generated countermeasure samples have higher mobility.

3.2. Adaptive Whitening

Blind source separation refers to the process of recovering the source signal only by using the observed signal according to the statistical characteristics of the signal without any prior knowledge of the source signal and transmission channel. It has important applications in wireless communication and voice signal and digital image processing [22]. As a necessary preprocessing step of blind source separation, whitening can identify the mixing matrix and directly realize the blind separation of non-stationary signals.

Currently, the whitening algorithm can be divided into a batch algorithm and an adaptive algorithm. The batch processing algorithm has good robustness, but it cannot meet the requirements of the system for real-time signal processing. The adaptive whitening algorithm, which is less complex, supports the online processing of mixed signals with effective real-time performance and has therefore been widely adopted and researched [23]. Therefore, when whitening the original signal, the whitening algorithm with an adaptive form [22] is often used. Since signal processing often involves processing signals with different characteristics and statistical properties, and these signals may have different distributions in time and frequency domains, adaptive whitening can better process different types and properties of signal data by adjusting the characteristics and statistical properties of the signal to preprocess the data, thus enhancing the overall effectiveness and quality of signal processing. Moreover, in feature extraction and pattern recognition, adaptive whitening can enhance the useful features in the signal, which is helpful for subsequent pattern recognition, classification, or prediction. Its structure is shown in Figure 4 [24].

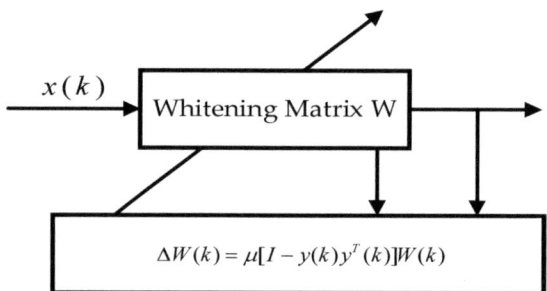

Figure 4. Structure of adaptive whitening algorithm.

$W \in R^{n \times m}$ is the whitening matrix with full rank, and the output whitening vector $y(k)$ meets the following characteristics:

$$E\{y(k)y^T(k)\} = WE\{x(t)x(t)^T\}W^T = I \quad (9)$$

$$R_{xx} = E\{x(k)x(k)^T\} = V_x H_x V_x^T \quad (10)$$

where $x(k)$ is the observation signal, I is the identity matrix, R_{xx} is the autocorrelation matrix of signal $x(k)$, and V_x and H_x are the eigenvector matrix and eigenvalue matrix of R_{xx}, respectively.

The adaptive whitening algorithm has excellent tracking performance and conditions for real-time signal processing. Its estimation of the whitening matrix $W(k)$ can be obtained by minimizing the cost function of Equation (11):

$$J(k) = -\frac{1}{2}\{\log[\det(W^T(k)W(k))] - \sum_{i=1}^{n} E(y_i^2(k))\} \tag{11}$$

where $\det(Z)$ represents the determinant operation on matrix Z. On the derivation of the instantaneous estimation of $W(k)$ over $J(k)$, there are the following:

$$\frac{\partial J(k)}{\partial W(k)} = -\left[I - y(k)y^T(k)\right]W(k) \tag{12}$$

Based on Equation (12), the updated formula of whitening matrix $W(k)$ in the adaptive algorithm can be obtained as follows:

$$W(k+1) = W(k) - \mu\frac{\partial J(k)}{\partial W(k)} = W(k) + \mu[I - y(k)y^T(k)]W(k) \tag{13}$$

where $y(k) = Wx(k)$ is the whitening signal and μ is the step size parameter. In order to ensure convergence, its value should meet $0 < \mu < \frac{2}{\sqrt{\lambda_{x-\max}}(1+\sqrt{\lambda_{y-\max}})}$, where $\lambda_{x-\max}$ and $\lambda_{y-\max}$ respectively represent the maximum eigenvalues of matrices R_{xx} and $R_{yy} = E\{y(k)y^T(k)\}$.

Different from the waveform of constant-frequency continuous signals, the waveform of frequency-hopping signals shows significant discontinuity, which leads to the inaccurate extraction of frequency-hopping signal features directly using the original signal and then affects the subsequent signal processing. However, gradient features are generally represented by high-dimensional data with high correlations and much redundant information, which not only increases the difficulty of data processing and model training but also reduces the amount of information on features, resulting in some gradient features being affected by abrupt points in the signal when representing modulated signals, making gradient calculation unstable. To solve the above problems, an adaptive whitening algorithm is introduced to minimize the interference between frequencies, effectively remove the correlation between data, improve the independence of sample features, and facilitate the accurate feature extraction of subsequent models. Additionally, the reduction in correlation reduces the dependence of the model on specific features, so the adversarial examples remain effective between different models, that is, there is a higher attack success rate between different models.

3.3. Feature Gradient Smoothing

Reference [25] pointed out that the local non-smoothness of the loss surface impairs the transferability of generated adversary samples. To solve this problem, this study used the local average gradient instead of the original gradient to generate countermeasure samples, as shown in Figure 5.

Source model a was used to generate countermeasure samples to attack target model B. g_A and G_A respectively represent the gradient of a corresponding point on the loss function surface of the two models. It can be seen that the loss function curve of model a showed an obvious oscillation phenomenon, which made the direction difference between g_A and g_B larger, which meant that the countermeasure samples generated on g_A could not effectively attack model B, and the migration of countermeasure samples was low. If the gradient smoothing process was applied to model a, the local average gradient G_A was obtained to replace the original g_A-generated countermeasure samples to attack model B. Since the directions of G_A and g_B were closer, the migration of countermeasure samples could be higher, and the attack performance for model B was stronger, that is, $\left\langle \hat{G}_A, \hat{g}_B \right\rangle > \left\langle \hat{g}_A, \hat{g}_B \right\rangle$.

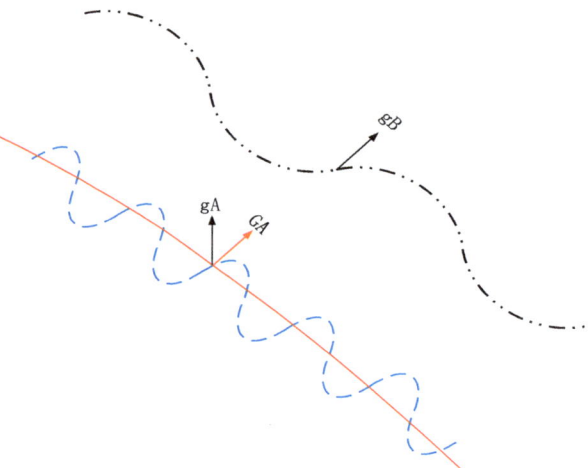

Figure 5. Example of non-smoothed lossy surface.

In this study, we approximated the mathematical expectation of the gradient in the neighborhood by sampling n times in the neighborhood of the sample x_s:

$$E_{\varepsilon'}(x_s) = \frac{1}{N} \sum_{i=1}^{n} f_L(x_s^i; \theta) \tag{14}$$

where $E_{\varepsilon'}(x_s)$ is the average value of characteristics in the x_s neighborhood and ε' is the upper boundary of the x_s neighborhood, set as $\varepsilon' = \beta \varepsilon$, where β is the super parameter.

At present, although modulated signals based on gradient have destructiveness against attacks, they also have a series of limitations and challenges. Compared with high-dimensional data such as pictures, the amount of information in the spectrum signal sample is smaller, and the high-dimensional vector of the middle layer of the deep learning model can magnify the key features of the input sample. If the middle layer features extracted by the DNN model are used as the attack object, and the average gradient of its neighborhood is used to replace its single-point gradient, the surface oscillation of the loss function can be effectively smoothed, the accuracy of the attack can be improved, and a more refined modulated signal can be generated against the sample. In addition, for the same type of modulated signal samples, after different DNN models are trained, the output characteristics of the intermediate layer usually show some similarity, and the characteristics of the samples are transferable. Therefore, the disturbance generated by the counterattacks based on the characteristics of the middle layer should have better mobility.

3.4. Description of Attack Methods

Algorithm 1 introduces the process of generating countermeasure samples based on adaptive whitening and feature gradient smoothing. Firstly, the signal samples are adaptively whitened before the original signal input model, so that the sample features extracted after the input model are more effective, and the gradient can be calculated by using the rich space–time features in the hidden layer of the DNN model. Then, n samples are taken within a certain domain of the current data point x_n^{adv}, n x_n^{adv} samples are input into the intercepted hidden layer model f_L, $E_{\varepsilon'}(x_n^{adv})$ is calculated according to Formula (14), and then the mathematical expectation $E_{\varepsilon'}(x)$ of the gradient in the neighborhood of the data point is used to replace the gradient value of the point for subsequent iterations to reduce unstable factors, avoiding the algorithm falling into local extreme points and effectively smoothing the oscillation of the loss function surface. Then, a new loss function J_L is constructed by Formula (15), and the characteristic gradient is calculated and the attenuation factor g_n is updated. Finally, x_{n+1}^{adv} is continuously updated to obtain the required countermeasure sample x^{adv}. The complete block diagram of the algorithm is shown in Figure 6.

Algorithm 1 AWFGS-MIFGSM adversarial example attacks

Input: Raw modulated signal sample x_S, Truncate hidden layer model f_L, New loss function J_L, Norm constraint p, Momentum decay factor μ, Disturbance size ε, Sampling times N, Iterations T, Attenuation factor g_n, Neighborhood range size β.
Output: Optimize adversarial example x^{adv}.

1:     Iteration step $\alpha = \varepsilon/T$, neighborhood boundary $\varepsilon' = \beta \cdot \varepsilon$

2:     $g_0 = 0$, $x_0^{adv} = x_S$

3:     **For** t = 0 **to** T − 1 **do**

4:     $(x_n^{adv})_{whitened}$ is obtained by adaptive whitening of x_n^{adv}

5:     Take N samples randomly for ε' neighborhood of $(x_n^{adv})_{whitened}$

6:     Input N samples into the hidden layer model f_L and obtain $E_{\varepsilon'}(x_n^{adv})_{whitened}$ according to Formula (13)

7:     Calculate new loss function $J_L(x_n^{adv}; \theta) = \left\| E_{\varepsilon'}(x_n^{adv})_{whitened} \right\|_p$

8:     Calculate characteristic gradient, update g_{n+1}

$$g_{n+1} = \mu \cdot g_n + \frac{\nabla_{x_n^{adv}} J_L(x_m^{adv}, \theta)}{||\nabla_{x_n^{adv}} J_L(x_m^{adv}, \theta)||_1}$$

9:     Update $x_{n+1}^{adv} = \text{Clip}_\varepsilon \left\{ x_n^{adv} + \alpha \cdot \text{sign}(g_{n+1}) \right\}$

10:    End for

11:    Obtain optimized adversarial example x^{adv}

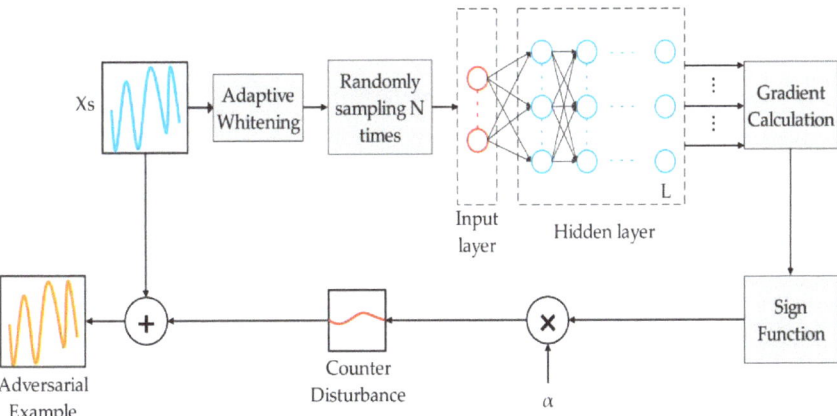

Figure 6. Anti sample attack based on adaptive whitening and feature gradient smoothing.

After obtaining the original signal sample feature $(x_S)_{whitened}$ after whitening, the average feature information is obtained. Different loss functions can be designed by using different p ($p = 0, 1, \ldots, \infty$) norms to constrain the features, as shown in Formula (15).

$$J_L(x_S, \theta) = ||E_{e'}(x_s)||_p \tag{15}$$

To verify the effectiveness of the experimental method, AWFGS is introduced into MI-FGSM to obtain the momentum iteration fast gradient sign method AWFGS-MIFGSM, which is based on adaptive whitening and feature gradient smoothing. The pseudo-code of the algorithm is shown in Algorithm 1.

3.5. Analysis of Attack Methods

1. In machine learning, input data typically consist of various measurements, and there is a significant correlation between adjacent sampling points. If unprocessed data are fed into the network, this creates excessive redundancy and lowers the network's training efficiency. A whitening operation before feature extraction can decrease data correlation and streamline the feature extraction process. Subsequently, the gradient calculated from these processed features is used to attack the DNN model. This approach enhances the mobility of the generated adversarial examples, increasing their attack success rate across different models. The reduction in correlation diminishes the model's reliance on specific features, thereby increasing the likelihood that an adversarial example will be effective across various models.
2. Most of the attacks based on label gradients are methods that attackers try to maximize the gradient of the loss function with respect to the input data so that the model can produce a false classification of the adversarial example. In this process, the optimization goal is to maximize the classification loss. Adjusting the input data thus generates classification errors in the adversarial examples. The proposed algorithm does not use the classification loss as the optimization goal but uses extensive high-dimensional feature data in the DNN hidden layer to design adversarial examples, which not only makes the obtained sample signal features richer but also produces finer disturbances.
3. At present, most of the methods that have been used to combat sample attacks use the single-point data gradient value on the optimized path. Because the surface oscillation of the loss function leads to the unreliability of the single-point gradient information, the method proposed in this paper helps the model make full use of the data point neighborhood gradient information by whitening and neighborhood sampling, making the gradient direction on the loss function of the source model and the attack model closer so that the disturbance generated by this has better mobility and the success rate of black box attacks is higher.

4. Experimental Results and Analysis

4.1. Experimental Setup

All experiments were calculated on NVIDIA GeForce GTX 1650 GPU and implemented by Tensorflow2.8 and cuda12.1.

4.1.1. Data Set

In this study, the frequency-hopping modulation signal was generated by MATLAB R2024a software simulation as the experimental data set. The data set covered four common modulation methods of frequency-hopping signals and simulated the Gaussian white noise in the real channel environment, which better restored the signals collected by the real communication. Using this data set, the recognition of the model for the basic modulation type signals and noise interference environment could be compared. The four modulation modes of the data set were divided into two digital modulation modes (QPSK and MFSK) and two analog modulation modes (AM and SSB). The frequency-hopping signal sampling rate was 40 KHz, the hopping speed was set to 500 hop/s, and eight frequency-hopping points were set, 250 points for each hopping. With the background of Gaussian white noise, the signal-to-noise ratio ranged from -20 dB to 18 dB, with an interval of 2 dB. The frequency-hopping signal of each modulation type generated 300 samples under each signal-to-noise ratio, including 24,000 signal samples in total. The data set was divided into a 70% training set, 20% verification set, and 10% test set.

4.1.2. DNN Model

Considering the characteristics of signal samples, model parameters, recognition effects under normal conditions, and other factors, ResNet, CLDNN, and LSTM were selected as modulation recognition models in this study. Each model was trained 500 times, and the learning rate was set to 0.001. If the training loss of the test set did not decrease for five consecutive times, the learning rate was halved.

4.1.3. Hyperparameter Settings

During the model training phase, to ensure the training's efficiency and consistency, the number of iterations, learning rate, and other hyperparameters were kept consistent. To set the maximum disturbance reference [19], PNR (perturbation-to-noise ratio) controlled ε under different signal-to-noise ratios, iteration times $M = 10$, the momentum attenuation factor $\mu = 0.7$, the step size of adaptive whitening was set to 0.001, sampling times N in the neighborhood was 30, and the neighborhood range size β was 11.

4.1.4. Evaluation Index

To effectively evaluate the AWFGS-MIFGSM method, three evaluation metrics—total attack time, attack success rate, and black box migration rate—were defined for the generated countermeasure samples.

The total attack time was represented by the time required by different algorithms in the white box scenario to complete the white box targetless attack on all samples on the model.

The attack success rate was expressed by the model recognition accuracy (MRA). The lower the recognition accuracy rate, the higher the attack success rate against the sample. If the total number of test samples was m and the number of samples successfully identified by the model was n, then the MRA was as follows:

$$MRA = \frac{N}{M} \times 100\% \qquad (16)$$

Black box mobility (BBM) refers to the ratio between the number of samples that can deceive both the white box model and the black box model in the countermeasure samples and the number of successful deceptions of the white box model. Let the number of samples that successfully deceive the white box model be D_w, and the number of samples that can also deceive the black box model among the samples that deceive the white box model be D_b. Then, BBM is as follows:

$$BBM = \frac{D_b}{D_w} \qquad (17)$$

4.2. Analysis of Results in Different Experimental Environments

In this study, the data set was tested with three models, and the modulation recognition accuracy of the three models was obtained, as shown in Figure 7. With the increase in the signal-to-noise ratio, the accuracy of the three models showed an upward trend and then tended to be stable. When the signal-to-noise ratio was negative because the noise power exceeded the signal power, the characteristics of the signal waveform itself were distorted, so the recognition rates of the three models were generally lower than those under the positive signal-to-noise ratio. When the signal-to-noise ratio was greater than 2 dB, the recognition effect was the best, and the curve tended to be stable. The recognition accuracies of CLDNN and ResNet were close at 2–18 dB.

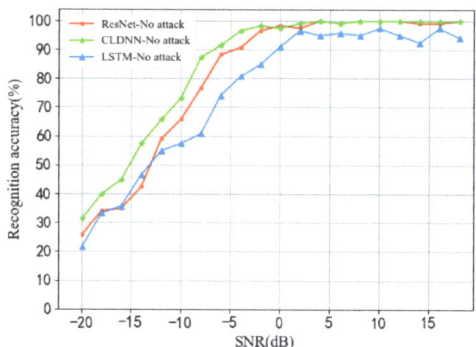

Figure 7. Modulation recognition accuracy of three models without attack.

4.2.1. Analysis of White Box Environment Experiment

The core purpose of generating adversarial examples was to cause the recognition model to misclassify the original samples. Based on this feature, this method only attacked the samples correctly classified in the original samples when carrying out white box attacks. In addition, considering the characteristics of modulated signals with different signal-to-noise ratios, it was also necessary to attack one by one for different signal-to-noise ratios when performing a counter sample attack.

Figure 8 shows the modulation recognition accuracy of the three models after generating adversarial examples from FGSM, I-FGSM, MI-FGSM and the algorithm AWFGS-MIFGSM proposed in this paper under the condition of no target in the white box. A comparison showed the following:

1. The white box no-target attack was relatively simple. Under low SNR, each attack method could make the recognition rate of the model reach less than 25%, but, under high SNR, the FGSM attack effect was the worst, and the accuracy rate of the model only decreased by about 35% at 10 dB, which was significantly weaker than other attack methods. The reason may be that FGSM covers single-step attacks, and the gradient direction of the generated disturbance was inaccurate for the nonlinear model.
2. MI-FGSM introduces momentum into I-FGSM to correct the gradient. Theoretically, the attack effect should be better than that of I-FGSM. However, in the LSTM and ResNet models, the attack effect of the two models was almost the same under low SNR. In the CLDNN model, the attack effect was not as good as that of I-FGSM when it was more than −2 dB. On the one hand, the difference in the model structure had an impact on the output. On the other hand, the amount of information in a single signal sample may have been too small, so there was no qualitative change to the gradient correction, or even the opposite effect.
3. PGD is recognized as the most effective first-order attack in the industry. It can be seen from the algorithm that PGD randomly added some noise to the attack destination samples and projected the gradient obtained in each iteration, which could retain more useful disturbance information. As a result, the attack effect was significantly better than that of FGSM, I-FGSM, and MI-FGSM, and the model recognition rate could be reduced to about 40%.
4. At 10 dB, the recognition rate of the CLDNN model, LSTM model, and ResNet model decreased by 71%, 66%, and 69%, respectively. However, at low SNR, the recognition rate of the CLDNN and LSTM models was slightly higher than that of the other attack methods. On the one hand, whitening and gradient smoothing may cause the method to generate more diversified countermeasure samples. At low SNR, this diversity may make it easier for countermeasure samples to escape from the detection or recognition system, thereby improving the recognition rate. On the other hand, the CLDNN and LSTM models may have certain robustness when processing sequence data, and

this method "corrects" some noise in the original signal to some extent at low SNR, making it easier to identify at low SNR.

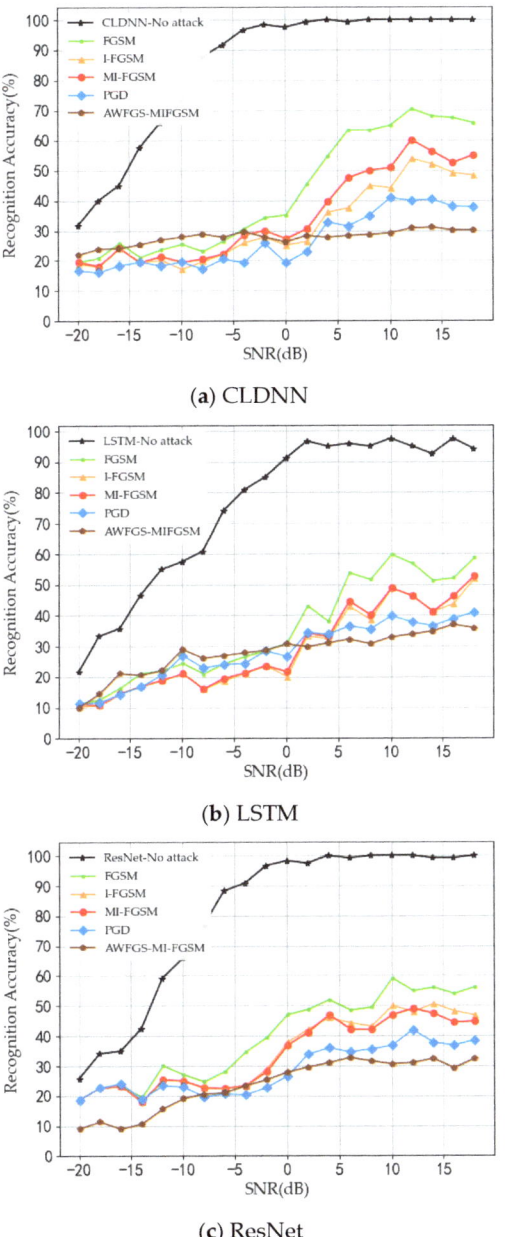

Figure 8. Recognition accuracy of three models under white box no-target attack.

From the previous analysis, the attack effect of FGSM was the worst, but, due to its one-step calculation characteristics, it took the least time to generate adversarial examples. I-FGSM, MI-FGSM, and PGD were all iterative attacks. With the same number of iterations, it took a relatively long time to generate adversarial examples, but the difference was not significant. Because the proposed algorithm AWFGS-MIFGSM needed to sample samples and calculate the feature gradient smoothing, it took the longest time to generate adversblearial examples, but the attack success rate was the highest (see Table 1).

Table 1. The time consumption of the three models to generate countermeasure samples under the white box no-target attack.

DNN Model	ATS (min)				
	FGSM	I-FGSM	MI-FGSM	PGD	AWFGS-MIFGSM
CLDNN	1.05	7.13	7.35	8.08	9.23
LSTM	0.91	7.31	7.47	7.44	48.09
ResNet	1.21	2.79	2.85	3.19	15.26

4.2.2. Experimental Analysis of Black Box Environment

In the real electronic warfare environment, the information related to the target model is often unknown to the communicators, that is, it is usually the case of a black box attack. At this time, the adversarial examples generated by the communicators must have good mobility.

Different from the traditional attack method of using an alternative model to replace the target black box model, to better verify the transferability of countermeasure samples, this study directly migrated the countermeasure samples generated in the CLDNN white box attack to the LSTM and ResNet models to execute the black box attack. The experimental results are shown in Figure 9.

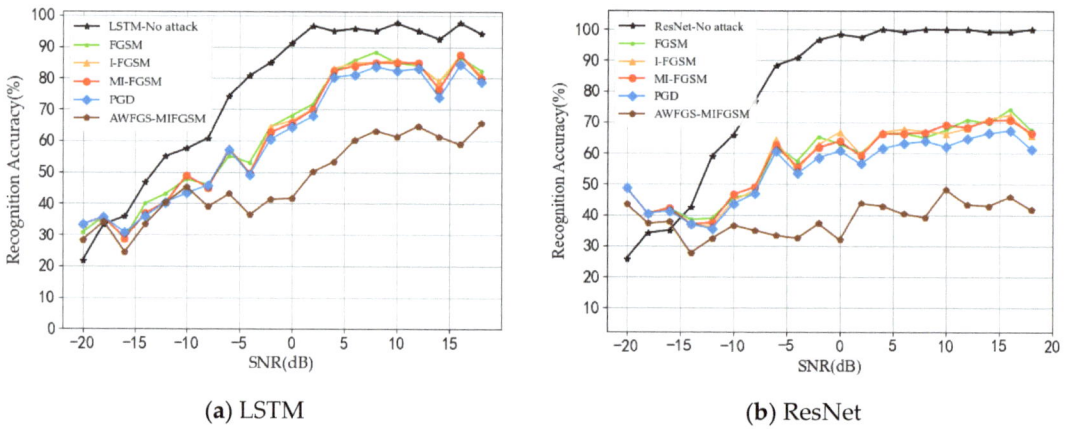

(a) LSTM   (b) ResNet

Figure 9. Recognition accuracy of two models under black box non-target attack.

As can be seen from Figure 9, due to the unknown black box information, the effect of all the anti-attack methods was reduced to varying degrees, but the attack performance of the method proposed in this paper remained optimal whether in low SNR or high SNR. It can be seen from Figure 9a that for the black box model of LSTM, the attack methods that could significantly reduce the recognition rate of the CLDNN model migrated to the LSTM model, and the attack effect was significantly worse. At 10 dB, FGSM, I-FGSM, and MI-FGSM only reduced the recognition rate of the LSTM model by about 13%. Although PGD achieved good results in the white box attack, its attack effect in the black box model was also unsatisfactory. In contrast, the attack method proposed in this paper still had a good effect. At 10dB, the recognition rate of the LSTM model was reduced by 37%.

It can also be seen from Figure 9b that the adversarial examples generated by the attack method based on adaptive whitening and feature gradient smoothing still had a strong attack effect when migrated to the ResNet black box model. At 10 dB, FGSM, I-FGSM, and MI-FGSM only reduced the recognition rate of the ResNet model by about 31%. The PGD method only reduced the recognition rate of the ResNet model by 36%. The recognition rate of the RESNET model was reduced by 51% by the proposed method.

Figure 10 shows the proportion of the counter samples that successfully attacked the white box model but also successfully attacked the black box model, that is, the comparison of black box mobility. It is evident that the black box mobility of the adversarial examples generated by the AWFGS-MIFGSM method was higher than that generated by the traditional method, whether using the LSTM model or the ResNet model, which shows that the adversarial example attack method proposed in this paper has superior attack migration performance, significantly improving the robustness of adversarial examples.

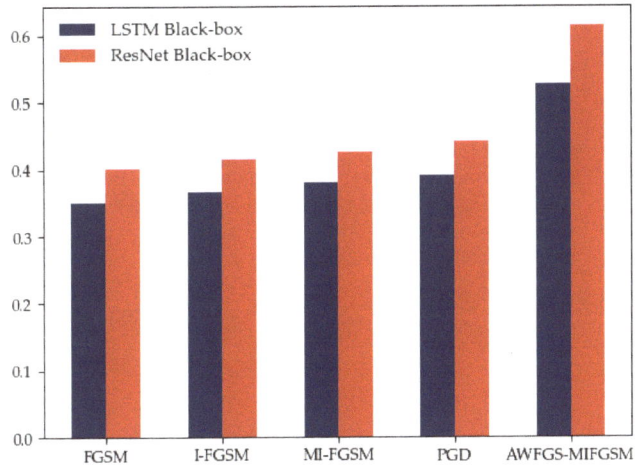

Figure 10. Black box mobility.

4.2.3. Experimental Performance Analysis under Mixed Signal-to-Noise Ratio

In the actual battlefield environment, the signal-to-noise ratio of the received frequency-hopping signal is not fixed. In order to better verify the attack performance of the method proposed in this paper under a mixed signal-to-noise ratio, the data set was processed as follows: 3000 samples were randomly extracted from each type of signal, and the training set and verification set were formed according to 4:1. The above three models of ResNet, CLDNN, and LSTM were trained, and the test set was composed of 10% of all test samples divided by 4.1. A comparison of the recognition results of the three models in the white box environment is shown in Table 2.

Table 2. Comparison of average recognition accuracy of three models under mixed SNR.

DNN Model	Recognition Accuracy under Different Attack Modes (%)					
	No Attack	FGSM	I-FGSM	MI-FGSM	PGD	AWFGS-MIFGSM
ResNet	82.08	39.77	34.43	33.61	28.67	23.66
CLDNN	84.17	42.67	31.57	34.66	26.50	27.75
LSTM	77.24	35.25	28.58	29.17	28.15	28.26

It can be seen from the results in Table 2 that for the mixed signal-to-noise ratio data, the three models had good recognition performance for frequency-hopping modulated signals under conventional conditions, and the average recognition accuracy was more than 77%. The FGSM, I-FGSM, and MI-FGSM attack methods significantly reduced the recognition rate of the model, and the PGD method had a better attack effect than the first three methods in the three models, but the attack effect of the AWFGS-MIFGSM method proposed in this paper was stronger than that of PGD method in the ResNet model, and was almost the same as that of the PGD method in the CLDNN and ResNet models, indicating that this method still had strong attack performance for mixed signal-to-noise ratio data.

4.2.4. Hyperparameters Analysis

The control variable method was used to study the hyperparameters. Therefore, except for the number of samples in neighborhood N and the size of neighborhood β, other parameters remained unchanged. At the same time, all signal samples under 10 dB were extracted from the original data set, and 600 signal samples with a signal-to-noise ratio of 10 dB were randomly selected from the training set to form a new test set, which was subjected to white box non-target attack.

First, the neighborhood size β was analyzed and the sampling times N were set in the neighborhood to 30. The experimental results are shown in Figure 11. It can be seen from the figure that when $\beta = 0$, the recognition accuracy was the highest and the attack effect was the worst. When increasing the value of β, the recognition rate of the model continued to decline until $\beta = 11$, when the curve reached the inflection point, but the recognition rate increased. According to this, when the neighborhood size β was set to 11 in the experiment, the attack effect was the best.

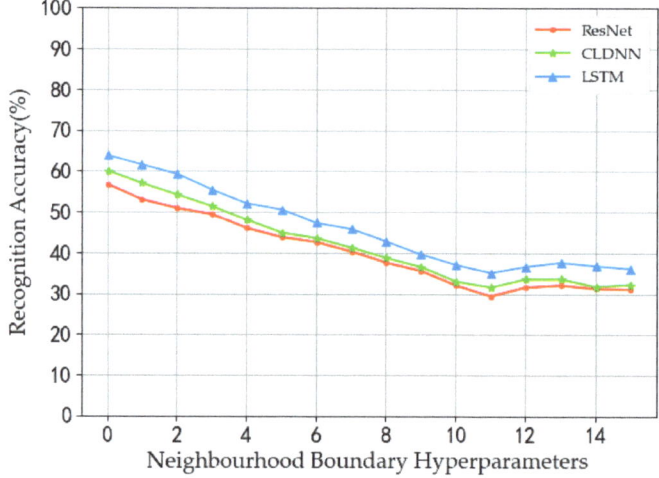

Figure 11. Relationship between neighborhood boundary and recognition accuracy at 10 dB.

We then analyzed the sampling times N within a specified neighborhood, setting the neighborhood range size to $\beta = 11$. The experimental results are shown in Figure 12. It can be seen from the figure that when $N = 0$, the recognition accuracy was the highest and the attack effect was the worst. When increasing the value of N, the recognition rate of the model continued to decline until $N = 30$, when the curve reached the inflection point, and the recognition rate tended to be stable. Considering that the larger N, the greater the computational overhead and time cost of the experiment, N was set to 30 in the experiment.

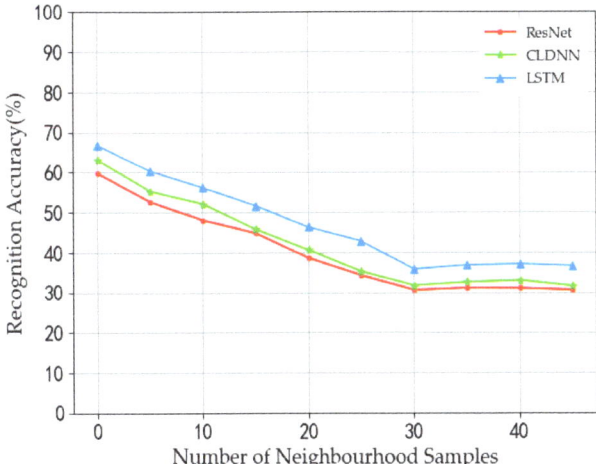

Figure 12. Relationship between sampling times and recognition accuracy in neighborhood under 10 dB.

5. Conclusions

Addressing the big gap in research on frequency-hopping modulation recognition in the field of anti-attack, this paper proposed a method of frequency-hopping modulation signal adversarial example attack based on adaptive whitening and characteristic gradients. Different from the conventional gradient attack, this study did not use classification confidence as the backpropagation data; instead, it employed the high-dimensional characteristics of the middle layer of the model to design the corresponding countermeasures. The simulation results show that the algorithm proposed in this paper achieves excellent results in both white box attack and black box attack. Although the algorithm has some advantages, there are still some further improvements: (1) like most adaptive algorithms, the adaptive whitening algorithm also has a contradiction between convergence speed and steady-state performance, which often cannot meet the requirements of the system for time-varying environment tracking ability, algorithm convergence speed, and steady-state error; (2) compared with the method of directly using tags to attack, the method proposed in this paper needs more time. How to reduce the complexity of the algorithm and improve efficiency is the main problem to be considered in the future.

Author Contributions: Conceptualization, Y.Z. and Y.L.; methodology, Y.Z., Y.L. and Z.D.; software, Y.Z. and Y.L.; validation, Y.Z., Y.L. and Z.D.; formal analysis, Y.Z., Y.L. and Z.D.; investigation, Y.Z. and Y.L.; resources, Y.Z.; data curation, Y.Z.; writing—original draft preparation, Y.Z.; writing—review and editing, Y.Z. and Y.L.; visualization, Y.Z.; supervision, Y.Z.; project administration, Y.Z.; funding acquisition, Y.L. All authors have read and agreed to the published version of the manuscript.

Funding: This research was funded by the National Natural Science Foundation of China, grant number 2022-SKJJ-B-112.

Data Availability Statement: The data presented in this study are not available due to privacy.

Conflicts of Interest: The authors declare no conflicts of interest.

References

1. Gummadi, R.; Wetherall, D.; Greenstein, B.; Seshan, S. Understanding and mitigating the impact of RF interference on 802.11 networks. In Proceedings of the ACM SIGCOMM Computer Communication Review, Kyoto, Japan, 27–31 August 2007; pp. 385–396.
2. Gao, Y.; Xiao, Y.; Wu, M.; Xiao, M.; Shao, J. Game theory-based anti-jamming strategies for frequency hopping wireless communications. *IEEE Trans. Wirel. Commun.* **2018**, *17*, 5314–5326. [CrossRef]

3. Zhang, J.; Yu, L. Frequency hopping signal modulation identification based on time-frequency characteristics. *J. Terahertz Sci. Electron. Inf.* **2022**, *20*, 40–46.
4. Panagiotou, P.; Anastasopoulos, A.; Polydoros, A. Likelihood ratio tests for modulation classification. In Proceedings of the MILCOM 2000 Proceedings. 21st Century Military Communications. Architectures and Technologies for Information Superiority (Cat. No. 00CH37155), Los Angeles, CA, USA, 22–25 October 2000; pp. 670–674.
5. Zhao, Y.; Jiang, H.; Qin, Y.; Xie, H.; Wu, Y.; Liu, S.; Zhou, Z.; Xia, J.; Zhou, F. Preserving minority structures in graph sampling. *IEEE Trans. Vis. Comput. Graph.* **2020**, *27*, 1698–1708. [CrossRef] [PubMed]
6. Abdel-Moneim, M.A.; Al-Makhlasawy, R.M.; Abdel-Salam Bauomy, N.; El-Rabaie, E.S.M.; El-Shafai, W.; Farghal, A.E.; Abd El-Samie, F.E. An efficient modulation classification method using signal constellation diagrams with convolutional neural networks, Gabor filtering, and thresholding. *Trans. Emerg. Telecommun. Technol.* **2022**, *33*, e4459. [CrossRef]
7. Li, H.G.; Guo, Y.; Sui, P. Convolutional neural network frequency hopping modulation identification based on time-frequency features. *J. Zhejiang Univ. (Eng. Ed.)* **1945**.
8. Liang, Y.X.; Tan, J.J.; Dusit, N. Research overview of smart wireless communication technology. *J. Commun.* **2020**, *41*, 1–17.
9. Szegedy, C.; Zaremba, W.; Sutskever, I. Intriguing properties of neural networks. In Proceedings of the 2nd International Conference on Learning Representations, Banff, AB, Canada, 14–16 April 2013; pp. 1–10.
10. Goodfellow, I.J.; Shlens, J.; Szegedy, C. Explaining and harnessing adversarial examples. In Proceedings of the 3rd International Conference on Learning Representations, ICLR 2015, San Diego, CA, USA, 7–9 May 2015.
11. Kurakin, A.; Goodfellow, I.J.; Bengio, S. Adversarial examples in the physical world. In *Artificial Intelligence Safety and Security*; Chapman and Hall/CRC: London, England, 2018; pp. 99–112.
12. Dong, Y.; Liao, F.; Pang, T.; Su, H.; Zhu, J.; Hu, X.; Li, J. Boosting adversarial attacks with momentum. In Proceedings of the IEEE conference on computer vision and pattern recognition, Salt Lake City, UT, USA, 18–23 June 2018; pp. 9185–9193.
13. Madry, A.; Makelov, A.; Schmidt, L. Towards Deep Learning Models Resistant to Adversarial Attacks. In Proceedings of the International Conference on Learning Representations, Vancouver, BC, Canada, 30 April–3 May 2018. Available online: https://openreview.net/forum?id=rJzIBfZAb (accessed on 7 December 2023).
14. O'Shea, T.J.; Corgan, J.; Clancy, T.C. Convolutional radio modulation recognition networks. In Proceedings of the Engineering Applications of Neural Networks: 17th International Conference, EANN 2016, Aberdeen, UK, 2–5 September 2016; pp. 213–226.
15. Ali, A.; Yang, Y.F.; Liu, S. Automatic modulation classification of digital modulation signals with stacked autoencoders. *Digit. Signal Process.* **2017**, *71*, 108–116. [CrossRef]
16. Xie, W.; Hu, S.; Yu, C.; Zhu, P.; Peng, X.; Ouyang, J. Deep learning in digital modulation recognition using high order cumulants. *IEEE Access* **2019**, *7*, 63760–63766. [CrossRef]
17. Zhan, J.M.; Zhao, Z.J. Modulation recognition algorithm for conventional modulation signals and spread spectrum signals. *Signal Process.* **2020**, *36*, 511–519.
18. Li, H.G.; Guo, Y.; Sui, P. Frequency hopping modulation mode identification based on time-frequency energy spectrum texture characteristics. *J. Commun.* **2019**, *40*, 20–29.
19. Sadeghi, M.; Larsson, E.G. Adversarial attacks on deep-learning based radio signal classification. *IEEE Wirel. Commun. Lett.* **2018**, *8*, 213–216. [CrossRef]
20. Zhao, H.; Lin, Y.; Gao, S.; Yu, S. Evaluating and improving adversarial attacks on DNN-based modulation recognition. In Proceedings of the GLOBECOM 2020-2020 IEEE Global Communications Conference, Taipei, Taiwan, 7–11 December 2020; pp. 1–5.
21. Lin, Y.; Zhao, H.; Ma, X.; Tu, Y.; Wang, M. Adversarial attacks in modulation recognition with convolutional neural networks. *IEEE Trans. Reliab.* **2020**, *70*, 389–401. [CrossRef]
22. Cichocki, A.; Amari, S. *Adaptive blind signal and image processing: Learning algorithms and applications*; John Wiley & Sons: Hoboken, NJ, USA, 2002.
23. Coviello, C.M.; Yoon, P.A.; Sibul, L.H. Source separation and tracking for time-varying systems. *IEEE Trans. Aerosp. Electron. Syst.* **2008**, *44*, 1198–1214. [CrossRef]
24. Ou, S.F.; Gao, Y.; Zhao, X.H. Adaptive whitening algorithm for variable factors based on random gradients. *J. Autom.* **2012**, *38*, 1370–1374.
25. Wu, L.; Zhu, Z.; Tai, C. Understanding and enhancing the transferability of adversarial examples. *arXiv* **2018**, arXiv:1802.09707.

Disclaimer/Publisher's Note: The statements, opinions and data contained in all publications are solely those of the individual author(s) and contributor(s) and not of MDPI and/or the editor(s). MDPI and/or the editor(s) disclaim responsibility for any injury to people or property resulting from any ideas, methods, instructions or products referred to in the content.

Review

Machine-Learning-Based Traffic Classification in Software-Defined Networks

Rehab H. Serag [1,2], Mohamed S. Abdalzaher [3,*], Hussein Abd El Atty Elsayed [4], M. Sobh [1], Moez Krichen [5,6] and Mahmoud M. Salim [7,8]

1. Department of Computer and Systems Engineering, Faculty of Engineering, Ain Shams University, Cairo 11566, Egypt; 2000764@eng.asu.edu.eg (R.H.S.)
2. Department of Electronics and Communications Engineering, Faculty of Engineering, Egyptian Russian University, Badr City 11829, Egypt
3. Department of Seismology, National Research Institute of Astronomy and Geophysics, Helwan 11421, Egypt
4. Department of Electronics and Communications Engineering, Faculty of Engineering, Ain Shams University, Cairo 11566, Egypt; helsayed@eng.asu.edu.eg
5. Department of Information Technology, Faculty of Computer Science and Information Technology, Al-Baha University, Al-Baha 65528, Saudi Arabia
6. ReDCAD Laboratory, University of Sfax, Sfax 3038, Tunisia
7. Interdisciplinary Research Center for Communication Systems and Sensing, King Fahd University of Petroleum & Minerals (KFUPM), Dhahran 31261, Saudi Arabia
8. Department of Electronics and Communications, Faculty of Engineering, October 6 University (O6U), Giza 12585, Egypt
* Correspondence: msabdalzaher@nriag.sci.eg

Citation: Serag, R.H.; Abdalzaher, M.S.; Elsayed, H.A.E.A.; Sobh, M.; Krichen, M.; Salim, M.M. Machine-Learning-Based Traffic Classification in Software-Defined Networks. *Electronics* **2024**, *13*, 1108. https://doi.org/10.3390/electronics13061108

Academic Editor: Christos J. Bouras

Received: 5 February 2024
Revised: 11 March 2024
Accepted: 13 March 2024
Published: 18 March 2024

Copyright: © 2024 by the authors. Licensee MDPI, Basel, Switzerland. This article is an open access article distributed under the terms and conditions of the Creative Commons Attribution (CC BY) license (https://creativecommons.org/licenses/by/4.0/).

Abstract: Many research efforts have gone into upgrading antiquated communication network infrastructures with better ones to support contemporary services and applications. Smart networks can adapt to new technologies and traffic trends on their own. Software-defined networking (SDN) separates the control plane from the data plane and runs programs in one place, changing network management. New technologies like SDN and machine learning (ML) could improve network performance and QoS. This paper presents a comprehensive research study on integrating SDN with ML to improve network performance and quality-of-service (QoS). The study primarily investigates ML classification methods, highlighting their significance in the context of traffic classification (TC). Additionally, traditional methods are discussed to clarify the ML outperformance observed throughout our investigation, underscoring the superiority of ML algorithms in SDN TC. The study describes how labeled traffic data can be used to train ML models for appropriately classifying SDN TC flows. It examines the pros and downsides of dynamic and adaptive TC using ML algorithms. The research also examines how ML may improve SDN security. It explores using ML for anomaly detection, intrusion detection, and attack mitigation in SDN networks, stressing the proactive threat-detection and response benefits. Finally, we discuss the SDN-ML QoS integration problems and research gaps. Furthermore, scalability and performance issues in large-scale SDN implementations are identified as potential issues and areas for additional research.

Keywords: software-defined networking (SDN); machine learning (ML); Quality of Service (QoS); traffic classification (TC); security

1. Introduction

The installation and configuration of network elements are complex tasks that require skilled personnel. When dealing with network nodes that interact with each other in complicated ways, a system-based approach involving simulation is necessary. However, the current programming interfaces of most networking equipment make it difficult to achieve this [1]. Furthermore, to manage large, multi-vendor networks, with various technologies becoming increasingly costly, service providers face resource shortages and rising real-estate expenses. A novel network paradigm is required to integrate network management and provisioning across many domains [2].

In network devices like switches and routers, SDN is a technique that separates the control plane from the data plane [3,4]. The control plane and data plane are tightly entwined in conventional networks, making it challenging to manage and scale the network [5]. In an SDN design, a central controller controls the network and communicates with switches and routers using a standard protocol, such as OpenFlow protocol [6].

Increased network scalability and flexibility are advantages of SDN. Network administrators may simply manage, configure, and enhance the network with a centralized controller. SDN additionally enables the development of virtual networks that can be altered to accommodate particular applications or traffic types. The SDN architecture is depicted in Figure 1, and is made up of the data plane, control plane, and application plane [7,8].

The data plane consists of network devices such as routers, switches, and access points that are accessed and managed through control–data-plane interfaces (C-DPIs) by SDN controllers. The most commonly used C-DPI is the OpenFlow protocol [6,9]. The implementation of the SDN architecture heavily relies on the control plane. Essentially, the control plane functions as a separate process that operates within the control layer. This layer consists of one or more controllers that offer a comprehensive perspective of the entire SDN system through C-DPI. The controllers consist of essential components, such as a coordinator and virtualizer, which are responsible for managing the behavior of the controller. Additionally, there is a control logic that translates the networking needs of applications into instructions for allocating network element resources. Finally, the application plane is made up of one or more network applications that communicate with the controller(s) in order to use an abstract view of the network for internal decision-making. These applications exchange data with the controller(s) using an open application–controller-plane interface (A-CPI), such as REST API [9].

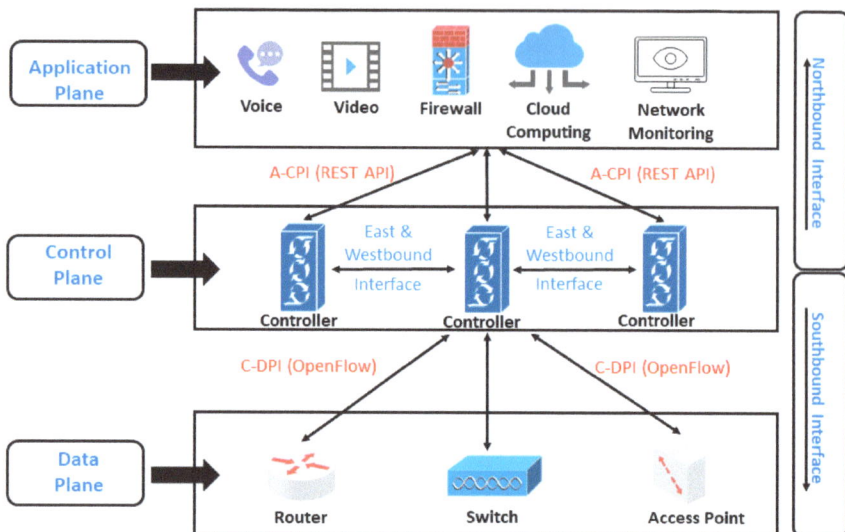

Figure 1. SDN architecture.

Table 1 presents the common existing SDN controllers: NOX [10], Floodlight [11], POX [12], OpenDayLight [13], RYU [14], and Beacon [15]. These controllers can be categorized as either centralized, in which a single control entity manages the entire network, or distributed, in which the network is divided into various sections for management [16,17].

Centralized controllers can be classified as either physically centralized or logically centralized. Physically centralized controllers are installed on a single server and are responsible for managing the entire network. The benefit of a physically centralized controller is its ease of use and management due to having only one controller [11]. A logically centralized controller utilizes numerous physical servers, with each controller of a specific network duty. They all, however, use a centralized data store to replicate a common network state [18].

Distributed controllers serve as a distributed control plane for network management. Nevertheless, the network is partitioned into multiple domains, with each domain being managed by its own controller [19,20]. Distributed controllers come in two forms: flat and hierarchical designs. In a flat design, the network is divided into separate domains, with each domain having its controller. Controllers utilizing the flat design communicate with each other using east–west interfaces to gain a global network view. In contrast, hierarchical design employs a two-layer controller model. The first layer is a domain controller that handles switches and runs applications in its local domain, while the second layer is a root controller that maintains the global network and manages the domain controllers [21].

Table 1. A summary of controller types and programming platforms used.

Controller	Programming Language Used	Created by	Architecture
NOX	Python	Nicira	Physically centralized
FloodLight	Java	Big Switch Networks	Physically centralized
POX	Python	Nicira	Physically and logically centralized
OpenDaylight	Java	Linux Foundation	Distributed flat design
Ryu	Python	NTT Labs	Physically centralized
Beacon	Java	Standford University	Physically centralized

One of the most important aspects of SDN is that it allows for network programmability, which enables the seamless integration of artificial intelligence (AI) into communication networks. By leveraging the application programming interface (API), SDN empowers network managers to send powerful programming instructions to network devices. With the help of AI, it can not only schedule automated and intelligent business orchestrators but also develop AI-optimized network strategies and automatically convert them into task scripts, which can be assigned to network allocation tasks via the API. Additionally, network statistics information can be automatically collected and processed to provide a solid foundation for ongoing network optimization. New functionalities can also be intelligently added as needed to the network environment via SDN applications [22].

Machine learning (ML) is a crucial tool for enabling AI [23] as it can effectively predict and schedule network resources based on the available data inputs [24,25]. It has applications in various areas providing data acquisition and analysis by emulating human learning behavior of knowledge [26]. ML aims to enable computers to determine and enhance their performance over time without being explicitly programmed to do so [27]. ML algorithms can be supervised, unsupervised, semi-supervised, or reinforcement, varying based on the type of data utilized for model training [28,29]. Supervised learning (SL) is the process of training a model using labeled data when the right output for each input is known. Unsupervised learning (USL) includes finding patterns and relationships in unlabeled data. Semi-supervised learning (SSL) is a set of both SL and USL. In reinforcement learning (RL), an agent learns to act in a given environment in order to maximize a reward [30].

Network managers may therefore create networks that are more flexible, efficient, and safe by integrating SDN and ML. According to Figure 2, In SDN, a variety of tasks can benefit from the utilization of ML algorithms, such as network resource management, where they can forecast traffic demand and dynamically assign network resources to satisfy it. This may result in greater network resource use, which would lower overall operation costs [26].

By examining user behavior, network anomalies, and traffic patterns, ML can be used to find potential security vulnerabilities [31]. This can lessen the threat of cyberattacks, particularly from malware, which is known for its ability to remain undetected in systems and execute automated coordinated attacks, making it particularly destructive for distributed systems such as IoT and Smart cities [32]. By providing real-time detection and mitigation assistance, this approach enhances cybersecurity measures. Additionally, ML can support the detection and isolation of network defects as well as the prediction of network performance decline, resulting in a more effective and dependable network [22,33].

Last but not least, ML can be used to categorize network traffic according to the kind of application or user behavior, enabling the prioritizing of high-priority traffic and assisting in making sure that vital applications obtain the necessary QoS levels. This can improve customer pleasure and experience, especially in applications that need real-time replies, high throughput, or low latency [34].

In conclusion, ML has the potential to be a potent tool for improving a number of SDN-related features, such as security, resource management, routing optimization, QoS prediction, and TC. Organizations may optimize their networks for greater performance, dependability, and security by utilizing ML techniques, which will ultimately improve their business outcomes.

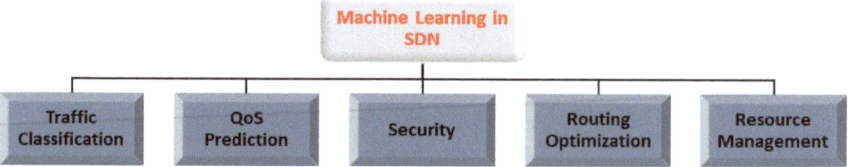

Figure 2. Machine learning applications in SDN.

Additionally, the SDN architecture's centralization and programmability, as well as the controller's capacity to gather real-time data, allow for the application of "intelligence" via ML approaches for effective routing and QoS provisioning [35].

SDN and ML have the ability to work together to build extremely intelligent and effective networks that can accommodate changing situations while delivering greater performance and security. We may anticipate seeing many more potential uses of this technology in the networking industry as ML develops.

1.1. Motivation

In [1], the focus is on the initial efforts to examine how AI is applied in the context of SDN. However, it is noteworthy that this paper does not specifically delve into TC in SDN using ML methods, but rather explores broader applications and implications of AI within the SDN framework. The overview presented in [33] provides a highly detailed introduction to basic ML algorithms and their applications in SDN networks, offering valuable references and guidance for further study. However, it is important to note that this paper covers studies only until 2018; thus, newer developments and advancements in the field may not be fully captured. The survey conducted by [26] serves as an introduction to relevant studies exploring the intersection of ML algorithms and SDN network applications, providing insights into their combined impact and potential in the field. While it may provide insights into the combined impact and potential of ML algorithms in SDN, it likely does not delve deeply into TC using ML methods. In [36], the focus is on IP TC using ML, although it does not delve into TC within the context of SDN. Our primary research objective is to offer a comprehensive overview of TC using ML techniques specifically applied in the context of SDN.

1.2. Contribution

The contributions of the paper can be listed as follows:
- Exploration of ML techniques for TC in SDN environments in a comprehensive manner.
- Incorporating the most recent research efforts in the SDN TC field.
- Including the most recent publicly available datasets suitable for training and evaluating ML models in SDN TC tasks.
- Highlighting the role of the ML model for mitigating the SDN security aspects.
- Discussing the limitations and open research issues in SDN TC.
- Providing insights into areas requiring further investigation and development.

Our paper is organized as follows. First, QoS in SDN using ML is discussed in Section 2. In Section 3, a comparison between traditional and ML TC methods is provided. Section 4 presents SDN TC using ML. Security in SDN using ML is presented in Section 5. Section 6 contains some useful datasets. Limitations and open research issues are introduced in Section 7. Finally, the paper is concluded in Section 8.

2. QoS in SDN Using Machine Learning

QoS is the ability of a network to give priority to selected network traffic and provide better service to users by ensuring dedicated bandwidth, controlling jitter and latency, and enhancing loss characteristics. QoS aims to provide end-to-end guarantees, and there are multiple technologies available to achieve this, which can be used individually or in combination. Resource reservation and allocation, prioritized scheduling, queue management, routing, and other services can be utilized by a network operating system to implement QoS.

Initially, the traditional network was not designed with QoS in mind, and various techniques were later introduced to improve performance tuning. These techniques allowed Internet Service Providers (ISPs) to optimize the internet as required. However, with emerging technologies like big data, cloud computing, and an increasing number of devices, the traditional internet faces new challenges that it struggles to cope with. SDN addresses these issues by making the internet more flexible and programmable [37]. So, as mentioned above, QoS refers to the ability to prioritize network traffic based on its importance and ensure that critical traffic receives preferential treatment over non-critical traffic. TC is one method that can be used to achieve this prioritizing [38,39].

In SDN, TC is often carried out by the controller, which can make use of ML algorithms to automatically recognize and categorize distinct forms of network traffic based on characteristics like packet size, protocol type, and application behavior. The controller can then apply QoS policies, such as giving priority to important traffic or limiting the bandwidth of specific categories of traffic, using this information.

3. Traffic Classification Using Traditional Methods vs. Machine Learning

3.1. Traditional Methods

In computer networks, traditional methods for TC imply the utilization of specific signatures, ports, or protocol headers to distinguish the traffic type. These methods are based on predefined rules that are used to distinguish between different types of traffic. Some of the commonly used techniques for TC include port-based, payload-based, deep packet inspection (DPI), and statistical-based techniques [40].

3.1.1. Port-Based TC

In the past, a widely adopted approach was port-based classification, which achieved some degree of success due to the prevalence of fixed port numbers assigned by the Internet Assigned Numbers Authority (IANA) [41]. However, this strategy revealed significant drawbacks over time. For instance, numerous applications emerged that did not possess registered port numbers, and many of them utilized dynamic port negotiation techniques to evade firewalls and network security measures. Additionally, the utilization of IP-layer encryption, obfuscation, and proxies can obscure the TCP or UDP header, rendering the original port numbers undetectable [42,43].

According to [44], utilizing the IANA list, port-based techniques achieved no more than 70% accuracy. Similarly, [45] discovered that such techniques were unable to identify 30–70% of the traffic flows they examined.

3.1.2. Deep Packet Inspection or Payload-Based TC

The deep packet inspection (DPI) technique, also known as the payload approach, was proposed to overcome the limitations of port-based classification techniques [43]. DPI classifies traffic by analyzing packet payloads and matching them with known protocol signatures [46–49]. Protocol signatures are established using regular expressions and evaluated by automata sequentially, requiring significant memory resources. Additionally, DPI is executed within the communication path, which can lead to scalability issues [42].

DPI tools such as L7-filter and OpenDPI [50,51] have been widely employed. In order to evaluate DPI techniques, in [52], it was discovered that even popular tools such as the L7-filter were only able to correctly classify 67.73% and 58.79% of bytes on the UNIBS and POLITO data sets, respectively.

Maintaining up-to-date signatures is essential for DPI techniques to remain effective, but this often requires manual effort. Unfortunately, as network applications continue to evolve, obtaining accurate signatures can become increasingly difficult [43]. In addition, introducing devices that support DPI into a network can be a costly and complex process. Also, DPI is often difficult or impossible to perform when working with encrypted traffic [33]. Furthermore, as network applications continue to proliferate rapidly and many of these applications offer similar services in practice, their QoS requirements tend to be alike. Attempting to identify each specific application using DPI becomes inefficient. Additionally, maintaining a database containing all web applications is impractical. In an operational SDN network, TC must be real-time and cost-effective. Utilizing simple DPI technology can exhaust significant controller computing resources and introduce noticeable delays to the network, thereby reducing network responsiveness [53,54].

3.1.3. Statistical-Based TC

This technique can categorize traffic streams by analyzing their statistical properties at the network layer rather than thoroughly examining the packet contents. It operates on the assumption that traffic with similar QoS requirements has comparable statistical features. As a result, several source applications can be recognized. The approach can classify flows into clusters with similar patterns by detecting trends in their properties such as the size of the initial few packets, arrival timings, packet length, IP address, round trip time, and source/destination ports [55,56].

3.2. TC Using Machine Learning

To overcome the limitations of traditional TC methods, ML algorithms are used [57,58]. The study and development of algorithms that can learn complicated correlations or patterns from empirical data, allowing them to make reliable decisions, is essential to the discipline of ML [59].

Figure 3 shows that ML typically involves several phases, including preprocessing, training, and testing. During preprocessing, data are prepared and processed, which can involve tasks such as filtering, imputation, and tuning for specific purposes. After preprocessing, the data are used to train ML methods. Finally, the system uses the trained data to make decisions based on input received during the training phase [39,56].

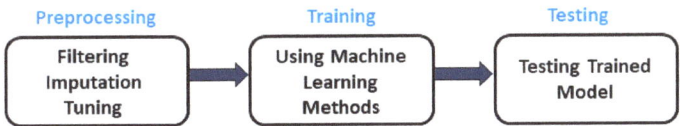

Figure 3. Machine learning phases.

ML algorithms exhibit variations in their methodology, and we classify them into four distinct categories according to the nature of the data they handle, the output they generate, and the specific task or problem they aim to address: supervised learning (SL), semi-supervised learning (SSL), unsupervised learning (USL), and reinforcement learning (RL) [26,42].

3.2.1. Supervised Learning

SL algorithms construct a mathematical model using a labeled training dataset that includes both inputs and their known outputs. These data are used by the algorithms to build a model that depicts the learned relationship between the input and output. Once trained, the model can be used to predict the output for new input data [60,61]. SL has become increasingly popular and is used in a diverse array of applications, including spam detection, speech, and object recognition [62]. SL can include both classification algorithms, which are used to predict discrete variables, and regression algorithms, which are used to predict continuous variables. These algorithms are acquired from the data and have the capability to generate predictions for novel, unseen data [26]. The drawback of the SL method is that it can attain a high level of accuracy in classifying known applications but is unable to identify unknown ones. Nonetheless, obtaining accurately labeled data can sometimes be challenging [43]. Additionally, SL not only requires a large number of data, but they must also be labeled [63]. An overview of some commonly used SL algorithms such as Decision Tree (DT), Random Forest (RF), Support Vector Machine (SVM), Naïve Bayes (NB), and Key Nearest Neighbor (KNN) will be provided.

- Decision Tree (DT)
  This method is represented by a tree structure in which the database features are represented by internal nodes and branches that specify decision criteria, and the outcome is expressed by each leaf node in a tree structure [64]. This approach computes entropy on the dataset to find information gains and classify the data. It computes entropy on the dataset to determine the root node with the maximum information gain. The technique is then repeated to separate branches and finish the tree [63].
  DT has several advantages, including its simplicity of interpretation and visualization, its ability to implicitly perform feature selection, and its ability to handle non-linear relationships among parameters. However, DT can be prone to overfitting the training data and can generate overly complex trees. It is also susceptible to instability as even little variations in the data lead to the generation of a fully contrasting tree. Furthermore, it is prone to instability because even minor changes in the data might result in the construction of an entirely different tree. Furthermore, DT may struggle to manage complex systems with inconsistent features [65,66].
- Random Forest (RF)
  The RF method is used to prevent over-fitting in the DT algorithm [33]. An RF is made up of numerous decision trees that are combined to produce a stable and trustworthy forecast. This prediction is then used for training and class prediction [67–69]. Each DT in the RF makes a class prediction, and the model prediction is made by choosing the class that has received the greatest number of votes [70].
  In addition to their capacity to manage noisy and correlated datasets and their capacity to increase classification accuracy, RF algorithms have a number of benefits [71]. In comparison to DT algorithms, they are also less prone to overfitting. In addition to offering very effective classification models, RF has the ability to assess the significance

and effects of each variable utilized in the classification procedure [72]. Additionally, it is capable of handling big datasets and missing values [63].

On the other hand, RF suffers from some disadvantages. Increasing the number of trees in RF can enhance prediction accuracy; however, this may lead to longer training times and higher memory requirements due to the large number of trees utilized. Also, RF may not produce accurate results for datasets with small sample sizes or low-dimensional data [73].

- Support Vector Machine (SVM)

  SVM is a widely used SL technique that was created by Vapnik and others [74]. It is a type of common linear classifier that implements binary classification.

  SVM seeks to find a feature space separation hyperplane that maximizes the margin between separate classes. It is worth noting that the margin refers to the distance between the hyperplane and the nearest data points of each class, and these data points are known as support vectors [75–77].

  SVM is a reliable algorithm that produces fewer false alarms in binary classification jobs. Its detection system can significantly reduce the amount of time necessary for attack identification and classification observation. Furthermore, when SVM is applied at the SDN controller level, its complexity shows a small impact on the total SDN framework [26].

- K Nearest Neighbor (KNN)

  KNN is an SL approach that employs the k nearest neighbors of an unclassified sample to determine its classification. As shown in Figure 4, the KNN algorithm is as follows: "if the majority of the k nearest neighbors belong to a particular class, the unclassified sample is classified into that class" [78]. So the detailed steps are

  1. Determine the value of the parameter "K" representing the number of neighbors.
  2. Calculate the Euclidean distance for the K neighbors.
  3. Identify the K nearest neighbors by considering the computed distance.
  4. Tally the occurrences of data points for each category within the K neighbors.
  5. Allocate the new data point to the category that has the highest frequency among the K neighbors.

  KNN is easy to implement, has high accuracy, calculates the features easily, and is suitable for multiclass classifications. However, for large datasets, KNN can be time-consuming [26].

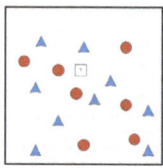 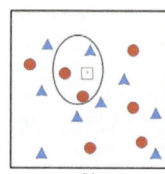 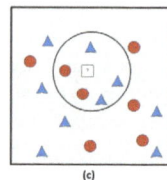

Figure 4. KNN algorithm example: (**a**) Before KNN ("?" represents the unclassified sample). (**b**) For K = 3, for the three nearest neighbors, one of them is classified as belonging to the class "Blue" while the remaining two neighbors are classified as belonging to the class "Red". As a result, the unclassified example will be categorized as class the "Red". (**c**) For K = 5, For the three nearest neighbors, three of them are classified as belonging to the class "Blue" while the remaining two neighbors are classified as belonging to the class "Red". As a result, the unclassified example will be categorized as class "Blue".

- Naïve Bayes (NB)

  NB is referred to as a probabilistic classifier because it depends on Bayes' Theorem. Bayes' theorem applies conditional probability to compute the chance of an event taking place based on the prior knowledge of conditions that may correlate with the event. Naïve Bayes theory can be represented as

$$P(X|Y) = \frac{P(Y|X)P(X)}{P(Y)} \tag{1}$$

where X and Y are events, P(X) is the prior probability of event X independent of event Y, P(Y) is the probability of event Y, P(X | Y) is called the posterior probability and it is the probability that event X will occur given the condition that Y is true, P(Y | X) is called the likelihood of X given fixed Y and can also be known as the probability that event Y will occur given the condition that X is true [79]. Those probabilities are calculated based on the training set. When classifying a fresh input data sample, the probability paradigm may generate different posterior probabilities for each class. The sample will be divided into classes based on the class with the greatest likelihood of succeeding.

The good side of Baye's theorem is that it only requires a dataset of a small size to learn the probability paradigm. On the other hand, it assumes that its predictors are conditionally independent, meaning they are not associated with any of the other features in the model. Additionally, it assumes that all features have an equal impact on the outcome. However, these assumptions are frequently not met in real-world situations [80].

3.2.2. Unsupervised Learning

To overcome the drawbacks of SL, USL is used. USL is utilized for clustering and data-aggregation tasks [61,81], where the data provided to the learner are unlabeled. In such scenarios, algorithms group the data into distinct clusters based on similarities found in the feature values [82].

USL models are required to establish relationships among elements in a dataset and classify raw data without external assistance [83]. USL algorithms can automatically discover patterns within unlabeled datasets. Nevertheless, the constructed clusters must still be mapped to their corresponding applications. Since the number of clusters is typically much greater than the number of applications, this can pose a challenge for TC tasks [43]. The algorithms commonly utilized in USL include K-Means and Self-Organizing Map (SOM).

- K-Means
  K-means is an unsupervised ML algorithm used for clustering data into groups or clusters based on similarity. The objective is to divide the data into K clusters, where each data point is assigned to the cluster whose mean or centroid is closest. The algorithm iteratively assigns data points to the nearest cluster centroid and adjusts the centroids until convergence, reducing the variance within each cluster. K-means finds applications in diverse fields like customer segmentation, image segmentation, and anomaly detection [84].
- Self-Organizing Map (SOM)
  A self-organizing map (SOM) serves as a USL technique utilized for reducing dimensionality and visualizing data. It functions by projecting high-dimensional input data onto a lower-dimensional grid of neurons, where each neuron represents a prototype or cluster within the original input space [85,86].
  In the SOM algorithm, neurons within the grid are organized based on similarities present in the input data. During the training process, input vectors are introduced to the network, and the neuron that closely matches the input vector is identified using a similarity metric, often derived from Euclidean distance. Subsequently, the weights of the winning neuron and its neighboring neurons are adjusted to move closer to the input vector, facilitating the self-organization of the map [87].
  SOMs offer a valuable means of visualizing high-dimensional data in a lower-dimensional space while retaining the topological characteristics of the original input space. They find applications across various domains, including data visualization, clustering, and pattern recognition [88].

3.2.3. Semi-Supervised Learning

Traditional ML technology is classified into two types: SL and USL. SL employs labeled sample sets for learning, while USL uses only unlabeled sample sets. However, in practical situations, the cost of labeling data can be very high, resulting in limited availability of labeled data, while a considerable number of unlabeled data are easily accessible [26]. Consequently, SSL techniques have gained popularity and are evolving rapidly, as they can utilize both labeled and unlabeled samples [89].

Typically, an SSL algorithm consists of two stages: the initial step involves analyzing labeled data to generate a general rule, which is subsequently utilized to deduce unlabeled data. Currently, the performance of SSL techniques is inconsistent and requires further enhancement [83]. Pseudo labeling [90,91], Expectation Maximization (EM), co-training, transductive SVM, and graph-based approaches are examples of SSL methods [92,93].

- Expectation Maximization (EM)

  Expectation maximization (EM) is a powerful algorithm used in statistical modeling, particularly in situations where data have missing or incomplete values or when there is a need to estimate the parameters of a probabilistic model. It is an iterative method that aims to find the maximum likelihood (ML) or maximum a posteriori (MAP) estimates of parameters in probabilistic models with latent variables [94].

  The EM algorithm consists of two main steps:

  (1) Expectation (E) step: In this step, the algorithm computes the expected value of the latent variables, given the observed data and the current estimates of the model parameters. It calculates the posterior probability distribution over the latent variables using the current parameter estimates and the observed data.

  (2) Maximization (M) step: In this step, the algorithm updates the model parameters to maximize the likelihood or posterior probability of the observed data, given the expected values of the latent variables computed in the E step. It finds the parameter values that increase the likelihood of the observed data, incorporating the information from the latent variables. The E and M steps are iteratively repeated until convergence, where the algorithm reaches a point where there is no significant improvement in the model parameters or likelihood of the data [95].

- Transductive SVM

  In traditional SL with SVMs, the algorithm learns from labeled data to classify new, unseen data points. However, in transductive SVMs, the algorithm aims to label the entire dataset, including both labeled and unlabeled instances, based on the structure of the data and the provided labels [96].

  Transductive SVMs use a combination of labeled and unlabeled data to create a decision boundary that separates different classes in the data space. By incorporating information from both labeled and unlabeled instances, transductive SVMs can potentially improve the accuracy of classification, especially when labeled data are limited or expensive to obtain [97].

  The transductive learning process in SVMs involves optimizing an objective function that considers both the labeled data's class labels and the model's predictions on the unlabeled data. This optimization aims to find the decision boundary that best fits the labeled data while also considering the distribution and structure of the unlabeled data [98].

- Co-training

  Co-training is an SSL algorithm designed for scenarios where a limited number of labeled data are available alongside a large number of unlabeled data. The key idea behind co-training is to leverage the unlabeled data to improve the performance of a classifier trained on the labeled data [99].

  The algorithm typically involves two classifiers, each trained on a different subset of features or views of the data. In each iteration of the algorithm, the classifiers are trained using the available labeled data, and then they make predictions on the unlabeled data. Instances with high-confidence predictions (i.e., predictions with high certainty) are then added to the labeled set, and the classifiers are retrained using the expanded labeled set. The co-training algorithm iterates between these steps, gradually incorporating more unlabeled data into the training process and refining the classifiers. The process continues until a stopping criterion is met, such as reaching a maximum number of iterations or when the performance of the classifiers stabilizes [99,100].

3.2.4. Reinforcement Learning

RL represents a form of ML training that relies on rewarding favorable behaviors and/or penalizing unfavorable ones. In general, an RL agent possesses the ability to perceive and interpret its environment, take actions, and acquire knowledge through the process of trial and error [101,102]. In the context of SDN implementation, RL is employed, with the controller assuming the role of the agent, while the network serves as the environment. The controller observes the state of the network and learns to make decisions regarding data forwarding. Figure 5 provides an overview of the ML algorithms.

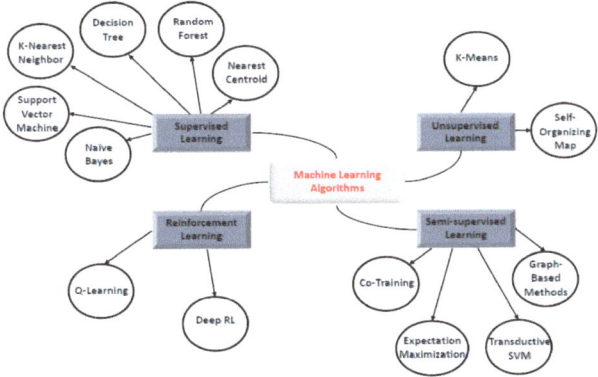

Figure 5. Machine Learning Algorithms.

3.2.5. Ensemble Learning

Ensemble learning is an ML technique that combines the predictions of multiple individual models to improve overall performance. Instead of relying on a single model, ensemble methods leverage the diversity and complementary strengths of multiple models to make more accurate predictions or decisions [103].

The primary categories of ensemble learning techniques include bagging, stacking, and boosting [104].

Bagging, short for Bootstrap Aggregating, is an ensemble learning technique used to improve the accuracy and robustness of ML models. It involves training multiple instances of a base model (DT, RF, SVM, KNN) on different subsets of the training data. These subsets are created by randomly sampling the training data with replacements (bootstrap samples). Once all the models are trained, their predictions are combined through averaging or voting to produce the final prediction. Bagging helps reduce overfitting and variance in the model by leveraging the diversity of the trained models [103]. One popular example of bagging is RF, which constructs multiple DTs trained on random subsets of the data and aggregates their predictions [67].

Boosting is an ML ensemble method used to improve the performance of weak learners (classifiers or regressors) and convert them into strong learners [105]. It works by sequentially training multiple models, where each subsequent model focuses on the examples that were misclassified by the previous ones. Through this process, misclassified instances are assigned higher weights to prioritize their inclusion in subsequent training sets, resulting in individual predictors specializing in different regions of the dataset [106]. In this way, boosting algorithms aim to reduce bias and variance. Some popular boosting algorithms include AdaBoost, Gradient Boosting Machines, and XGBoost.

(1) XGBoost is a modern tree classifier that enhances gradient boosting with optimizations for speed and scalability, allowing it to efficiently handle large-scale datasets [107].
(2) Gradient Boosting Machines (GBM) iteratively build a sequence of DTs, each correcting errors made by previous trees [108]. GBM demonstrates strong performance, but it faces challenges such as overfitting and computational speed [109].
(3) AdaBoost combines weak learners to create a strong learner, giving more weight to misclassified examples [110].

Stacking, also known as stacked generalization, is an ensemble learning technique that involves training multiple models and combining their predictions to make a final prediction. In stacking, the predictions made by each base model are used as features to train a meta-model, which learns how to best combine these predictions to make the final prediction. This meta-model is often a simple linear model or another ML algorithm [106,107].

Among the powerful ensemble learning techniques available, the Voting Classifier is a simple ensemble learning method that combines the predictions of multiple base classifiers (e.g., logistic regression, SVMs, DTs) and predicts the class with the most votes [111,112].

These ensemble learning models are widely used in various ML tasks such as classification, regression, and anomaly detection, and they often achieve higher predictive performance compared to individual models.

Table 2 presents a comparison of various ML models.

Table 2. Comparison between different ML models.

Learning Type	Definition	Task Type	Applications	Advantages	Disadvantages
Supervised Learning	Builds a mathematical model with a labeled training dataset that consists of both inputs and their known outputs	Classification, Regression	Spam detection, Speech recognition, object recognition	Accurate predictions for known applications, fast convergence, can handle multi-class classification	Requires labeled data which can be expensive and time-consuming, unable to identify unknown applications, requires large number of data, can suffer from overfitting when the model is too complex
Unsupervised Learning	Learning from unlabeled data without predefined output	Clustering, data aggregation	Anomaly detection	Automatically discover patterns within unlabeled datasets, discover hidden patterns and structures, Can handle large datasets	May produce ambiguous/difficult results interpretation, difficult to evaluate performance, the built clusters must still be mapped to their applications, and the number of clusters is much greater than the number of applications, which can pose a challenge for TC tasks

Table 2. Cont.

Learning Type	Definition	Task Type	Applications	Advantages	Disadvantages
Semi-Supervised Learning	Learning from a combination of labeled and unlabeled data	Classification, regression, clustering	Speech recognition	Utilize both labeled and unlabeled samples, can reduce the cost of labeling data	SSL means performance is inconsistent and needs enhancement, performance may depend on the quality of labeled data, to be effective may require a larger amount of unlabeled data
Reinforcement Learning	Learning through trial and error that involves rewarding desired behaviors and/or penalizing undesired ones	Decision making	Gaming	Can learn complex decision-making	Slow convergence, Requires a reward function, which may be difficult to design

4. SDN Traffic Classification Using ML

In [113], TC within an SDN/cloud environment was investigated through the application of SL. Four distinct algorithms (SVM, NB, RF, and J48 tree (C4.5)) were employed, utilizing two sets of features: features collected from observed data and default features generated from Netmate. The results for collected features indicate accuracy rates of 79.49% (SVM), 82.05% (NB), 97.44% (RF), and 82.05% (J48 tree (C4.5)), while for the generated dataset, the accuracy became 85.29% (SVM), 84.87% (NB), 95.8% (RF), and 92.86% (J48 tree (C4.5)).

Detecting and classifying conflicting flows in SDNs were discussed in [64] based on some features (action, protocol, MAC address, and IP address) using various ML algorithms (DT, SVM, EFDT, and Hybrid (DT-SVM)), and EFDT and hybrid DT-SVM algorithms were designed based on DT and SVM algorithms to achieve higher performance. The studies were carried out on two network topologies (simple tree and fat tree) with flow volumes ranging from 1000 to 100,000. The results demonstrate that EFDT has the highest accuracy.

In [114], the authors proposed a model that integrates SDN and ML algorithms for TC. SL algorithms (SVM, NB, and Nearest Centroid) were used, and the results show that the supervised models used have an accuracy of more than 90%.

In [63], it has been focused on examining and creating a TC solution using ML that could be integrated into an SDN platform. The research presented an ML-driven TC solution for SDN, leveraging existing network statistics and an offline procedure to understand network traffic patterns with the aid of a clustering algorithm. Instead of predefining a fixed number of network traffic classes, an unsupervised learning (USL) algorithm was employed to determine the most suitable number of network traffic classes, thereby offering a more customized TC approach for network operators. To accomplish this, the dataset was initially clustered and annotated using an unsupervised ML algorithm, followed by training multiple classification models based on the resulting dataset.

In Table 3, we thoroughly examine the aforementioned related works and offer a detailed comparison with respect to objective, classification models, features, dataset (topology), controller, and accuracy achieved.

Table 3. Summary of common classification ML models for SDN.

Ref.	Year	Objective	Classification Models	Required Features	Dataset	Topology Used	Controller	Accuracy
[113]	2023	Addresses TC in an SDN/cloud platform	SVM, NB, RF, and J48 tree (C4.5)	Nine features were used for the first iteration, but for the second iteration, a set of default features provided by Netmate tool were used	manually collected using the tcpdump tool	–	OpenDaylight controller	Accuracy rates are up to 97% with the studied features and exceeding 95% with the generated features
[64]	2021	Detection and classification of conflict flows in SDN	SVM, DT, Hybrid DT-SVM, Extremely Fast Decision Tree (EFDT)	Action, Protocol, MAC address, and IP	Dataset From their previous work	Fat Tree and Simple Tree Topologies	Ryu controller	98.53%, 99.27%, 99.27%; 99.49%
[114]	2020	Classification of data traffic based on the applications in an SDN platform	SVM, Nearest centroid, Naïve Bayes (NB)	Generated using the "netmate" flow generator	Generated using the "netmate" flow generator	Single switch with "n" host topology, linear topology with the same number of switches as the host, tree topology.	POX controller	92.3%, 91.02%; 96.79%
[63]	2020	Analyzing network data and deploying an ML-based network TC solution, followed by the integration of the model within an SDN platform	SVM (RBF), SVM (Linear), DT, RF, KNN	MAC addresses of source and destination, port addresses, flow duration, flow byte count, flow packet count, and average packet size	IP Network Traffic Flows dataset, labeled with 75 Apps from Kaggle	Tree Topology is used for Simulation Testbed	Ryu controller	70.40%, 96.37%, 95.76%, 94.92%; 71.47%
[115]	2020	Data Classification	RF, LDA, DNN are tested for two Scenarios	time, bytesReceived, bytesSent, durationSec, packetRxDropped, packetsRxError, packetsSent, packetsTxDropped, packetsTxError, packetsReceived, rx throughput, tx throughput	Used their own dataset	Single OVS switch with two sender nodes and a receiver	ONOS controller	Scenario A: RF 95%, LDA 98% and DNN 69%, Scenario B: RF 42%, LDA 76% and DNN 74%
[116]	2017	Traffic Classification	SVM, K-Means	30 features were used	Dataset from [117]	–	–	SVM has higher accuracy than K-Means
[118]	2016	Classify traffic for SDNs in a QoS-aware manner	Laplacian SVM, KMeans	10 features	Real internet dataset captured by the Broadband Communication Research group in UPC, Barcelona, Spain	–	–	Laplacian SVM approximately ranges from 80 to 90%

Table 3. Cont.

Ref.	Year	Objective	Classification Models	Required Features	Dataset	Topology Used	Controller	Accuracy
[42]	2016	Classify traffic for SDNs in an application-aware manner	RF, Stochastic Gradient Boosting (SGB), and Extreme Gradient Boosting (EGB)	Size, interarrival time, and timestamps of first 5 packets. Src/Dst MAC and IP addresses. Src/Dst ports. The duration, packet, and byte counts.	Labeled dataset using their own topology created an SDN application designed to collect OpenFlow statistics from the controlled switches.	–	–	RF and EGB has the highest accuracy
[119]	2014	Application-layer Classification	DPI, ML, and Multi-classifier (combination between DPI and ML)	–	Five datasets collected from their own topology	Single switch with two hosts topology	Floodlight controller	MultiClassifier has high accuracy

In [115], the authors applied various ML algorithms to classify real network traffic data automatically. To assess the performance of these algorithms on actual physical and virtual networks, two different scenarios were implemented. The first scenario involves regular data delivery over the network, while the second scenario simulates a malicious network, where the receiver node is periodically flooded with excessive requests. Results show that the second scenario has an overall lower accuracy than the first scenario.

The work performed in [116] examined two ML algorithms (SVM and K-means) for TC. The dataset used is from [117]. The results show that the overall accuracy achieved is greater than 95%.

In [118], a QoS-aware TC system was proposed that combines DPI and semi-supervised ML algorithms. DPI labels certain traffic flows that belong to known applications. The labeled data are subsequently employed by a SSL algorithm comprising Laplacian SVM and K-Means to categorize traffic flows from unknown applications. By doing so, the system can classify both known and unknown traffic flows into distinct QoS classes. Simulation results show that Laplacian SVM accuracy ranges from approximately 80% to 90%.

In [42], an application-aware TC system 2qw introduced. SDN topology is implemented to gather traffic data. Following that, multiple SL algorithms are applied to categorize traffic flows into different applications.

The work performed in [119], proposed a MultiClassifier system that identifies applications through the integration of an ML-based classifier and a DPI-based classifier. When a new flow arrives, the ML-based classifier is first used for classification. If the reliability of its classification result exceeds a predetermined threshold value, it is considered the final result of the MultiClassifier system. However, if the ML-based classifier's result's reliability is beneath the threshold, the system will resort to DPI-based classification. If the DPI-based classification returns "UNKNOWN", the classification results from the ML-based classifier will still be selected. Otherwise, the classification results from the DPI-based classifier will be selected.

From Table 3 it can be seen that the collective findings from the reviewed papers underscore the significant impact and versatility of ML techniques in the domain of TC within SDNs. The integration of SVM and DT in [64] is motivated by several reasons. One primary advantage is that DTs excel at capturing complex decision boundaries, while SVMs are adept at handling high-dimensional spaces. By combining these strengths, the hybrid model can better accommodate diverse datasets, capturing both linear and non-linear relationships effectively. Additionally, the hybrid model offers robustness to noise, drawing on SVM's noise tolerance while still leveraging DTs to discern intricate patterns. The interpretability of the model is enhanced, as DTs inherently provide clear rules for decision making, contributing to a more understandable and interpretable model.

Moreover, the hybrid model can exploit the non-linear capabilities of both SVM and decision trees, proving advantageous in scenarios where intricate relationships need to be captured. The combination also enables insights into feature importance, a benefit derived from the inherent property of DTs. The ensemble effect, derived from combining SVM and DTs, is another notable advantage, often leading to improved model performance. Additionally, the hybrid model can handle imbalanced data effectively, benefiting from decision trees' ability to address such scenarios. Lastly, the computational efficiency of the hybrid model is enhanced, with DTs being less computationally intensive compared to certain SVM configurations. Overall, the adoption of the hybrid SVM and DT model is driven by a strategic amalgamation of these advantages to address the specific requirements of the research problem at hand. In [114], the showcase emphasized the applicability of diverse ML algorithms, revealing varying performance across scenarios, while [63] uses SVM with both linear and Radial Basis Function (RBF) kernels. The observed outcomes reveal a notable performance discrepancy between the two kernels. The decision to employ the linear SVM kernel may stem from the dataset's characteristics, where the underlying relationships between features and the target variable are more effectively captured by a linear decision boundary.

Linear SVMs are particularly potent when dealing with linearly separable data, and the high accuracy achieved with this kernel in this paper underscores its appropriateness for the given context. On the other hand, the observed low accuracy with the RBF kernel suggests that the inherent flexibility and capacity to capture non-linear relationships might not be beneficial for this specific dataset. The RBF kernel introduces additional complexity, and in situations where a simpler model suffices, it may lead to overfitting or suboptimal performance. The choice between linear and RBF kernels often hinges on the characteristics of the data, and the results highlight the significance of this consideration in determining the most suitable kernel for the given research context. The achievement in [116] demonstrated impressive accuracy using SVM and K means. In [118], the proposal of a QoS-aware TC system combining DPI and semi-supervised ML algorithms demonstrated the successful categorization of known and unknown traffic flows. The application-aware TC system in [42], leveraging SDN topology, and the MultiClassifier system in [119], combining ML-based and DPI-based classifiers, further contribute to the diversity of ML approaches. In summary, putting all these studies together shows that using ML is really effective for sorting out different types of traffic in SDNs. However, it also suggests that we need to keep looking into it and make it better to deal with specific problems and work well in real-world networks.

5. Security in SDN Using ML

ML algorithms play an important role in security and TC by analyzing network traffic patterns to discern normal behavior from potential security threats. By leveraging ML for TC, SDN can precisely identify and categorize various types of network traffic, enabling targeted security measures. The integration of ML-driven TC with security protocols ensures a dynamic defense mechanism against evolving threats, as the network can adapt in real time to anomalies. This seamless collaboration between security and TC in SDN not only enhances threat-detection and -response capabilities but also contributes to the overall robustness and reliability of modern network architectures.

The implementation of a threat-aware system, known as Eunoia, as proposed by [62], utilizes ML to counter network intrusion in SDN. Initially, the data preprocessing subsystem employs a forward feature selection strategy to choose relevant feature sets. Subsequently, the predictive data modeling subsystem utilizes DT and RF algorithms to identify malicious activities. A dataset of 30,000 entries was randomly selected from 10% of the KDD99 intrusion-detection dataset based on the 1998 DARPA initiative. Results demonstrate that RF achieves an accuracy of 98.75% when using the entire dataset, 99.4% when excluding ambiguous data, and 45% when only ambiguous data are selected. Meanwhile, accuracy for DT was measured using ambiguous data only for different numbers of features, yielding 82.48% and 91.17% for the selection of 10 and 15 features, respectively.

The data presented in Table 4 highlight the substantial influence and flexibility of ML methods in the field of TC for security in SDNs, as indicated by the collective results of the reviewed papers. In [120], ML techniques to counteract Denial of Service (DoS) and Distributed Denial of Service (DDoS) attacks in SDN are proposed and assessed. The evaluation of these techniques takes place in a realistic scenario where the SDN controller is exposed to DDoS attacks, with the aim of deriving crucial insights to enhance the security of future communication networks through ML-based approaches. The ML techniques utilized include SVM, NB, DT, and Logistic Regression, with corresponding accuracy rates of 97.5%, 96.03%, 96.78%, and 89.98%, respectively.

Table 4. Summary of common classification ML models for Security in SDN.

Ref.	Year	Objective	Classification Models	Required Features	Dataset	Accuracy
[120]	2020	Propose and evaluate the use of ML techniques to address Denial of Service (DoS) and Distributed Denial of Service (DDoS) attacks in SDN environments	SVM, NB, DT, and Logistic Regression	-	Created with the traffic flow generated by Scapy	97.5%, 96.03%, 96.78%; 89.98%
[62]	2017	Implementation of a threat-aware system, known as Eunoia	DT, RF	Data preprocessing subsystem employs a forward feature-selection strategy to choose relevant feature sets.	Intrusion-detection dataset based on the 1998 DARPA initiative	RF achieves accuracies of 98.75% (full dataset), 99.4% (excluding ambiguous data), and 45% (only ambiguous data), DT accuracy was assessed using ambiguous data with 10 and 15 features, resulting in 82.48% and 91.17%, respectively
[121]	2016	Investigated DDoS attacks by analyzing traffic flow patterns	NB, KNN, K-means, and K-medoids	Request time, source host, destination host, and flag bit (referred to as "fg") represent the connection request time, the originating host, the target host, and the flag bit, respectively	Real-time dataset, which is a traced file obtained from TCP traffic between Lawrence Berkley Laboratory and the rest of the world	94%, 90%, 86%; 88%
[122]	2016	Introducing an enhanced behavior-based SVM for classifying network attacks to improve the accuracy of intrusion detection and speed up the learning process for distinguishing between normal and intrusive patterns	SVM	DT used for feature reduction: prioritizes relevant features, selecting suitable ones as input for SVM	KDD1999 dataset	Average accuracy of 97.55%

The examination of DDoS attacks, as explored in [121], involves the analysis of traffic flow patterns. The focus is on distinguishing between normal and abnormal traffic by utilizing various ML algorithms, including NB, KNN, K-means, and K-medoids. The accuracy rates for the ML methods are 94%, 90%, 86%, and 88%, respectively.

In [122], an improved behavior-based SVM is introduced for the classification of network attacks. To enhance the accuracy of intrusion detection and accelerate the learning of normal and intrusive patterns, DT is employed as a feature-reduction technique. This involves prioritizing relevant features and selecting the most qualified ones, which are then utilized as input data for training the SVM classifier. The results demonstrate an average accuracy of 97.55%.

From Table 4, it is evident that the papers reviewed present various approaches and techniques for utilizing ML in countering network intrusion in SDN environments. The study proposing the threat-aware system Eunoia [62] utilizes ML, specifically DT, and RF, to identify malicious activities in SDN. The results demonstrate high accuracy rates for RF, particularly when excluding ambiguous data. However, the accuracy significantly decreases when only ambiguous data are considered, highlighting the importance of data preprocessing and feature selection in enhancing model performance. The findings from the study outlined in [120] underscore the effectiveness of employing ML techniques to combat DoS and DDoS attacks in SDN environments. Through the utilization of SVM, NB, DT, and Logistic Regression, the study achieved notable accuracy rates, ranging from 89.98% to 97.5%. These results highlight the potential of ML-based approaches to significantly enhance the security posture of future communication networks, offering robust defenses against malicious cyber threats such as DDoS attacks. The achievement in [122] introduces an enhanced behavior-based SVM for classifying network attacks. By leveraging DT as a feature-reduction technique, the model prioritizes relevant features to enhance intrusion-detection accuracy and expedite the learning process for normal and intrusive patterns. The findings reveal an impressive average accuracy of 97.55%, showcasing the efficacy of the proposed SVM approach in accurately identifying and classifying network attacks.

In conclusion, the reviewed papers collectively demonstrate the effectiveness of ML techniques, particularly ensemble methods like RF and SVM, in detecting and mitigating network intrusion in SDN environments. Additionally, the importance of data preprocessing, feature selection, and model optimization is emphasized in improving the accuracy and robustness of ML-based intrusion detection systems.

6. Datasets

This section presents a concise overview of several recently used datasets that are valuable resources for researchers and practitioners in the field of security and network analysis using ML. These datasets encompass diverse characteristics such as benign traffic, common attacks, and network flow analysis results. Table 5 summarizes key attributes of each dataset, aiding researchers in selecting appropriate datasets for their specific needs and analyses.

Table 5. Summary of some publicly available datasets.

Ref.	Dataset Name	Year	Description	No. of Features	Created by
[123]	DDOS attack SDN Dataset	2020	This dataset is specifically designed for SDN applications, created using the Mininet emulator, and employed for TC using ML and deep learning algorithms	23 features	Mendley data
[124]	A Novel SDN Intrusion Dataset	2020	SDN dataset tailored to attacks, openly accessible to researchers, providing a comprehensive resource for evaluating intrusion detection system performance	More than 80 features	Authors of [124]
[125]	CSE-CIC-IDS2018 on AWS	2018	The project aims to create a varied and extensive benchmark dataset for intrusion detection. This involves building user profiles representing network events and behaviors, which are then combined to produce diverse datasets covering different evaluation aspects	80 features	A joint project involving the Communications Security Establishment (CSE) and the Canadian Institute for Cybersecurity (CIC)

Table 5. Cont.

Ref.	Dataset Name	Year	Description	No. of Features	Created by
[126]	IP Network Traffic Flows Labeled with 75 Apps	2017	This dataset extends its capability by creating ML models that can identify specific applications, including Facebook, YouTube, and Instagram, among others, using IP flow statistics (currently covering 75 applications)	87 features	Universidad Del Cauca, Popayán, Colombia
[127]	CIC-IDS2017	2017	The dataset comprises benign traffic and recent common attacks, mirroring real-world PCAP data. It incorporates network traffic analysis outcomes from CICFlowMeter, featuring labeled flows categorized by timestamps, source and destination IPs, ports, protocols, and attack types in CSV format	More than 80 features	Canadian Institute for Cybersecurity (CIC)

7. Limitations and Open Research Issues

Emerging technologies, such as SDN and ML, have the potential to greatly enhance network automation and management. However, there are several limitations associated with the integration of SDN and ML. Addressing these limitations will be crucial to realizing the full potential of these technologies and achieving more efficient network management.

7.1. Limitations

7.1.1. Datasets Availability

The availability of high-quality datasets is a critical factor in the development and evaluation of ML algorithms. However, the lack of openly accessible and standardized datasets poses a significant challenge, not only in the field of SDN but also in various domains [33,128].

To address this challenge, researchers have proposed different methods for generating the necessary datasets to assess various ML algorithms in the context of SDN. One approach is the implementation of testbeds, which involve setting up real-world network environments specifically designed for data collection and experimentation [129]. Testbeds provide researchers with the flexibility to control network parameters and collect data under specific conditions, allowing for the generation of customized datasets that reflect real-world network characteristics.

Another approach is the use of standard network simulators or emulators, such as Mininet, NS3, or EstiNet [130–133]. These simulators and emulators provide virtualized environments where network behaviors can be simulated, allowing researchers to generate datasets that capture various network scenarios and conditions. Simulators and emulators enable reproducibility and scalability, as experiments can be easily replicated and expanded upon.

While these approaches offer valuable means of generating datasets, it is important to note that they have their limitations. Testbeds may require significant resources and infrastructure, making them costly and challenging to set up. Simulators and emulators, on the other hand, may introduce certain simplifications and assumptions that do not perfectly reflect the complexities of real-world network environments.

7.1.2. Datasets Quality

The quality and availability of datasets play a critical role in the training and performance of ML models, and this holds true in the context of SDN environments as well.

However, there are specific challenges associated with dataset quality in SDN that need to be addressed for effective ML-based solutions [134,135].

One of the primary challenges is the scarcity of labeled data in SDN environments. ML models typically require large numbers of accurately labeled data for training. However, in the context of SDN, acquiring such labeled datasets can be challenging due to the complexity and dynamic nature of network traffic. The manual labeling of data is time-consuming, expensive, and prone to errors. Additionally, the diversity and scale of network traffic in SDN make it difficult to gather representative and comprehensive datasets that capture all relevant traffic patterns.

To overcome the challenge of limited labeled data, researchers and practitioners in SDN have explored various approaches. One approach is to leverage transfer learning, where models trained on related datasets or domains are fine-tuned or used as a starting point for training in the target SDN environment. This allows for the transfer of knowledge and experiences from existing labeled datasets to the target scenario, reducing the reliance on scarce labeled data.

7.1.3. High-Bandwidth Traffic Classification

A significant challenge for TC systems is the significant progress in the network, which may need to process traffic at gigabit speeds in some instances. Ref. [43] proposed two solutions to address this challenge:

1. Utilizing specialized hardware or parallel processing architecture.
2. To enhance the scalability of SDN classification, it is recommended that the architecture of SDN be restructured. Relevant studies have suggested practical techniques [136,137].

7.1.4. Interpretability and Clarity

One of the challenges associated with many ML algorithms, especially those based on deep learning, is their inherent lack of interpretability, often referred to as the "black box" nature of these models [138]. This lack of interpretability makes it difficult to comprehend and explain the decision-making processes of the models, hindering their transparency and understandability.

In the context of TC in SDN, interpretability and clarity are crucial, particularly in scenarios where transparency is essential, such as network security. Understanding why and how a particular traffic flow is classified as belonging to a specific class becomes crucial for network administrators and security analysts to make informed decisions and take appropriate actions.

The ability to interpret ML models' decisions can provide valuable insights into the reasoning behind TC outcomes. It allows network operators to understand the factors and features that contribute to the classification decision, enabling them to validate the accuracy of the classifications and gain confidence in the model's performance. Interpretability also facilitates the identification of potential biases or shortcomings in the model's training data or architecture, allowing for improvements and adjustments to be made.

Addressing the challenge of interpretability and clarity in ML-based TC requires the development of techniques and methodologies that can provide meaningful explanations for the model's decisions. This involves exploring approaches such as model-agnostic interpretability techniques, rule-extraction methods, and feature importance analysis. By leveraging these techniques, it becomes possible to extract interpretable rules or explanations from complex ML models, shedding light on the factors influencing the classification outcomes.

7.1.5. Ideal Network Assumption

Many existing research studies in the field of ML-based TC and SDN assume ideal network conditions where complete and accurate information about traffic flow is readily available. However, in reality, real-world networks often encounter various anomalies and challenges that can significantly impact network performance and the effectiveness of

ML-based approaches. These anomalies include packet loss, packet retransmission, delay, and jitter, which can lead to deviations from the expected traffic patterns and introduce uncertainties in the classification process.

The presence of these abnormal conditions poses significant challenges to the efficiency and accuracy of ML-based TC models. ML algorithms trained on ideal network assumptions may struggle to handle the complexities and variations introduced by real-world network conditions. As a result, classification accuracy may suffer, and the reliability of the TC system may be compromised.

To address this issue, it is crucial to develop robust traffic classifiers that can effectively handle and adapt to abnormal network conditions. These classifiers should be designed to be resilient to packet loss, retransmission, delays, and jitter, ensuring accurate classification even in the presence of such anomalies. Additionally, techniques such as anomaly detection and outlier handling can be incorporated into the ML algorithms to identify and mitigate the impact of abnormal network behavior on the classification process.

7.1.6. Resources Limitations

ML algorithms may require significant computational resources. In SDN environments with limited resources, this may be a constraining factor [139].

7.2. Open Research Issues

7.2.1. Real-World Challenges

While much of the existing research in this field has focused on simulating ML algorithms on simple network topologies and assessing the accuracy of the models, it is essential to acknowledge that real-world networks present significantly greater complexity. Merely achieving high accuracy in a controlled environment is insufficient when it comes to practical implementation. Real-world network performance is influenced by a multitude of factors, such as scalability, availability, and adaptability to dynamic conditions.

In order to address the challenges of real-world network environments, it is imperative to consider the scalability of ML-based solutions. As network sizes and traffic volumes increase, the algorithms must be able to handle the corresponding growth without compromising efficiency or accuracy. Additionally, the availability of ML models is crucial, as the network must continue to operate reliably even in the face of failures or disruptions.

Another critical aspect to consider is the utilization of larger and more diverse datasets. While many studies have demonstrated the effectiveness of ML algorithms using relatively small and homogeneous datasets, real-world networks exhibit a wide range of traffic patterns, protocols, and applications. By incorporating more comprehensive datasets that capture this diversity, ML models can be trained to better handle the complexities and idiosyncrasies of real-world traffic.

Furthermore, it is important to consider the practical implementation challenges associated with integrating ML algorithms into existing network infrastructures. Network operators must navigate issues related to the deployment, management, and maintenance of ML models in a live network environment. These challenges include issues such as computational requirements, model updates, and integration with existing network management systems.

To overcome these real-world challenges, future research should focus on developing ML algorithms that are specifically designed for complex network topologies and can effectively address scalability, availability, and adaptability concerns. Furthermore, efforts should be made to collect and analyze larger and more diverse datasets that accurately represent real-world network traffic. Only by addressing these challenges can ML-based solutions be successfully deployed and utilized in practical network environments, leading to improved network performance and enhanced QoS.

7.2.2. Architecture Generalization

In traditional networks, communication between non-adjacent layers is typically restricted, limiting the potential for information exchange and collaboration across different network domains [140]. However, enabling cross-domain generalization is crucial when applying ML models trained on one specific SDN architecture to diverse network types or architectures.

To achieve effective generalization, it is necessary to conduct research and develop approaches that can seamlessly adapt ML models to various network architectures. This entails designing models that can capture the underlying principles and patterns common to different SDN architectures, enabling the transfer of knowledge and experiences gained from one architecture to another. By doing so, ML models trained on a specific SDN architecture can be effectively applied to different network environments, reducing the need for extensive retraining or model redesign.

Furthermore, it is important to explore techniques that facilitate the transfer of learned knowledge from one SDN architecture to another. This includes investigating methods for extracting and abstracting architectural-agnostic features and representations that capture the essential characteristics of network behavior. By focusing on these architecture-agnostic features, ML models can better adapt to diverse network architectures, allowing for more efficient and generalized deployment.

Additionally, the development of standardized interfaces and protocols across different SDN architectures can greatly facilitate architecture generalization. By establishing common standards for communication and information exchange between various layers and domains, ML models can seamlessly integrate with different architectures, promoting interoperability and flexibility.

Overall, conducting research on approaches that enable cross-domain generalization in ML-based SDN applications is crucial for advancing the practicality and scalability of these technologies. By developing models and techniques that can effectively adapt to diverse network architectures, we can unlock the full potential of ML in SDN and reap the benefits of improved network performance, enhanced resource utilization, and enhanced QoS across a wide range of network environments.

7.2.3. Use of Formal Methods and Model-Based Testing

Formal methods and model-based testing play a crucial role in the context of ML-based TC techniques in SDNs [141]. Formal methods provide a rigorous framework for specifying and verifying the properties of network protocols and algorithms, enabling the detection of potential vulnerabilities or design flaws in SDN-based TC systems, and ensuring their correctness and reliability [142]. By employing formal methods, researchers and practitioners can mathematically analyze the behavior and performance of the ML models and algorithms used for TC. This analysis helps in identifying potential limitations, biases, or vulnerabilities in the models and enables the development of robust and accurate TC solutions [143]. Additionally, model-based testing techniques allow for systematic and automated testing of the TC algorithms against well-defined models or specifications, helping in validating the behavior and performance of the algorithms under different traffic scenarios, enhancing their effectiveness, and ensuring their suitability for real-world deployment in SDN environments [144]. Overall, the use of formal methods and model-based testing contributes to the reliability, accuracy, and efficiency of ML-based TC techniques in SDNs.

7.2.4. Use of Ensemble Learning Models

Ensemble models, which combine the predictions of multiple individual models, have emerged as powerful tools in ML for improving predictive accuracy and robustness [103,109]. Ensemble learning, despite being a potent tool in ML, poses numerous research challenges that demand deeper exploration. One critical concern concentrates on the scalability and efficiency of ensemble methods, especially in dealing with large-scale datasets and real-time applications. With datasets continually expanding in size and complexity, there is a pressing need to devise ensemble learning strategies capable of efficiently managing such extensive data volumes without sacrificing predictive accuracy [145]. Moreover, the interpretability and transparency of ensemble models pose significant challenges. This is particularly evident in ensemble methods where multiple base learners are combined, each with distinct parameters and decision-making approaches. Enhancing the interpretability of ensemble models is essential for extracting insights into the underlying data relationships and instilling confidence in the model's predictions [146]. Addressing these open research issues in ensemble learning will not only advance the field but also enhance the applicability and robustness of ensemble methods across various domains and applications.

7.2.5. Routing Optimization and Resource Management

Routing optimization and resource management in SDN present intriguing avenues for exploration, particularly in the context of leveraging ML techniques. One of the open research issues in this domain is the development of ML-based algorithms for routing optimization. Traditional routing protocols within SDN might not fully exploit the dynamic nature of network traffic and changes in network topology. ML algorithms can adaptively learn from network data to optimize routing decisions, leading to improved network performance, reduced latency, and enhanced QoS [147,148].

Resource management poses another challenge, as efficiently allocating network resources based on varying demand patterns is crucial for maintaining network reliability and efficiency. ML models can analyze historical traffic patterns and resource usage data to predict future demand and dynamically adjust resource allocations accordingly [149].

Overall, delving into ML applications for optimizing routing and managing resources in SDN presents an exciting area for future research and innovation, with the potential to significantly enhance the performance and scalability of modern networks.

8. Conclusions

SDN and ML are innovative technologies that have the potential to greatly enhance network performance and QoS. SDN facilitates centralized and programmable network management, enabling efficient resource utilization and dynamic adaptation to changing traffic demands. ML, on the other hand, can analyze network data to identify patterns and forecast future traffic behavior, offering proactive QoS management capabilities. When combined with TC, SDN and ML can accurately identify and prioritize different traffic types, optimizing network performance, mitigating congestion, and improving the overall user experience.

However, the effectiveness of this approach heavily relies on the quality and quantity of data used for analysis. By leveraging larger and more diverse datasets, the accuracy and robustness of these technologies can be significantly enhanced, unlocking their full potential in improving network performance and QoS management. Therefore, future research should focus on collecting and utilizing comprehensive datasets to further advance the application of ML algorithms in the context of SDN.

This paper provided a comprehensive survey of the application of ML algorithms in the domain of SDN, with a specific emphasis on TC. We discussed the differences between traditional and ML-based TC methods, highlighting the advantages offered by ML techniques. Additionally, we provided an overview of various ML algorithms that have been applied in SDN environments. By examining the existing literature, we explored the current state of the field and identified key research limitations and open issues that require further investigation.

Despite the progress made, there are still several challenges that need to be addressed in the field of ML and SDNs. Collaboration among researchers is crucial in overcoming these challenges and advancing the field. By working together, we can make new discoveries and develop innovative approaches that will shape the future of traffic categorization in

SDNs. This survey serves as a valuable reference, providing insights into the current state of the field and inspiring further exploration in this rapidly evolving area.

Author Contributions: Conceptualization, R.H.S., M.S.A., H.A.E.A.E., M.S. and M.M.S.; Methodology, R.H.S., M.S.A., H.A.E.A.E. and M.K.; Formal analysis, R.H.S., M.S.A., M.K. and M.M.S.; Investigation, R.H.S., M.S.A., H.A.E.A.E. and M.K.; Resources, R.H.S., M.S.A., M.S., M.K. and M.M.S.; Data curation, R.H.S. and M.S.A.; Writing—original draft, R.H.S., M.S.A., H.A.E.A.E., M.S., M.K. and M.M.S.; Writing—review & editing, R.H.S., M.S.A., H.A.E.A.E., M.S., M.K. and M.M.S.; Visualization, R.H.S., M.S.A., M.K. and M.M.S.; Supervision, M.S.A., H.A.E.A.E. and M.S. All authors have read and agreed to the published version of the manuscript.

Funding: This research received no external funding.

Data Availability Statement: Data sharing is not applicable.

Conflicts of Interest: The authors declare no conflicts of interest.

Abbreviations

The following abbreviations are used in this manuscript:

A-CPI	Application-Controller Plan Interface
AI	Artificial Intelligence
API	Application Programming Interface
C-DPI	Control-Data Plane Interface
DPI	Deep Packet Inspection
DT	Decision Tree
EFDT	Extremely Fast Decision Tree
IANA	Internet Assigned Numbers Authority
ISP	Internet Service Provider
KNN	Key Nearest Neighbor
ML	Machine Learning
NB	Naïve Bayes
QoS	Quality of Service
RBF	Radial Basis Function
RF	Random Forest
SDN	Software Defined Network
SL	Supervised Learning
SOM	Self-Organizing Map
SSL	Semi-Supervised Learning
SVM	Support Vector Machine
TC	Traffic Classification
USL	Unsupervised Learning

References

1. Latah, M.; Toker, L. Application of artificial intelligence to software defined networking: A survey. *Indian J. Sci. Technol.* **2016**, *9*, 1–7. [CrossRef]
2. Sezer, S.; Scott-Hayward, S.; Chouhan, P.K.; Fraser, B.; Lake, D.; Finnegan, J.; Viljoen, N.; Miller, M.; Rao, N. Are we ready for SDN? Implementation challenges for software-defined networks. *IEEE Commun. Mag.* **2013**, *51*, 36–43. [CrossRef]
3. Rowshanrad, S.; Namvarasl, S.; Abdi, V.; Hajizadeh, M.; Keshtgary, M. A survey on SDN, the future of networking. *J. Adv. Comput. Sci. Technol.* **2014**, *3*, 232–248. [CrossRef]
4. Huo, L.; Jiang, D.; Qi, S.; Miao, L. A blockchain-based security traffic measurement approach to software defined networking. *Mob. Netw. Appl.* **2021**, *26*, 586–596. [CrossRef]
5. Wang, Y.; Jiang, D.; Huo, L.; Zhao, Y. A new traffic prediction algorithm to software defined networking. *Mob. Netw. Appl.* **2021**, *26*, 716–725. [CrossRef]
6. McKeown, N.; Anderson, T.; Balakrishnan, H.; Parulkar, G.; Peterson, L.; Rexford, J.; Shenker, S.; Turner, J. OpenFlow: Enabling innovation in campus networks. *ACM SIGCOMM Comput. Commun. Rev.* **2008**, *38*, 69–74. [CrossRef]
7. Farhady, H.; Lee, H.; Nakao, A. Software-defined networking: A survey. *Comput. Netw.* **2015**, *81*, 79–95. [CrossRef]
8. Shu, Z.; Wan, J.; Li, D.; Lin, J.; Vasilakos, A.V.; Imran, M. Security in software-defined networking: Threats and countermeasures. *Mob. Netw. Appl.* **2016**, *21*, 764–776. [CrossRef]

9. Karakus, M.; Durresi, A. Quality of service (QoS) in software defined networking (SDN): A survey. *J. Netw. Comput. Appl.* **2017**, *80*, 200–218. [CrossRef]
10. Gude, N.; Koponen, T.; Pettit, J.; Pfaff, B.; Casado, M.; McKeown, N.; Shenker, S. NOX: Towards an operating system for networks. *ACM SIGCOMM Comput. Commun. Rev.* **2008**, *38*, 105–110. [CrossRef]
11. Gupta, N.; Maashi, M.S.; Tanwar, S.; Badotra, S.; Aljebreen, M.; Bharany, S. A comparative study of software defined networking controllers using mininet. *Electronics* **2022**, *11*, 2715. [CrossRef]
12. Kaur, S.; Singh, J.; Ghumman, N.S. Network programmability using POX controller. In Proceedings of the ICCCS International Conference on Communication, Computing & Systems, Chennai, India, 20–21 February 2014; Volume 138, p. 70.
13. Medved, J.; Varga, R.; Tkacik, A.; Gray, K. Opendaylight: Towards a model-driven sdn controller architecture. In Proceedings of the IEEE International Symposium on a World of Wireless, Mobile and Multimedia Networks, Sydney, Australia, 19 June 2014; pp. 1–6.
14. Albu-Salih, A.T. Performance evaluation of ryu controller in software defined networks. *J. Qadisiyah Comput. Sci. Math.* **2022**, *14*, 1. [CrossRef]
15. Erickson, D. The beacon openflow controller. In Proceedings of the 2nd ACM SIGCOMM Workshop on Hot Topics in Software Defined Networking, Hong Kong, 16 August 2013; pp. 13–18.
16. Blial, O.; Ben Mamoun, M.; Benaini, R. An overview on SDN architectures with multiple controllers. *J. Comput. Netw. Commun.* **2016**, *2016*, 9396525. [CrossRef]
17. Paliwal, M.; Shrimankar, D.; Tembhurne, O. Controllers in SDN: A review report. *IEEE Access* **2018**, *6*, 36256–36270. [CrossRef]
18. Tadros, C.N.; Mokhtar, B.; Rizk, M.R. Logically centralized-physically distributed software defined network controller architecture. In Proceedings of the 2018 IEEE Global Conference on Internet of Things (GCIoT), Alexandria, Egypt, 5–7 December 2018; pp. 1–5.
19. Chaudhry, S.; Bulut, E.; Yuksel, M. A Distributed SDN Application for Cross-Institution Data Access. In Proceedings of the 2019 28th International Conference on Computer Communication and Networks (ICCCN), Valencia, Spain, 29 July–1 August 2019; pp. 1–9.
20. Ahmed, H.G.; Ramalakshmi, R. Performance analysis of centralized and distributed SDN controllers for load balancing application. In Proceedings of the 2018 2nd International Conference on Trends in Electronics and Informatics (ICOEI), Tirunelveli, India, 11–12 May 2018; pp. 758–764.
21. Hu, T.; Guo, Z.; Yi, P.; Baker, T.; Lan, J. Multi-controller based software-defined networking: A survey. *IEEE Access* **2018**, *6*, 15980–15996. [CrossRef]
22. Xu, G.; Mu, Y.; Liu, J. Inclusion of artificial intelligence in communication networks and services. *ITU J. ICT Discov. Spec* **2017**, *1*, 1–6.
23. Zhang, J.; Guo, H.; Liu, J. Adaptive task offloading in vehicular edge computing networks: A reinforcement learning based scheme. *Mob. Netw. Appl.* **2020**, *25*, 1736–1745. [CrossRef]
24. Moustafa, S.S.; Mohamed, G.E.A.; Elhadidy, M.S.; Abdalzaher, M.S. Machine learning regression implementation for high-frequency seismic wave attenuation estimation in the Aswan Reservoir area, Egypt. *Environ. Earth Sci.* **2023**, *82*, 307. [CrossRef]
25. Hamdy, O.; Gaber, H.; Abdalzaher, M.S.; Elhadidy, M. Identifying exposure of urban area to certain seismic hazard using machine learning and GIS: A case study of greater Cairo. *Sustainability* **2022**, *14*, 10722. [CrossRef]
26. Zhao, Y.; Li, Y.; Zhang, X.; Geng, G.; Zhang, W.; Sun, Y. A survey of networking applications applying the software defined networking concept based on machine learning. *IEEE Access* **2019**, *7*, 95397–95417. [CrossRef]
27. Namasudra, S.; Lorenz, P.; Ghosh, U. The New Era of Computer Network by using Machine Learning. *Mob. Netw. Appl.* **2023**, *28*, 764–766. [CrossRef]
28. Abdalzaher, M.S.; Soliman, M.S.; El-Hady, S.M.; Benslimane, A.; Elwekeil, M. A Deep Learning Model for Earthquake Parameters Observation in IoT System-Based Earthquake Early Warning. *IEEE Internet Things J.* **2022**, *9*, 8412–8424. [CrossRef]
29. Salazar, E.; Azurdia-Meza, C.A.; Zabala-Blanco, D.; Bolufé, S.; Soto, I. Semi-supervised extreme learning machine channel estimator and equalizer for vehicle to vehicle communications. *Electronics* **2021**, *10*, 968. [CrossRef]
30. Sarker, I.H. Machine learning: Algorithms, real-world applications and research directions. *SN Comput. Sci.* **2021**, *2*, 160. [CrossRef]
31. Abdalzaher, M.S.; Elwekeil, M.; Wang, T.; Zhang, S. A Deep Autoencoder Trust Model for Mitigating Jamming Attack in IoT Assisted by Cognitive Radio. *IEEE Syst. J.* **2022**, *16*, 3635–3645. [CrossRef]
32. Shafin, S.S.; Karmakar, G.; Mareels, I. Obfuscated Memory Malware Detection in Resource-Constrained IoT Devices for Smart City Applications. *Sensors* **2023**, *23*, 5348. [CrossRef]
33. Xie, J.; Yu, F.R.; Huang, T.; Xie, R.; Liu, J.; Wang, C.; Liu, Y. A survey of machine learning techniques applied to software defined networking (SDN): Research issues and challenges. *IEEE Commun. Surv. Tutor.* **2018**, *21*, 393–430. [CrossRef]
34. Dias, K.L.; Pongelupe, M.A.; Caminhas, W.M.; de Errico, L. An innovative approach for real-time network traffic classification. *Comput. Netw.* **2019**, *158*, 143–157. [CrossRef]
35. Owusu, A.I.; Nayak, A. An intelligent traffic classification in sdn-iot: A machine learning approach. In Proceedings of the 2020 IEEE International Black Sea Conference on Communications and Networking (BlackSeaCom), Odessa, Ukraine, 26–29 May 2020; pp. 1–6.
36. Nguyen, T.T.; Armitage, G. A survey of techniques for internet traffic classification using machine learning. *IEEE Commun. Surv. Tutor.* **2008**, *10*, 56–76. [CrossRef]

37. Thazin, N. QoS-based Traffic Engineering in Software Defined Networking. In Proceedings of the 2019 25th Asia-Pacific Conference on Communications (APCC), Ho Chi Minh City, Vietnam, 6–8 November 2019.
38. Tahaei, H.; Afifi, F.; Asemi, A.; Zaki, F.; Anuar, N.B. The rise of traffic classification in IoT networks: A survey. *J. Netw. Comput. Appl.* **2020**, *154*, 102538. [CrossRef]
39. Mohammed, A.R.; Mohammed, S.A.; Shirmohammadi, S. Machine learning and deep learning based traffic classification and prediction in software defined networking. In Proceedings of the 2019 IEEE International Symposium on Measurements & Networking (M&N), Catania, Italy, 8–10 July 2019; pp. 1–6.
40. Rojas, J.S.; Gallón, Á.R.; Corrales, J.C. Personalized service degradation policies on OTT applications based on the consumption behavior of users. In Proceedings of the Computational Science and Its Applications—ICCSA 2018: 18th International Conference, Melbourne, Australia, 2–5 July 2018; Springer: Berlin/Heidelberg, Germany, 2018; pp. 543–557.
41. Fernández, D.P. Restraining ICANN: An analysis of OFAC sanctions and their impact on the Internet Corporation for Assigned Names and Numbers. *Telecommun. Policy* **2023**, *47*, 102614. [CrossRef]
42. Amaral, P.; Dinis, J.; Pinto, P.; Bernardo, L.; Tavares, J.; Mamede, H.S. Machine learning in software defined networks: Data collection and traffic classification. In Proceedings of the 2016 IEEE 24th International conference on network protocols (ICNP), Singapore, 8–11 November 2016; pp. 1–5.
43. Yan, J.; Yuan, J. A survey of traffic classification in software defined networks. In Proceedings of the 2018 1st IEEE International Conference on Hot Information-Centric Networking (HotICN), Shenzhen, China, 15–17 August 2018; pp. 200–206.
44. Moore, A.W.; Papagiannaki, K. Toward the accurate identification of network applications. In Proceedings of the Passive and Active Network Measurement: 6th International Workshop, PAM 2005, Boston, MA, USA, 31 March–1 April 2005; Proceedings 6; Springer: Berlin/Heidelberg, Germany, 2005; pp. 41–54.
45. Madhukar, A.; Williamson, C. A longitudinal study of P2P traffic classification. In Proceedings of the 14th IEEE International Symposium on Modeling, Analysis, and Simulation, Monterey, CA, USA, 11–14 September 2006; pp. 179–188.
46. Finsterbusch, M.; Richter, C.; Rocha, E.; Muller, J.A.; Hanssgen, K. A survey of payload-based traffic classification approaches. *IEEE Commun. Surv. Tutor.* **2013**, *16*, 1135–1156. [CrossRef]
47. Sen, S.; Spatscheck, O.; Wang, D. Accurate, scalable in-network identification of p2p traffic using application signatures. In Proceedings of the 13th international conference on World Wide Web, New York, NY, USA, 19–21 May 2004; pp. 512–521.
48. Goo, Y.H.; Shim, K.S.; Lee, S.K.; Kim, M.S. Payload signature structure for accurate application traffic classification. In Proceedings of the 2016 18th Asia-Pacific Network Operations and Management Symposium (APNOMS), Kanazawa, Japan, 5–7 October 2016; pp. 1–4.
49. Fu, Z.; Liu, Z.; Li, J. Efficient parallelization of regular expression matching for deep inspection. In Proceedings of the 2017 26th International Conference on Computer Communication and Networks (ICCCN), Vancouver, BC, Canada, 31 July–3 August 2017; pp. 1–9.
50. Gabilondo, Á.; Fernández, Z.; Viola, R.; Martín, Á.; Zorrilla, M.; Angueira, P.; Montalbán, J. Traffic classification for network slicing in mobile networks. *Electronics* **2022**, *11*, 1097. [CrossRef]
51. Guo, D.; Liao, G.; Bhuyan, L.N.; Liu, B.; Ding, J.J. A scalable multithreaded l7-filter design for multi-core servers. In Proceedings of the 4th ACM/IEEE Symposium on Architectures for Networking and Communications Systems, San Jose, CA, USA, 6–7 November 2008; pp. 60–68.
52. Gringoli, F.; Salgarelli, L.; Dusi, M.; Cascarano, N.; Risso, F.; Claffy, K. Gt: Picking up the truth from the ground for internet traffic. *ACM SIGCOMM Comput. Commun. Rev.* **2009**, *39*, 12–18.
53. Yu, C.; Lan, J.; Xie, J.; Hu, Y. QoS-aware traffic classification architecture using machine learning and deep packet inspection in SDNs. *Procedia Comput. Sci.* **2018**, *131*, 1209–1216. [CrossRef]
54. Parsaei, M.R.; Sobouti, M.J.; Javidan, R. Network traffic classification using machine learning techniques over software defined networks. *Int. J. Adv. Comput. Sci. Appl.* **2017**, *8*.
55. Ibrahim, H.A.H.; Al Zuobi, O.R.A.; Al-Namari, M.A.; MohamedAli, G.; Abdalla, A.A.A. Internet traffic classification using machine learning approach: Datasets validation issues. In Proceedings of the 2016 Conference of Basic Sciences and Engineering Studies (SGCAC), Khartoum, Sudan, 20–23 February 2016; pp. 158–166.
56. Audah, M.F.; Chin, T.S.; Zulfadzli, Y.; Lee, C.K.; Rizaluddin, K. Towards efficient and scalable machine learning-based QoS traffic classification in software-defined network. In Proceedings of the Mobile Web and Intelligent Information Systems: 16th International Conference, MobiWIS 2019, Istanbul, Turkey, 26–28 August 2019; Proceedings 16; Springer: Berlin/Heidelberg, Germany, 2019; pp. 217–229.
57. Dainotti, A.; Pescape, A.; Claffy, K.C. Issues and future directions in traffic classification. *IEEE Netw.* **2012**, *26*, 35–40. [CrossRef]
58. Xue, Y.; Wang, D.; Zhang, L. Traffic classification: Issues and challenges. In Proceedings of the 2013 International Conference on Computing, Networking and Communications (ICNC), San Diego, CA USA, 28–31 January 2013; pp. 545–549.
59. Nikravesh, A.Y.; Ajila, S.A.; Lung, C.H. An autonomic prediction suite for cloud resource provisioning. *J. Cloud Comput.* **2017**, *6*, 1–20. [CrossRef]
60. Kotsiantis, S.B.; Zaharakis, I.; Pintelas, P. Supervised machine learning: A review of classification techniques. *Emerg. Artif. Intell. Appl. Comput. Eng.* **2007**, *160*, 3–24.
61. Hastie, T.; Tibshirani, R.; Friedman, J. *The Elements of Statistical Learning*; Springer Series in Statistics; Springer: New York, NY, USA, 2001.

62. Song, C.; Park, Y.; Golani, K.; Kim, Y.; Bhatt, K.; Goswami, K. Machine-learning based threat-aware system in software defined networks. In Proceedings of the 2017 26th International Conference on Computer Communication and Networks (ICCCN), Vancouver, BC, Canada, 31 July–3 August 2017; pp. 1–9.
63. Perera Jayasuriya Kuranage, M.; Piamrat, K.; Hamma, S. Network traffic classification using machine learning for software defined networks. In Proceedings of the Machine Learning for Networking: Second IFIP TC 6 International Conference, MLN 2019, Paris, France, 3–5 December 2019; Springer: New York, NY, USA, 2020; pp. 28–39.
64. Khairi, M.H.H.; Ariffin, S.H.S.; Latiff, N.M.A.; Yusof, K.M.; Hassan, M.K.; Al-Dhief, F.T.; Hamdan, M.; Khan, S.; Hamzah, M. Detection and classification of conflict flows in SDN using machine learning algorithms. *IEEE Access* **2021**, *9*, 76024–76037. [CrossRef]
65. Quinlan, J.R. Induction of decision trees. *Mach. Learn.* **1986**, *1*, 81–106. [CrossRef]
66. Maimon, O.Z.; Rokach, L. *Data Mining with Decision Trees: Theory and Applications*; World Scientific: Singapore, 2014; Volume 81.
67. Biau, G.; Scornet, E. A random forest guided tour. *Test* **2016**, *25*, 197–227. [CrossRef]
68. Genuer, R.; Poggi, J.M.; Genuer, R.; Poggi, J.M. *Random Forests*; Springer: Berlin/Heidelberg, Germany, 2020.
69. Liaw, A.; Wiener, M. Classification and regression by randomForest. *R News* **2002**, *2*, 18–22.
70. Ridwan, M.A.; Radzi, N.A.M.; Abdullah, F.; Jalil, Y. Applications of machine learning in networking: A survey of current issues and future challenges. *IEEE Access* **2021**, *9*, 52523–52556. [CrossRef]
71. Haddouchi, M.; Berrado, A. A survey of methods and tools used for interpreting random forest. In Proceedings of the 2019 1st International Conference on Smart Systems and Data Science (ICSSD), Rabat, Morocco, 3–4 October 2019; pp. 1–6.
72. Torizuka, K.; Oi, H.; Saitoh, F.; Ishizu, S. Benefit segmentation of online customer reviews using random forest. In Proceedings of the 2018 IEEE International Conference on Industrial Engineering and Engineering Management (IEEM), Bangkok, Thailand, 16–19 December 2018; pp. 487–491.
73. Aria, M.; Cuccurullo, C.; Gnasso, A. A comparison among interpretative proposals for Random Forests. *Mach. Learn. Appl.* **2021**, *6*, 100094. [CrossRef]
74. Vapnik, V. *Statistical Learning Theory*; Wiley: New York, NY, USA, 1998; Volume 1, p. 2.
75. Steinwart, I.; Christmann, A. *Support Vector Machines*; Springer Science & Business Media: New York, NY, USA, 2008.
76. Martínez-Ramón, M.; Christodoulou, C. Support vector machines for antenna array processing and electromagnetics. In *Synthesis Lectures on Computational Electromagnetics*; Springer: Cham, Switzerland, 2005; Volume 1, pp. 1–120.
77. Hu, H.; Wang, Y.; Song, J. Signal classification based on spectral correlation analysis and SVM in cognitive radio. In Proceedings of the 22nd International Conference on Advanced Information Networking and Applications (AINA 2008), Okinawa, Japan, 28–31 March 2008; pp. 883–887.
78. Cover, T.; Hart, P. Nearest neighbor pattern classification. *IEEE Trans. Inf. Theory* **1967**, *13*, 21–27. [CrossRef]
79. Box, G.E.; Tiao, G.C. *Bayesian Inference in Statistical Analysis*; John Wiley & Sons: Hoboken, NJ, USA, 2011.
80. Bayes, T. Naive Bayes Classifier. In *Article Sources and Contributors*; BIOMISA, Department of Computer and Software Engineering, College of Electrical and Mechanical Engineering, National University of Sciences and Technology (NUST): Islamabad, Pakistan, 1968; pp. 1–9.
81. Alpaydin, E. *Introduction to Machine Learning*; MIT Press: Cambridge, MA, USA, 2020.
82. Williams, N.; Zander, S.; Armitage, G. A preliminary performance comparison of five machine learning algorithms for practical IP traffic flow classification. *ACM SIGCOMM Comput. Commun. Rev.* **2006**, *36*, 5–16. [CrossRef]
83. Liu, J.; Xu, Q. Machine learning in software defined network. In Proceedings of the 2019 IEEE 3rd Information Technology, Networking, Electronic and Automation Control Conference (ITNEC), Chengdu, China, 15–17 March 2019; pp. 1114–1120.
84. Kanungo, T.; Mount, D.M.; Netanyahu, N.S.; Piatko, C.D.; Silverman, R.; Wu, A.Y. An efficient k-means clustering algorithm: Analysis and implementation. *IEEE Trans. Pattern Anal. Mach. Intell.* **2002**, *24*, 881–892. [CrossRef]
85. Stefanovič, P.; Kurasova, O. Visual analysis of self-organizing maps. *Nonlinear Anal. Model. Control* **2011**, *16*, 488–504. [CrossRef]
86. Van Hulle, M.M. Self-organizing Maps. In *Handbook of Natural Computing*; Springer: Berlin/Heidelberg, Germany, 2012.
87. Ghaseminezhad, M.; Karami, A. A novel self-organizing map (SOM) neural network for discrete groups of data clustering. *Appl. Soft Comput.* **2011**, *11*, 3771–3778. [CrossRef]
88. Xu, L.; Xu, Y.; Chow, T.W. PolSOM: A new method for multidimensional data visualization. *Pattern Recognit.* **2010**, *43*, 1668–1675. [CrossRef]
89. Zhu, X.J. *Semi-Supervised Learning Literature Survey*; University of Wisconsin-Madison Department of Computer Sciences: Madison, WI, USA, 2005.
90. Lee, D.H. Pseudo-label: The simple and efficient semi-supervised learning method for deep neural networks. In Proceedings of the Workshop on Challenges in Representation Learning, ICML, Atlanta, GA, USA, 16–21 June 2013; Volume 3, p. 896.
91. Wu, H.; Prasad, S. Semi-supervised deep learning using pseudo labels for hyperspectral image classification. *IEEE Trans. Image Process.* **2017**, *27*, 1259–1270. [CrossRef] [PubMed]
92. Chapelle, O.; Scholkopf, B.; Zien, A. Semi-supervised learning (chapelle, o. et al., eds.; 2006)[book reviews]. *IEEE Trans. Neural Netw.* **2009**, *20*, 542. [CrossRef]
93. Pise, N.N.; Kulkarni, P. A survey of semi-supervised learning methods. In Proceedings of the 2008 International Conference on Computational Intelligence and Security, Suzhou, China, 13–17 December 2008; Volume 2, pp. 30–34.
94. Moon, T.K. The expectation-maximization algorithm. *IEEE Signal Process. Mag.* **1996**, *13*, 47–60. [CrossRef]

95. Ng, S.K.; Krishnan, T.; McLachlan, G.J. The EM algorithm. In *Handbook of Computational Statistics: Concepts and Methods*; Springer: Berlin/Heidelberg, Germany, 2012; pp. 139–172.
96. Chen, Y.; Wang, G.; Dong, S. Learning with progressive transductive support vector machine. *Pattern Recognit. Lett.* **2003**, *24*, 1845–1855. [CrossRef]
97. Singla, A.; Patra, S.; Bruzzone, L. A novel classification technique based on progressive transductive SVM learning. *Pattern Recognit. Lett.* **2014**, *42*, 101–106. [CrossRef]
98. Bruzzone, L.; Chi, M.; Marconcini, M. A novel transductive SVM for semisupervised classification of remote-sensing images. *IEEE Trans. Geosci. Remote Sens.* **2006**, *44*, 3363–3373. [CrossRef]
99. Nassar, I.; Herath, S.; Abbasnejad, E.; Buntine, W.; Haffari, G. All labels are not created equal: Enhancing semi-supervision via label grouping and co-training. In Proceedings of the IEEE/CVF Conference on Computer Vision and Pattern Recognition, Seattle, WA, USA, 17–21 June 2021; pp. 7241–7250.
100. Han, W.; Coutinho, E.; Ruan, H.; Li, H.; Schuller, B.; Yu, X.; Zhu, X. Semi-supervised active learning for sound classification in hybrid learning environments. *PLoS ONE* **2016**, *11*, e0162075. [CrossRef]
101. Sutton, R.S.; Barto, A.G. *Introduction to Reinforcement Learning*; MIT Press: Cambridge, MA, USA, 1998; Volume 135.
102. Kaelbling, L.P.; Littman, M.L.; Moore, A.W. Reinforcement learning: A survey. *J. Artif. Intell. Res.* **1996**, *4*, 237–285. [CrossRef]
103. Dong, X.; Yu, Z.; Cao, W.; Shi, Y.; Ma, Q. A survey on ensemble learning. *Front. Comput. Sci.* **2020**, *14*, 241–258. [CrossRef]
104. Syarif, I.; Zaluska, E.; Prugel-Bennett, A.; Wills, G. Application of bagging, boosting and stacking to intrusion detection. In Proceedings of the Machine Learning and Data Mining in Pattern Recognition: 8th International Conference, MLDM 2012, Berlin, Germany, 13–20 July 2012; Proceedings 8; Springer: Berlin/Heidelberg, Germany, 2012; pp. 593–602.
105. Bartlett, P.; Freund, Y.; Lee, W.S.; Schapire, R.E. Boosting the margin: A new explanation for the effectiveness of voting methods. *Ann. Stat.* **1998**, *26*, 1651–1686. [CrossRef]
106. Graczyk, M.; Lasota, T.; Trawiński, B.; Trawiński, K. Comparison of bagging, boosting and stacking ensembles applied to real estate appraisal. In Proceedings of the Intelligent Information and Database Systems: Second International Conference, ACIIDS, Hue City, Vietnam, 24–26 March 2010; Proceedings, Part II 2; Springer: Berlin/Heidelberg, Germany, 2010; pp. 340–350.
107. Rashid, M.; Kamruzzaman, J.; Imam, T.; Wibowo, S.; Gordon, S. A tree-based stacking ensemble technique with feature selection for network intrusion detection. *Appl. Intell.* **2022**, *52*, 9768–9781. [CrossRef]
108. Natekin, A.; Knoll, A. Gradient boosting machines, a tutorial. *Front. Neurorobotics* **2013**, *7*, 21. [CrossRef] [PubMed]
109. Eom, W.J.; Song, Y.J.; Park, C.H.; Kim, J.K.; Kim, G.H.; Cho, Y.Z. Network traffic classification using ensemble learning in software-defined networks. In Proceedings of the 2021 International Conference on Artificial Intelligence in Information and Communication (ICAIIC), Jeju Island, Republic of Korea, 13–16 April 2021; pp. 89–92.
110. Lee, W.; Jun, C.H.; Lee, J.S. Instance categorization by support vector machines to adjust weights in AdaBoost for imbalanced data classification. *Inf. Sci.* **2017**, *381*, 92–103. [CrossRef]
111. Dagnew, G.; Shekar, B. Ensemble learning-based classification of microarray cancer data on tree-based features. *Cogn. Comput. Syst.* **2021**, *3*, 48–60. [CrossRef]
112. Kim, H.; Kim, H.; Moon, H.; Ahn, H. A weight-adjusted voting algorithm for ensembles of classifiers. *J. Korean Stat. Soc.* **2011**, *40*, 437–449. [CrossRef]
113. Belkadi, O.; Vulpe, A.; Laaziz, Y.; Halunga, S. ML-Based Traffic Classification in an SDN-Enabled Cloud Environment. *Electronics* **2023**, *12*, 269. [CrossRef]
114. Raikar, M.M.; Meena, S.; Mulla, M.M.; Shetti, N.S.; Karanandi, M. Data traffic classification in software defined networks (SDN) using supervised-learning. *Procedia Comput. Sci.* **2020**, *171*, 2750–2759. [CrossRef]
115. Kwon, J.; Jung, D.; Park, H. Traffic data classification using machine learning algorithms in SDN networks. In Proceedings of the 2020 International Conference on Information and Communication Technology Convergence (ICTC), Jeju Island, Republic of Korea, 21–23 October 2020; pp. 1031–1033.
116. Fan, Z.; Liu, R. Investigation of machine learning based network traffic classification. In Proceedings of the 2017 International Symposium on Wireless Communication Systems (ISWCS), Bologna, Italy, 28–31 August 2017; pp. 1–6.
117. Moore, A.; Hall, J.; Kreibich, C.; Harris, E.; Pratt, I. Architecture of a network monitor. In Proceedings of the Passive & Active Measurement Workshop, San Diego, CA, USA, 6–8 April 2003 2003; Volume 2003.
118. Wang, P.; Lin, S.C.; Luo, M. A framework for QoS-aware traffic classification using semi-supervised machine learning in SDNs. In Proceedings of the 2016 IEEE International Conference on Services Computing (SCC), San Francisco, CA, USA, 27 June–2 July 2016; pp. 760–765.
119. Li, Y.; Li, J. MultiClassifier: A combination of DPI and ML for application-layer classification in SDN. In Proceedings of the 2014 2nd International Conference on Systems and Informatics (ICSAI 2014), Shanghai, China, 15–17 November 2014; pp. 682–686.
120. Ahmad, A.; Harjula, E.; Ylianttila, M.; Ahmad, I. Evaluation of machine learning techniques for security in SDN. In Proceedings of the 2020 IEEE Globecom Workshops (GC Wkshps), Taipei, Taiwan, 7–11 December 2020; pp. 1–6.
121. Barki, L.; Shidling, A.; Meti, N.; Narayan, D.; Mulla, M.M. Detection of distributed denial of service attacks in software defined networks. In Proceedings of the 2016 International Conference on Advances in Computing, Communications and Informatics (ICACCI), Jaipur, India, 21–24 September 2016; pp. 2576–2581.

122. Wang, P.; Chao, K.M.; Lin, H.C.; Lin, W.H.; Lo, C.C. An efficient flow control approach for SDN-based network threat detection and migration using support vector machine. In Proceedings of the 2016 IEEE 13th International Conference on E-Business Engineering (ICEBE), Macau, China, 4–6 November 2016; pp. 56–63.
123. Ahuja, N.; Singal, G.; Mukhopadhyay, D. DDOS attack SDN dataset. *Mendeley Data* **2020**, *1*, 17632.
124. Elsayed, M.S.; Le-Khac, N.A.; Jurcut, A.D. InSDN: A novel SDN intrusion dataset. *IEEE Access* **2020**, *8*, 165263–165284. [CrossRef]
125. CSE-CIC-IDS 2018 on AWS. Available online: https://www.unb.ca/cic/datasets/ids-2018.html (accessed on 2 March 2024).
126. IP Network Traffic Flows Labeled with 75 Apps. Available online: https://www.kaggle.com/datasets/jsrojas/ip-network-traffic-flows-labeled-with-87-apps/data (accessed on 2 March 2024).
127. Intrusion Detection Evaluation Dataset. Available online: https://www.unb.ca/cic/datasets/ids-2017.html (accessed on 2 March 2024).
128. Bakker, J.N.; Ng, B.; Seah, W.K. Can machine learning techniques be effectively used in real networks against DDoS attacks? In Proceedings of the 2018 27th International Conference on Computer Communication and Networks (ICCCN), Hangzhou, China, 30 July–2 August 2018; pp. 1–6.
129. Gebremariam, A.A.; Usman, M.; Du, P.; Nakao, A.; Granelli, F. Towards e2e slicing in 5g: A spectrum slicing testbed and its extension to the packet core. In Proceedings of the 2017 IEEE Globecom Workshops (GC Wkshps), Singapore, 4–8 December 2017; pp. 1–6.
130. Hussain, M.; Shah, N.; Amin, R.; Alshamrani, S.S.; Alotaibi, A.; Raza, S.M. Software-defined networking: Categories, analysis, and future directions. *Sensors* **2022**, *22*, 5551. [CrossRef] [PubMed]
131. Ivey, J.; Yang, H.; Zhang, C.; Riley, G. Comparing a scalable SDN simulation framework built on ns-3 and DCE with existing SDN simulators and emulators. In Proceedings of the 2016 ACM SIGSIM Conference on Principles of Advanced Discrete Simulation, Banff Alberta, AB, Canada, 15–18 May 2016; pp. 153–164.
132. De Oliveira, R.L.S.; Schweitzer, C.M.; Shinoda, A.A.; Prete, L.R. Using mininet for emulation and prototyping software-defined networks. In Proceedings of the 2014 IEEE Colombian Conference on Communications and Computing (COLCOM), Bogota, Colombia, 4–6 June 2014; pp. 1–6.
133. Wang, S.Y.; Chou, C.L.; Yang, C.M. EstiNet openflow network simulator and emulator. *IEEE Commun. Mag.* **2013**, *51*, 110–117. [CrossRef]
134. Singla, A.; Bertino, E.; Verma, D. Overcoming the lack of labeled data: Training intrusion detection models using transfer learning. In Proceedings of the 2019 IEEE International Conference on Smart Computing (SMARTCOMP), Washington, DC, USA, 12–15 June 2019; pp. 69–74.
135. Al-Gethami, K.M.; Al-Akhras, M.T.; Alawairdhi, M. Empirical evaluation of noise influence on supervised machine learning algorithms using intrusion detection datasets. *Secur. Commun. Netw.* **2021**, *2021*, 1–28. [CrossRef]
136. Hayes, M.; Ng, B.; Pekar, A.; Seah, W.K. Scalable architecture for SDN traffic classification. *IEEE Syst. J.* **2017**, *12*, 3203–3214. [CrossRef]
137. Bianco, A.; Giaccone, P.; Kelki, S.; Campos, N.M.; Traverso, S.; Zhang, T. On-the-fly traffic classification and control with a stateful SDN approach. In Proceedings of the 2017 IEEE International Conference on Communications (ICC), Paris, France, 21–25 May 2017; pp. 1–6.
138. von Eschenbach, W.J. Transparency and the black box problem: Why we do not trust AI. *Philos. Technol.* **2021**, *34*, 1607–1622. [CrossRef]
139. Jurado-Lasso, F.F.; Marchegiani, L.; Jurado, J.F.; Abu-Mahfouz, A.M.; Fafoutis, X. A survey on machine learning software-defined wireless sensor networks (ml-SDWSNS): Current status and major challenges. *IEEE Access* **2022**, *10*, 23560–23592. [CrossRef]
140. She, C.; Yang, C.; Quek, T.Q. Cross-layer optimization for ultra-reliable and low-latency radio access networks. *IEEE Trans. Wirel. Commun.* **2017**, *17*, 127–141. [CrossRef]
141. Souri, A.; Norouzi, M.; Asghari, P.; Rahmani, A.M.; Emadi, G. A systematic literature review on formal verification of software-defined networks. *Trans. Emerg. Telecommun. Technol.* **2020**, *31*, e3788. [CrossRef]
142. Yao, J.; Wang, Z.; Yin, X.; Shi, X.; Wu, J.; Li, Y. Test oriented formal model of SDN applications. In Proceedings of the 2014 IEEE 33rd International Performance Computing and Communications Conference (IPCCC), Austin, TX, USA, 5–7 December 2014; pp. 1–2.
143. Albert, E.; Gómez-Zamalloa, M.; Rubio, A.; Sammartino, M.; Silva, A. SDN-Actors: Modeling and verification of SDN programs. In Proceedings of the International Symposium on Formal Methods, Oxford, UK, 12 July 2018; Springer: Berlin/Heidelberg, Germany, 2018; pp. 550–567.
144. Li, Y.; Yin, X.; Wang, Z.; Yao, J.; Shi, X.; Wu, J.; Zhang, H.; Wang, Q. A survey on network verification and testing with formal methods: Approaches and challenges. *IEEE Commun. Surv. Tutor.* **2018**, *21*, 940–969. [CrossRef]
145. Aswini, K.; Reddy, U.; Nagpal, A.; Rana, A.; Abood, B.S.Z. Ensemble Learning Approaches for Big Data Classification Tasks. In Proceedings of the 2023 10th IEEE Uttar Pradesh Section International Conference on Electrical, Electronics and Computer Engineering (UPCON), Gautam Buddha Nagar, India, 1–3 December 2023; Volume 10, pp. 1545–1550.
146. Pintelas, E.; Livieris, I.E.; Pintelas, P. A grey-box ensemble model exploiting black-box accuracy and white-box intrinsic interpretability. *Algorithms* **2020**, *13*, 17. [CrossRef]
147. Amin, R.; Rojas, E.; Aqdus, A.; Ramzan, S.; Casillas-Perez, D.; Arco, J.M. A survey on machine learning techniques for routing optimization in SDN. *IEEE Access* **2021**, *9*, 104582–104611. [CrossRef]

148. Abdalzaher, M.S.; Salim, M.M.; Elsayed, H.A.; Fouda, M.M. Machine learning benchmarking for secured iot smart systems. In Proceedings of the 2022 IEEE International Conference on Internet of Things and Intelligence Systems (IoTaIS), Bali, Indonesia, 24–26 November 2022; pp. 50–56.
149. Schneider, S.; Satheeschandran, N.P.; Peuster, M.; Karl, H. Machine learning for dynamic resource allocation in network function virtualization. In Proceedings of the 2020 6th IEEE Conference on Network Softwarization (NetSoft), Ghent, Belgium, 29 June–3 July 2020; pp. 122–130.

Disclaimer/Publisher's Note: The statements, opinions and data contained in all publications are solely those of the individual author(s) and contributor(s) and not of MDPI and/or the editor(s). MDPI and/or the editor(s) disclaim responsibility for any injury to people or property resulting from any ideas, methods, instructions or products referred to in the content.

Article

Towards Implementation of Emotional Intelligence in Human–Machine Collaborative Systems

Miroslav Markov [1], Yasen Kalinin [2], Valentina Markova [2,*] and Todor Ganchev [3]

1. Department of Software and Internet Technologies, Technical University of Varna, 9010 Varna, Bulgaria; m.markov@tu-varna.bg
2. Department of Communication Engineering and Technologies, Technical University of Varna, 9010 Varna, Bulgaria; yasenkalinin@tu-varna.bg
3. Department of Computer Science and Engineering, Technical University of Varna, 9010 Varna, Bulgaria; tganchev@tu-varna.bg
* Correspondence: via@tu-varna.bg

Abstract: Social awareness and relationship management components can be seen as a form of emotional intelligence. In the present work, we propose task-related adaptation on the machine side that accounts for a person's momentous cognitive and emotional state. We validate the practical significance of the proposed approach in person-specific and person-independent setups. The analysis of results in the person-specific setup shows that the individual optimal performance curves for that person, according to the Yerkes–Dodson law, are displaced. Awareness of these curves allows for automated recognition of specific user profiles, real-time monitoring of the momentous condition, and activating a particular relationship management strategy. This is especially important when a deviation is detected caused by a change in the person's state of mind under the influence of known or unknown factors.

Keywords: emotional intelligence; arousal; valence; attention; adaptation strategies; emotional and cognitive states; personal profiles; MorphCast; RapidMiner

Citation: Markov, M.; Kalinin, Y.; Markova, V.; Ganchev, T. Towards Implementation of Emotional Intelligence in Human–Machine Collaborative Systems. *Electronics* **2023**, *12*, 3852. https://doi.org/10.3390/electronics12183852

Academic Editors: Francisco Falcone, Teodor Iliev, Lorant Andras Szolga and Gani Balbayev

Received: 5 August 2023
Revised: 6 September 2023
Accepted: 8 September 2023
Published: 12 September 2023

Copyright: © 2023 by the authors. Licensee MDPI, Basel, Switzerland. This article is an open access article distributed under the terms and conditions of the Creative Commons Attribution (CC BY) license (https://creativecommons.org/licenses/by/4.0/).

1. Introduction

The evolution of human–machine collaborative systems undoubtedly demands the creation of advanced human-friendly artificial intelligence (AI) architectures capable of person-specific adaptations, endowing the machines with the ability to adequately interpret human inputs, intentions, actions, and behaviors, allowing them to make decisions that are transparent to humans and also conform to societal and moral constraints. These are required for achieving the acceptability of technology and simultaneously for managing the effectiveness of collaborative systems.

Recent scientific studies in this regard are focusing on the intelligence of the machines, presented by their so-called cognitive component, including the ability to acquire information necessary for the achievement of a specific goal, processing this information through various machine learning (ML) methods, shaping a domain-specific knowledge, and as a result, implementation of respective action. The effectiveness of the ML process, measured through feedback from the machine, forms its individual intelligence quotient (IQ) [1], just like the IQ scoring for human individuals.

Human general intelligence also has a second component, emotional intelligence (EI), formulated and studied first by J. Miller and P. Salovey [2] and additionally developed by D. Goleman [3]. EI describes the ability to understand and manage one's own emotions and the ability to perceive and interpret the emotional states of surrounding individuals correctly and subsequently to shape proper behavior toward them to achieve successful collaboration, i.e., the degree of EI or the emotional quotient (EQ) is directly related to

the ability to collaborate. The contemporary understanding of EI from the perspective of psychology includes four components and the corresponding abilities:
- Self-awareness.
- Self-management.
- Social awareness.
- Relationship management.

From the perspective of computer science and human–machine interaction (HMI), these could be interpreted as the following.

Self-awareness: As the machine does not possess inherent feelings and emotions to be aware of, this component represents the ability of the machine to interpret each situation inherent in the dynamics of the collaboration process: the performance of the system (including the individual performance of the human user, participating in the system); phase/stage of the collaborative task; detected deviations, etc.

Self-management: Self-management relates to the machine's adaptive abilities in response to the interpreted situation regarding the parameters of the collaborative task.

Social awareness: This component represents the ability of the machine to perceive and correctly interpret the emotional and cognitive states of its human partner during the implementation of a particular task, as well as to assess and forecast the influence of the changes in these human states on the task results.

Relationship management: Relationship management relates to the ability of the machine to adaptively change its behavior to ensure a positive impact on the human user (respectively, to the HMI collaborative system), relevant to their emotional and cognitive dynamics.

The latter two components are of particular interest in the current research. Concerning the social awareness of a machine, we consider its abilities for verbal and non-verbal perception (recognition and interpretation) of the human state through various technologies. Specifically, the verbal category involves natural language understanding and processing based on the recent advances in large language models (LLMs) [4–11], speech-to-text [12] and text-to-speech [13] conversion, translation [14], etc. The non-verbal category concerns cognitive state detection methods based on biosensors and visual and tactile input. The diversity of contemporary technologies providing the means of such awareness on the machine side includes:

- Eye tracking—for attention recognition and state detection, by assessment of some parameters [15], e.g., pupil dilation [16,17], saccade and fixation duration [18];
- Facial expression recognition—for emotional and cognitive state detection [19–21];
- Electrocardiography (ECG), electrodermal activity (EDA) [22–26], and skin temperature sensors [27]—for assessment of the human body's physiological reactions related to stress, anxiety, agitation, cognitive load, etc. It was also shown that the detection of heart rate variability could be based on photoplethysmography (PPG) sensors integrated into wearable devices [28,29], as well as on traditional electrode-based technology integrated into plasters [30] or smart textiles [31,32];
- Electroencephalography (EEG) [33–38]—for capturing the cognition processes, even in cases of a lack of behavioral reaction caused by a specific stimulus. The potential of this technology is promising, primarily through the development of brain–computer interfaces (BCIs) [39–42] in that number those with direct brain connection [43].
- Equipment-extensive technologies for human state assessment, such as functional near-infrared spectroscopy (fNIRS) [44,45], capturing the hemodynamics in different parts of the brain; magnetic resonance imaging (MRI) [46], enabling the creation of a digital twin of a human brain [47]; electromyographic sensors [48–50] for detection as well as activation of controlled activities of a particular muscle group.

Despite these and other technological advances, recent research on integrating human emotional and cognitive states in adaptive HMI is still fragmented, and social awareness and especially relationship management, based on this awareness, remain neglected. Accounting for this gap, the reported research offers an advance toward enabling social awareness of machines, which opens the opportunity for integrating relationship management strategies. This article presents recent advances in integrating a multimodal emotion recognition component in the intelligent human–machine interface framework—iHMIfr [51], which enables adaptation on the machine side for the implementation of intelligent performance management functionality. The experimental evaluation in a person-independent and person-specific scenario reported in Section 3 validates the proposed approach.

2. Materials and Methods

2.1. Background

The research reported here builds on the conceptual architecture of the intelligent human–machine interface framework (IHMIfr) [51], the workflow adaptation for intelligent human–machine interfaces [52], and the implemented task-related transformation of a collaborative system [53]. The proposed unified view contributes to creating social awareness and relationship management strategies for machines. The proposed advance, which in this research is seen as the second phase, is focused on including a representative user model based on assessing the human state of mind in consistency with iHMIfr. The concept of the experimental validation was upgraded as a second phase of the task-related adaptation presented in [53].

2.2. Research Design

In the following, we present the conceptual design (Section 2.2.1), the experimental protocol, and the dataset used for its experimental validation (Sections 2.2.2–2.2.4).

2.2.1. Conceptual Design

The collaborative system implemented in the first phase of our research was based on using two components: the application and the decision manager. The simplified workflow concerning the decision for adaptation is shown in Figure 1. At this end, a methodology for task-related ex-post transformation was formulated, including a definition of success criteria based on a particular task, a definition of task parameters (speed, complexity, etc.) thresholds, a description of task adaptation strategy based on an estimation of the current performance of the user, and implementation of the selected strategy in the application manager.

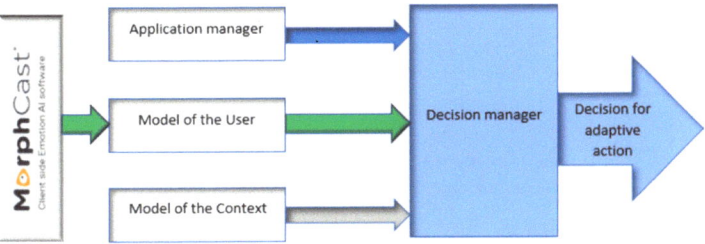

Figure 1. Workflow for decision for adaptation.

The advance proposed here includes a representative user model that consistently assesses the human state of mind with iHMIfr. The human emotional and cognitive state is then interpreted, and a profiling strategy is applied to achieve personalized adaptation. In the present work, the analysis and interpretation of the momentous cognitive state are based on well-known psychological concepts, including the Yerkes–Dodson law and statistical data processing. The methodology followed at this phase includes the acquisition of multimodal input signals during the implementation of the collaborative task; interpretation and assessment of emotional and cognitive states and their registration and monitoring in the human model; definition of criteria for assessment of the emotional and cognitive state; creation of a personalized profile of the users, based on the selected criteria; design of adaptive strategy, based on the current value of the selected criteria; and implementation of the strategy in the application manager.

2.2.2. Experimental Setup

A purposely developed web-based application was used to acquire user data for experimental validation. The web application is coded in JavaScript v. ES12 as a primary language, and ReactJS v. 18.2.0 is used for the reactive rendering of components. Styling is done with Cascading Style Sheets (CSS) in combination with the Material UI library3. The browser's local memory is used for real-time cashing, and after the end of the task, all the data are saved in a .csv file format.

The input, as seen in Figure 1, is based on the MorphCast platform v.1.16 [54] through the integration of the SDK offered by the manufacturer. MorphCast provides real-time measurements of various psychological parameters, such as emotional valence, arousal, attention, and basic emotional states. These serve as multimodal input streams for user data modeling and interpretation components.

2.2.3. Dataset

Twenty-one volunteers took part in the experiment. All of them were students or researchers at the Technical University of Varna. All participants were informed in detail about the study's substance and the data collected throughout the experiment. Each one signed written informed consent for inclusion before initiating their participation. In addition, all of the participants completed a questionnaire including data about their age, gender, handedness (left or right), experience in computer games (rarely/moderately/often), weekly time spent on computer/mobile phone/other gaming devices games (under 10 h/between 10 and 20 h/over 20 h), night sleeping time—usually and the last night (in hours) and self-assessment of the current working capacity/efficiency (low/medium/high).

The data were collected from all 21 participants from the Emotional and Cognitive State Tracking Dataset (ETICS). It consists of three .csv files for each individualization level from the second part of the test and correspondingly three files for the third part (with task adaptation), containing:

- Timestamp/stimuli/answer (user response)/performance/speed/reaction time—from the application manager.
- Timestamp/arousal/valence/attention/angry/disgust/fear/happy/neutral/sad/surprise—from MorphCast platform.
- Data fusion of the above, matched by timestamp in the moment of user response.

In addition, synchronized high-resolution video and audio from the PC camera, capturing the user's face (and face expressions) and screen capture video from the application (the stimuli of the cognitive test), are available in .mp4 file format. Additional information about our research and the presented dataset can be found on Supplementary Materials.

2.2.4. Experimental Protocol

The web-based application and data acquisition platform (Section 2.2.2) were installed on a computer equipped with a high-resolution camera. Each volunteer was left alone during recordings, except the experiment manager, who remained in the room. Each participant completed the informed consent and the questionnaire (Section 2.2.3).

The experimental protocol consisted of three parts—introduction to the rules, individualization phase, and testing phase. The task that the volunteers had to fulfill represented a cognitive T-load D-back test proposed in [55] and explained in detail in [53]. In brief, the T-load D-back test is a two-component task in which the machine provides the user with stimuli from two characters: letters and numbers. The submission sequence is letter–number–letter–number. The user must respond to the numbers, whether they are even or not, by pressing the keys. Regarding letters, a reaction (again by pressing a key) is necessary only if the current letter is the same as the previous one. The first part introduces the participants to the task's separate components (allowing them to try and receive feedback about the success) and their combination (i.e., the actual test).

The individualization of the task (i.e., the second part) is tailored so that it is initially adapts to the individual characteristics of the specific person, such as cognitive capacity, emotional involvement, concentration, level of fatigue, etc. Individualization consists of successive blocks of the same number of symbols, with the task speed increasing with each subsequent block. The goal is to detect for each user a certain threshold at which the performance drops below a preliminarily defined success criterion (85% in this case). A score above 85% is considered task completion. Each user's individualized (in terms of speed) charge is then used to place them in a high-stress (high workload) situation where the probability of errors is high. Task-specific parameters—current stage (level speed), performance (% errors), and response time (in milliseconds)—are considered, as they are necessary in forming the decision for task-related adaptation. During the individualization stage, there is a minimum break of 1 min after each level. The participant can prolong the break at their discretion.

The third part consists of a 15-minute test with a constant task-related adaptation based on the current performance (estimated as the average on each sequence of 10 stimuli) and the selected settings of the application adaptive strategy. The selected, in this case, adaptive process is purely reflective, as follows: when the current performance is below the success criterion (85%), the application manager slows the process (by adding 100 ms between the stimuli); if the performance drops below a critical threshold (50%), the speed is decreased by a double step (200 ms); when the performance is above the success criterion, the speed remains the same; and when the performance is above the criterion for excellent performance (95%), the speed increases with a single step (100 ms) to raise the efficiency of the HMI system.

During the second and third parts of the test, data fusion on the decision level is performed, matching the data from the application manager and the data from the MorphCast platform and synchronizing them by timestamps.

3. Results

The experimental results reported here have been obtained using the RapidMiner platform for data science and machine learning [56].

3.1. Results in Person-Independent Scenario

In this scenario, all the fused .csv files pertaining to the 21 volunteers are united in a common dataset. Some of the statistical parameters calculated in relation to the data attributes are presented in Table 1.

First, we need to acknowledge that the observed average value in terms of user effectiveness was impressive—0.879 ± 0.116, i.e., 87.9%. The system's adaptability can explain the high average value of this parameter concerning the task. Depending on the estimation of the current performance (averaged for the last 10 stimuli, according to the adaptive strategy chosen in the case), the time step was dynamic and readjusted. The low standard deviation value of ± 0.116 among different volunteers indicates that the system adapted accordingly to each person's individuality. The mean interstimulus interval (defining the speed of stimuli appearance) is 965.401 ms, and the mean user response time is 612.346 ms, with a variance of 160–170 ms due to individual participant differences.

The average for all participants' estimated arousal and emotional valence are -0.391 ± 0.223 and -0.311 ± 0.101, respectively. The standard deviation values indicate a certain degree of similarity among different people's cognitive and emotional states due to their involvement in the same task in a common setup.

Table 1. Statistical analysis in the person-independent scenario.

Name	Type	Histogram	Min	Max	Average	Deviation
Av. Perf	Real		0.400	1	0.879	0.116
speed	Integer		600	1600	985.401	176.338
reaction time	Integer		4	1380	612.346	165.508
arousal	Real		−0.775	0.389	−0.391	0.223
valence	Real		−0.866	0.462	−0.311	0.101
attention	Real		0	1	0.495	0.401

Because values of attention tracking were normalized to the interval [0, 1], an average value of about 0.5 was observed, which is in the center of this interval. At the same time, the histogram shows a non-Gaussian distribution of values, with two large clusters around 0 and 1. These extreme values correspond to the momentary values of attention and inattention during the task execution. The intermediate values most probably correspond to transition episodes between the two extremes, and thus are relatively rare.

Of considerable interest in our analysis is the interrelationship between cognitive and emotional states on the one hand and the participant's performance on the other. In cognitive psychology, this relationship is represented by the Yerkes–Dodson law, shown in Figure 2.

The experimental results have been analyzed in two different ways. In the first, the arousal values were juxtaposed against the cumulative performance following the data processing algorithm:

- Data extraction from all participants in the experiment (the sample).
- Combining the data (in RapidMiner—through the "Append" operator).
- Sorting the data in ascending order concerning the attribute "arousal".
- Setting the values of the "success" attribute as follows: 1 on success and −1 on failure.
- Creating a new attribute, "cumulative performance", and applying a cumulative function about the "performance" attribute (taking values −1 and 1).
- Using the cumulative performance rate values to establish arousal dependence.

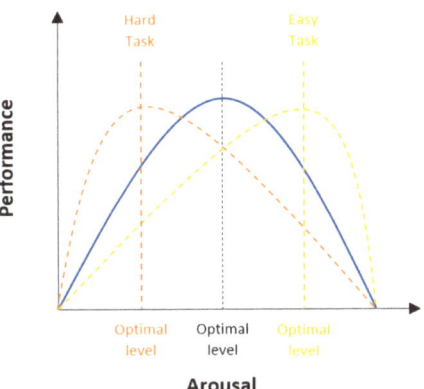

Figure 2. The Yerkes–Dodson law—tasks of different difficulty. (Blue line—the relationship during normal task; Yellow line—the relationship during easy task; Orange line—the relationship during hard task).

The result is shown in Figure 3, where the interrelationship between arousal and cumulative performance is in good agreement with the Yerkes–Dodson law. At the same time, the adaptability of the task (through the preset strategy) ensures movement along the curve in the zone of optimal performance and does not let it drop.

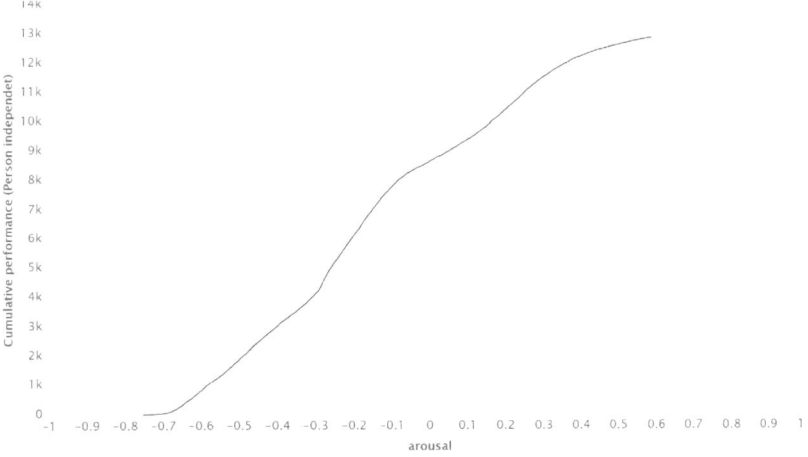

Figure 3. Arousal–cumulative performance relationship.

The second analysis considers the users' performance as consisting of two components—their attention and personal abilities to implement a particular task. While the latter depends strongly on the user's personality (and is expected to show different patterns), the first could represent the cognitive part of the performance, i.e., it should also follow the Yerkes–Dodson law. In Figure 4, we show the obtained relationship between the arousal and attention values.

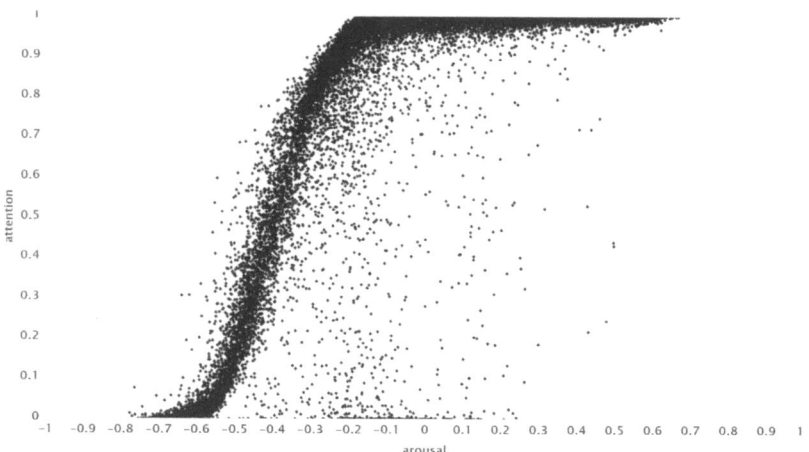

Figure 4. Arousal–attention relationship.

As shown in the figure, at low arousal values, attention is very close to zero (i.e., absent), then, as arousal increases, it also increases until reaching saturation (values close to 1). The graph is in good agreement with the Yerkes–Dodson law, as the optimal average level of arousal to maintain the maximum degree of attention, based on the considered data set, can be determined in the interval $[-0.25; 0.25]$.

3.2. Results in Person-Specific Scenario

In the person-specific scenario, the log files were processed per participant to extract regularities related to creating adequate user profiles. This included calculating and visualizing specific parameters and their subsequent comparison among the participants. We aimed to investigate the availability of characteristics relevant to factors such as gender, age, acquired skills, etc.

3.2.1. Valence–Arousal Relationship

The relationship between emotional valence and arousal was investigated to analyze the participants' emotional states. It is presented in Figure 5, and the individual participants are distinguished by color. For comparison, Figure 6 shows a column graph of the average performance rate and the average level of attention, again by participants. When analyzing the data, it was observed that the participants with the highest average levels of attention (id_3, id_6, id_8, id_9, id_11, id_12, id_16, id_18, id_20) are predominantly present in the fourth quadrant of the valence—arousal scale, i.e., they are closer to conditions associated with stress. Participants with low levels of attention (id_1, id_4, id_15) mostly fill the second and third quadrants (probably due to their experience in computer games and acceptance of the test as a similar activity and due to the individual specificity of their perceptions). The routineness of task solving, especially for id_1 and id_4, was also confirmed by the high-performance rates accompanied by the lowest reaction times (Figure 7), with a low degree of dispersion presented by the standard deviation (Figure 8). In the first quadrant, there are relatively few data belonging to participants from all groups, and they are somewhat sporadic.

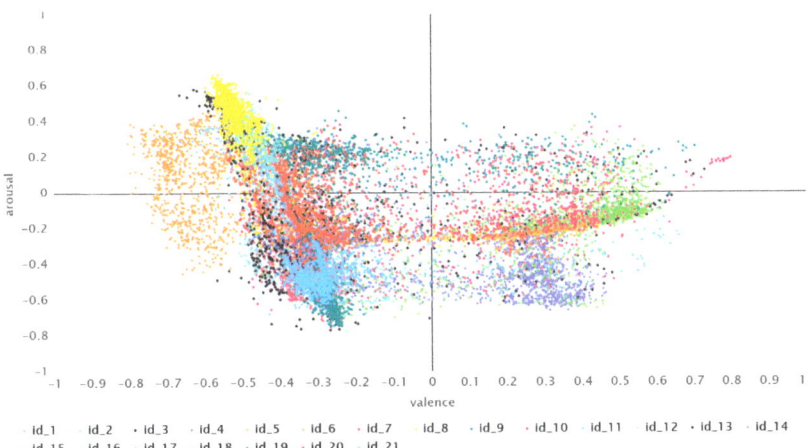

Figure 5. Arousal–valence relationship in participants.

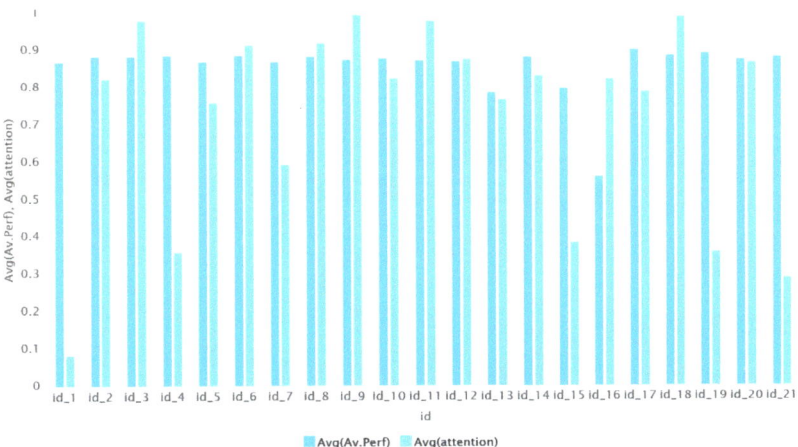

Figure 6. Average performance rate and intermediate level of attention by participants.

3.2.2. Arousal–Performance Relationship

As in the case of person-independent analysis, the relationship between emotional arousal and performance is established for the cumulative performance or through the attention component. In the first case, the following algorithm is used:

- Data extraction from all participants in the experiment.
- Sorting of the data of each participant in ascending order regarding the attribute "arousal".
- Setting the values of the "performance" attribute as follows: 1 on success and −1 on failure.
- Creating a new attribute, "cumulative performance rate", and applying a cumulative function concerning the "success rate" attribute (accepting values −1 and 1).
- Creating a new attribute "id_" and setting unique values for each participant.
- Combining the data (in RapidMiner—by using the "Append" operator).
- Use of cumulative performance rate values to establish dependence on arousal.

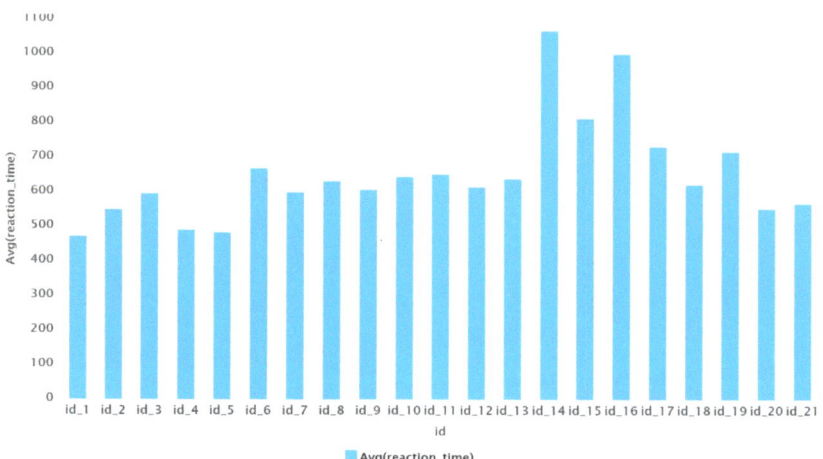

Figure 7. Average reaction time of participants.

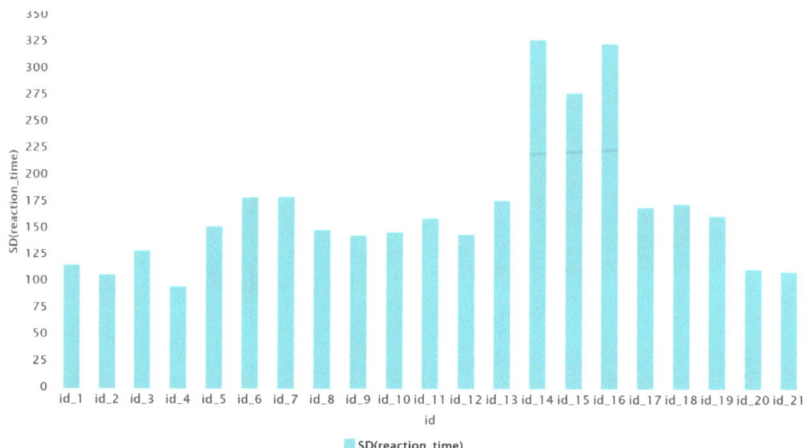

Figure 8. Standard deviation of reaction time of participants.

The results obtained by implementing this algorithm are shown in Figure 9.

The analysis of results per participant shows the individual optimal performance curves for that person according to the Yerkes–Dodson law. These curves create opportunities for recognition by the machine of specific profiles of the participants, as well as for real-time monitoring and activating a particular type of strategy when a deviation is detected. A change in the person's state of mind under the influence of some factor might cause variations that can be detected automatically.

3.2.3. Arousal–Attention Relationship

Another exciting aspect of the participant analysis is related to the arousal–attention relationship. This dependence is presented in Figure 10, with each participant's data in a different color.

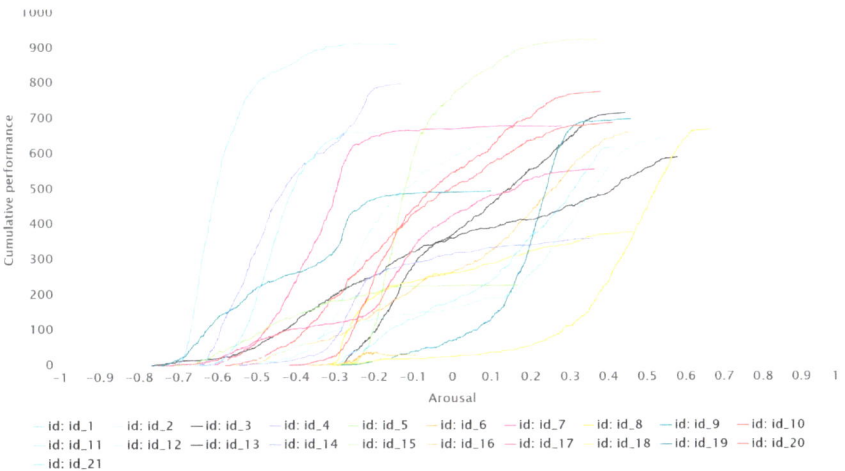

Figure 9. Arousal–cumulative performance of participants.

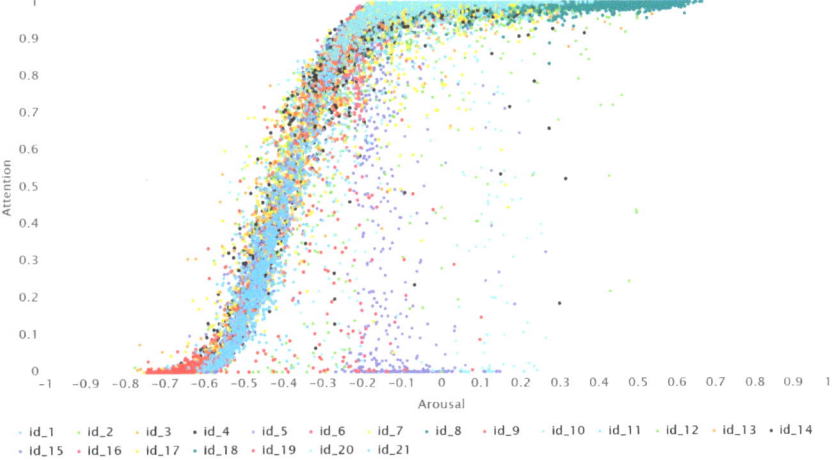

Figure 10. Arousal–attention of participants.

As in the person-independent analysis, the relation between arousal and attention again conformed to the Yerkes–Dodson law. However, a significant scatter of these data is also visible. Presenting the data by participants in the experiment and comparing them with the data from the conducted survey, some exciting regularities were revealed. As shown in Figure 11, a significant portion of the scattered data belongs to two profiles. After analysis of the survey data, it was clarified that these two profiles belong to participants with a dominant left hand.

Although all participants differed significantly in the levels of emotional arousal within the test, most of the observed curves follow a trajectory compliant with the Yerkes–Dodson law. The two profiles of left-handed participants differ significantly, which warrants a machine learning model to be elaborated for recognizing atypical profiles, such as a person's left-handedness, as one of these atypical manifestations. The availability of potential atypicality linked to conditions such as dyslexia, autism, etc. was not investigated in our study.

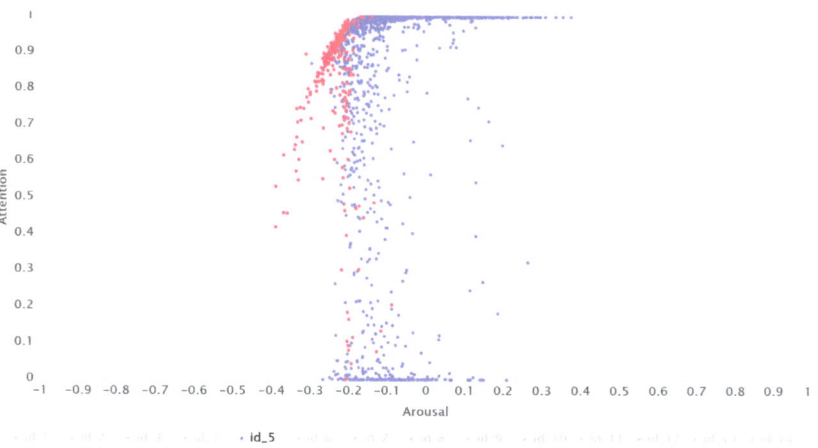

Figure 11. Arousal–attention of participants—left-handedness.

4. Conclusions

The present research contributes toward developing an emotion modeling component to enhance machines with emotional intelligence functionality. Our concept builds on multimodal input concerning the user's momentous cognitive and emotional conditions and the intelligent human–machine interface framework—iHMIfr. The experimental validation confirms that the automated recognition of mental states could help achieve awareness about the human condition in collaborative human–machine interaction.

The detection and profiling of personal traits during the execution of a given task and the corresponding activation of adequate adaptive strategies establish the ground for machine-to-human relationship management. Achieving social awareness and relationship management functionality, accompanied by a task-related adaptation (based on self-awareness and self-management on the machine side), contributes directly towards machine emotional intelligence.

Supplementary Materials: The following supporting information can be downloaded at http://isr.tu-varna.bg/ihmi/index.php/resursi (accessed on 7 September 2023).

Author Contributions: Conceptualization, M.M., V.M. and T.G.; methodology, M.M. and Y.K.; software, Y.K.; validation, M.M., Y.K. and V.M.; formal analysis, M.M.; investigation, M.M.; resources, V.M.; data curation, M.M.; writing—original draft preparation, M.M.; writing—review and editing, T.G.; visualization, M.M.; supervision, T.G.; project administration, T.G.; funding acquisition, T.G. All authors have read and agreed to the published version of the manuscript.

Funding: This research was supported by the Bulgarian National Science Fund (BNSF), with grant agreement FNI KP-06-N37/18, entitled "Investigation on intelligent human-machine interaction inter-faces, capable of recognizing high-risk emotional and cognitive conditions".

Data Availability Statement: The data presented in this study are available in Supplementary Materials.

Conflicts of Interest: The authors declare no conflict of interest. The funders had no role in the design of the study, in the collection, analyses, or interpretation of data, in the writing of the manuscript, or in the decision to publish the results.

References

1. Liu, F.; Liu, Y.; Shi, Y. Three IQs of AI systems and their testing methods. *J. Eng.* **2020**, *2020*, 566–571. [CrossRef]
2. Salovey, P.; Mayer, J.D. Emotional Intelligence. *Imagin. Cogn. Personal.* **1990**, *9*, 185–211. [CrossRef]
3. Goleman, D. *Emotional Intelligence*; Bantam Books: New York, NY, USA, 2005.

4. Hazarika, D.; Poria, S.; Zimmermann, R.; Mihalcea, R. Conversational transfer learning for emotion recognition. *Inf. Fusion* **2021**, *65*, 1–12. [CrossRef]
5. Mohammadi Baghmolaei, R.; Ahmadi, A. TET: Text emotion transfer. *Knowl-Based Syst.* **2023**, *262*, 110236. [CrossRef]
6. You, L.; Han, F.; Peng, J.; Jin, H.; Claramunt, C. ASK-RoBERTa: A pretraining model for aspect-based sentiment classification via sentiment knowledge mining. *Knowl-Based Syst.* **2022**, *253*, 109511. [CrossRef]
7. Zhang, X.; Ma, Y. An ALBERT-based TextCNN-Hatt hybrid model enhanced with topic knowledge for sentiment analysis of sudden-onset disasters. *Eng. Appl. Artif. Intell.* **2023**, *123*, 106136. [CrossRef]
8. Vekkot, S.; Gupta, D. Fusion of spectral and prosody modelling for multilingual speech emotion conversion. *Knowl-Based Syst.* **2022**, *242*, 108360. [CrossRef]
9. Leippold, M. Sentiment spin: Attacking financial sentiment with GPT-3. *Financ. Res. Lett.* **2023**, *55*, 103957. [CrossRef]
10. Gupta, A.; Singhal, A.; Mahajan, A.; Jolly, A.; Kumar, S. Empirical Framework for Automatic Detection of Neural and Human Authored Fake News. In Proceedings of the 2022 6th International Conference on Intelligent Computing and Control Systems (ICICCS), Madurai, India, 25–27 May 2022; IEEE: Madurai, India, 2022; pp. 1625–1633.
11. Malhotra, A.; Jindal, R. Deep learning techniques for suicide and depression detection from online social media: A scoping review. *Appl. Soft Comput.* **2022**, *130*, 109713. [CrossRef]
12. Mi, C.; Xie, L.; Zhang, Y. Improving data augmentation for low resource speech-to-text translation with diverse paraphrasing. *Neural Netw.* **2022**, *148*, 194–205. [CrossRef] [PubMed]
13. Korzekwa, D.; Lorenzo-Trueba, J.; Drugman, T.; Kostek, B. Computer-assisted pronunciation training—Speech synthesis is almost all you need. *Speech Commun.* **2022**, *142*, 22–33. [CrossRef]
14. Zhang, H.; Yang, X.; Qu, D.; Li, Z. Bridging the cross-modal gap using adversarial training for speech-to-text translation. *Digit. Signal Process.* **2022**, *131*, 103764. [CrossRef]
15. Lim, Y.; Gardi, A.; Pongsakornsathien, N.; Sabatini, R.; Ezer, N.; Kistan, T. Experimental characterisation of eye-tracking sensors for adaptive human-machine systems. *Measurement* **2019**, *140*, 151–160. [CrossRef]
16. Shi, L.; Bhattacharya, N.; Das, A.; Gwizdka, J. True or false? Cognitive load when reading COVID-19 news headlines: An eye-tracking study. In Proceedings of the CHIIR '23: ACM SIGIR Conference on Human Information Interaction and Retrieval, Austin, TX, USA, 19–23 March 2023; ACM: Austin, TX, USA, 2023; pp. 107–116.
17. Erdogan, R.; Saglam, Z.; Cetintav, G.; Karaoglan Yilmaz, F.G. Examination of the usability of Tinkercad application in educational robotics teaching by eye tracking technique. *Smart Learn. Environ.* **2023**, *10*, 27. [CrossRef]
18. Li, S.; Duffy, M.C.; Lajoie, S.P.; Zheng, J.; Lachapelle, K. Using eye tracking to examine expert-novice differences during simulated surgical training: A case study. *Comput. Hum. Behav.* **2023**, *144*, 107720. [CrossRef]
19. Fernandes, A.S.; Murdison, T.S.; Proulx, M.J. Leveling the Playing Field: A Comparative Reevaluation of Unmodified Eye Tracking as an Input and Interaction Modality for VR. *IEEE Trans. Visual. Comput. Graphics* **2023**, *29*, 2269–2279. [CrossRef] [PubMed]
20. Shadiev, R.; Li, D. A review study on eye-tracking technology usage in immersive virtual reality learning environments. *Comput. Educ.* **2023**, *196*, 104681. [CrossRef]
21. Pan, H.; Xie, L.; Wang, Z. C3DBed: Facial micro-expression recognition with three-dimensional convolutional neural network embedding in transformer model. *Eng. Appl. Artif. Intell.* **2023**, *123*, 106258. [CrossRef]
22. Sung, G.; Bhinder, H.; Feng, T.; Schneider, B. Stressed or engaged? Addressing the mixed significance of physiological activity during constructivist learning. *Comput. Educ.* **2023**, *199*, 104784. [CrossRef]
23. Campanella, S.; Altaleb, A.; Belli, A.; Pierleoni, P.; Palma, L.A. Method for Stress Detection Using Empatica E4 Bracelet and Machine-Learning Techniques. *Sensors* **2023**, *23*, 3565. [CrossRef]
24. Chen, K.; Han, J.; Baldauf, W.; Wang, Z.; Chen, D.; Kato, A.; Ward, J.A.; Kunze, K. Affective Umbrella—A Wearable System to Visualize Heart and Electrodermal Activity, towards Emotion Regulation through Somaesthetic Appreciation. In Proceedings of the AHs '23: Augmented Humans Conference, Glasgow, UK, 12–14 March 2023; ACM: Glasgow, UK, 2023; pp. 231–242.
25. Sagastibeltza, N.; Salazar-Ramirez, A.; Martinez, R.; Jodra, J.L.; Muguerza, J. Automatic detection of the mental state in responses towards relaxation. *Neural Comput. Appl.* **2023**, *35*, 5679–5696. [CrossRef] [PubMed]
26. Stržinar, Ž.; Sanchis, A.; Ledezma, A.; Sipele, O.; Pregelj, B.; Škrjanc, I. Stress Detection Using Frequency Spectrum Analysis of Wrist-Measured Electrodermal Activity. *Sensors* **2023**, *23*, 963. [CrossRef] [PubMed]
27. Castro-García, J.A.; Molina-Cantero, A.J.; Gómez-González, I.M.; Lafuente-Arroyo, S.; Merino-Monge, M. Towards Human Stress and Activity Recognition: A Review and a First Approach Based on Low-Cost Wearables. *Electronics* **2022**, *11*, 155. [CrossRef]
28. Mach, S.; Storozynski, P.; Halama, J.; Krems, J.F. Assessing mental workload with wearable devices—Reliability and applicability of heart rate and motion measurements. *Appl. Ergon.* **2022**, *105*, 103855. [CrossRef]
29. Ngoc-Thang, B.; Tien Nguyen, T.M.; Truong, T.T.; Nguyen, B.L.-H.; Nguyen, T.T. A dynamic reconfigurable wearable device to acquire high quality PPG signal and robust heart rate estimate based on deep learning algorithm for smart healthcare system. *Biosens. Bioelectron. X* **2022**, *12*, 100223. [CrossRef]
30. Wang, Z.; Matsuhashi, R.; Onodera, H. Towards wearable thermal comfort assessment framework by analysis of heart rate variability. *Build. Environ.* **2022**, *223*, 109504. [CrossRef]
31. Goumopoulos, C.; Stergiopoulos, N.G. Mental stress detection using a wearable device and heart rate variability monitoring. In *Edge-of-Things in Personalized Healthcare Support Systems*; Elsevier: Amsterdam, The Netherlands, 2022; pp. 261–290.

32. Chen, Y.; Wang, Z.; Tian, X.; Liu, W. Evaluation of cognitive performance in high temperature with heart rate: A pilot study. *Build. Environ.* **2023**, *228*, 109801. [CrossRef]
33. Du, H.; Riddell, R.P.; Wang, X. A hybrid complex-valued neural network framework with applications to electroencephalogram (EEG). *Biomed. Signal Process. Control.* **2023**, *85*, 104862. [CrossRef]
34. Soni, S.; Seal, A.; Mohanty, S.K.; Sakurai, K. Electroencephalography signals-based sparse networks integration using a fuzzy ensemble technique for depression detection. *Biomed. Signal Process. Control.* **2023**, *85*, 104873. [CrossRef]
35. Zali-Vargahan, B.; Charmin, A.; Kalbkhani, H.; Barghandan, S. Deep time-frequency features and semi-supervised dimension reduction for subject-independent emotion recognition from multi-channel EEG signals. *Biomed. Signal Process. Control.* **2023**, *85*, 104806. [CrossRef]
36. Liu, S.; Zhao, Y.; An, Y.; Zhao, J.; Wang, S.-H.; Yan, J. GLFANet: A global to local feature aggregation network for EEG emotion recognition. *Biomed. Signal Process. Control.* **2023**, *85*, 104799. [CrossRef]
37. Gong, L.; Li, M.; Zhang, T.; Chen, W. EEG emotion recognition using attention-based convolutional transformer neural network. *Biomed. Signal Process. Control.* **2023**, *84*, 104835. [CrossRef]
38. Quan, J.; Li, Y.; Wang, L.; He, R.; Yang, S.; Guo, L. EEG-based cross-subject emotion recognition using multi-source domain transfer learning. *Biomed. Signal Process. Control.* **2023**, *84*, 104741. [CrossRef]
39. Baradaran, F.; Farzan, A.; Danishvar, S.; Sheykhivand, S. Automatic Emotion Recognition from EEG Signals Using a Combination of Type-2 Fuzzy and Deep Convolutional Networks. *Electronics* **2023**, *12*, 2216. [CrossRef]
40. Baradaran, F.; Farzan, A.; Danishvar, S.; Sheykhivand, S. Customized 2D CNN Model for the Automatic Emotion Recognition Based on EEG Signals. *Electronics* **2023**, *12*, 2232. [CrossRef]
41. Cardona-Álvarez, Y.N.; Álvarez-Meza, A.M.; Cárdenas-Peña, D.A.; Castaño-Duque, G.A.; Castellanos-Dominguez, G.A. Novel OpenBCI Framework for EEG-Based Neurophysiological Experiments. *Sensors* **2023**, *23*, 3763. [CrossRef]
42. Li, X.; Chen, J.; Shi, N.; Yang, C.; Gao, P.; Chen, X.; Wang, Y.; Gao, S.; Gao, X. A hybrid steady-state visual evoked response-based brain-computer interface with MEG and EEG. *Expert Syst. Appl.* **2023**, *223*, 119736. [CrossRef]
43. Musk, E. Neuralink. An Integrated Brain-Machine Interface Platform with Thousands of Channels. *J. Med. Internet. Res.* **2019**, *21*, e16194. [CrossRef]
44. Zhou, L.; Wu, B.; Deng, Y.; Liu, M. Brain activation and individual differences of emotional perception and imagery in healthy adults: A functional near-infrared spectroscopy (fNIRS) study. *Neurosci. Lett.* **2023**, *797*, 137072. [CrossRef]
45. Karmakar, S.; Kamilya, S.; Dey, P.; Guhathakurta, P.K.; Dalui, M.; Bera, T.K.; Halder, S.; Koley, C.; Pal, T.; Basu, A. Real time detection of cognitive load using fNIRS: A deep learning approach. *Biomed. Signal Process. Control.* **2023**, *80*, 104227. [CrossRef]
46. Roberts, G.S.; Hoffman, C.A.; Rivera-Rivera, L.A.; Berman, S.E.; Eisenmenger, L.B.; Wieben, O. Automated hemodynamic assessment for cranial 4D flow MRI. *Magn. Reson. Imaging* **2023**, *97*, 46–55. [CrossRef]
47. Paul, G. From the visible human project to the digital twin. In *Digital Human Modeling and Medicine*; Elsevier: Amsterdam, The Netherlands, 2023; pp. 3–17.
48. Bangaru, S.S.; Wang, C.; Busam, S.A.; Aghazadeh, F. ANN-based automated scaffold builder activity recognition through wearable EMG and IMU sensors. *Autom. Constr.* **2021**, *126*, 103653. [CrossRef]
49. Nicholls, B.; Ang, C.S.; Kanjo, E.; Siriaraya, P.; Mirzaee Bafti, S.; Yeo, W.-H.; Tsanas, A. An EMG-based Eating Behaviour Monitoring system with haptic feedback to promote mindful eating. *Comput. Biol. Med.* **2022**, *149*, 106068. [CrossRef] [PubMed]
50. Tian, H.; Li, X.; Wei, Y.; Ji, S.; Yang, Q.; Gou, G.-Y.; Wang, X.; Wu, F.; Jian, J.; Guo, H.; et al. Bioinspired dual-channel speech recognition using graphene-based electromyographic and mechanical sensors. *Cell Rep. Phys. Sci.* **2022**, *3*, 101075. [CrossRef]
51. Markov, M.; Ganchev, T. Intelligent human-machine interface framework. *Int. J. Adv. Electron. Comput. Sci.* **2022**, *9*, 41–46.
52. Markov, M. Workflow adaptation for intelligent human-machine interfaces. *Comput. Sci. Technol. J. Tech. Univ. Varna* **2022**, *1*, 51–58.
53. Markov, M.; Kalinin, Y.; Ganchev, T. A Task-related Adaptation in Intelligent Human-Machine Interfaces. In Proceedings of the 2022 International Conference on Communications, Information, Electronic and Energy Systems (CIEES), Veliko Tarnovo, Bulgaria, 24–26 November 2022; IEEE: Veliko Tarnovo, Bulgaria, 2022; pp. 1–4.
54. Anon. Emotion AI Provider. *Facial Emotion Recognition MorphCast*. 2023. Available online: https://www.morphcast.com (accessed on 7 September 2023).
55. O'Keeffe, K.; Hodder, S.; Lloyd, A. A comparison of methods used for inducing mental fatigue in performance research: Individualised, dual-task and short duration cognitive tests are most effective. *Ergonomics* **2020**, *63*, 1–12. [CrossRef]
56. Anon RapidMiner | Amplify the Impact of Your People, Expertise & Data RapidMiner. Available online: https://www.rapidminer.com (accessed on 7 September 2023).

Disclaimer/Publisher's Note: The statements, opinions and data contained in all publications are solely those of the individual author(s) and contributor(s) and not of MDPI and/or the editor(s). MDPI and/or the editor(s) disclaim responsibility for any injury to people or property resulting from any ideas, methods, instructions or products referred to in the content.

Article

An Efficient Classification of Rice Variety with Quantized Neural Networks

Mustafa Tasci [1,*], Ayhan Istanbullu [2], Selahattin Kosunalp [1], Teodor Iliev [3], Ivaylo Stoyanov [4] and Ivan Beloev [5]

1. Department of Computer Technologies, Gönen Vocational School, Bandırma Onyedi Eylül University, 10200 Bandırma, Türkiye; skosunalp@bandirma.edu.tr
2. Department of Computer Engineering, Faculty of Engineering, Balıkesir University, 10145 Balıkesir, Türkiye; iayhan@balikesir.edu.tr
3. Department of Telecommunication, University of Ruse, 7017 Ruse, Bulgaria; tiliev@uni-ruse.bg
4. Department of Electrical and Power Engineering, University of Ruse, 7017 Ruse, Bulgaria; stoyanov@uni-ruse.bg
5. Department of Transport, University of Ruse, 7017 Ruse, Bulgaria; ibeloev@uni-ruse.bg
* Correspondence: mtasci@bandirma.edu.tr

Abstract: Rice, as one of the significant grain products across the world, features a wide range of varieties in terms of usability and efficiency. It may be known with various varieties and regional names depending on the specific locations. To specify a particular rice type, different features are considered, such as shape and color. This study uses an available dataset in Turkey consisting of five different varieties: Ipsala, Arborio, Basmati, Jasmine, and Karacadag. The dataset introduces 75,000 grain images in total; each of the 5 varieties has 15,000 samples with a 256 × 256-pixel dimension. The main contribution of this paper is to create Quantized Neural Network (QNN) models to efficiently classify rice varieties with the purpose of reducing resource usage on edge devices. It is well-known that QNN is a successful method for alleviating high computational costs and power requirements in response to many Deep Learning (DL) algorithms. These advantages of the quantization process have the potential to provide an efficient environment for artificial intelligence applications on microcontroller-driven edge devices. For this purpose, we created eight different QNN networks using the MLP and Lenet-5-based deep learning models with varying quantization levels to be trained by the dataset. With the Lenet-5-based QNN network created at the W3A3 quantization level, a 99.87% classification accuracy level was achieved with only 23.1 Kb memory size used for the parameters. In addition to this tremendous benefit of memory usage, the number of billion transactions per second (GOPs) is 23 times less than similar classification studies.

Keywords: rice classification; deep learning; Quantized Neural Network; LeNet-5

Citation: Tasci, M.; Istanbullu, A.; Kosunalp, S.; Iliev, T.; Stoyanov, I.; Beloev, I. An Efficient Classification of Rice Variety with Quantized Neural Networks. *Electronics* **2023**, *12*, 2285. https://doi.org/10.3390/electronics12102285

Academic Editor: Alberto Fernandez Hilario

Received: 19 April 2023
Revised: 11 May 2023
Accepted: 16 May 2023
Published: 18 May 2023

Copyright: © 2023 by the authors. Licensee MDPI, Basel, Switzerland. This article is an open access article distributed under the terms and conditions of the Creative Commons Attribution (CC BY) license (https://creativecommons.org/licenses/by/4.0/).

1. Introduction

Rice, as one of the most produced and consumed cereal products, has the highest production capacity following wheat and corn. It has historically been a food item with thousands of varieties. In 2022, the production capacity of rice was 513 million tons in approximately 119 countries [1]. The classification of rice varieties is an attractive research topic due to its important place among nutrients and trade role throughout the world. The determination of rice variety before the production process has the potential to enhance the quality of the final product satisfying the requirements of food safety. The applications of the classification phase can possibly distinguish the solid products from the form of seeds. Recent technological developments based on image processing have resulted in efficient and intelligent classification methods for all branches of agriculture [2–4]. These novel methods provide fast decisions while satisfying time and resource constraints [5]. Therefore, the drawbacks of manual strategies under the responsibility of human control in classifying grains are eliminated.

In recent years, machine learning (ML) algorithms have been successfully applied to operate classification tasks with high accuracy [6,7]. The basic idea relies on collecting a sufficient number of images of the products to be processed. This process extracts specific parameters about the product to enable the classification operation, such as texture, size, and shape. An important efficiency of ML is its ability to analyze a huge amount of information in a reliable way. In rice classification, ML methods have been a popular way of enhancing the final performance with the capability of extracting a lot of physical features from a specified dataset.

Deep Learning (DL), as a sub-section of ML, is a concept with the aid of artificial neural networks through advancing learning capabilities in object detection and image recognition. DL approaches have a complex structure as it requires a high volume of training data and high-performance computing resources [8–10]. To improve the performance accuracy for the classification of three rice groups, a deep convolutional neural network (DCNN) based structure is proposed with a key focus on minimizing training errors [11]. The training operation is integrated with a stochastic gradient descent structure to avoid the problem of heuristics and arrange system parameters in a smart vision. The dataset includes 5554 and 1845 images for training and validation, respectively. Another work designs a DL-based cost-effective solution using AlexNet architecture with two public datasets from Asia [12]. It extracts the features by applying a transfer learning approach with data augmentation in the training phase. A three-dimensional view from the surface of rice seeds, in place of two-dimensional images, is associated with a DL network for fast and more accurate identification of rice varieties [13]. For the feature extraction, PointNet platform targeting at 3D classification and segmentation is used and improved through employing a cross-level feature connection property. For 8 rice varieties, the dataset was experimentally generated and contains 210 samples (150 samples for training and 60 samples for validation). A recent study created DL models based on Artificial Neural Networks (ANNs), Deep Neural Networks (DNNs), and Convolutional Neural Networks (CNNs) to perform classification tasks with 75,000 samples of the dataset for five rice varieties [14]. The performance outputs indicate that the best classification accuracy value is achieved by CNN.

An underlying drawback of DL-based models is the high computational burden as such models involve intensive mathematical operations [15]. The duration of a training phase may take several days with respect to network depth and parameters. The parameters in a trained network can reach GigaByte or even TeraByte levels depending on the size of the model. Therefore, these models often require computing devices with high resources which makes the implementation of the models a difficult task in resource-constrained devices [16,17]. Nowadays, edge devices such as mobile phones and Internet of Things (IoT) devices are designed to be able to run DL algorithms or train the models. The edge devices are usually equipped with limited facilities with the purpose of providing connection to service providers and other edge devices [18–20]. This brings a necessity to take the limited resources such as processing capacity, operating frequency, memory size, and power consumption into consideration for a perpetual operation of DL [21]. In this article, eight various QNN networks are constructed at W1A1, W2A2, W3A3, and W8A8 quantization levels using Pytorch framework and Xilinx Brevitas library [22] on MLP and Lenet-5 models. Each network quantizes the image input to 8 bits. In general, the complete workflow for each QNN is demonstrated in Figure 1. The whole process for building a QNN network model consists of three steps, as presented in the figure. The first step includes the preparation of the dataset used by resizing the dimensions of the images from $3 \times 256 \times 256$ to $3 \times 32 \times 32$ in RGB format. This is then followed by dividing the dataset for training and validation. In the second step, the QNN network is created by determining the required parameters, such as weights and activation. Then, the hyperparameters are defined to be used for the training of the QNN model. The final step includes the evaluation of the constructed QNN models. Later, the performance results prove the efficiency of the proposed models. Performance comparisons with well-known existing studies indicate the superiority of the proposed study in terms of resource consumption. To sum up, the main contributions of this paper can be summarized by following:

- The primary contribution is to develop a solution for an efficient classification strategy for rice variety classification, taking advantage of Quantized Neural Network (QNN) models.
- The main emphasis has been placed on the utilization of limited resources for edge devices in IoT applications to reduce the high level of the computational burden of DL models.
- The proposed QNN networks with various quantization levels benefit from the Pytorch framework and Xilinx Brevitas library on MLP and Lenet-5 models.
- The performance efficiency of the proposed idea has been extensively tested using a real-world dataset with five different varieties, in comparison to state-of-the-art approaches.

The forthcoming parts of the article are organized as follows. The second part describes the definition of the models, including the dataset, performance measurement metrics, and the proposed QNN networks. In third section of the article, the performance evaluations are presented with a deep analysis. We finally conclude the paper in the last part.

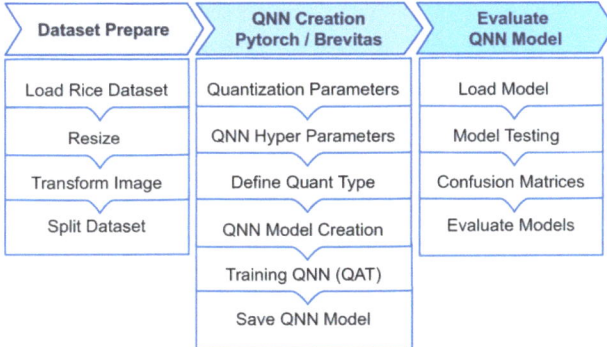

Figure 1. The workflow for QNN design and evaluation.

2. Definition of Models

2.1. Preparation of Dataset

In this study, a recent dataset comprising five rice varieties (Ipsala, Arborio, Basmati, Yasemin, and Karacadagas as depicted in Figure 2) is selected due to its high number of sample images [23]. The number of samples for each class is 15,000, with a pixel size of 256 × 256.

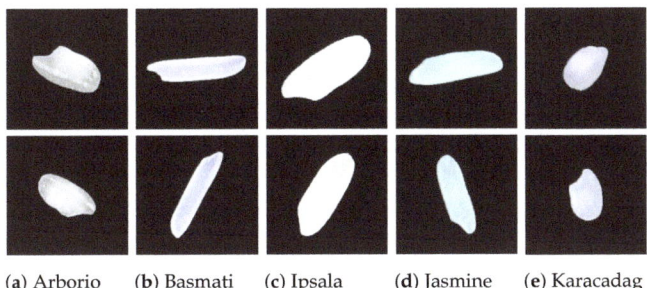

(a) Arborio   (b) Basmati   (c) Ipsala   (d) Jasmine   (e) Karacadag

Figure 2. Rice varieties in the dataset.

A preprocessing is applied to resize the images to 32 × 32 as the main emphasis of this study is placed on the implementation of QNN models using resource-constrained devices. A view of both original and resized images can be seen in Figure 3.

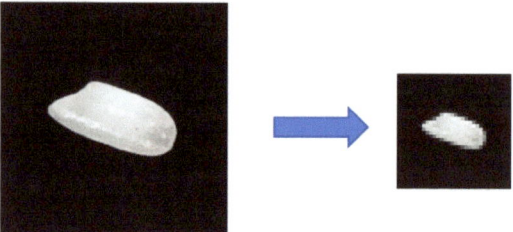

Figure 3. A view of the image after resizing the original image.

The advantage of reducing the size of the images on the LENET-5-based CNN model is presented in Table 1, which shows the memory allocation, the number of parameters, and the billion floating point operations (GFLOPs) per second. With this reduction, the proposed model is capable of performing approximately 110 times less than the number of floating-point operations. Memory usage is also decreased almost 460 times. The dataset is partitioned into 60,000 images for training, 5000 images for validation, and 10,000 images for testing.

Table 1. Changing features on Lenet-5 according to the size of the input images.

Input Size	Parameters	Bias	GFLOPs	Memory (KB)
3 × 256 × 256	7,157,901	227	142.9	28,632
3 × 32 × 32	61,581	227	1.3	62

2.2. Multi-Layer Perceptron (MLP) Model

Multi-layer Perceptron Network (MLP) is a simple neural network with multiple hidden layers of perceptrons among the input and output layers [24]. A typical MLP network is composed of a minimum of three layers beginning with an input layer to forward the processed data by the hidden layers to the output layer. The classification task is finalized by the output layer. The number of hidden layers is an application-specific property acting as computational units in a feed-forward fashion. In this study, the MLP network contains a flattened layer to shape the incoming image matrix in linear form. After linearization step, the one-dimensional data are fed to the next two hidden layers with 128 and 64 neurons. It is then captured by a Softmax layer with 5 outputs as the number of rice varieties to calculate the probability of membership for each rice class. The whole MLP model described is shown in Figure 4.

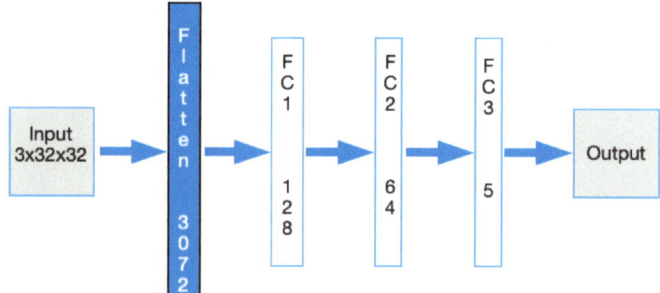

Figure 4. MLP neural network model for rice classification.

2.3. LeNet-5 Model

LeNet-5 is a pioneering CNN structure that has had a great impact on the evolution of Deep Learning. It has the fundamental cells of CNN with a multi-layer convolution and pooling. In total, LeNet-5 comprises 7 layers with the exception of the input layer allowing the parameters to be trained in each layer. The input in this model is a 32×32-pixel image. The rationale behind the popularity of LeNet-5 is its simplicity and easy architecture. This study utilizes the original LeNet-5 model proposed in [25] as depicted in Figure 5.

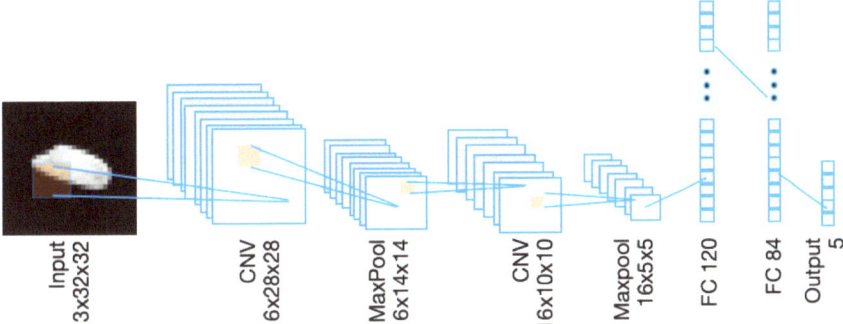

Figure 5. Lenet-5 based CNN model.

2.4. Quantized Neural Network (QNN) Model

Quantization in DL models is defined as a process of reducing the memory requirement and computational burden by executing low-bit width values instead of floating-point values. To ensure a high-performance accuracy for applications run on-device, Quantization becomes a critical technique to supply a compact model leading to a reasonable size of neural network. Quantized Neural Network (QNN) is a special type of CNN without sacrificing performance. There are two types of quantization: Post-Training Quantization (PTQ) and Quantization-Aware-Training (QAT) [26].

PTQ has a straightforward implementation process requiring no quantization in the training part benefitting from a pre-trained network. The parameters can be quantized based upon completion of the training of the floating-point network, subject to a quantization error on parameters. This may result in incorrect classification with increased quantization error. QAT is used to recover this error by computing the parameters during the training. As QAT performs the quantization process while training the model and calculating the parameters, one advantage of QAT is to raise the optimization to greater extents [27]. The all steps of both quantization techniques are shown in Figure 6.

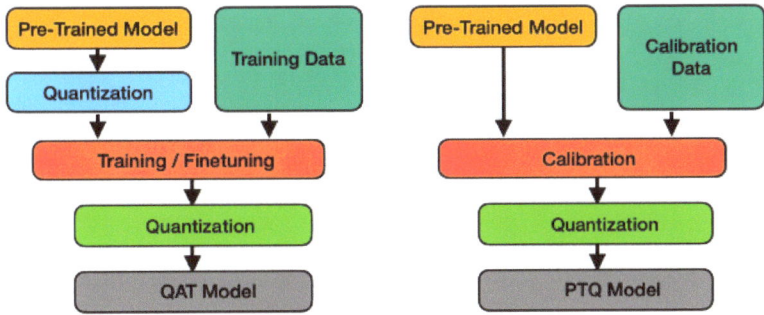

Figure 6. The block diagrams of QAT and PTQ quantization processes.

CNN algorithms can include millions of floating-point parameters and billions of floating-point operations to recognize a single image [28]. The winner of the ImageNet competition performed 244 MB of parameters and 1.4 GFLOPs in 2012 and 552 MB of parameters and 30.8 GFLOPs per image in 2014 [29]. This requirement of high computing and memory capacities of deep neural networks hinders the utilization of these applications on mobile devices. To deal with this issue, quantization allows a model to consume less computing and memory resources while keeping its accuracy close to the original model [30]. The quantization process is performed on the weight (W), input (I), bias (B), and output (O) data. The maximum value in the data to be quantized is calculated with the following equation.

$$Qnt_{th} = 2^{N-1} \tag{1}$$

N indicates the bit width to be quantized, Qnt_{th} represents the maximum value to have occurred as a result of the quantization process. Here th is the value of the element with the highest absolute value according to the i and j indices of the matrix A to be quantized.

$$th = max|A_{i,j}| \tag{2}$$

Then, a specific scale, k, is defined by dividing th by Qnt_{th}:

$$k = \frac{th}{Qnt_{th}} \tag{3}$$

The quantization process is finalized, taking the ratio between A and k.

$$QntA = \frac{A}{k} \tag{4}$$

2.5. Quantization in Brevitas

Brevitas is a PyTorch library developed by Xilinx Research Lab for QAT-type quantification, introducing a quantized version of PyTorch layers. The layers in a neural network developed by PyTorch are replaced with Brevitas layers, resulting in the creation of the quantized model. Due to the interoperability of Brevitas with PyTorch layers, it makes the implementation of hybrid models feasible, thereby making the utilization of quantized and unquantized layers together. Consequently, this library quantizes the relevant parts of the layers with the parameters (W, I, B, O) aforementioned above. The frequently-used quantization techniques in Brevitas are:

- *INT*: it returns the input tensor to the quantized integer at the specified bit width.
- *BINARY*: it returns the input tensor quantized at $(-1,1)$ values.
- *TERNARY*: it returns the input tensor quantized at $(-1,0,1)$.

Binary quantization represents the FP32 type in the W, I, B, O parameters as a 1-bit number. For example, after a bit quantization, the value of 0.127478 becomes 1, while the value of -0.05439 is quantized to -1. In the other quantization levels, the parameter value is converted to the closest number that can be represented by a selected number. The 4-bit quantization operation is shown on the matrix A given below as a numerical example.

$$A = \begin{bmatrix} -0.235 & 0.205 & -0.654 \\ 0.567 & 0.709 & 0.432 \\ 0.032 & 0.456 & -0.623 \end{bmatrix}, \quad th = 0.709, \quad N = 4, \quad Qnt_{th} = 8$$

$$k = \frac{0.709}{8}$$

$$QntA \approx \begin{bmatrix} -3 & 2 & -7 \\ 6 & 8 & 5 \\ 0 & 5 & -7 \end{bmatrix}$$

It can be seen that after the quantization of the input matrix, its largest value is 8, and the smallest value is −7. These values are a range of signed numbers that can be written with a data width of 4 bits. In our study, quantization levels are used in WxAx format. Here, W represents the weight, A indicates the activation process, and x represents the bit width at which the quantization process will be performed.

This study implements BINARY for the W1A1 model and INT for the rest of the models. The networks developed for the MLP and Lenet-5 models are trained with quantized values at the W1A1, W2A2, W3A3, and W8A8 quantization levels. The complete process of building the MLP model is provided in Algorithm 1.

Algorithm 1 MLP Quantize model generator algorithm

1: $X \leftarrow inputData$
2: $W \leftarrow weightBitWidth$
3: $A \leftarrow activationBitWidth$
4: $I \leftarrow inputBitWidth$
5: $C \leftarrow numberofClasses$
6: $O_F \leftarrow outputFeatures(128, 64)$
7: **Require:** *Brevitas Modules (QuantIdentity, QuantLinear, Dropout, BatchNorm1D, TensorNorm)*
8: **procedure** MLP
9:     **append** *QuantIdentity(I)* **to** Model
10:     **append** *DropOut* **to** Model
11:     **for** outputFeatures **do**
12:         **append** *QuantLinear(W)* **to** Model
13:         **append** *BatchNorm1D* **to** Model
14:         **append** *QuantIdentity(A)* **to** Model
15:         **append** *DropOut* **to** Model
16:     **end for**
17:     **append** *QuantLinear(W)* **to** Model
18:     **append** *TensorNorm* **to** Model
19:     $X \leftarrow X \times 2 - 1$
20:     **for** Model **from** MLP **do**
21:         $X \leftarrow Modul(X)$
22:     **end for**
23: **end procedure**

The trained QNN networks are converted to ONNX (Open Neural Network Exchange) format using the BrevitasToONNX module. The complete flowchart of the MLP model in ONNX format can be seen in Figure 7.

In this figure, X represents the quantized input file of the output layer, which then takes Y as a power. In the input section, image data in the range of 0–255 is initially normalized to the range of −127–127. Then, the second normalization is performed on the normalized data to the range of (−1,1) with FP32 bit data type. In the second step, the linearized input matrix is multiplied by the weights on the 128-layer MLP block. It is then followed by multiple thresholding components and matrix transposing operations. After completing the same operations in the 64-layer MLP block, the classification scores are generated for the five rice grades.

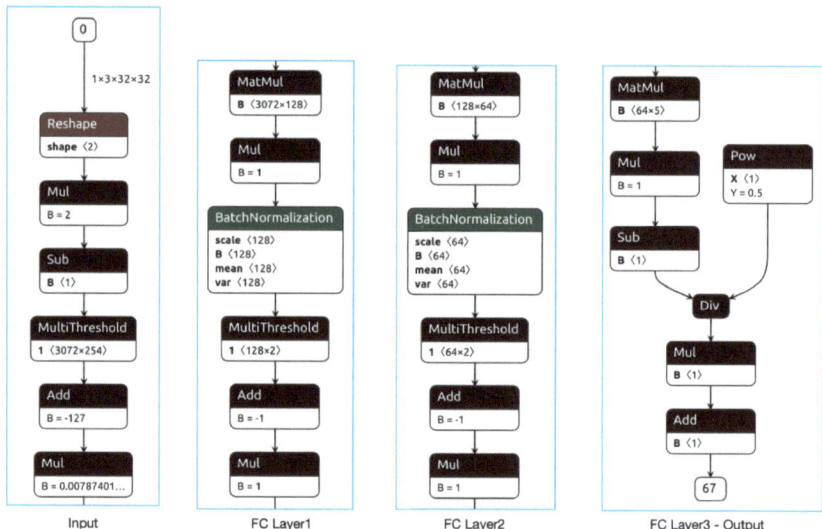

Figure 7. The quantized MLP model with Brevitas.

The model created with the Brevitas library on the Lenet-5 model is seen in Figure 8 after the ONNX transformation. In the introductory part of the Lenet-5-based QNN model, the image data are normalized in the range of (−1,1) in the FP32 bit data type. In the second and third transaction blocks, the QuntConv2d convolution layer, transpose operation, multi-threshold, and QuantMaxpool2d pooling operations are performed with the quantized data. At the entrance of the fourth block, the 2D matrix is flattened into 1D. After this stage, the operations made as in the quantified MLP model are performed. The pseudo-code of the entire Lenet-5 model is presented in Algorithm 2.

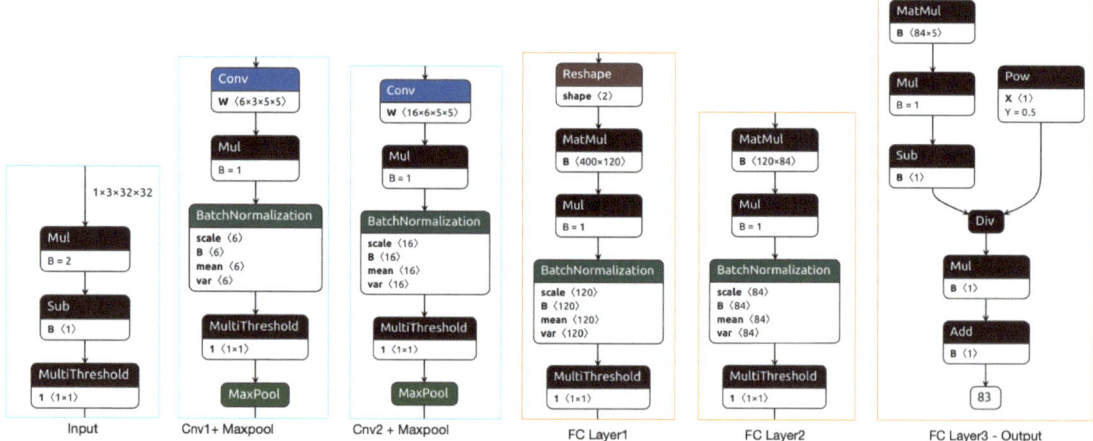

Figure 8. The quantized Lenet-5 model with Brevitas.

Algorithm 2 LENET-5 quantize model generator algorithm

1: $X \leftarrow inputData$
2: $W \leftarrow weightBitWidth$
3: $A \leftarrow activationBitWidth$
4: $I \leftarrow inputBitWidth$
5: $C \leftarrow numberOfClasses$
6: $C_F \leftarrow ConvFeatures(16, 6)$
7: $Fc_F \leftarrow FcFeatures(120, 84)$
8: **Require:** *Brevitas Modules (QuantConv2d,MaxPool2D,QuantIdentity,*
9: *QuantLinear,BatchNorm2D,BatchNorm1D,TensorNorm)*
10: **procedure** LENET
11:     **append** *QuantIdentity(I)* **to** Model
12:     **for** ConvFeatures **do**
13:         **append** *QuantConv2d(W)* **to** Model
14:         **append** *BatchNorm2D* **to** Model
15:         **append** *QuantIdentity(A)* **to** Model
16:         **append** *MaxPool2D* **to** Model
17:     **end for**
18:     **for** FcFeatures **do**
19:         **append** *QuantLinear(W)* **to** Model
20:         **append** *BatchNorm1D* **to** Model
21:         **append** *QuantIdentity(A)* **to** Model
22:     **end for**
23:     **append** *QuantLinear(W)* **to** Model
24:     **append** *TensorNorm* **to** Model
25:     $X \leftarrow X \times 2 - 1$
26:     **for** Model **from** Lenet **do**
27:         $X \leftarrow Model(X)$
28:     **end for**
29: **end procedure**

2.6. Performance Criterions

In the developed models of this study, the weight and activation parameters conduct the classification task at four different quantification levels. One of the most significant tools used in evaluating the performance of a model in AI-Based classification applications is the confusion matrix [31]. It paves a way to explore the relationships between the performance and test outputs better. The knowledge regarding the accurate and inaccurate classification for both positive and negative samples can be obtained by the confusion matrix as presented in Table 2 for a two-class confusion matrix.

Table 2. Binary class confusion matrix.

		Predicted Class	
		Positive	Negative
Actual Class	P (Positive)	TP (True Positive)	FN (False Negative)
	N (Negative)	FP (False Positive)	TN (True Negative)

Due to the five classes of rice in the dataset, the classification task of this study for each model includes a five-class confusion matrix. The terms of the confusion matrix are shown in Table 3. The performances of the two models at all quantization levels are analyzed using the metrics of accuracy (ACC), precision (Pre), recall (Rec), F1-Score (F1S), operations per second, and memory usage. The metrics for each class in the multi-class confusion matrix can be calculated using the equations given below.

Table 3. Five class confusion matrix.

		Predicted Classes				
		C1	C2	C3	C4	C5
Actual Classes	C1	T11	F12	F13	F14	F15
	C2	F21	T22	F23	F24	F25
	C3	F31	F32	T33	F34	F35
	C4	F41	F42	F43	T44	F45
	C5	F51	F52	F53	F54	T55

$$ACC_k = \frac{TP_k + TN_k}{TP_k + TN_k + FP_k + FN_k} \tag{5}$$

$$Pre_k = \frac{TP_k}{TP_k + FP_k} \tag{6}$$

$$Rec_k = \frac{TP_k}{TP_k + FN_k} \tag{7}$$

$$F1S_k = 2 \times \frac{Pre_k \times Rec_k}{Pre_k + Rec_k} \tag{8}$$

Accuracy denotes the success level of the classification. Precision stores the number of positive predictions, and Recall holds the number of positive samples to be identified. By combining precision and recall metrics, F1-Score is defined as the predictive ability through detailing a class-wise performance manner instead of accuracy that relies on the entire performance. The calculations of the values of TP, FP, TN, FN, and the criteria are shown by Algorithm 3.

Algorithm 3 Multiclass Confusion Matrix Evaluate Algorithm

1: $CM \Leftarrow ConfusionMatrix$
2: $GT \Leftarrow SumofCM$
3: $N \Leftarrow Numberofclasses$
4: **for** $i = 1, 2, \ldots, N$ **do**
5:     **for** $j = 1, 2, \ldots, N$ **do**
6:         **if** i is Not equal j **then**
7:             $fn[i] = fn[i] + CM[i, j]$
8:             $fp[i] = fp[i] + CM[j, i]$
9:         **end if**
10:     **end for**
11:     $tp[i] = CM[i, i]$
12:     $tn[i] = GT - tp[i] - fp[i] - fn[i]$
13:     $acc[i] = (tp[i] + tn[i])/GT$
14:     $pre[i] = tp[i]/(tp[i] + fp[i])$
15:     $rec[i] = tp[i]/(tp[i] + fn[i])$
16:     $f1s[i] = 2 * (pre[i] * rec[i])/(pre[i] + rec[i])$
17: **end for**
18: $acc = tp/GT$

---

3. Experimental Results

This section presents the outputs of the classification process carried out by MLP ve Lenet-5 models. The dataset included as input in QNN models covers 75,000 rice images, and the size of each image is resized from 256 × 256 to 32 × 32. The names of the five rice varieties are Ipsala, Arborio, Basmati, Yasemin, and Karacadag, acting as classification outputs. The hardware specifications, software platforms, and hyperparameters are summarized in Table 4 running on Google Colab.

The first experiment presents the performance accuracy of the Lenet-5 model with no quantization. The models created with the dimension of 32 × 32 images on the Pytorch framework are trained for 200 epochs. In the model constructed by the MLP, the classification accuracy was obtained as 96.45%. The classification success of the model created by Lenet-5 reached 99.99% in the Lenet-5 model, as demonstrated in Figure 9.

The next figure indicates the records of accuracy and loss values during the training phase for the two models at four quantization levels. These outputs are shown in Figure 10 with a duration of 200 epochs. It is worth noting that all models in Lenet-5, with the exception of the 1-bit quantization model (W1A1), achieve a classification accuracy of nearly 98% for 50 epochs. The reason behind taking longer training time at a 1-bit quantization level is because of the low weight and activation sensitivity level in the backpropagation algorithm. We, therefore, set the training epoch duration as 200 for all models, in accordance with the duration at which the W1A1 model reached maximum learning. This permits us to visualize the results of all models on the same figure.

Table 4. Hardware features and all parameters.

Parameters	Specifications
GPU Model Name	Nvidia Tesla K80
GPU Memory	12 GB
GPU Memory Clock	0.82 GHZ
GPU Performance	4.1 TFLOPs
CPU Model Name	Intel ® Xeon ®
CPU Frequency	2.30 GHz
Number Of CPU Cores	2
Available RAM	12 GB
Operating System	Linux
Programing Language	Python 3.9
Framework	Pytorch, Brevitas
Batch Size	100
Learning Rate	0.02
Epoch	200

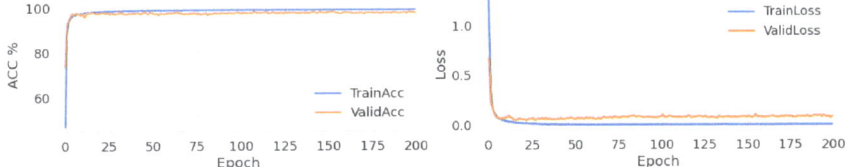

Figure 9. Performance accuracy and loss of Lenet-5 model with no quantization.

In total, 8 neural networks were trained according to the model and quantification levels with 60,000 training images and 5000 validation images in the dataset, and these network models were recorded with their weights. These eight network models were tested with 10,000 test images specifically dedicated to only the training phase. To compare the quantized neural networks with 32-bit floating point MLP and Lenet-5 networks, the same dataset was applied to test the performance. As a result of the test phase, the value of ACC, the amount of memory used, the weight and activation parameters of the model, and the number of billion transactions per second (GOPs) are presented in Table 5. In this table, the first row of the models indexed by the FP32 term represents the models with no quantization. It is clearly seen that the accuracy of both models without quantization offers the best performance but at the expense of a very high memory usage property.

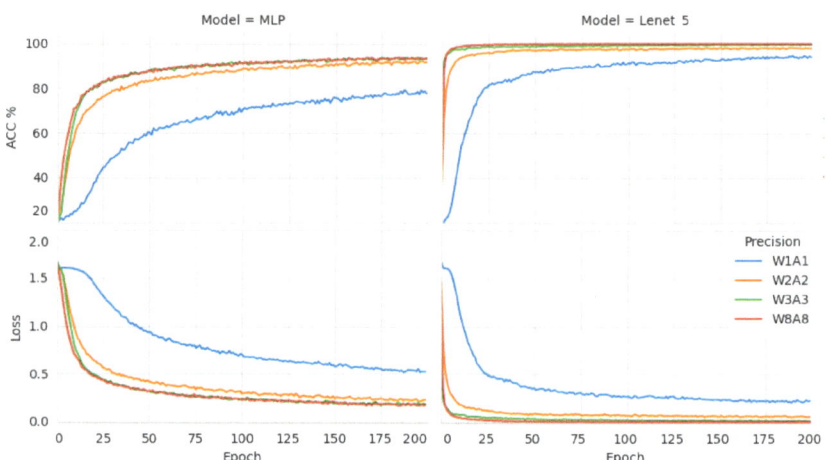

Figure 10. Accuracy and loss plots for MLP and Lenet-5 models for the training phase.

Table 5. The accuracy, number of transactions, and the amount of memory usage for eight models in the test implementation.

Model	Parameters	Bias	GOPs	Precision	Memory (Kb)	ACC%
MLP	401,925	193	0.8	32 Fp	1608	96.45
				W8A8	402	94.72
				W3A3	150	93.88
				W2A2	100	92.23
				W1A1	50	79.16
Lenet-5	61,581	227	1.3	32 Fp	247	99.99
				W8A8	61	99.99
				W3A3	**23**	**99.87**
				W2A2	15	98.20
				W1A1	7.7	94.40

MLP-based models, as an overall trend, consume approximately seven times higher memory usage when compared with Lenet-5 models that achieve better accuracy. On the other hand, MLP-based quantized models attain 0.8 GOPs per second to quantize an image, while Lenet-5-based QNN models use 1.3 GOPs. QNN-W1A1 consumes only 7 KB of memory with a performance accuracy of 94.40%. However, MLP-FP32 achieves a similar performance accuracy using 1.6 MB memory which is almost 228 times larger than Lenet-5-W1A1. This particular result proves the superior practicality of the proposed model on resource-constrained edge devices. In addition, since the proposed model is suitable for data flow, it can reach very high speeds on parallel processing platforms such as FPGA. In this study, the highest efficiency in terms of memory consumption and accuracy was obtained in the Lenet-5-W3A3 network, with a memory consumption of 23 KB and an accuracy of 99.87%.

High accuracy when evaluating an AI model would partly indicate a proper success level of the network. For a full assessment of the network performance, the scores of Pre, Rec, and F1S are some examples of metrics to assess the reliability of the model. It can be inferred from these metrics that an inference regarding the performance accomplishment of the model is acquired. To extract these metrics, the confusion matrices for the eight QNN models are constructed from the statistical evaluation of the dataset. We chose to show the confusion matrices of the best and worst networks instead of presenting eight confusion matrices. The confusion matrix of the best network in terms of success/resource utilization ratio, Lenet-5-W3A3, is shown in Figure 11. The accuracy for all rice types is similarly high, corresponding to a minor level of interference. In particular, for the Ipsala type, one sample is only classified wrongly.

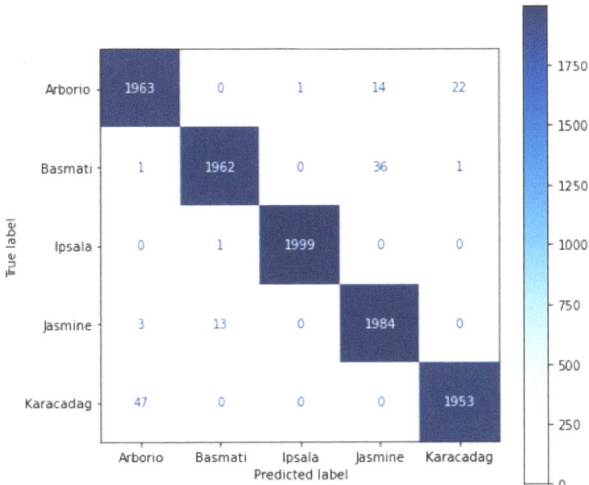

Figure 11. The confusion matrix of Lenet-5-W3A3 model.

The confusion matrix of MLP-W1A1 exhibits the worst performance, as presented in Figure 12. It is important mentioning that MLP-W1A1 actually overcomes the classification of four types with success. However, it has a terrifying classification accuracy for the Arborio type because an incorrect classification for 1764 Arborio samples was observed. Nevertheless, the total accuracy drops partly even though mislabeling of the majority of Arborio samples among 10,000 samples. To further analyze this error, the values of F1 for all classes are calculated using Algorithm-1, which is presented in Table 6. The F1 scores confirm the suitability of the seven networks to be applied. On the one hand, although the MLP-W1A1 network approaches a performance accuracy close to 0.8, the network faces a very low F1 score of 0.16 caused by improper prediction of Arborio type, as outlined above. Ipsala type experiences the best F1 score, with almost all scores being equal to 1.

Table 6. F1 scores for the eight networks for each type of rice.

Classes	MLP W1A1	MLP W2A2	MLP W3A3	MLP W8A8	Lenet-5 W1A1	Lenet-5 W2A2	Lenet-5 W3A3	Lenet-5 W8A8
Arborio	0.16	0.84	0.95	0.93	0.88	0.97	0.98	0.98
Basmati	0.98	0.98	0.98	0.98	0.95	0.98	0.99	0.99
Ipsala	1	1	1	1	0.99	1	1	1
Jasmine	0.97	0.94	0.97	0.97	0.93	0.97	0.98	0.98
Karacadag	0.69	0.82	0.97	0.95	0.91	0.98	0.98	0.98

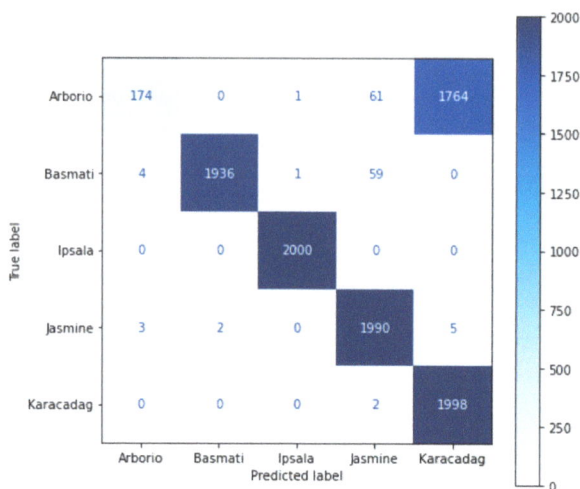

Figure 12. The confusion matrix of the MLP-W1A1 model.

4. Conclusions and Discussion

This study investigates the potential of a high-performance classification approach through quantized deep learning for different rice varieties. The proposed idea has the key benefit of providing efficient and intelligent utilization of capacity in terms of memory, power, and processing speed. The main theme of the present work is, therefore, to design models running on edge devices that require low resource utilization. The confusion matrices of the developed models were constructed in connection with class-based F1 scores and accuracy levels. Eight Quantized Neural Network (QNN) networks were created using the environments of multilayer perceptron (MLP) and LeNet-5 with respect to various quantization levels. The results verify a successful classification of the seven models, except the MLP model at 1 quantization precision. We compare the results of the proposed best model with different studies in the literature as presented in Table 7.

Table 7. Performance comparisons to existing studies in the literature.

References	Class	Classifier	Bit Size	ACC	GOPs	Memory
Koklu2021 [14]	5	CNN (VGG16)	Fp32	100%	30.9	537 Mb
Lin2018 [11]	3	DCNN	Fp32	95.5%	4.2	98 Mb
Prakash2022 [32]	5	CNN (VGG16)	Fp32	99.5%	30.9	537 Mb
Poudel2022 [33]	4	CNN-SVM	Fp32	91.0%	30.9	537 Mb
Lakshmi2022 [34]	5	CNN (Resnet-50)	Fp32	98.9%	8.3	102 Mb
This Study	5	QNN (Lenet-5)	W3A3	99.8%	1.3	23.1 Kb
This Study	5	QNN (Lenet-5)	W1A1	94.4%	1.3	7.7 Kb

It is observed that most studies in classifying rice were carried out by using the Convolutional Neural Network (CNN) models with the examples of VGG-16, ResNet-50, and LeNet-5. Looking at Table 7, the best classification accuracy is obtained by [14] on VGG-16 with a 100% accuracy level consuming 537 MB memory and 30.9 GFLOPs. In our model, the Lenet-5-W3A3 model achieved 99.87% accuracy with only 23.1 Kb of memory and 1.3 GOPs processing. This reveals that the proposed model performs the classification with 23 times less processing and much less memory usage without sacrificing too much accuracy. Another model proposed by [32] with an accuracy level of 99.5% is built on VGG-16 with 23 times more resource consumption than our study. To sum up Table 7, as an overall trend, all compared schemes exhibit a high accuracy level at an unacceptable amount of memory usage and GFLOPs transactions for resource-limited edge devices.

As a result, instead of an input image of 3 × 256 × 256 dimensions, the input image of 3 × 32 × 32 dimensions was quite sufficient for rice classification with this dataset. In addition, it is observed that Lenet-5, which is a simpler model compared to models such as VGG-16 and Resnet-50, successfully classifies this dataset. QNN models can be used by choosing the quantization level according to the source size and preferred accuracy level in the edge devices.

Author Contributions: Conceptualization, M.T. and A.I.; methodology, M.T.; software, M.T., A.I. and S.K.; validation, M.T., A.I., S.K., T.I., I.S. and I.B.; investigation, M.T., A.I., S.K., T.I., I.S. and I.B.; writing—original draft preparation, M.T., A.I., S.K., T.I., I.S. and I.B.; writing—review and editing, M.T., A.I., S.K., T.I., I.S. and I.B.; visualization, M.T., A.I., S.K., T.I., I.S. and I.B. All authors have read and agreed to the published version of the manuscript.

Funding: This research received no external funding.

Institutional Review Board Statement: Not applicable.

Informed Consent Statement: Not applicable.

Data Availability Statement: This dataset was collected from Kaggle; this can be found at: https://www.kaggle.com/datasets/muratkokludataset/rice-image-dataset (accessed on 5 April 2023).

Conflicts of Interest: The authors declare no conflict of interest.

References

1. FAO. Available online: https://www.fao.org/worldfoodsituation/csdb/en/ (accessed on 4 March 2023).
2. Fabiyi, S.D.; Vu, H.; Tachtatzis, C.; Murray, P.; Harle, D.; Dao, T.K.; Andonovic, I.; Ren, J.; Marshall, S. Varietal Classification of Rice Seeds Using RGB and Hyperspectral Images. *IEEE Access* **2020**, *8*, 22493–22505. [CrossRef]
3. Gulzar, Y.; Hamid, Y.; Soomro, A.B.; Alwan, A.A.; Journaux, L. A convolution neural network-based seed classification system. *Symmetry* **2020**, *12*, 2018. [CrossRef]
4. Singh, D.; Taspinar, Y.S.; Kursun, R.; Cinar, I.; Koklu, M.; Ozkan, I.A.; Lee, H.N. Classification and Analysis of Pistachio Species with Pre-Trained Deep Learning Models. *Electronics* **2022**, *11*, 981. [CrossRef]
5. Ruslan, R.; Khairunniza-Bejo, S.; Jahari, M.; Ibrahim, M.F. Weedy Rice Classification Using Image Processing and a Machine Learning Approach. *Agriculture* **2022**, *12*, 645. [CrossRef]
6. Shaikh, T.A.; Rasool, T.; Lone, F.R. Towards leveraging the role of machine learning and artificial intelligence in precision agriculture and smart farming. *Comput. Electron. Agric.* **2022**, *198*, 107119. [CrossRef]
7. Liakos, K.G.; Busato, P.; Moshou, D.; Pearson, S.; Bochtis, D. Machine Learning in Agriculture: A Reviews. *Sensors* **2018**, *18*, 2674. [CrossRef]
8. Kiratiratanapruk, K.; Temniranrat, P.; Sinthupinyo, W.; Prempree, P.; Chaitavon, K.; Porntheeraphat, S.; Prasertsak, A. Development of Paddy Rice Seed Classification Process using Machine Learning Techniques for Automatic Grading Machine. *J. Sens.* **2020**, *2020*, 7041310. [CrossRef]
9. Menghani, G. Efficient deep learning: A survey on making deep learning models smaller, faster, and better. *ACM Comput. Surv.* **2022**, *55*, 3578938. [CrossRef]
10. Nguyen, T.; Paik, I.; Watanobe, Y.; Thang, T.C. An Evaluation of Hardware-Efficient Quantum Neural Networks for Image Data Classification. *Electronics* **2022**, *11*, 437. [CrossRef]
11. Lin, P.; Li, X.L.; Chen, Y.M.; He, Y. A Deep Convolutional Neural Network Architecture for Boosting Image Discrimination Accuracy of Rice Species. *Food Bioprocess Technol.* **2018**, *11*, 765–773. [CrossRef]
12. Jeyaraj, P.R.; Asokan, S.P.; Nadar, E.R.S. Computer-Assisted Real-Time Rice Variety Learning Using Deep Learning Network. *Rice Sci.* **2022**, *29*, 489–498. [CrossRef]
13. Qian, Y.; Xu, Q.; Yang, Y.; Lu, H.; Li, H.; Feng, X.; Yin, W. Classification of rice seed variety using point cloud data combined with deep learning. *Int. J. Agric. Biol. Eng.* **2021**, *14*, 206–212. [CrossRef]
14. Koklu, M.; Cinar, I.; Taspinar, Y.S. Classification of rice varieties with deep learning methods. *Comput. Electron. Agric.* **2021**, *187*, 106285. [CrossRef]
15. Al-Andoli, M.N.; Tan, S.C.; .; Sim, K.S.; Lim, C.P.; Goh, P.Y. Parallel Deep Learning with a Hybrid BP-PSO Framework for Feature Extraction and Malware Classification. *Appl. Soft Comput.* **2022**, *12*, 109756. [CrossRef]
16. Kosunalp, S.; Mitchell, P.D.; Grace, D.; Clarke, T. Practical implementation issues of reinforcement learning based ALOHA for wireless sensor networks. In Proceedings of the The Tenth International Symposium on Wireless Communication Systems (ISWCS), Ilmenau, Germany, 27–30 August 2013.
17. Kosunalp, S.; Mitchell, P.D.; Grace, D.; Clarke, T. Practical Implementation and Stability Analysis of ALOHA-Q for Wireless Sensor Networks. *ETRI J.* **2016**, *38*, 911–921. [CrossRef]

18. Li, H.; Ota, K.; Dong, M. Learning IoT in Edge: Deep Learning for the Internet of Things with Edge Computing. *IEEE Netw.* **2018**, *32*, 96–101. [CrossRef]
19. Kosunalp, S.; Kaya, Y. IoT-TDMA: A performance evaluation of TDMA scheme for wireless sensor networks with Internet of Things. *Concurr. Comput. Pract. Exp.* **2022**, *34*, e7063. [CrossRef]
20. Batzolis, E.; Vrochidou, E.; Papakostas, G.A. Machine learning in embedded systems: Limitations, solutions and future challenges. In Proceedings of the IEEE 13th Annual Computing and Communication Workshop and Conference (CCWC), Las Vegas, NV, USA, 8–11 March 2023. [CrossRef]
21. Pham, P.; Chung, J. Improving Model Capacity of Quantized Networks with Conditional Computation. *Electronics* **2021**, *10*, 886. [CrossRef]
22. Pappalardo, A. Xilinx/Brevitas. Available online: https://zenodo.org/record/7875571#.ZGNzL3bP2Uk (accessed on 18 March 2023).
23. Cinar, I.; Koklu, M. Identification of Rice Varieties Using Machine Learning Algorithms. *J. Agric. Sci.* **2022**, *28*, 307–325. [CrossRef]
24. Narmadha1, R.; Sengottaiyan, N.; Kavitha, R. Deep Transfer Learning Based Rice Plant Disease Detection Model. *Intell. Autom. Soft Comput.* **2022**, *31*, 1257–1271. [CrossRef]
25. LeCun, Y.; Jackel, L.D.; Bottou, L.; Cortes, C.; Denker, J.S.; Drucker, H.; Guyon, I.; Muller, U.A.; Sackinger, E.; Simard, P.; et al. Learning algorithms for classification: A comparison on handwritten digit recognition. *Neural Netw. Stat. Mech. Perspect.* **1995**, *261*, 2.
26. Weng, O. Neural Network Quantization for Efficient Inference: A Survey. *arXiv* **2023**, arXiv:2112.06126.
27. Gholami, A.; Kim, S.; Dong, Z.; Yao, Z.; Mahoney, M.W.; Keutzer, K. A Survey of Quantization Methods for Efficient Neural Network Inference. In *Low-Power Computer Vision*; CRC: Boca Raton, FL, USA, 2022; pp. 291–326. [CrossRef]
28. Umuroglu, Y.; Fraser, N.J.; Gambardella, G.; Blott, M.; Leong, P.; Jahre, M.; Vissers, K. Finn: A framework for fast, scalable binarized neural network inference. In Proceedings of the 2017 ACM/SIGDA International Symposium on Field-Programmable Gate Arrays, Monterey, CA, USA, 22–24 February 2017; pp. 65–74.
29. Russakovsky, O.; Deng, J.; Su, H.; Krause, J.; Satheesh, S.; Ma, S.; Huang, Z.; Karpathy, A.; Khosla, A.; Bernstein, M.; et al. ImageNet Large Scale Visual Recognition Challenge. *Int. J. Comput. Vis.* **2015**, *115*, 211–252. [CrossRef]
30. Jain, A.; Bhattacharya, S.; Masuda, M.; Sharma, V.; Wang, Y. Efficient Execution of Quantized Deep Learning Models: A Compiler Approach. *arXiv* **2020**, arXiv:2006.10226.
31. Korkmaz, A.; Buyukgoze, S. Detection of Fake Websites by Classification Algorithms. *Eur. J. Sci. Technol.* **2019**, *16*, 826–833. [CrossRef]
32. Prakash, N.; Rajakumar, R.; Madhuri, N.L.; Jyothi, M.; Bai, A.P.; Manjunath, M.; Gowthami, K. Image Classification for Rice varieties using Deep Learning Models. *YMER Digit.* **2022**, *21*, 261–275. [CrossRef] [PubMed]
33. Poudel, A.; Devkota, B. Varietal Identification of Rice Seed Using Deep Convolutional Neural Network. *J. Eng. Sci.* **2022**, *267*, 378–384.
34. Lakshmi, V.; Seetharaman, K. Rice Classification and Quality Analysis using Deep Neural Network. In Proceedings of the 2022 International Conference on Intelligent Innovations in Engineering and Technology (ICIIET), Coimbatore, India, 22–24 September 2022; pp. 307–314.

Disclaimer/Publisher's Note: The statements, opinions and data contained in all publications are solely those of the individual author(s) and contributor(s) and not of MDPI and/or the editor(s). MDPI and/or the editor(s) disclaim responsibility for any injury to people or property resulting from any ideas, methods, instructions or products referred to in the content.

Article

ML-Based Traffic Classification in an SDN-Enabled Cloud Environment

Omayma Belkadi [1,*], Alexandru Vulpe [2,3], Yassin Laaziz [1] and Simona Halunga [2]

1. National School of Applied Sciences Tangier, LabTIC, Abdelmalek Essaadi University, Tetouan 93002, Morocco
2. Telecommunications Department, University Politehnica of Bucharest, 060042 Bucharest, Romania
3. R&D Department, Beam Innovation SRL, 041386 Bucharest, Romania
* Correspondence: belkadi.omayma@gmail.com

Abstract: Traffic classification plays an essential role in network security and management; therefore, studying traffic in emerging technologies can be useful in many ways. It can lead to troubleshooting problems, prioritizing specific traffic to provide better performance, detecting anomalies at an early stage, etc. In this work, we aim to propose an efficient machine learning method for traffic classification in an SDN/cloud platform. Traffic classification in SDN allows the management of flows by taking the application's requirements into consideration, which leads to improved QoS. After our tests were implemented in a cloud/SDN environment, the method that we proposed showed that the supervised algorithms used (Naive Bayes, SVM (SMO), Random Forest, C4.5 (J48)) gave promising results of up to 97% when using the studied features and over 95% when using the generated features.

Keywords: traffic classification; machine learning; SDN; cloud computing

Citation: Belkadi, O.; Vulpe, A.; Laaziz, Y.; Halunga, S. ML-Based Traffic Classification in an SDN-Enabled Cloud Environment. *Electronics* **2023**, *12*, 269. https://doi.org/10.3390/electronics12020269

Academic Editors: Teodor Iliev, Lorant Andras Szolga, Gani Balbayev and Francisco Falcone

Received: 11 November 2022
Revised: 15 December 2022
Accepted: 28 December 2022
Published: 5 January 2023

Copyright: © 2023 by the authors. Licensee MDPI, Basel, Switzerland. This article is an open access article distributed under the terms and conditions of the Creative Commons Attribution (CC BY) license (https://creativecommons.org/licenses/by/4.0/).

1. Introduction

Nowadays, we can see a drastic increase in access to internet applications as people rely more and more on the internet. Consequently, there is a significant demand for good management and classification of network traffic [1]. Our research falls into the area of network traffic classification, which has been extremely active for more than a decade. The applications of traffic analysis range from security and anomaly detection to network management and traffic engineering [2]. The uses of the internet have undergone several changes in recent years; starting as a network for the simple transfer of binary and textual data without constraints of time or speed, the internet experienced its first revolution with the appearance and democratization of the web and a demand for more and more important bandwidth. Nowadays, with the appearance of streaming applications, such as real-time video transmission, IP telephony, and internet television, its use obliges even stronger constraints. The internet must, therefore, be able to provide users and their applications with the quality of service (QoS) they need. It must evolve from the offering of a single "best effort" service to a multi-service offering. Over the last few years, QoS has emerged as a major issue in the internet [3].

Furthermore, the increase in the complexity of the internet and its numerous interconnections, the heterogeneity of its resources in terms of technologies, but also in terms of dimensions, and the characteristics of its traffic, as well as new applications with diverse and evolving needs, add many characteristics to internet traffic that are far from the traditional ones. In particular, it has been shown that applications used to exchange large data, for example, change the distribution of file sizes [3], which has the particularity of creating long dependency properties and self-similarity in traffic. The latter translate into high traffic variability, which affects the stability and quality of services offered, decreases overall network performance, and, thus, results in QoS/performance degradation. The improvement of internet architectures and protocols (e.g., software-defined networks—SDN, an emerging technology for solving network complexity, by basically separating the data and control planes to allow better management and innovation) is closely linked to the knowledge and understanding of the characteristics of internet traffic because they indicate the types of mechanisms to be deployed to adequately address user needs and network constraints. Consequently, the development of tools based on intelligent metrology, technologies allowing the collection of information in internet traffic, and methods allowing the analysis and classification of its characteristics by using, for example, machine learning are very important subjects for the fields of network engineering and research. Accurate traffic classification, especially for real-time traffic, is very important for not only network management, but also for intrusion detection and security monitoring in order to discover abnormal behaviors and prevent data breaches.

There are multiple approaches to traffic classification [1], as shown in Figure 1, such as the port-based method, which utilizes the port numbers that an application uses to match traffic to its corresponding source. Even though it was previously the quickest and most effective method, the latter is used less with all of the current changes in the field. In addition to that, there is the payload-based technique. It uses measurable packets' payload properties, but it faces many restrictions, such as encryption and confidentiality issues. The last method of classification in the schema, which is based on flow statistics combined with machine learning, is the most promising technique. This is the approach used in our work.

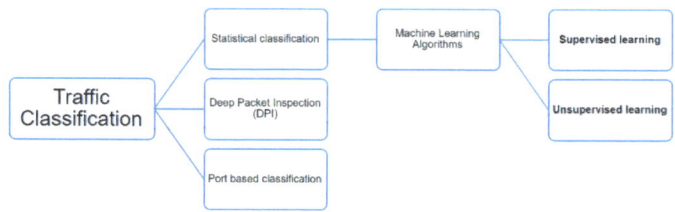

Figure 1. Traffic classification methods.

Machine learning (ML) is a field of artificial intelligence and a scientific discipline that covers several areas of study: mathematics, statistics, and algorithms [1]. The diversity of these anchors contributes most certainly to the success of this discipline, whose work has been characterized by great creativity in the design of algorithmic methods, the search for a solid mathematical foundation to support the methods developed, and attention to natural mechanisms of learning and generalization.

A great deal of attention has been given to the natural fields of applications, as evidenced by the exponential growth of learning in areas such as data mining and pattern recognition. Their aim is to improve the performance of a machine when performing a task by using a set of exercises. The multiple ways of expressing this triplet (performance, task, exercise) make it possible to develop many theoretical frameworks for a field, including that of statistical learning, to develop different models by using generative or discriminant examples, and to apply them to various tasks, such as chess, driving, and classification.

Machine learning algorithms can be categorized according to the type of learning that they employ:

- **Supervised learning** includes the tasks of classification, regression, and ranking. It usually involves dealing with a prediction problem. Supervised classification consists of analyzing new data and assigning them to a predefined class according to their characteristics or attributes. The algorithms are based on decision trees, neural networks, the Bayes rule, and k-nearest neighbors. Moreover, an expert is employed to correctly label examples. The learning must then find or approximate the function that allows the assignment of the correct label to these examples. Linear discriminant analysis and the support vector machine (SVM) are typical examples.

- **Unsupervised learning** (clustering, segmentation) differs in that there are no predefined classes; the objective is to group records that appear to be similar into the same class. The problem is that of finding homogeneous groups in a population. Techniques for aggregation around mobile centers or hierarchical bottom-up classification are often used. The essential difficulty in this type of construction is validation. No experts are required. The algorithm must discover the structure of data by itself. Clustering and Gaussian mixtures are examples of unsupervised learning algorithms.

The main contribution of this paper is the study of the classification of cloud network traffic managed by an SDN by using machine learning techniques. There is a rising number of papers working separately on traffic classification in SDNs or cloud traffic, but as our proposed integration of the two environments (an SDN controller and cloud platform) has not been discussed before, our goal in this work is to tackle this traffic and study it for classification within our deployed testbed's real traffic. The generated traffic flows belonged to a Linux virtual machine that was installed and run from a cloud platform whose network was managed by the OpenDaylight SDN controller. We conducted controlled experiments to build models for four different supervised ML algorithms (Naive Bayes, SVM, Random Forest, and C4.5) with the aim of having the most accurate model for classifying an application's traffic. These experiments consisted of the separate use of two applications (YouTube and Facebook), where the user interacted in each case to generate traffic flows, enabling the knowledge of what application was actually in use. The data collected in each experiment were considered as training data, and test data were randomly collected to test the trained modules. Moreover, we showed how the selection of features could affect the final results by using two different sets in this paper.

This paper is organized as follows. Section 2 describes related work on traffic classification in SDN and cloud environments and the latest trends and challenges, while Section 3 details the process of collecting traffic data and selecting traffic features for the experiments. Section 4 describes the methodology of the training and classification process, as well as the experimental design, while in Section 5, the results are analyzed and discussed in more detail. Finally, Section 6 concludes the paper.

2. Related Work

The literature on traffic classification alone is extremely rich; however, the methods proposed in the papers that we reviewed vary from one to another, while the common fact is that they all combine more than one algorithm to achieve better classification and accuracy. We observed that the number of articles related to this theme was limited, and they were already summarized in a previous survey [1] (August 2018). Then, in a more recent study, the authors of [4] (September 2022) updated the survey.

For instance, in [5], the authors used ML algorithms to classify network traffic by application, similarly to the approach in this study, but in a traditional network. By using data labeled by application, they trained some ML models that were recognized by the classifier, including Skype, Post Office Protocol 3 (POP3), the Domain Name System (DNS), Torrent, and Telnet. They tested the following six different classification models and compared their accuracy: Support Vector Machine (SVM), Random Forest, C4.5, AdaBoost, MLP, and Radial Biased Function (RBF).

At this point, we can also say that few papers have discussed traffic classification in SDNs. Papers mentioning the SDN controller OpenDaylight were mainly focused on security and anomaly detection, rather than classifying traffic.

However, in [6], the authors used both statistical and deep packet inspection (DPI)-based approaches in their classification model. They assumed that using DPI techniques and a machine learning classifier would help achieve a higher accuracy. However, that did not change the fact that DPI techniques require more calculation time and face encryption issues. In this paper, they did not mention what SDN controller they used, and they only mentioned that their classifier was implemented in the control plane.

On the other hand, the authors of [7] claimed to propose a new method for classifying traffic in an SDN by using four different neural network algorithms: feedforward, multi-layer perceptron (MLP), nonlinear autoregressive exogenous multilayer perceptron (NARX (Levenberg–Marquardt)), and Naive Bayes. They also mentioned using the OpenDaylight controller with real-time campus traffic to test their model (but this was not a cloud-based environment), and they used 13 features in their training set. However, the last feature that they used (AppPRO: protocol of the application layer) was said to be added manually, and the utility and values of this were not clear, nor if it affected the final results.

In [2], the authors tackled traffic classification in an SDN by using a network application to collect traffic flows—exclusively transmission control protocol (TCP) traffic. Several packets of information were gathered by using different methods, such as Packet IN messages, to extract source/destination IP addresses and port addresses. Then, they used the controller to collect the first five packet sizes and timestamps as the next five packets after the initial handshake between the server and client flow went through the controller. The flow duration was calculated by subtracting the timestamp of the initial packet and the timestamp of the message received by the controller regarding the removal of the flow entry. So, overall, they used 12 features, which were slightly similar to the features studied in this work; then, they compared the accuracies of three ML algorithms' models, which were lower than those in our tests: Random Forest (highest 96%), Stochastic Gradient Boost (highest 93%), and Extreme Gradient Boost (highest 95%).

In [8], Eom, Won-Ju et al. proposed a machine learning network classification system that used a software-defined (SDN only) technique that was implemented at the network controller level (RYU). The system was used for traffic classification, and the overall system performance significantly improved in terms of some standard QoS parameters, such as accuracy, precision, and training and classification time, in comparison with other classifiers under the same testing conditions. However, the highest accuracy reached was 96.15% when using the LightGBM algorithm model.

In [9], based on the POX controller and mininet network emulator, the authors studied traffic classification in an SDN by using three supervised learning algorithms: SVM, Naive Bayes, and the nearest centroid. They classified various applications based on the number of collected flow instances for the first five minutes and for ten minutes. The highest obtained accuracy was 96.79% with Naive Bayes, but they basically used the ICMP ping traffic generated with mininet.

Furthermore, multiple recent papers studied traffic in complex environments. In [10], the authors performed a systematic review of the use of artificial intelligence (AI) in SDNs, outlining the latest achievements in the field. The authors of [11] presented the results obtained by applying a deep learning recurrent algorithm for classifying traffic over cloud-implemented Internet of Things (IoT) systems, and they came to the conclusion that the results outperformed those of other similar implementations with respect to latency, throughput, and transmission rate. In [12], the authors defined, implemented, and evaluated the performance of a deep learning SDN used for the detection of several security threats in an IoT environment, and they validated the algorithm by using the CICIDS2018 dataset, showing that the proposed algorithm achieved better results with respect to accuracy, precision, speed, and other evaluation metrics, while the authors of [13] highlighted the effectiveness of applying artificial intelligence models as an answer to the security issues raised by the development of IoT, namely, the neural network. Indeed, a neural network is applicable in the analysis of intrusions. In addition, in this work, there was a further use of genetic algorithms, which allowed the improvement of the performance of the neural network through the optimization of its parameters, which was achieved through a trial-and-error approach. In [14], the authors presented a comprehensive overview of a large number of classification metrics and compared them by means of standard QoS metrics, such as speed, accuracy, recall, etc.

In [15], the authors proposed traffic classification by using supervised machine learning techniques in an SDN-enhanced FiWi–IoT environment. The tests showed the Random

Forest algorithm to be the best classifier (with an accuracy of 99%), followed by the KNN Tree, Neural Network, Naïve Bayes, Logistic Regression, and SVM, as in our findings. Different data were captured from IoT and non-IoT devices as PCAP files, similarly to in our procedure, but the authors did not list the exact list of features used. The authors of [16] presented a framework based on SDN by using a machine learning classification model. This was intended to detect and mitigate DDoS attacks for IoT devices. A new approach was proposed in [17] to detect DDoS attacks in SDNs by employing six classifiers (SVMs, Random Forests, and Gradient-Boosted Machines) by using an optimal set of weights. They developed a testbed with mininet and a POX controller loaded with different datasets, and the accuracy of their tests went up to 99%. On the other hand, in [18], supervised machine learning models were also used to detect DDoS attacks. This time, the authors only compared two algorithms—SVM (showed 80% accuracy) and Naive Bayes (76%)—and they used mininet and an RYU controller for their testbed.

Furthermore, the authors of [19] proposed an integrated approach to benchmarking and profiling vertical industrial applications with regard to resource utilization, capacity limits, and reliability characteristics. This was based on data analysis to extract information, as well as the benchmarking of experiments, which would be used later in the development of artificial intelligence algorithms. This was all done with the purpose of optimizing the use of the infrastructure, providing a guarantee of the quality of the service (QoS) presented, and, obviously, supporting Industry 4.0 in its evolution. The authors of [20] suggested a mechanism for addressing the problem of optimal resource allocation by profiling services and predicting the resources that guaranteed the desired service quality. To do so, the approach adopted was based on the collection of data from the hardware and the virtual and service infrastructure, the study of well-known implementations based on containers according to the microservice paradigm, and the use of machine learning algorithms for the prediction of resources required for service requests. Moreover, the authors of [21] presented a subsystem of the METRO-HAUL tool that enabled network resource optimization according to two different perspectives: offline network design and online resource allocation. Indeed, the offline network design algorithms aimed at planning the resource allocation, while the online resource allocation took the different requirements of end-user services in terms of bandwidth, delay, QoS, and the set of VNFs into account.

The motivation behind our study was the development of an application for traffic classification within our implemented SDN/cloud environment, which is where the novelty resides. So, the first step presented in this paper consisted of demonstrating how we could use the traditional way of classifying traffic by using supervised ML algorithms. Thus, unlike in the studied papers, we based our study, on the one hand, on controlled experiments in order to concretely label training traffic data and have robust models with our set of algorithms. On the other hand, our study was completed by comparing two sets of different features in a search for better results, as the choice of features is a very important parameter in classification.

3. Traffic Data

3.1. Dataset

During data collection, we used our integrated platforms of OpenDaylight and OpenNebula [22]; then, we created an Ubuntu 16.06 desktop virtual machine within OpenNebula, as shown in Figure 2.

Unlike in previous work, we rather manually collected our dataset by running one type of experiment for five minutes or more in parallel with the separate collection of the full transmitted and received packets, traces, and logs for each experiment over the network by using the *tcpdump* tool [23] (version 4.3.0) at the level of the command line, and we used a script that simultaneously executed the *lsof* command every second. The *lsof* command helped to list open connections by providing the program names and their source/destination addresses and ports.

The goal of running controlled experiments was to collect network traces in which we knew exactly what application was used. With that, we would be able to accurately label our training dataset, which explains our small training set for this demonstration. However, we intended to use a slightly larger dataset to test the classifiers. Moreover, as we studied traffic in our implemented environment, which was recently discussed in our previous publication [22], this made our studied classification a more specific use case, as we could not find large public databases for this particular network traffic.

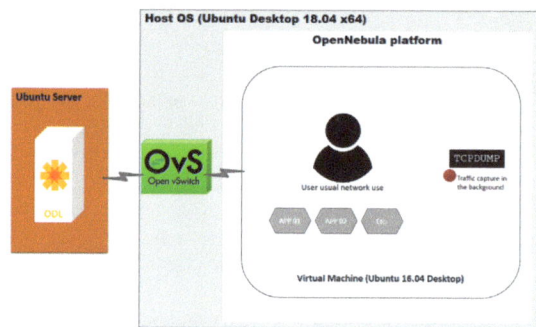

Figure 2. Data collection process.

Here, we describe both the setup and data collection for the controlled experiments, giving details about the different types that we included to build our ground truth in addition to each application run. We conducted experiments with two popular applications (Facebook and YouTube). At the start of each experiment, we first opened the application, logged into it, and then simulated a set of interactions.

Here are details for the use of each application:

- Facebook: We opened the Facebook web page on a Chrome browser, and we simulated typical behaviors that a user would have by posting something, liking a publication, having a chat conversation (sending and receiving messages), seeing the last news feed, and then visiting a random page.
- YouTube: We opened this on a Chrome browser, and then we chose a video of five minutes to watch.

To summarize the data collected in our experiments, in Table 1, we have provided the metrics of one run of each experiment and its duration, packet count, and total size in bytes.

Table 1. Data set.

Experiment	Duration	# of Packets	Bytes
Facebook	5 m 12 s	21,354	16.92 MB
YouTube	5 m 14 s	61,157	60.30 MB
Test data	14 m 54 s	179,190	153.61 MB

The first two experiments consisted of collecting the traffic data of each application separately and making sure that no other applications were in use on the network other than the browser. In this way, we were able to label the flows. Then, a third experiment was run by using both applications, and the obtained dataset was used for classification.

We used the output of the *lsof* command to label the experiment packets with their corresponding applications. However, to extract the flow information, we worked directly on the PCAP files (Figure 3) by using tcptrace [24]; then, we labeled each flow with its application by using the *lsof* output. At the end of the experiment, we obtained two files: a PCAP one containing the packet information and another containing the output of the *lsof* command. From the PCAP file, we extracted the packets' time, source address, source port, destination address, destination port, protocol, and length in bytes.

```
14:53:03.687920000  188.125.82.39     443    132.227.127.148  49214  6  52
14:53:03.690622000  188.125.82.39     443    132.227.127.148  49209  6  52
14:53:03.694117000  188.125.66.236    443    132.227.127.148  49207  6  52
14:53:03.863089000  132.227.127.148   49204  69.147.76.52     443    6  40
14:53:03.954086000  69.147.76.52      443    132.227.127.148  49204  6  52
14:53:03.964260000  132.227.127.148   49237  23.55.155.27     80     6  40
14:53:03.964276000  132.227.127.148   49231  173.194.40.110   80     6  40
14:53:03.966150000  173.194.40.110    80     132.227.127.148  49231  6  52
14:53:03.966154000  23.55.155.27      80     132.227.127.148  49237  6  52
14:53:04.065402000  132.227.127.148   49191  66.196.66.213    443    6  40
```

Figure 3. Example of a PCAP file output.

From the *lsof* output (as shown in Figure 4), we extracted the application name, its source address, source port, destination address, destination port, and protocol.

```
Google  640 omega   60u  IPv4  0x448722b59263ac7b   0t0  TCP  132.227.127.148:49306->173.194.40.120:443  (ESTABLISHED)
Google  640 omega   62u  IPv4  0x448722b59305dc7b   0t0  TCP  132.227.127.148:49327->50.16.202.95:443    (CLOSE_WAIT)
Google  640 omega   66u  IPv4  0x448722b592639c7b   0t0  TCP  132.227.127.148:49307->173.194.40.115:443  (ESTABLISHED)
Google  640 omega   67u  IPv4  0x448722b592611c7b   0t0  TCP  132.227.127.148:49330->2.22.48.178:443     (ESTABLISHED)
Google  640 omega   68u  IPv4  0x448722b5925e9c7b   0t0  TCP  132.227.127.148:49331->31.13.81.7:443      (ESTABLISHED)
Google  640 omega   69u  IPv4  0x448722b5925be463   0t0  TCP  132.227.127.148:49332->193.51.224.8:443    (ESTABLISHED)
Google  640 omega   70u  IPv4  0x448722b5925ea463   0t0  TCP  132.227.127.148:49333->88.221.14.105:443   (ESTABLISHED)
Google  640 omega   76u  IPv4  0x448722b5811f6c7b   0t0  TCP  132.227.127.148:49313->173.194.40.102:443  (ESTABLISHED)
Google  640 omega   131u IPv4  0x448722b5930b0c7b   0t0  TCP  132.227.127.148:49329->173.194.40.127:443  (ESTABLISHED)
```

Figure 4. Example of an output of the *lsof* command.

By using a script, we parsed the packet information file with the *lsof* output to get each application packet in a separate file; then, we extracted and calculated the selected features, which are discussed in the next section.

3.2. Features Selection

After building the ground truth of our experiments, we needed to find features that we could extract from packet headers and that would allow us to distinguish the traffic of user activity from the rest.

Even though we had the full packets of our experiments, we worked only on packet headers because, in the online case, we would not have access to the full packets, as it is known that deep packet inspection that includes packet payloads is an issue for many researchers [25]. One cannot access this due to encryption or privacy, and it is even illegal in some cases. For now, this work studied the offline case with packet headers, and in this section, we classify features from previous work; then, we present the ones that are helpful for us.

Through the selection of features from our collected data, we had many choices to make to find the most exhaustive ones. Choosing which one to try from the hundreds was very important to us. We could not try all of the possible features, since it would be inefficient to try a feature that we knew would not be useful for detecting a changing behavior, so our choice was logically based on the question of if these features would be related to a user changing their behavior or not.

We categorized many features that were discussed in other papers—for example, in [26], there were more than 250 features, which we summarized by avoiding those based on packet payloads, and we included them in our list. In [3,27–29], the authors mentioned features that they worked with, which were not all useful for us, so we took the flow- and packet-based ones. We show the wide variety of those for characterizing flows, including the simple statistics of packets, in eight categories in Table 2.

From all of the features above, the packet and flow-level ones were the most important for us, since we wanted to identify flows generated by interactions with the desired application. There were features from the list that would not help distinguish if a flow was generated by an interaction or not. For example, ports are helpful for application identification [30], but in our case, we could not use them because, in the browser in which we ran our applications, the same port numbers were used, and there would not be a difference in which one is used. The TCP window level and round-trip time (RTT) should not change if users are interacting with the same browser. These features are more about computer performance. For the rest of the categories, we took some features from each. For example, in timing, all of the features sound helpful, but the packet and flow inter-arrival times, packets, bytes, and DNS requests per second, in addition to the duration, are the most exhaustive. In the packet count, the number of flow packets was the only feature that sounds helpful; therefore, we included it in our choice. Another exhaustive feature that we took was the total size of a flow's packets in the packet size category, and both features were added in the application.

Table 2. Feature categories.

Category	Features
Ports	Client port, server port
Timing	statistics of packet inter-arrival time
	statistics of flow inter-arrival time
	FFT of packet inter-arrival time (frequency: 1 to 10)
	total transmit time (difference between the times of the first and last packet)
	time since last connection
	packets per second
	bytes per second
	DNS requests per second
	TTL
	flow duration
	idle time
Packet count	total number of packets
	number of packets per flow
	number of out-of-order packets
	truncated packets
	packets with PUSH bits
	packets with SYN bits
	packets with FIN bits
	total number of ACK packets seen
	pure ACK packets
	number of packets carrying SACK blocks
	number of packets carrying DSACK blocks
	number of duplicate ACK packets received
	number of all window probe packets seen
Packet size	number of unique bytes sent
	truncated bytes
	sum of a flow's packet size
	effective bandwidth
	throughput
	total bytes of data sent
	size of packets with URG bit turned on
TCP	statistics of retransmission
	segment statistics
	request statistics
	bulk mode
	statistics of control bytes in the packet
Window level	statistics of window advertisements seen
	number of times a zero-receive window was advertised
	number of bytes sent in the initial window
	number of segments sent in the initial window
RTT	total number of RTTs
	RTT sample statistics
	Full-size RTT sample
	RTT value calculated from the TCP three-way handshake
Application	number of new flows per second
	number of active flows per second

Consuming a connection will definitely have an effect on packets and flows, which means that any interaction with the application will be logically related to a packet or flow changing; for example, there will be more packets received and transmitted while checking the Facebook news feed or during a video call, and since a flow is, by definition, a sequence of packets, this level will be affected too. This is why we divided the nine features that we previously selected into these two levels. Table 3 shows these features and their descriptions.

Table 3. Studied features.

Feature	Description
Flow level	
Active flows per second	The number of active flows appearing in one second
New flows per second	The number of new flows appearing in one second
Flow size	The size of a flow in bytes
Flow duration	The time between the first and last packets seen in a flow in seconds
Flow inter-arrival time	Difference between the arrival times of two successive flows
Packet level	
Packet inter-arrival time	Difference between the arrival times of two successive packets
Packets per second	Number of packets appearing in one second
Bytes per second	Sum of bytes in one second
Number of packets	The count of packets in one flow

4. Methodology

Classification is the most studied challenge in the field of ML. Its concept is simple; it gives the right label or class to an item of data according to its characteristics, and many tasks can be reduced. To define a classification problem, one starts by representing the data in the vector space of their characteristics; then, one carries out calculations on this representation of data and assigns a score that can be translated to a certain class, followed by identifying the number of existing classes.

This work presents a set of machine learning algorithms used with a labeled dataset that we trained in order to identify and classify the flows of the studied applications on an SDN/cloud platform. This research aims to give an overview of traffic classification in such an environment. As shown in Figure 5, the generation of the classification training model was performed by using the trained data. In the classification phase, a sample of traffic was used with the chosen features to classify the entire stream.

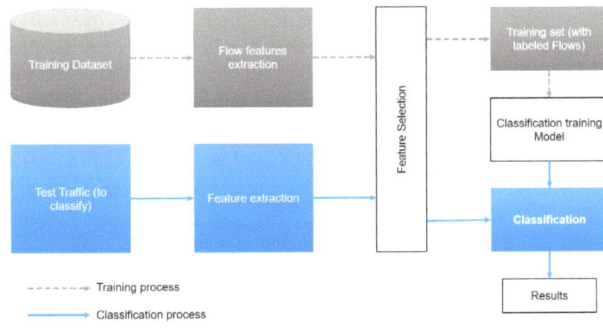

Figure 5. Training and classification process.

After the data collection and feature calculation, we generated a file that had a csv extension at the end. This type of file is usually accepted by Weka, but we decided to convert it into the ARFF format, since this is the default input in Weka. In addition, the size of the file decreased considerably compared to that of the file that we obtained with a csv extension. The structure of a file in ARFF format is very simple. ARFF files are divided into three parts: @relation, @attribute, and @data.

- @relation <name>: Every ARFF file must start with this declaration on its first line, ideally with the name of the file (one cannot leave blank lines at the beginning). <name> will be a string, and if it contains spaces, it should be enclosed in quotes.
- @attribute <name> <data_type>: This section includes a line for each attribute existing in the dataset to indicate its name and the type. With <name>, the name of the attribute will be indicated, and it must begin with a letter; if it contains spaces, it must be enclosed in quotation marks. For <type_of_data>, the type of data for this attribute can be:
    - numeric, meaning that the attribute is a number.
    - an integer, indicating that this attribute contains whole numbers.
    - a string, indicating that this attribute represents text strings.
    - a date [<date-format>]; in <date-format>, we indicate the date format, which is of the type "yyyy-MM-dd'T'HH:mm:ss".
    - <nominalspecification>. These are data types defined by the user and can take the indicated values. Each of the values must be separated by commas.
- @data: This section includes the data themselves. Each element is separated by commas, and all lines must have the same number of elements, which is a number that matches the number of declarations in @attribute, which was added in the previous section. If no data are available, a question mark (?) is written in their place, since this character represents the absence of a value in Weka. The decimal separator must be a period, and strings must be enclosed in single quotes.

There is a large set of classifying algorithms in Weka, but we limited the algorithms that we used to the most widely used algorithms for traffic classification in most of the related work listed in Section 2. Thus, we only made use of the following ones:

- **Naive Bayes**—Naive Bayes is a supervised classification and prediction technique that builds probabilistic models; it is based on Bayes' theorem and on data independence. It is a supervised technique, since it requires previously classified examples for its operation. In general terms, Bayes' theorem expresses the probability that an event occurs when it is known that another event also occurs. Bayesian statistics are used to calculate estimates based on prior subjective knowledge.
The implementations of this theorem are adapted with use and allow the combination of data from various sources and their expression in the degree of probability.
- **SVM**—Support Vector Machines and wide-margin separators are a set of supervised learning techniques designed to solve problems of discrimination and regression. SVMs were developed in the 1990s based on the theoretical considerations of Vladimir Vapnik [31] concerning the development of a statistical theory of learning: the Vapnik–Chervonenkis theory. SVMs were quickly adopted for their ability to work with large data sizes and low numbers of hyperparameters due to the fact that they are well founded in theory and their good results in practice.
Wide-margin separators are classifiers that rely on two key ideas to deal with nonlinear discrimination problems and to reformulate classification problems as quadratic optimization problems. The first key idea is the notion of the maximum margin. The margin is the distance between a separation boundary and the nearest samples. The latter are called support vectors.
In order to be able to deal with cases in which the data are not linearly separable, the second key idea of SVMs is to transform the representation space of the input data

into a larger (possibly infinite) dimensional space in which a linear separator is likely to exist.
- **Random Forest**—This algorithm is a combination of predictor trees in such a way that each tree depends on the values of a random vector that is tested independently and with the same distribution for each of these.
Random Forest makes use of an aggregation technique developed by Leo Breiman that improves the classification precision by incorporating randomness into the construction of each individual classifier. This randomization is introduced both in the construction of the tree and in the training samples. This classifier, which is simple to train and adjust, is often used.
- **J48 tree (C4.5)**—This is one of the most widely used ML algorithms. Its operation is based on generating a decision tree from the data through partitions that are made recursively according to the depth-first strategy. Before each data partition, the algorithm considers all of the possible tests that can divide the dataset and selects the test that produces the highest information gain.
For each discrete attribute, a test with "n" results was considered, where "n" was the number of possible values that the attribute could take. For each continuous attribute, a binary test was performed on each of the values that the attribute took from the data.

Furthermore, to take a deep dive into our results, we ran the same tests for a second iteration by changing the features that we selected. This time, we used the Netmate [32] tool, which generated a set of default features provided by the tool [33]; then, we used this set of features as the flow attributes on which to base the classification with the same four algorithms. Figure 6 illustrates the steps of our methodology.

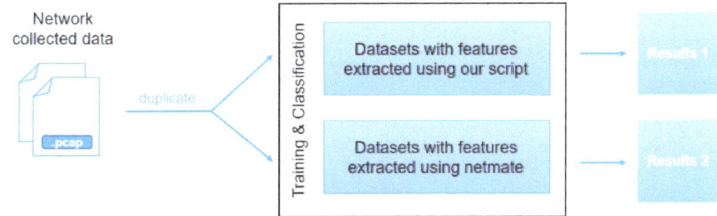

Figure 6. Second iteration of the classification tests.

The captured traffic data remained the same; then, they were duplicated to run the same experiment while following the same training and classification processes as those explained in the beginning of this section, but with different sets of features. The first set contained the features that we selected from the studies of the literature, for which we developed a script to calculate each metric of the nine features. The second set was generated by Netmate with a total of 44 features. The results of our approach will be presented and discussed in the next section.

5. Results and Discussion

This section describes the results of the experiments that were carried out to show which model was the best for classifying our traffic data. As mentioned in the previous sections, the results presented for our experiments were based on a training set of evaluations of labeled data that were used to build the classification model for each algorithm used; then, they were loaded into the Weka classification as a training set. It should be noted that the percentage of success of each algorithm varied depending on the type of evaluation that was performed. Typically, when we used a training file as an evaluation method, we obtained a higher precision in the percentage of hits than when we used cross-validation, because through cross-validation, a part of the dataset was used to train and another was used for testing, so we could obtain a lower percentage of correctly classified data.

For the following results, we used the default settings of Weka for each algorithm both to build the trained model and for the classification tests with the different feature cases. Table 4 lists the two sets of features used.

Table 4. Feature sets.

Features	Definition	Count
Studied Features	Selected as in Section 3.2	9
Netmate Features	Generated by the Netmate tool [33]	44

All classifiers were tested with the trained data. Figure 7 shows the results for the accuracy of the different algorithms that were tested on the first set of features under study based on Equation (1):

$$Accuracy = \frac{TP + TN}{TP + TN + FP + FN} \qquad (1)$$

where:

- TP: true positive—reflects the average number of samples that the model correctly classified from the positive class.
- TN: true negative—reflects the average number of samples that the model correctly classified from the negative class.
- FP: false positive—reflects the average number of samples that the model incorrectly classified from the positive class when, in fact, it was from the negative class.
- FN: false negative—reflects the average number of samples that the model incorrectly classified from the negative class when, in fact, it was from positive class.

After running these tests for each of the selected algorithms, we believe that the best model was the one obtained with the Random Forest as the classifier, since it gave a very good percentage of accuracy (∼97%) compared to those of the other algorithms, followed by Naive Bayes and C4.5 (∼82%), and then the SVM.

There were two algorithms in Weka that we made use of: SMO (79.49%) and LibSVM (76.92%); the first one was developed within the tool and was automatically available in the UI; its accuracy results were around 79%. It used J. Platt's sequential minimal optimization algorithm [34] with the RBF kernel by default. LibSVM was developed separately from the platform by Chih-Chung Chang and Chih-Jen Lin [35], and it is simply integrated with a .jar call. It is a wrapper class for the libsvm library [36] within the tool. This showed a slightly lower accuracy (of ∼77%) compared to that of SMO.

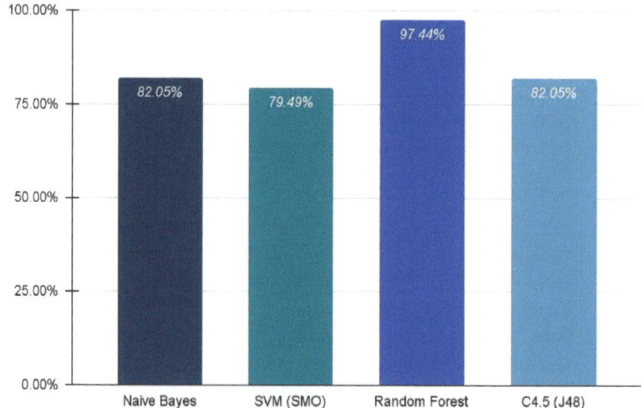

Figure 7. Comparison of the classification algorithms with the studied features and the accuracy results.

SVM algorithms' results can vary and can be affected by the implementation and settings of the kernel configuration used, the dataset size, and the features used. Even though the results were expected to be similar when using the SVM method with the same dataset and features in the first iteration, the observed difference was mainly explained by the default settings of the two algorithms within the tool. Still, they seemed to have the lowest accuracies in our tests with the set of studied features compared to the other classifiers.

Otherwise, in Figure 8, we show the accuracy of the same four algorithms on the second set of features in our experiments. As we can see, Random Forest still showed the best classification results for our data.

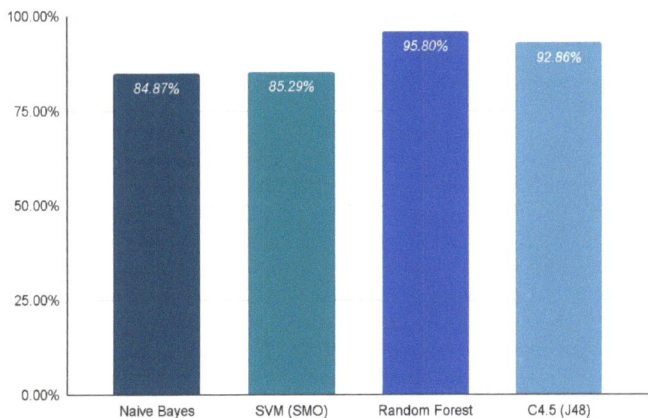

Figure 8. Comparison of the classification algorithms with the Netmate features and accuracy results.

However, it slightly decreased compared to the first results, so we can say that it showed better classification with our selected features. However, for the remaining three algorithms, it was obvious that they performed a better classification with the Netmate features, as they showed an increased accuracy. In particular, C4.5 jumped to 92.86% (more than a 10% difference) and the SVM jumped to 85.29% (a difference of 6%).

In terms of the average recall and precision of the classification algorithms, Figures 9 and 10 confirm the Random Forest's high rates for correctly classifying the applications' different flows, with the highest precision and recall compared to those of the other algorithms with both the studied and Netmate features.

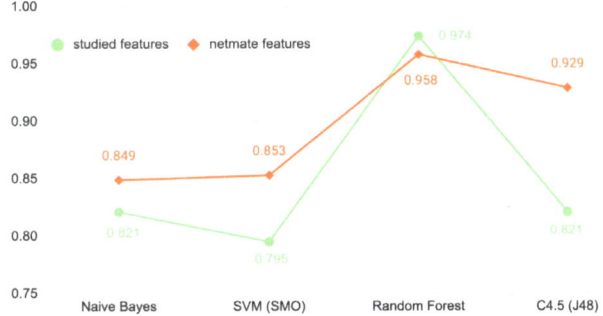

Figure 9. Average recall of the classifiers on both sets of features.

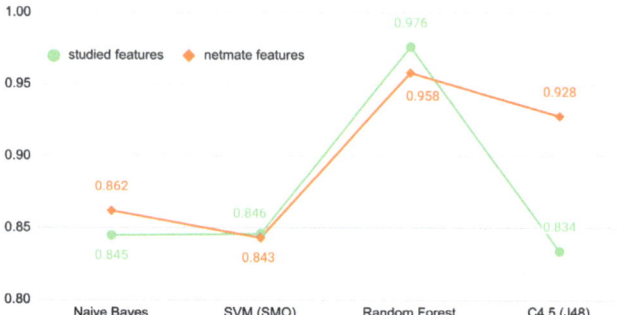

Figure 10. Average precision of the classifiers on both sets of features.

We also observed that SMO had a good precision of 0.846 with the studied features and 0.843 with the Netmate features, but the poor recall for the same algorithm indicated the large number of false negatives in the case of the studied features, which explained the low overall accuracy of the classifier when using this set of features compared to the other. We found that SMO showed better results with a bigger number of features, as there were four times as many Netmate features as there were features developed in this study.

On the other hand, we found that Naive Bayes and C4.5 (J48 in Weka) showed exactly the same average recall when classifying our data and a small difference in precision when it came to the studied features. However, with the Netmate features, C4.5 showed a higher precision and recall—over 0.9—which explained the increased accuracy of the classifier with this set of features. The same went for Naive Bayes, with a smaller difference in the metrics between the use of the two different sets of features.

Classifiers can also be compared according to their ability to individually classify matrix classes; in our case, this would be the flows belonging to each application and their exact precision and recall based on Equations (2) and (3):

$$Precision = \frac{TP}{TP + FP} \quad (2)$$

$$Recall = \frac{TP}{TP + FN} \quad (3)$$

To look further at the given results, in Table 5, we present these metrics for each classifier for the Facebook and YouTube flows regarding the two features sets (S_f refers to the studied features, while N_f refers to Netmate's features).

Table 5. Precision and recall results for each application.

	YouTube				Facebook			
	Precision		Recall		Precision		Recall	
	S_f	N_f	S_f	N_f	S_f	N_f	S_f	N_f
Naive Bayes	0.8	0.781	0.667	0.758	0.545	0.542	0.542	0.650
SVM (SMO)	0.833	0.806	0.417	0.758	0.5	0.636	0.875	0.525
Random Forest	0.923	0.924	1	0.924	1	0.875	0.875	0.875
C4.5 (J48)	0.727	0.905	0.667	0.864	0.6	0.780	0.75	0.800

Precision gave us the number of correctly classified traffic flows for each application over all of the existing flows for that specific application. For instance, we can see that all Facebook flows were correctly classified by the Random Forest algorithm as Facebook flows, while SMO showed the lowest precision other than that of Naive Bayes in the case of the studied features. Nevertheless, the three algorithms showed better classification with the Netmate features, except for Random Forest. However, in the case of YouTube,

Random Forest kept showing the best results in comparison with the rest of the classifiers when using the studied and Netmate features, and it was ranked before SMO with 0.833 (versus Netmate's 0.806) and Naive Bayes with 0.8 (versus Netmate's 0.781).

Moreover, we had the recall metric, which showed the number of correctly classified flows over all of the two applications flows. For example, in the case of the YouTube application, all flows were correctly classified with the Random Forest algorithm when using the studied features. The poorest recall went to the SVM algorithm (SMO) when using the same set of features. Nevertheless, Facebook flows' recall showed more persistent results for the four algorithms when using studies features, but SMO and Naive Bayes showed less of an ability to correctly classify the Facebook flows when using the Netmate features.

To sum up the obtained results, we can say that Random Forest showed the best results for both applications with both feature sets, but the results were more significant with our studied and selected features, which gave the highest accuracy. The accuracy obtained in our tests was as efficient as that stated in previous papers on SDN traffic classification [2,6–9]. However, the remaining three algorithms—SVM, Naive Bayes, and C4.5—were able to better classify the network flows of our dataset when using the Netmate features. In the experiments in [5], Random Forest and C4.5 were also the classifiers that gave the best accuracy, while SVM did not show good results when using Weka. In addition, the authors of [7] claimed that of all of the proposed methods for classifying traffic in SDNs, theirs gave the highest accuracy (97%), similarly to the results in this paper with the Random Forest algorithm (97.44%). In [6], the authors included a study about the appropriate number of features to use for better results, and they concluded that the number should be equal to or higher than eight features, which was the case in our experiments. The Netmate features (44 in total) were four times more numerous than those that we selected (nine features). Most papers using supervised learning have stated the use of the Netmate features for their classification studies, but did not compare them with other sets of features. Their comparisons were only based on the chosen algorithms' metrics (i.e., accuracy, recall, precision, etc.).

Overall, this work's originality can be reduced to three main pillars:

- First: An undiscussed platform setup that included two known platforms of the SDN/cloud fields (OpenDaylight and OpenNebula) was studied. As the integration of the cloud and an SDN is a great facilitator when it comes to moving towards automation, artificial intelligence and machine learning techniques were used to ensure that all digitization initiatives were integrated in a coherent way. This was all with the ultimate goal of delivering the best end-user experience and quality via traffic classification mechanisms.
- Second: An accurate training data was created, where we knew exactly which traffic was generated by each application, and this was then used to train our classifiers.
- Third: Not only were four popular algorithms that are commonly used in related work compared, but a further comparison based on two sets of features was also included. Therefore, the increased performance observed for classifying application flows in our tests was basically related to the set of features, as the whole configuration remained unchangeable, except for the change in the feature set in each iteration.

6. Conclusions

In this paper, we studied traffic classification in an SDN/cloud environment by using the approach of supervised learning through different four algorithms. We discussed the methodology used based on the Weka tool and how the testbed was deployed by using two sets of features. We proved how efficient these algorithms could be in correctly classifying the network traffic in such an environment and how the choice of features impacted the results, which could be an extended research topic.

This work could have many possible extensions due to the richness of the topic. For example, a larger dataset could be a very good start in order to see how the classifiers' performance would be. This could be done by using the two mentioned applications (Facebook and YouTube) or by extending the use to more popular applications. Furthermore, Weka provides a significant set of algorithms that could also be customized by changing their settings, which would open up many possible scenarios of tests. Feature selection and its impact on the final results should not be forgotten, as the latter could be extended or changed with the aim of finding the best possible features for enhancing a classifier's performance for later integration into a platform. Weka also provides many facilities for analyzing these attributes and classifying them before working on the data themselves, which could be of use.

Author Contributions: Conceptualization, S.H. and Y.L.; methodology, A.V.; software, O.B.; validation, O.B. and A.V.; investigation, O.B.; writing—original draft preparation, O.B.; writing—review and editing, A.V. and Y.L.; supervision, S.H.; funding acquisition, A.V. and S.H. All authors have read and agreed to the published version of the manuscript.

Funding: This work was supported by a grant from the Ministry of Research and Innovation, UEFISCDI Romania, project no. ERANET-ERAGAS-ICT-AGRI3-FarmSusteinaBl-1.

Data Availability Statement: The data presented in this study are available on request from the corresponding author.

Acknowledgments: This work was a cooperation between Abdelmalek Essaadi University, Morocco, and University Politehnica of Bucharest (UPB), Romania. The authors are grateful for the support offered by the Agence Universitaire de la Francophonie (AUF) via their Eugene Ionesco scholarship program, which made this joint work possible.

Conflicts of Interest: The authors declare no conflicts of interest.

Abbreviations

The following abbreviations are used in this manuscript:

ARFF	Attribute-Relation File Format
DPI	Deep Packet Inspection
ML	Machine Learning
MLP	Multilayer Perceptron
NARX	Nonlinear Autoregressive Exogenous Multilayer Perceptron
PCAP	Packet Capture
POP3	Post Office Protocol 3
QoS	Quality of Service
PCA	Principal Component Analysis
RBF	Radial Biased Function
SDN	Software-Defined Network
SMO	Sequential Minimal Optimization
SVM	Support Vector Machines
UI	User Interface

References

1. Zander, S.; Nguyen, T.; Armitage, G. Automated traffic classification and application identification using machine learning. In Proceedings of the IEEE Conference on Local Computer Networks 30th Anniversary (LCN'05), Sydney, NSW, Australia, 17 November 2005; pp. 250–257. [CrossRef]
2. Amaral, P.; Dinis, J.; Pinto, P.; Bernardo, L.; Tavares, J.; Mamede, H.S. Machine learning in software defined networks: Data collection and traffic classification. In Proceedings of the IEEE 24th International conference on network protocols (ICNP), Singapore, 8–11 November 2016; pp. 1–5. [CrossRef]
3. Nguyen, T.T.; Armitage, G. A survey of techniques for internet traffic classification using machine learning. *IEEE Commun. Surv. Tutor.* **2008**, *10*, 56–76. [CrossRef]
4. Azab, A.; Khasawneh, M.; Alrabaee, S.; Raymond, C.K.K.; Sarsour, M. Network traffic classification: Techniques, datasets, and challenges. *Digit. Commun. Netw.* **2022**. ISSN 2352-8648. [CrossRef]
5. Jaiswal, R.C.; Lokhande, S.D. Machine learning based internet traffic recognition with statistical approach. In Proceedings of the 2013 Annual IEEE India Conference (INDICON), Mumbai, India, 13–15 December 2013; pp. 1–6. [CrossRef]

6. Yu, C.; Lan, J.; Xie, J.; Hu, Y. QoS-aware traffic classification architecture using machine learning and deep packet inspection in SDNs. *Procedia Comput. Sci.* **2018**, *131*, 1209–1216. [CrossRef]
7. Parsaei, M.R.; Sobouti, M.J.; Khayami, S.; Javidan, R. Network traffic classification using machine learning techniques over software defined networks. *Int. J. Adv. Comput. Sci. Appl. (IJACSA)* **2017**, *8*, 220–225. [CrossRef]
8. Eom, W.J.; Song, Y.J.; Park, C.H.; Kim, J.K.; Kim, G.H.; Cho, Y.Z. Network Traffic Classification Using Ensemble Learning in Software-Defined Networks. In Proceedings of the 2021 International Conference on Artificial Intelligence in Information and Communication (ICAIIC), Jeju Island, Korea, 13–16 April 2021; pp. 89–92. [CrossRef]
9. Raikar, M.M.; Meena, S.M.; Mulla, M.M.; Shetti, N.S.; Karanandi, M. Data traffic classification in software defined networks (SDN) using supervised-learning. *Procedia Comput. Sci.* **2020**, *171*, 2750–2759. [CrossRef]
10. Zhao, P.; Zhao, W.; Liu, Q. Research on SDN Enabled by Machine Learning: An Overview. In *International Conference on 5G for Future Wireless Networks*; Springer: Cham, Switzerland, 2020; pp. 190–203.[CrossRef]
11. Patil, S.; Raj, L.A. Classification of traffic over collaborative IoT and Cloud platforms using deep learning recurrent LSTM. *Comput. Sci.* **2021**, *22*. [CrossRef]
12. Javeed, D.; Gao, T.; Khan, M.T.; Ahmad, I. A Hybrid Deep Learning-Driven SDN Enabled Mechanism for Secure Communication in Internet of Things (IoT). *Sensors* **2021**, *21*, 4884. [CrossRef] [PubMed]
13. Oreski, D.; Androcec, D. Genetic algorithm and artificial neural network for network forensic analytics. In Proceedings of the 43rd International Convention on Information, Communication and Electronic Technology (MIPRO), Opatija, Croatia, 28 September–2 October 2020; pp. 1200–1205. [CrossRef]
14. Alzahrani, R.J.; Alzahrani, A. Survey of Traffic Classification Solution in IoT Networks. *Int. J. Comput. Appl.* **2021**, *183*, 37–45. [CrossRef]
15. Ganesan, E.; Hwang, I.-S.; Liem, A.T.; Ab-Rahman, M.S. SDN-Enabled FiWi-IoT Smart Environment Network Traffic Classification Using Supervised ML Models. *Photonics* **2021**, *8*, 201. [CrossRef]
16. Aslam, M.; Ye, D.; Asad, M.; Hanif, M.; Ndzi, D.; Chellouq, S.A.; Elaziz, M.A.; Al-Qaness, M.A.A.; Jilani, S.F. Adaptive Machine Learning Based Distributed Denial-of-Services. *Sensors* **2022**, *22*, 2697. [CrossRef]
17. Maheshwari, A.; Mehraj, B.; Khan, M.S.; Idrisi, M.S. An optimized weighted voting based ensemble model for DDoS attack detection and mitigation in SDN environment. *Microprocess. Microsyst.* **2022**, *89*, 104412. ISSN 0141-9331. [CrossRef]
18. Mishra, A.; Gupta, N. *Supervised Machine Learning Algorithms Based on Classification for Detection of Distributed Denial of Service Attacks in SDN-Enabled Cloud Computing*; Springer: Singapore, 2022; Volume 370, pp. 165–174.[CrossRef]
19. Zafeiropoulos, A.; Fotopoulou, E.; Peuster, M.; Schneider, S.; Gouvas, P.; Behnke, D.; Müller, M.; Bök, P.B.; Trakadas, P.; Karkazis, P.; et al. Benchmarking and Profiling 5G Verticals' Applications: An Industrial IoT Use Case. In Proceedings of the 6th IEEE Conference on Network Softwarization (NetSoft), Ghent, Belgium, 29 June–3 July 2020; pp. 310–318. [CrossRef]
20. Uzunidis, D.; Karkazis, P.; Roussou, C.; Patrikakis, C.; Leligou, H.C. Intelligent Performance Prediction: The Use Case of a Hadoop Cluster. *Electronics* **2021**, *10*, 2690. [CrossRef]
21. Troia, S.; Martinez, D.E.; Martín, I.; Zorello, L.M.M.; Maier, G.; Hernández, J.A.; de Dios, O.G.; Garrich, M.; Romero-Gázquez, J.L.; Moreno-Muro, F.J.; et al. Machine Learning-assisted Planning and Provisioning for SDN/NFV-enabled Metropolitan Networks. In Proceedings of the European Conference on Networks and Communications (EuCNC), Valencia, Spain, 18–21 June 2019; pp. 438–442. [CrossRef]
22. Belkadi, O.; Laaziz, Y.; Vulpe, A.; Halunga, S. An Integration of OpenDaylight and OpenNebula for Cloud Management Improvement using SDN. In Proceedings of the 27th Telecommunications Forum (TELFOR), Belgrade, Serbia, 26–27 November 2019; pp. 1–4. [CrossRef]
23. Tcpdump Tool. Available online: https://www.tcpdump.org/ (accessed on 18 July 2021).
24. Tcptrace Tool. Available online: https://github.com/blitz/tcptrace (accessed on 18 July 2021).
25. Carela-Español, V.; Bujlow, T.; Barlet-Ros, P. Is our ground-truth for traffic classification reliable? In *International Conference on Passive and Active Network Measurement*; Springer: Cham, Switzerland, 2014; pp. 98–108. [CrossRef]
26. Moore, A.; Zuev, D.; Crogan, M. *Discriminators for Use in Flow-Based Classification. s.l.*; Department of Computer Science, Queen Mary and Westfield College: London, UK, 2005.
27. Das, A.K.; Pathak, P.H.; Chuah, C.N.; Mohapatra, P. Contextual localization through network traffic analysis. In Proceedings of the IEEE INFOCOM 2014—IEEE Conference on Computer Communications, Toronto, ON, Canada, 27 April–2 May 2014; pp. 925–933. [CrossRef]
28. Kim, H.; Claffy, K.C.; Fomenkov, M.; Barman, D.; Faloutsos, M.; Lee, K. Internet traffic classification demystified: Myths, caveats, and the best practices. In Proceedings of the 2008 ACM CoNEXT Conference, Madrid, Spain, 9–12 December 2008; pp. 1–12.
29. Basher, N.; Mahanti, A.; Mahanti, A.; Williamson, C.; Arlitt, M. A comparative analysis of web and peer-to-peer traffic. In Proceedings of the 17th international conference on World Wide Web, Beijing China, 21–25 April 2008; pp. 287–296. [CrossRef]
30. Moore, A.W.; Papagiannaki, K. Toward the accurate identification of network applications. In *International Workshop on Passive and Active Network Measurement*; Springer: Berlin/Heidelberg, Germany, 2005; pp. 41–54.[CrossRef]
31. Cortes, C.; Vapnik, V. Support-vector networks. *Mach. Learn.* **1995**, *20*, 273–297. [CrossRef]
32. Dupay, A.; Sengupta, S.; Wolfson, O.; Yemini, Y. NETMATE: A network management environment. *IEEE Netw.* **1991**, *5*, 35–40. [CrossRef]

33. Netmate Features. Available online: https://github.com/DanielArndt/netmate-flowcalc/blob/master/doc/user_manual.pdf (accessed on 20 September 2021).
34. Platt, J. *Sequential Minimal Optimization: A Fast Algorithm for Training Support Vector Machines*; Microsoft: Redmond, WA, USA, 1998.
35. LibSVM Algorithm Used in WEKA. Available online: https://waikato.github.io/weka-wiki/lib_svm (accessed on 20 September 2021).
36. Chang, C.C.; Lin, C.J. LIBSVM: A library for support vector machines. *ACM Trans. Intell. Syst. Technol. (TIST)* **2011**, *2*, 1–27. [CrossRef]

Disclaimer/Publisher's Note: The statements, opinions and data contained in all publications are solely those of the individual author(s) and contributor(s) and not of MDPI and/or the editor(s). MDPI and/or the editor(s) disclaim responsibility for any injury to people or property resulting from any ideas, methods, instructions or products referred to in the content.

MDPI AG
Grosspeteranlage 5
4052 Basel
Switzerland
Tel.: +41 61 683 77 34

Electronics Editorial Office
E-mail: electronics@mdpi.com
www.mdpi.com/journal/electronics

Disclaimer/Publisher's Note: The title and front matter of this reprint are at the discretion of the Guest Editors. The publisher is not responsible for their content or any associated concerns. The statements, opinions and data contained in all individual articles are solely those of the individual Editors and contributors and not of MDPI. MDPI disclaims responsibility for any injury to people or property resulting from any ideas, methods, instructions or products referred to in the content.

www.ingramcontent.com/pod-product-compliance
Lightning Source LLC
LaVergne TN
LVHW072346090526
838202LV00019B/2492